WITHOUT HATREDS OR FEARS

JORGE ARTEL and the Struggle

for Black Literary Expression

in Colombia

LAURENCE E. PRESCOTT

 Wayne State University Press   Detroit

AFRICAN AMERICAN LIFE SERIES

A complete listing of the books in this series can be found
at the back of this volume.

SERIES EDITORS:

Melba Joyce Boyd *Department of Africana Studies, Wayne State University*

Ron Brown *Department of Political Science, Wayne State University*

Library of Congress Cataloging-in-Publication Data

Prescott, Laurence E. (Laurence Emmanuel)
    Without hatreds or fears : Jorge Artel and the struggle for black
literary expression in Colombia / Laurence E. Prescott.
        p.   cm.—(African American life series)
    Includes bibliographical references (p.   –   ) and index.
    ISBN 0-8143-2751-6 (alk. paper).—ISBN 0-8143-2878-4 (pbk. :
alk. paper)
    1. Artel, Jorge—Criticism and interpretation.   2. Artel, Jorge.
Tambores en la noche.   3. Blacks in literature.   3. Blacks—Cuba—
History.   5. Blacks—Colombia—History.   I. Title.   II. Series.
PQ8180.1.R77Z85   2000
868—dc21   99-39371

Designed by: S. R. Tenenbaum

Wɪᴛʜᴏᴜᴛ ʜᴀᴛʀᴇᴅs ᴏʀ ꜰᴇᴀʀs

Jorge Artel, 1930s. *Courtesy of Sra. Zoila Esquivia Vásquez de Artel.*

To my family,

present and departed, near and far,

and especially to Rosalía, for spurring me on,

and to Alexandre and Andrea, for enriching my life

and giving it new meaning.

First we must unflinchingly face our fears
and honestly ask ourselves why we are afraid.
This confrontation will, to some measure, grant
us power. We shall never be cured of fear by
escapism or repression, for the more we attempt
to ignore and repress our fears, the more we
multiply our inner conflicts.

Martin Luther King Jr.

We hate what we fear and so where hate is, fear is lurking.

Cyril Connolly

CONTENTS

ACKNOWLEDGMENTS

This book is the culmination of research carried out mainly between 1981 and 1993 in Colombia, Mexico, Panama, Venezuela, Costa Rica, Puerto Rico, the Dominican Republic, and Cuba, and in various libraries of the United States while I was a visiting scholar in the Program in Atlantic History, Culture, and Society at the Johns Hopkins University (1987–88) and on other occasions. My original intention was to complete and publish a study of the poetry of Jorge Artel during his lifetime. Regrettably, long years spent documenting and locating sources, pursuing new leads, and finally writing the drafts, took more time than anticipated. Nevertheless, this book is the first comprehensive study of Jorge Artel, his work, and their contribution to Colombian and Spanish American literatures.

In the course of my investigation I received assistance from numerous institutions and individuals who deserve recognition. I am indebted to the Fulbright-Hays Program, which enabled me to conduct essential field research; to the University of Kentucky for Summer Fellowships that supported research travel; to the Organization of American States for a PRA Fellowship that allowed me to collect crucial data; to the Ford Foundation Fellowship Program, which enabled me to enhance the comparative and interdisciplinary aspects of the study; to the College of Liberal Arts, the Department of Spanish, Italian, and Portuguese, and the Department of African and African American Studies of the Pennsylvania State University for an endowed fellowship leave and for generous financial support.

Many libraries, archives, and research centers allowed me access to their holdings. I wish to thank particularly the administrators and staff of the following: in Colombia, the Biblioteca Nacional, the Biblioteca Luis-Angel Arango, the Biblioteca de la Universidad de Cartagena, the Biblioteca de la Inquisición de Cartagena, the Biblioteca Departamental del Atlántico, the Biblioteca de la Universidad de Antioquia, the Biblioteca del Centenario, the Biblioteca de la Universidad Industrial de Santander, and the Instituto Caro y Cuervo; in Mexico, the Biblioteca Nacional, the Hemeroteca Nacional, the Biblioteca de la Universidad de Guanajuato, the Biblioteca de la Universidad de Nuevo León, and the Biblioteca de la Universidad Veracruzana; in Panama, the Biblioteca de la Universidad de Panama, the Biblioteca Nacional, and the Archivo Nacional; the Biblioteca Nacional of Costa Rica; in Venezuela, the Biblioteca Nacional and the Hemeroteca Nacional; the Biblioteca de la Universidad de Puerto Rico; in the Dominican Republic, the Archivo General de la Nación; the Biblioteca Nacional "José Martí" of Cuba; the Casa Hispánica of Columbia University; the New York Public Library (especially the Schomburg Center for Research in Black Culture); and the Library of Congress.

Also, I gratefully acknowledge the kindness of the publishers and editors of *El Universal* of Cartagena, *El Heraldo* of Barranquilla, and *La Patria* of Manizales, who permitted me to examine their archives, and the assistance of their helpful employees.

Many of the findings, ideas, and interpretations contained herein were first presented publicly through invited lectures and papers at colloquia, symposia, and professional meetings. Some portions of chapters have appeared as journal articles and parts of books. I am grateful to the University of Kentucky for permission to use material that originally appeared in *Perspectives on Contemporary Literature*; to Alfred A. Knopf, Inc., and Harold Ober Associates for permission to use Langston Hughes's "Danse Africaine" and "Our Land"; to the Schomburg Center for Research in Black Culture for permission to use Claude McKay's "The Harlem Dancer." I thank also Dr. Manuel Zapata Olivella for allowing me to cite from his books *¡Levántate, mulato!* and *El hombre colombiano*, and other writings.

For supporting my efforts over the years or for reading and commenting on the manuscript I owe many thanks to Professors Russell Salmon, Daniel R. Reedy, Héctor H. Orjuela, Henry Richards, and especially Marvin A. Lewis. I appreciate also the comments and questions of students in my classes at Penn State University and the University of New Mexico; their readings and discussions of works by Artel and other poets stimulated new perceptions and quickened the development of my ideas.

I could not have carried out this study without the cooperation of Jorge Artel, his wife Ligia Alcázar, and their children, Jorge Nazim and Miguel, who took me into their home, their hearts, and their trust, and graciously shared with me albums of clippings and rare photographs, personal correspondence, and stimulating recollections, all of which have provided invaluable insights into the poet, his circumstances, and his writings. To them I express profound gratitude and the hope that the quality of this book will compensate somewhat for its delay.

Space does not allow me to mention by name the many persons who showed genuine interest in my work. I would be remiss, however, if I did not acknowledge certain friends who encouraged and nourished me at crucial stages of this project: Gary and Carol, Mary and Augusto, Inez and Edwin, Marianne, LaVerta, and Frank M., my heartfelt appreciation.

I am also grateful to Manuel Zapata Olivella, Winston Caballero S., Indalecio Camacho, Gonzalo González (R.I.P.), Rogelio Castillo C., and their families for hospitality, learning experiences, and helpful suggestions; and to the Esquivia Vásquez family (Aníbal, Zoila, Candelaria, and Selma) who received me not as a stranger but as a friend and made available priceless documents.

A word of thanks also to Kathryn Wildfong, managing editor of the Wayne State University Press, whose sensitive and patient guidance was instrumental in converting the manuscript into book form.

Finally, to the members of my family—by birth, extension, and marriage—whose love, patience, and faith sustained me throughout this entire undertaking, I extend my deepest thanks and affection.

To the reader, I offer my apologies for any errors or oversights that I may have committed in writing this book.

INTRODUCTION

In almost any study, anthology, or class dealing with twentieth-century Afro-Hispanic poetry the names and works of certain Caribbean authors—notably Nicolás Guillén and Emilio Ballagas of Cuba, and Luis Palés Matos of Puerto Rico—are treated as canonical. The many book-length studies, monographs, articles, and anthology entries devoted to Guillén and Palés Matos evince their standing and acceptance as the exemplars of Spanish-American poetic *negrismo*. As one student of the literature has shown, Cuban anthologists laid the foundation for the black literary canon (Mullen 436, 449–50).[1] Although other contemporary poets, especially South American authors of African descent, have lacked neither lyrical talent nor racial commitment, they have often found themselves—to paraphrase a study on postcolonial literatures—"doubly marginalized," that is, pushed to the cultural and intellectual fringe of societies that themselves have experienced the dilemma of colonial alienation (Ashcroft, Griffiths, and Tiffin 144). As a consequence, these writers are often ignored or only cursorily mentioned by critics and anthologists.

Studies by scholars such as Richard L. Jackson and Marvin A. Lewis have done much to reveal the ethnic dimension and literary significance of works of lesser known Peruvian, Ecuadorian, Uruguayan, Venezuelan, and Colombian poets. Of these too often overlooked and underestimated poets, Jorge Artel of Colombia is particularly deserving of individual study and attention. Although Jackson and Lewis devote significant space to Artel's poetry, the nature and scope of their books preclude a thorough discussion of the artist and his work within a proper national context.

Jorge Artel is widely regarded as the preeminent poet of black expression in contemporary Colombia, a reputation based largely on his first two books of poetry, titled *Tambores en la noche* [*Drums in the Night*] (1940; 2nd ed., 1955). This recognition notwithstanding, Artel, much like his nineteenth-century racial confrère and countryman Candelario Obeso, remains a fairly isolated figure within the literature of his native land. In fact, his name is conspicuously absent from recent studies of contemporary Colombian poetry and other books that deal with important national poets of this century. On the other hand, Spanish-American literary historians and critics, in general—and some Colombian critics, in particular—too often have regarded Artel as a mere epigone of the more famous *negrista* poets. During the height of literary *negrismo*, for example, the eminent Peruvian critic and bibliophile Luis Alberto Sánchez dubbed Artel "the Colombian Nicolás Guillén," a description frequently and unquestioningly repeated by others (e.g., Auqué Lara). Whether intended as a compliment, dismissal, or accurate assessment of the poet and his work, that designation ignores the historical and literary reality of Colombia and overlooks Artel's particularity as an Afro-Colombian author. Indeed, by identifying Artel as a Colombian version of the Cuban mulatto poet, Sánchez, in effect, reduced Artel to the limited orbit and perspective of Afro-Cubanism or Afro-Antilleanism, thereby precluding a fair and balanced appreciation of the Afro-Colombian's poetry on its own terms.

While these objections do not negate the existence of real and important similarities between Cuba and Colombia or, for that matter, of affinities between Guillén and Artel, the nature and implications of these similarities have yet to be fully explored.[2] With regard to Cuba and Colombia, for example, it is evident that both countries share a common heritage of early Spanish colonization, large-scale enslavement of Africans, and outstanding literary tradition. Moreover, both have produced major authors of African descent as well as significant works related to their respective African populations. Nevertheless, the realities of race and writing in the two nations have resulted in notable differences with respect to the literary profile and output of Afro-Colombians and Afro-Cubans. As for the two poets, it is important to point out that in spite of Artel's unique position in Colombian letters, he has enjoyed neither the national esteem nor the international prominence of his Cuban contemporary. Although his poetry appears in many anthologies of Colombia and Spanish America and has been the subject of scores of critical articles in books, journals, and newspapers of many countries, until now no scholarly book or monograph on Artel and his work has ever seen print.[3]

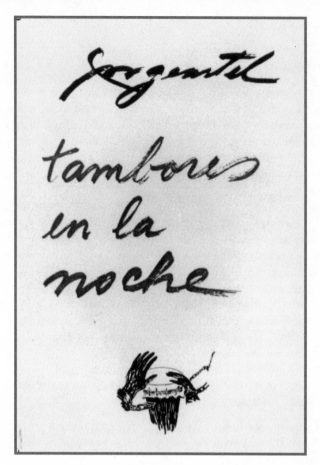

Cover of the second edition of *Tambores en la noche*, 1955.

Several obstacles have hampered an extensive investigation and study of Artel's poetry and related prose, thereby hindering a full appraisal of his significance within Colombian and Spanish-American literatures. They include the inaccessibility of his printed books; the dispersion of published texts by and about the poet throughout numerous newspapers and periodicals of the Americas, some of which have long ceased production; and the lack of readily available bibliographical sources pertinent to his writings, experiences, and ideas. Furthermore, Artel's own erratic, often bohemian, lifestyle, and his twenty-three years of self-imposed exile from Colombia (1948–71), spent traveling and sojourning in various American republics, present for even the most meticulous researcher a formidable task of time-consuming investigation.

While close study of primary sources is indispensable, a wider, more comprehensive approach to Artel's work is needed. Indeed, to arrive at a more penetrating grasp of Artel's poetry, to understand both the individual and collective forces and the intrinsic and extrinsic factors that shaped

15

it and that also have affected the development of a discourse of literary blackness in Colombia, it is necessary also to consider the social, cultural, and historical contexts from which Artel's poetry and Afro-Colombian writing, in general, have emerged. In that respect, I share the opinion of the authors of *The Empire Writes Back* regarding "the need to incorporate cultural context into any assessment of literary worth" (Ashcroft, Griffiths, and Tiffin 183).

Important forces and factors that I identify and discuss in this book include the impact of geography and inveterate regionalism; the unique patterns of black slavery in Colombia and the resultant racial configurations and attitudes; the absence of a strong, cohesive group consciousness among Afro-Colombians; the "genteel tradition" of Colombian literature (J. C. Brown); and the weaknesses and limitations of Colombia's publishing enterprise. In light of Sánchez's aforementioned description of Artel, it has also been instructive to compare aspects of Cuban and Colombian history, society, and culture that elucidate the emergence of writers of African descent and the evolution of black writing within the two countries.

This study, then, addresses several questions of fundamental importance to an appreciation of the poetry of Jorge Artel and the problems of black literary expression in Colombia:

1. What explains the historically low profile of Colombian writers of African descent in their own country and in the history of Spanish-American literature by and about blacks?

2. What factors have tended to hinder or promote the development of black literary expression in Colombia? Specifically, how have geography, history, and the realities of race and ethnicity in Colombia influenced the creation, development, and dissemination of writing by black Colombians, and especially of literary texts that confront and explore the meaning and significance of the African presence and heritage in that nation?

3. What differences between the demographic and historical situation of Cuba and that of Colombia help to explain and clarify the relatively late emergence and less prominent profile of Afro-Colombian writers and literature?

4. What role have the publishing industry and the national print media in Colombia played in these matters?

5. How have these factors informed and shaped the poetic expression of Jorge Artel?

6. What contribution have Artel and his work made to the development of an assertive tradition of black writing in Colombia?

In tackling these questions, I hope also to shed light on other related enigmas, such as the underrepresentation of Colombia in Latin American anthologies and collections of black, or even *negrista,* literature, and the absence of a published anthology of black-inspired poetry in a country whose citizens of African descent constitute approximately one-fourth of the total population.

The purpose of this book, in short, is twofold: to study the poetry of Jorge Artel that treats the African heritage and the black presence in Colombia and America; and to reveal the various factors that have hindered a sharper, more pronounced profile of writers of African descent and their works in the nation of Colombia. While each aim perhaps could be the basis for a separate study, I believe that the two are not only inextricably related, but even interdependent.[4] I am hopeful that a detailed exposition of the two topics will make this book more interesting and more useful to scholars, students, and general readers of Latin American literature and civilization, of Afro-Hispanic literature and civilization, and of African-American literature in the broadest sense. In addition, it will become evident, I believe, that the experiences, ideas, and locations contained in the poetry and related prose writings of Jorge Artel are not limited to the field of literary studies, but are relevant also to other traditional disciplines (e.g., history) and to new areas of intellectual inquiry, such as cultural studies.

I have arranged this study into seven chapters and a concluding section. Chapter 1 discusses geographical, historical, and racial conditions in Colombia and shows their relation to literary production therein. Continuing the preliminary grounding, chapter 2 contrasts slavery and race relations in Colombia and Cuba to show their impact upon writing and writers in both countries, and also explores the publishing industry's role in hampering Afro-Colombian literary expression. Chapter 3 offers a detailed presentation of Artel's literary career, journalistic activities, and travel experiences, with emphasis on the period from 1930 to 1955, when he produced most of his major writings on black culture and related concerns. Chapter 4 examines some of Artel's early, uncollected poems for the purpose of revealing the literary and aesthetic foundations of his poetry. Chapter 5 analyzes the poems of the first edition of *Tambores en la noche* and shows their kinship with works of other black poets and writers. Chapter 6 discusses critics' reactions to Artel's first book and to his identification as Colombia's preeminent black poet, looks at the controversy of black poetry (*poesía negra*) in Colombia, and contrasts the racial and political stance of Artel and Guillén in their respective poetry. Chapter 7 explains the lack of critical attention to the second edition of *Tambores en la noche,* discusses revisions and innovations that distinguish this volume from the previous book, and studies thematic and stylistic elements of the new poems. At the same time it shows the continuity between the two books, unveils the author's subtle confrontation with the critics' assessments, and reveals the impact of Artel's travel experiences on his wider racial vision and more overt display of a steadfast commitment to a literature of liberation. The concluding section recapitulates the main points of the preceding chapters, underscores Artel's literary significance and legacy, and speculates on the prospects of Afro-Colombian authors and writing gaining a more prominent position within the national literary canon.

No one theoretical approach has dominated the writing of this book. Several key texts (e.g., Ashcroft, Griffiths, and Tiffin; Ortega y Gasset; Braithwaite), however, have afforded valuable insights and perspectives, which, in turn, have shaped the readings herein. If this book succeeds in promoting a fair assessment and more perceptive appreciation of Jorge Artel's literary achievements, a greater awareness of the rich diversity of Colombia's peoples and cultures, and a better understanding of the expanse and experiences of the African diaspora, it will have fulfilled its purpose.

All translations, unless otherwise noted, are mine. For the sake of space and style, most secondary sources are quoted in English only.

1

$\mathcal{F}$OUNDATIONAL REALITIES:

Geography and Regionalism, Slavery, *Mestizaje,*

and Black Identity in Colombia

> We are struggling for the freedom to reflect our reality, that is, to be authentic. . . . To liberate the mind from the colonial burden is no easy undertaking, especially when our own thinking has no other measurement than the norm inherited from the [Spanish] conquistador.
>
> Manuel Zapata Olivella (1963)

Literary expression by Colombian writers of African descent, like Colombian literature in general, has been influenced by many factors, not the least of which have been the country's geography and regionalism. By specifically shaping, however, the experience and perception of peoples of African descent, several other factors, such as slavery, *mestizaje* (racial mixing or amalgamation and cultural blending) and race relations, have influenced significantly the manner in which Afro-Colombian poets and writers have confronted and represented the black presence and black culture in their writings. This chapter and the following one will demonstrate the role that these and other elements of historical and contemporary Colombian reality have played in the development of black literary expression in Colombia and, consequently, in the poetry of Jorge Artel.

GEOGRAPHY AND REGIONALISM

Colombia, as geographers have long pointed out, is a land of varied contrasts—cool, dry mountains; hot, humid coasts; long river valleys; flat expansive plains (Carlson 306; James 137–38). This geographic diversity has affected profoundly the nature of the population and culture of Colombia. Consequently, any discussion of factors that have influenced Colombian life and culture—including ethnicity and race relations—must take into account the role of the country's geography. If it is true, as Colombian writer Manuel Zapata Olivella has observed, that "A culture cannot be understood without a geography" (*El hombre colombiano* 11), the geographic factor and its impact are crucial to understanding the question of black literary expression in Colombia.

Located in the northwest corner of South America (see Map), the Republic of Colombia occupies a space of some 440,000 square miles, making it the third-largest Spanish-speaking country of that continent. Its territory borders on the Caribbean Sea to the north; Venezuela to the east; Brazil, Peru, and Ecuador to the south; and the Pacific Ocean to the west. With the distinction of being the only South American country with coasts on both the Atlantic and Pacific Oceans, Colombia uniquely shares in both the Andean and the Caribbean worlds. Historically, however, Colombia's population of African descent has tended to occupy the hot lowlands of the Pacific and Atlantic coasts and the warm valleys, especially of the Magdalena, Cauca, and Patía Rivers. For that reason, these areas will be the primary, but by no means exclusive, focus of our discussion of geography.

The Western or Pacific Region

The western portion of Colombia (consisting today of the departments of Nariño, the Cauca, the Valle, and the Chocó) is dominated by the Andes Mountains, which enter from the south (Ecuador) and separate into three ranges: the western, the central, and the eastern. With the Pacific Ocean on the far west and the central Andean range on the east, this area abounds in natural resources (minerals, wood, fish) and boasts the arable lands of the fertile Cauca Valley. On the other hand, much of the Pacific coastline is dominated by thick, wooded growth and swamps, and frequent, torrential rainfalls (Góez 33; Carlson 308, 309–10). One geographer describes it as "a stormy region, with an unusual frequency in lightning flashes, suffocating heat; high atmospheric and ground humidity, and many rivers traversing the jungle towards the sea" (Góez 33). These conditions, and the changes that the tidal movements effect upon the shore, no doubt inhibited the establishment of many permanent Spanish settlements and cities similar to those that were founded on the Atlantic coast and in the interior highlands. Consequently, social and cultural development in the Pacific has characteristically lagged behind that of these other areas. In addition, as we shall see later, after the abolition of slavery in 1852 and the subsequent emigration of many ex-slaves to the uninhabited areas of the coast, the central government seemed less inclined to support and stimulate the social, cultural, and economic development of what had become a heavily Negroid area (E. Romero 28). It certainly requires no great intelligence to

CANAL ZONE

COSTA
RICA

CARIBBEAN SEA

Colón
Panama seceded
in 1903
Barranquilla
ATLÁNTICO
Santa Marta
Riohacha
Cartagena
Ciénaga
GUAJIRA
Golfo
de Urabá
Golfo
de Panamá

PACIFIC
OCEAN

CÓRDOBA
SUCRE
CÉSAR

BOLÍVAR
Petrólea
ANTIOQUIA
NORTE
DE SANTANDER
Barrancabermeja
Cúcuta
Quibdó
Medellín
El Centro
RISARALDA
SANTANDER
Bucaramanga
CALDAS
Arauca
Pereira
Manizales
QUINDIO
Buenaventura
Armenia
CUNDINAMARCA
Tunja
ARAUCA
VALLE
DEL CAUCA
Ibagué
BOYACÁ
Cali
Girardot
BOGOTÁ
TOLIMA
Tumaco
CAUCA
CASANARE
Neiva
Popayán
SPECIAL
DISTRICT
Villavicencio
NARIÑO
HUILA
Puerto López
Pasto
META
VICHADA
Orito

PUTUMAYO
CAQUETÁ
GUAVIARE
GUAINÍA

ECUADOR

VAUPÉS

Territory lost
to Ecuador
from 1880 to 1942

AMAZONAS

PERU

Río Napo

Territory lost
to Brazil
in 1904 and 1905

Leticia

The Republic of
COLOMBIA

Political divisions

BRAZIL

Source – Instituto Geográfico "Agustín Codazzi", Colombia, 1989

Kilometres
0   100   200   300   400   500
0   100   200   300
Miles

understand that such a situation was hardly conducive to the development of a scribal culture. As a result, there is little evidence of published creative writing by blacks in this area prior to the twentieth century.[1]

The Atlantic Region

Colombia's Atlantic region, extending southward from the Caribbean Sea, differs significantly from the Pacific in climate, topography, and natural resources. Here the temperatures, while still tropical, are not as high, nor are the rains as frequent or as heavy, as in some western areas. Furthermore, the northern coastline, unlike that of the Pacific, is less affected by the tides, and therefore suffers less erosion and change (Góez 27, 34, 64). This fact, along with the natural harbors and strategic location of the region, favored the rise and development of important commercial centers and international ports. Santa Marta, Colombia's oldest settlement, was founded in 1525; Cartagena, located further west, was settled eight years later, in 1533. During the seventeenth century, Cartagena, known as the "Queen of the Indies," became a principal port of entry for captive Africans destined for slavery in the areas under Spanish domination. According to Manuel Zapata Olivella, who has studied and written a great deal on ethnic groups in Colombia, this fact had a profound effect on the character and people of the Atlantic region:

> The notable importance of Cartagena as the first slave port of the conti-
> nent contributed to the increase of the African population on the coast
> and to its mixing with the Indian and Hispanic elements. (*El hombre
> colombiano* 279)[2]

As the Spanish conquerors moved inland they found not so much a mass of dense jungle and ubiquitous waterways, as great expanses of pasturelike land. To be sure, there were occasional swamps, thickets, and even arid conditions (Carlson 309), but by and large the invaders found the land suitable for raising cattle and for agriculture. These physical conditions, as well as the commercial factors mentioned above, made for a more hospitable and inviting environment, which, in turn, promoted the rapid economic development of the Atlantic region. Also, proximity to both European and North American markets, as well as to Africa, made Colombia's northern coast an important sector within the mercantile Atlantic community, with whose interests—not the least of which was the slave trade—it became heavily involved. Moreover, the Magdalena River, the country's primary navigable artery, traversing from south to north much of the inhabited sections of the region and emptying into the Caribbean Sea, was a natural highway for the transportation and exchange of goods, services, and culture not only between the coastal regions and the interior but also between colonial Colombia (New Granada) and the European world. Understandably, blacks residing in this more prosperous and developing region would more likely be exposed to and benefit from the social and economic advances and opportunities existing there.

Regional Divisions and Identities

Prior to the arrival of the Spanish, commerce between the indigenous inhabitants of different areas apparently was quite common, in spite of the high, imposing cordilleras (Mina 45). Spanish colonization of the land, however, abetted by the natural barriers to easy trade, communication, and travel, promoted both "the isolation of the separate areas of settlement" and the creation of "strongly contrasted regions" (James 146, 145; Góez 94) while also hindering economic development in certain sections (Bushnell 16, 79). Even decades after the winning of independence (1819) and throughout the nineteenth century, travel and commerce between regions, hampered by the lack of an adequate road system, remained low (Melo 150–151; J. M. Samper, *Ensayo* 260, 265).

Within the different regions of the country, distinguished to a great extent not only by climate and topography, but also by ethnicity and racial concentration, inhabitants generally have developed distinct economic pursuits, social customs, speech patterns, and forms of dress that still characterize them today. As historian Jaime Jaramillo explains,

Colombia is a country of strong regions. Our federal states of the nineteenth century . . . corresponded to regions not only with their own geography, but with their individual economic and social structure and their typical cultural features. . . . With good reason our anthropologists have been able to speak of real subcultures. ("Regiones y nación" 191–92)[3]

These various distinctions often tended to foster or exacerbate regional identities, loyalties, competition, *caudillismo*, drives for autonomy, and subsequent conflict with the central authority. Frequently they led to revolts, secessionist movements, and civil wars, thus weakening or delaying the development of a broad, inclusive sense of national feeling and identity (Bushnell 36–37; James 145). Even today Colombians are still classified by ethno-regional nomenclature, such as "el antioqueño, el costeño, el cundinamarqués, el santandereano y el nariñense" (Góez 144; Zapata Olivella, *El hombre colombiano* 211–378). As late as 1964 Preston James noted that the people of Antioquia "continue to think of themselves as Antioqueños first, and Colombians second" (149).[4]

Regionalism and Black Colombians

Topography and regionalism have also had a direct and decisive impact upon the composition of Colombia's population. Climate, terrain, and natural resources determined which economic activities (e.g, agriculture, mining, fishing) could be pursued. The exploitation of the natural wealth of the land—be it gold, silver, pearls, grazing pastures, or fertile farmlands—the decline and protection of indigenous peoples, and the desires and needs of the ruling class (e.g., the need for a readily available supply of cheap labor), led to the importation of thousands of African men, women, and children and their enslavement in a wide variety of occupations (J. King 297).

Historically, African people have been less numerous and less visible in the urban centers of the highland interior, such as Tunja, Popayán, and, particularly, the savannah and capital city of Bogotá, where the Spanish and the *mestizo*—the offspring of unions between Hispanic and native populations—have predominated. Although African slaves were also found in these areas, employed largely as domestic servants, as a rule their numbers never reached proportions large enough to impact profoundly the cultural identity and human element of the mountainous interior. Thus while the concentration and often numerically superior presence of blacks, mulattoes, and zambos—the name given to the offspring of unions between Africans and Amerindians—in places such as Cartagena, the Chocó, and the valleys of the Cauca and lower Magdalena Rivers gave a decidedly and indelibly African flavor and tinge to the culture and population of the Atlantic and Pacific littorals and other warm climes,[5] the cities and settlements of the interior and cool mountain highlands largely bore the cultural stamp and human face of European settlers, the assimilated mestizo, and Amerindian groups. As a consequence of this demographic configuration, there developed, as many have noted, a certain form of geographical separation or regional segregation of the black and white populations of the country (Sharp, "Una imagen del negro" 172).[6] White apprehension about the perils of living and working in hot tropical climates and the belief that blacks were innately or better suited for such conditions justified the enslavement of African peoples and contributed further to a geo-racial dichotomy of warm-coastal-Negroid lowlands and cool-interior-Caucasian and mestizo highlands.[7]

As stated above, until the coming of modern, rapid means of transportation and communication—namely, the automobile and the airplane—coast and interior existed and developed, to a great degree, independently of and in relative isolation from each other. This geo-racial-cultural separation, as well as the centralist character of Colombian government and the hegemony of Bogotá, not only rendered blacks as exotic in many areas, but also reinforced white and mestizo attitudes of superiority towards *costeños* (coastal people) in general and toward the descendants of Africans in particular, and have been the cause of frequent misunderstanding and distortion of Afro-Colombian peoples and their cultural creations (see Artel, "Leyenda y realidad" 4–5; Guzmán Izquierdo 2525; Whitten 108).[8] The civil wars that plagued Colombia during the nineteenth century and often masked regional rivalries further exacerbated ethnic suspicions and racial tensions. Thus the presence of large numbers of black soldiers among armies of occupation in areas where people of African descent were hardly seen or were primarily household servants tended to revive or strengthen old fears and stereotypes, especially regarding black men (Rivera y Garrido 70–73; Vélez 65–76).[9]

Notwithstanding the profound African presence that marks the character of much of the Pacific and Atlantic regions, these two areas also differ significantly from one other, as we have seen, in geography and regional development. As a result, for Afro-Colombians, too, identification with the native region or homeland has often taken precedence over other forms of identity, including common racial (African) background and shared political affiliation.[10] For example, although blacks as a whole tended to identify with and support the Liberal Party after its successful campaign to abolish slavery, ex-slaves and their descendants were used as foot soldiers by regional caudillos of both the Liberal and Conservative camps interested in promoting their own causes.[11] Even troops on the same side but from different regions were known to fight each other (Tirado Mejía, *Aspectos sociales* 45, 47). It comes as no surprise, then, that blacks of the Atlantic region generally have identified more with fellow northern *costeños* than with their racial confreres of the Pacific coast or other areas. Although geographical separation accounts for much of this attitude, regional differences in the nature and conditions of slavery and in the process of *mestizaje* also seem to have played a significant role. These divergent experiences, as the next two sections will show, would also impact cultural development and black identity in Colombia.

Slavery in Colombia

The Western Region

During colonial times African slaves in the western region were commonly used in domestic service and at times in small-scale agriculture. They were primarily employed, however, in the labor and supportive network necessary for extracting gold from placer mines and river beds, an activity that kept blacks toiling in bondage until the middle of the nineteenth century. According to one scholar, the enormous mansions and opulent churches constructed in the city of Popayán during the colonial period, and the sumptuous religious festivals that took place there, owe their origin to the labor of black slaves who were worked and driven hard to maintain a high output of gold (Crist 10).[12] Increasing the misery of the slaves was the lack of a proper diet and even starvation conditions that they suffered on account of the distance separating the mining camps from the food-growing centers, and the avaricious masters' failure "to establish proper supply lines or food sources" (Sharp, "Manumission" 92). Of gold-washing in Barbacoas, located in what is today the Department of Nariño, one early nineteenth-century observer wrote:

> the principal labour is done by negro [sic] slaves, who are treated here with greater cruelty by their masters than in any other part of the colonies that I visited; . . . [food] is really distributed to them very sparingly. (Stevenson 2: 421)[13]

Given the harsh treatment and other intolerable conditions, it is not surprising that many slaves sought freedom from bondage by escaping—individually, in pairs, or in groups—into the surrounding dense forests and jungles. There, some of these fugitives took refuge in remote Indian villages while others went it alone. Still others (generally called *cimarrones*) banded together for mutual help and defense, joining or establishing fugitive slave, or maroon, communities known as *palenques,* from which they raided small white settlements and supply trains (Escalante, *El negro en Colombia* 118; Sharp "Manumission" 100; Rout 100–01; J. King 310–11). Available evidence indicates that the *palenques* of the Pacific region, especially the large or threatening ones, were eventually destroyed or otherwise abandoned, although not all of the runaways were captured and returned to slave status. On the other hand, settlements of free or manumitted blacks and mulattoes managed to survive in spite of attempts by the whites to reenslave or abuse their inhabitants. During the 1800s this seems to have been the case particularly in the fertile Cauca Valley, which, as Mateo Mina points out, "was converted into a battle ground between wealthy whites and black peasants during more than fifty years" (49).[14] In general, though, as blacks in western New Granada gained their freedom, they tended to separate themselves from the whites, choosing to lead a simple but autonomous existence (Sharp, *Slavery* 153).

All of the above factors tended to preclude large-scale miscegenation between blacks and whites in many parts of the Pacific region (Zapata Olivella, *El hombre colombiano* 310, 313). Likewise, it seems that mixing between blacks and Indians took place on a relatively small scale since the latter either worked in the distant agricultural areas or resided in the thick forests in order to avoid contact with both whites and blacks.

The hardships and privations that these Negroid peoples—both slave and free—had to endure, their relatively limited mixing with white and indigenous populations, and the overt discrimination and exploitation that they suffered because of their class, skin color, and lack of education (Sharp, *Slavery* 149–52) would seem to have created conditions leading to the preservation or development of an ethnic identity in which racial background, group pride and solidarity, and cultural distinctions were important elements. Yet while strong racial group identification appears to have been common among blacks in the rich Cauca Valley, it does not seem to have characterized their free counterparts in the Chocó, at least during most of the slavery period. Sharp contends that "there is little evidence that the free black population ever formed anything approaching a free colored community in the Chocó. Only in rare instances did the freedmen demonstrate any signs of interest-group orientations" (*Slavery* 153). Opportunities for self-purchase and the possibility of manumission probably encouraged many slaves in the Chocó to concentrate on gaining their individual liberty rather than on undertaking collective efforts for freedom and economic improvement (Sharp, "Manumission" 106). Moreover, the black and mulatto population in the minerally rich but socially and economically impoverished Chocó soon came to outnumber whites, who regarded the area as unhealthy and largely abandoned it after slavery was abolished. In sum, racial antagonism in the Chocó probably was not as chronic nor as open as in the Cauca Valley.[15] Nevertheless, when taken together, the circumstances of slavery and its aftermath in western Colombia no doubt contributed to a retarding in black communities—whether more or less racially conscious—of the development of a tradition of written literature through which they might express themselves individually and collectively.

The Atlantic Region

Although slave labor was used in the mining carried out in the Atlantic region, the majority of the African bondmen and their descendants were employed in rural areas as field hands, herdsmen, semiskilled laborers (e.g., in sugar cane presses), and domestics; and in urban centers as tradesmen, peddlers, mechanics, domestics, and menial laborers (Juan and Ulloa 28–29, 44; Escalante, *El negro en Colombia* 130–31; Mörner 120).[16] Blacks also replaced Indians, it will be recalled, as *bogas,* or boatmen, on the vessels (e.g., *bongo, champán*) that carried merchandise and passengers on the Magdalena and other rivers. All of these forms of employment allowed for greater contact between persons of varying places, classes, and ethnic groups, which, in turn, stimulated the growth and diversification of the region. Blacks and whites in the Atlantic region tended to live closer together and to interact more often and under more varied circumstances than in areas of the west. Consequently, relationships between master and slave were inclined to be more relaxed, which could mean less hardship for the slave and, possibly, manumission for the female slave or her offspring, if fathered by the master. Concubinage was not uncommon and could gain the female slave special favors or privileges (e.g., food, clothing, status). Also, as the eighteenth-century travelers Juan and Ulloa observed in Cartagena, a poor, sick Spaniard who was taken in and cared for by a woman of color frequently married "his benefactress, or one of her daughters" (32–33).

In general, blacks—both slave and free—benefited from the economic prosperity that characterized the region. In particular, slaves in urban areas such as Cartagena, Barranquilla, and Santa Marta had more opportunities to gain their freedom through self-purchase than their rural counterparts.[17] On the other hand, in rural areas, where the hacienda was an almost self-contained unit, the opportunity to earn and save money with which to purchase one's freedom was not as great. Thus, a rural slave might seek freedom by escape into the hinterland, where he could live among the Indians or join a maroon community. Safety in an urban setting might also be feasible for a rural bondsman, especially one with a valuable skill or aptitude, who might succeed in passing as a freeman or in persuading some craftsman to take him on as an apprentice or journeyman.[18]

At the moment of abolition, the number of persons (2,405) held as slaves in the northern coastal region was approximately one fourth of the number of those in the western region (10,621) (Galvis Noyes 230–32). This suggests that a larger percentage of the population of African descent in the Atlantic coast was free. That fact, combined with the greater social and economic opportunities that existed there, probably would allow for a higher rate of literacy among the people of color, which, in turn, could mean a greater likelihood of the emergence of a tradition of black writing. Those same conditions, however, and the not unrelated low incidence of racial antagonism, may well have thwarted or rendered unnecessary both individual and group expression of blackness in literature.

Although racial conflict was not absent in the Atlantic region, neither did it take the open, caustic form that raged in the Cauca. A study of contemporary racial attitudes and discrimination in Cartagena by Mauricio Solaún and Sidney Kronus may provide some insights. According to these writers, the ambiguous nature of racial discrimination, the tendency of nonwhites to marry persons of lighter complexion in order to "improve" the race, and the close economic ties between nonwhites and whites have averted the creation of overt racial hostility among economically and politically successful people of African descent (127–28). Furthermore, given the absence of spokespersons and racially committed leaders of the advantaged classes who could "articulate grievances and mobilize support among high proportions of the black masses" (130), a broad social movement along racial lines has also failed to develop. Of course the existence of such attitudes and behavior is not a recent phenomenon but extends back centuries. Thus those who enjoyed the advantages of education were often the least likely to speak out in racial terms.[19]

MESTIZAJE AND BLACK IDENTITY

Sexual union between the three principal ethnic groups of Colombia—Amerindians, Europeans, and Africans—has been a common and constant occurrence since colonial times. Although the Spanish Crown generally prohibited or strongly opposed unions of peoples of African origin with whites and Indians, the conditions and circumstances of (black) life, particularly in the Atlantic region, fostered a high degree of miscegenation between Africans, Europeans, Amerindians, and their resulting mixtures (Zapata Olivella, *El hombre colombiano* 168; Escalante, *El negro en Colombia* 116; Mörner 122). The variety of human types resulting from the various crossings (mestizos, mulattoes, zambos, etc.) tended to blur physical differences and create a color continuum that made difficult the enforcement of sharp distinctions based on racial origin and color.[20] Although the word *negro* came to refer primarily to those black persons—slave or free—whose physical features (i.e., dark complexion, broad nose, full lips, woolly hair, etc.) denoted a direct or unmixed African background and who were regarded by some as aesthetically repulsive (Gilij 245), the term was also loosely applied as an epithet to mixed-race and swarthy-skinned persons.[21] Consequently, the constant mingling of whites with blacks, mulattoes, and *mestizos* created difficulty not only in determining who was "pure" white but also in determining who was "black."[22]

Colonial laws designed to protect the privileged position and "pure" lineage of the white minority discriminated against people of color, thus preventing all but a few from gaining the perquisites of whiteness. Officially, the masses of mixed-bloods were labeled *castas*. Popularly there developed a complicated and often outlandish nomenclature for the mixtures, based on the degree of whiteness one had. As Juan and Ulloa observed in Cartagena:

> Every person is so jealous of the order of their tribe or cast [*sic*], that if, through inadvertence, you call them by a degree lower than what they actually are, they are highly offended, never suffering themselves to be so deprived of so valuable a gift of fortune. (27)

White identity, as another observer noted, implied a certain nobility of lineage and, therefore, a measure of respect not accorded to persons of indigenous or African background (Gilij 251).[23]

In short, color and race were basic elements in the socioeconomic structure of colonial society and determined to a great extent a person's real and potential status, thereby creating no little tension between the groups. As Zapata Olivella has noted,

> The result of the forced socioeconomic union [between blacks, whites and Indians] will be the interracial tensions expressed in subtle distinctions of color. While whites claimed nobility, setting forth their "purity of blood," mixed-race persons alleged to be more [worthy] according to the lesser degree of black or Indian blood they possessed. (*El hombre colombiano* 197)

Not surprisingly, the advantages and prerogatives of lighter skin and Caucasian features in colonial society stimulated many nonwhite individuals to change or modify their racial identity in order to improve their social status and gain better opportunities. A certificate of whiteness known as *cédula de gracias al sacar*, a change of residence, occupational mobility, and acquisition of wealth occasionally were effective methods of obtaining a lighter identity and, thereby, higher status. *Mestizaje*, or biological and cultural mixing, became a common means by which people of color might better their status and also that of their offspring. Marital or free unions with fairer-skinned and socially or economically superior persons could better a dark-skinned person's status, help rid the lineage of "bad" blood, and improve the progeny's chances for greater acceptance and tolerance.

On rare occasions advancement into the ranks of the privileged was permitted to colored individuals (i.e., men) who achieved noteworthy financial success or who demonstrated a potential for popular leadership. Marriage to fair-skinned daughters of good families helped to seal acceptance and to put distance between such individuals and the colored masses. In this way colonial and—in later years—national elites could maintain control of the wealth and power, thereby strengthening their own position, and prevent the emergence of strong leaders or wealthy malcontents who might pose a threat to their authority or otherwise challenge the status quo.

As a result of the constant, centuries-old mingling of African, European, and indigenous peoples and their issue, Colombia's population is commonly described as triethnic (Zapata Olivella, *El hombre colombiano* 277). That is, the majority of Colombians are believed to be of mixed racial origin, having at least two blood lines flowing within their veins (Smith 57). Thus many might agree that Colombians constitute "a general race whose elements mix in the majority of the inhabitants in such a manner that to figure it out would pose a difficult problem of ethnology" ("Problema Racial"). The pervasive reality and awareness of this *mestizaje* has led to strange and far-fetched notions, or, in a word, mythologizing. Specifically, some Colombians have assumed that the predominance of a mixed-race population in their nation obviates or precludes the existence of racial problems, especially where blacks are concerned and when contrasted with the apparent lack of racial mixing in the United States. For example, referring to black-white conflicts, chronicler J. M. Cordovez Moure (1835–1918) asserted: "There is no danger of collision between the two races nor with any of the others which make up the great mass of our inhabitants, because the great movement of fusion takes place without stress" (*Reminiscencias* 485).[24]

As in Venezuela (see Wright), the expression *café con leche* (café au lait), a colorful indicator of racial blending and harmony, is occasionally heard in Colombia.[25] According to this metaphorical description, some persons are seen as having more *café* (coffee), while others are viewed as having more *leche* (milk). All, however, supposedly are equal citizens of the nation. Afro-Colombians and other blacks who have challenged such widespread assumptions by raising questions of race, or who have charged the existence of racial discrimination in some public or private activity, sphere, or policy, have themselves been quickly accused of disturbing the nation's racial tranquillity, of being social misfits, or even of promoting discrimination and racism.[26] In fact, until very recently, demonstrations of racial pride and solidarity by Afro-Colombians, efforts on their part to promote the scholarly study of the African heritage in Colombia, and calls for incorporation of the black presence in school and university curricula, as occurred in 1943, were met with denunciation, ridicule, and warnings of racial division and turmoil.[27] In this way the pervasive concept and reality of *mestizaje* as an agglutinative or national characteristic of Colombian society and culture may well have served to inhibit upwardly mobile blacks who have gained educational and economic opportunity from warmly and openly identifying with their African heritage and asserting or embracing a strong black identity. It is unlikely, too, that such alienated individuals would create literary texts that confronted and expressed blackness in an affirmative and positive manner.

In spite of denials to the contrary, the existence in Colombia of attitudes of racial superiority and of racially discriminatory practices is unquestionable. According to one contemporary observer, "Collectively, nationally, racial discrimination is [considered] outrageous; but on an individual basis it is considered just. The important thing is not in thinking that way but in mentioning it" (Londoño 141–42). Indeed, these attitudes and practices, which also informed colonial society, have continued unabated since independence. As anthropologist Aquiles Escalante has noted:

[T]hat mighty force bestowed by the fact of being white maintains all of its power in Colombia. White skin, blue eyes and blonde hair are magic wands which like art of enchantment make all socio-economic barriers fall automatically. (*El negro en Colombia* 138)

It would not be surprising, then, to find that much racial mixing in Colombia has been subliminally motivated by a desire to overcome barriers and to achieve a greater measure of acceptance, respect, and self-esteem, which may be denied to black and indigenous persons of unmixed ancestry.[28]

While officials and elites in postindependence Colombia have tended to exalt and exploit *mestizaje* as cultural heritage or ethos, presenting it as a symbol or reflection of national identity, on another level it has meant denial or disregard of the black presence. As in other lands of Spanish America, blackness or Africanness in Colombia has too frequently been seen as synonymous with inferior ancestry, lower-class status, innate laziness, cultural backwardness, and savage barbarism (Escalante, *El negro en Colombia* 108; Guzmán Izquierdo 2525; Wade, *Blackness and Race Mixture* 20).[29] It is especially noteworthy that during the colonial period, the word *mandinga*, referring to enslaved Africans of the Mande group from the Guinea Coast area, came to be associated with "devil" (H. Restrepo 37–38; B. Davidson 103).[30] It should come as no surprise, therefore, that many persons of African descent, harboring deep-seated feelings of inferiority and self-hatred, and despising the negative images of black people and culture that have existed and been widely disseminated, would resent being identified as a black (*negro*) or being associated with an African heritage.[31] Writer Zapata Olivella's comments on a relative of his and on the attitude of most African-descended people in twentieth-century Cartagena can probably be applied to a great number of Afro-Colombians:

> She remembered nothing about her distant forebears, nor did she acknowledge any linkage with those blacks with whom she had no family ties. The majority of African descendants in Cartagena, eager to find a place in a discriminatory society, dragged this lack of identity around like a shield.
>
> . . . .
>
> Reasons abound, then, why the ideal of dignity and pride held by Cartagena's mulattoes and mestizos cannot take sustenance from their tragic and wretched African or indigenous ancestry. Their aspirations and impulses of identification, like the few unmixed descendants of Spaniards, are directed at seeing themselves as representatives of peninsular [i.e., Iberian] culture. Led by ideals imposed by the dominant group, Indians and blacks looking at their mirror images hardly had or have eyes to discover the ethnic features of their true race. (*¡Levántate, mulato!* 59, 65)

Consequently, since the colonial beginnings of Colombia, many persons of African descent have not only moved away from their ancestral origins by dint of forced migration and acculturation, but also via miscegenation. They have learned all too well that lighter skin and non-Negroid features may assist in obtaining job and educational opportunities often denied to those of darker pigmentation and African features, and that with education, wealth, a good job, and a nonblack identity an individual can, to some extent, improve his or her social status. Clearly, literature that openly espouses black identity or proudly proclaims an African cultural background is not likely to emerge from persons eager to escape or hide blackness.

The conditions described above—and particularly prevalent during the colonial era in the Atlantic region, where social interaction between peoples of African, European, and native American background easily occurred— would seem to have attenuated in many Negroids a need for racial solidarity and impeded the development of a vital, aggressive sense of black or African identity. Furthermore, inasmuch as expressions of ethnicity that authorities considered lewd, pagan, or threatening (e.g., language, certain religious practices, funeral rites, scarification, use of magic herbs and potions) were forbidden, punished, and suppressed, many aspects of African heritage gradually disappeared from sight and memory or were merged with other cultural forms.[32]

With its underlying implication of biological and cultural whitening, the reality of *mestizaje* also seems to have impeded at times the maintenance or development of strong group consciousness or identity among peoples of African origin. As in the Pacific region, a more viable African-based cultural identity could be expressed only outside of the larger Hispanic society, as in the maroon settlement of Palenque de San Basilio, whose inhabitants maintained a strict practice of endogamy.[33] Such communities, however, separated from and at odds with mainstream Hispanic culture and lacking educational opportunities, were not likely either to produce a tradition of scribal literature. On the other hand, for the few racially conscious Colombian writers of African descent who did emerge before the early twentieth century, there were other conditions arising from slavery and race relations that hindered an overt expression of literary blackness in their homeland. To demonstrate this more effectively, the following chapter compares the impact of slavery and race relations on the development of black literary expression in Cuba and Colombia.

2

COMPARATIVE PERSPECTIVES:

Slavery, Race Relations, and Black Literary Expression

in Early Cuba and Colombia

> If we aspire to the survival of democracy, we must become
> participants in the struggle that is now taking place in the world,
> to achieve democratic ideals, for which we need the feeling of in-
> feriority that has worked upon our psychology like a tremendous
> weight, to disappear. And we understand that one of the means
> of making it disappear is that of being able to shout "Long live
> the black race."
>
> Natanael Díaz (1943)

Cuba and Colombia share a common background of Span-
ish colonization, African slavery, and significant literary production. Within
both countries peoples of African descent comprise a significant proportion
of the population. Moreover, both nations have produced important writers
of African descent, as well as prominent works on their respective African
populations. Nevertheless, while black and mulatto writers in Cuba began
emerging in the early nineteenth century and have been a fairly constant and
conspicuous presence since then, Colombian writers of African descent did
not become visible until the second half of that century and even then their
presence tended to be rather sporadic and their voices somewhat muffled.
Furthermore, while there developed as early as the seventeenth century a
marked literary interest in representing blacks as an integral element of Cuba,
no similarly noteworthy concern has been evident in Colombia.

Through the methodology of comparison and contrast, this chapter will
show how slavery and race relations influenced the development of literature
by and about blacks in the two countries. More precisely, this discussion will
serve as a necessary and useful backdrop to understanding and appreciating
the poetry of Jorge Artel as a unique Colombian expression and not as a mere
extension of Afro-Cuban writing. My hypothesis is threefold: first, I contend
that in Cuba the rapid decline of the Indian population, the protraction of
slavery and the slave trade, and the growth of a large mulatto group fostered
there both an early interest in blacks as a literary subject and a precedence

in the development of literary expression by persons of African descent. Second, I maintain that the lengthy period of Spanish colonial domination and later foreign intervention on the island tended to promote a strong national consciousness that, at times, united blacks and whites in a common struggle. Third, I hold that the nature of race relations in Cuba encouraged a more assertive—if not direct—literary response by Afro-Cuban writers. As a consequence of these circumstances three important developments occurred: in the first place, the African presence became an essential—albeit often begrudged—feature of Cuban identity; second, a strong tradition of literature by and about people of African descent became inextricably intertwined with the national literature and history; and third, Afro-Cuban writing became a viable and frequent conduit for overt expression of an oppositional discourse of racial pride and ethnic challenge to the racial status quo.

Conversely, in Colombia—whose more ethnically diverse population reflects the mingling of Indian, African, and European groups; whose independence from Spain was achieved early in the nineteenth century but whose sense of national unity was delayed and periodically threatened by regional factionalism and internecine conflicts; and whose culture exhibits a historical as well as ethno-geographical dichotomy of coast versus interior— black literary expression not only evolved more slowly, but also was perceived as exotic, out of step with majority concerns and tastes, and less worthy of national regard and respect. Moreover, the black presence was not considered or treated by writers and intellectuals of the dominant classes as a fundamental element of Colombia's human and cultural landscape. In addition, the deep-rooted (albeit contradictory) ethos of *mestizaje* and the less violent and confrontational nature of race relations between blacks and dominant white-mestizo groups in Colombia also contributed to a less racially assertive posture by writers of African descent. I shall begin this discussion with an examination of the institution of slavery in the two countries and continue it with a brief review of race relations.

Before comparing the institution of slavery in the two countries, a few general words about Cuban geography are in order. Unlike Colombia, which is situated on the South American mainland, Cuba is an island nation in the Caribbean. Reached by Colombus during his maiden voyage to the New World, the narrow island contains many excellent harbors, which no doubt facilitated contraband trade. Cuba's proximity to Hispaniola, Jamaica, and Puerto Rico, as well as to Florida and Mexico on the North American mainland, permitted relatively easy communication with and travel to these sites and fostered early Spanish settlement.

Comprising a total area of 44,218 square miles, Cuba is about one-fourth the size of Colombia. While its topography is certainly diverse, it consists largely of plain and rolling land. Mountainous terrain occupies only about one-fourth of the land and its altitude does not compare to that of the Colombian Andes. This geographical configuration abetted "the development of a good overland transport system" (Blutstein et al. 10) and no doubt facilitated communication throughout the island. This did not preclude, however, regional variations in economic pursuits, customs, political loyalties, and racial concentrations. In fact, the strength of such regionalism was made manifest during the War of Independence (Helg 58, 72, 74). It would appear, however, that the geography of Cuba has been less a barrier to national unity than that of Colombia.

SLAVERY PERIOD

The presence of peoples of African descent in the Americas is largely the result of the transatlantic slave trade. Millions of men, women, and children were forcibly taken from their homelands to serve as the primary labor force in the New World. Although African slavery was widespread, certain variables—such as the kind of labor performed, the location of the slave (e.g., urban vs. rural setting, island vs. mainland), the number of slaves or their ratio within the total population, and the length of duration of slavery—could and did affect the institution and, in turn, its impact upon the people and culture of a given area. These variables account for some of the major differences between the experiences of enslaved Africans in Cuba and their counterparts in Colombia.

Cuba

Prior to the nineteenth century, the Spanish-controlled island of Cuba was largely a permanent settler society, characterized by "[s]mall towns and insignificant class and caste distinctions" (Knight, "Slavery" 206; Knight, *African Dimension* 38).[1] Cuba's population as a whole was relatively small, with whites holding a slight majority (Masferrer and Mesa-Lago 353). Between 1791 and 1820, however, Cuba transformed from a settler society to a plantation society based on sugarcane production. The unquenchable demand for more laborers increased slave numbers to such an extent that for several decades (1817–61) Afro-Cubans constituted the majority of the island's population (Knight, "Slavery" 206; Masferrer and Mesa-Lago 357).[2] Concomitantly, white fears of black revolt and resistance, fueled by the success of the revolution in neighboring Haiti, also grew. With this fear, more restrictive and discriminatory measures were imposed on both the slave and free colored communities throughout much of the nineteenth century (Knight, "Slavery" 211–12). In addition, as Knight points out, "The plantation fostered two separate societies in Cuba. For those whites caught in the penumbra of sociocultural divisions, the only recognition was race, which allowed them to escape from the discrimination, the segregation, and the coercion of the system" ("Slavery" 222).

Owing to their employment in the sugarcane industry, the majority of slaves, throughout much of the nineteenth century, were situated in the rural areas of the island (Knight, "Slavery" 206–07). Although education was generally beyond the reach of bondmen of the rural plantations, under propitious circumstances an urban house slave might manage to acquire the rudiments of learning. Such was the case with the slave-poet Juan Francisco Manzano (1797?–1854), whose poetic ability was instrumental in obtaining his freedom. During his lifetime Manzano published at least two books of poetry and other works.[3] He is remembered especially, however, for his now famous and unique *Autobiography*, written at the request of the Creole leader Domingo del Monte (Manzano, *Obras* 85; Schulman 27; Jackson, *Black Writers* 27–28), but not published in Spanish until 1937. Both the autobiography and several of Manzano's poems were translated into English in 1840 by the British abolitionist Richard R. Madden, who sought to publicize and disseminate the abuses of slavery as a means of ending the slave trade. Consequently, Manzano's fame as a slave and a literary writer spread beyond his native land and served to preserve his name for posterity.[4]

Notwithstanding the hardships and obstacles that Afro-Cubans faced, their preponderance in the population no doubt increased the likelihood that a good number of them would be drawn, as Manzano was, to the art of writing.[5] Moreover, literature, and particularly poetry, offered an indirect and less obvious means of denouncing the inhumanity and injustice of slavery and (racial) oppression. Through the ambiguity of metaphor and the disguise of evasion, Afro-Cuban writers could express their collective and individual frustrations and anger vis-à-vis the injustices of society. This technique seems to be characteristic especially of one of the most celebrated of the early Cuban poets of color, Gabriel de la Concepción Valdés (1809–44), a free mulatto (or quadroon) known popularly as "Plácido."[6] As José Antonio Portuondo observes,

> Plácido calls attention to the impossibility of singing openly the most fervent longings of his soul, and therefore he conceals them, in accordance with Spanish models, in poems to Greece, to Poland . . . [etc.], among the stanzas of which there is always some arrogant affirmation of his hatred for tyrants and of his love for freedom. . . . (*Bosquejo* 22)[7]

It must also be noted that Plácido identified with his racial confreres and sympathized with the plight of colored bondmen. Although his poetry does not evince a direct attack on black slavery nor an overt statement of racial pride and solidarity, within his poetic denunciation of tyranny and exaltation of liberty can be found a subtle, carefully wrought antislavery message (Castellanos and Castellanos 213–14). Moreover, his verses titled "Epigrama satírico" ridicule the fatuousness of color prejudice.

If the uneven quality of Plácido's verses did not earn him distinction as a superior poet, his rebelliousness, arrest, and subsequent execution by firing squad for alleged participation in the infamous "Conspiracy of the Ladder" of 1844 certainly enhanced his fame. In the decades following Plácido's death, new editions of his poems were published in New York (1854), Paris (1857), and Havana (1886) and some of his works were translated into English. Indubitably, Plácido's heroically tragic fate made him a martyr for Cuban liberty, helping to ensure a permanent and respected place for him in the hearts and memory of many Cubans, as well as in the Cuban Parnassus. As we shall see later, Candelario Obeso, Colombia's first known poet of African descent, who was born five years after Plácido's execution in 1844, also suffered a tragic existence. Unlike Plácido's heroic end, however, Obeso's death was shrouded in ignominious speculation and condemnation, and bore the stigma of suicide.

Fear of slave revolts and black conspiracies, such as that of 1844, prompted Spanish authorities to impose stricter regulatory controls on the Cuban colored population (Corwin 81; Knight, *Slave Society in Cuba* 95; Knight, "Slavery" 211–13).[8] As Knight observes, the prejudices of slavery and race were inescapable. Racial prejudice and the policy of legal discrimination and segregation created, in turn, greater resentment among Afro-Cubans, who "turned inward to themselves and their own community" ("Slavery" 216).[9] Therefore, Afro-Cubans organized themselves, developed their own institutions, including newspapers and printing presses, and promoted their own values of racial pride, which, no doubt, increased their sense of group identity and solidarity.[10] This would lead—as Trelles's "Bibliografía" demonstrates—to a more self-conscious ethnic awareness and a more prominent profile for writers, poets, and intellectuals of African descent, who often articulated and symbolized the plight and struggle of their people.

As the examples of Manzano and Plácido show, in nineteenth-century Cuba, literature by writers of African descent and the institution of slavery—or, more precisely, resistance to slavery—were often closely linked. The efforts of white intellectuals also strengthened these ties. Francisco Calcagno's publication in 1868 of a series of bio-critical essays on several Afro-Cuban poets no doubt served as an acknowledgment of the presence, literary talents, and artistic potential of Cubans of African ancestry.[11] In addition, the profits of a third edition of Calcagno's work, which appeared in book form in 1879, went toward purchasing the freedom of another slave poet, José del Carmen

Díaz, of Güines (Coulthard 19).[12] Such natural or cultivated ability, it could be argued, deserved to be released from the shackles of slavery. Once again, literary creativity and the cause of black freedom were intertwined.

Although the slave trade to Cuba was officially ended in 1866, it appears that enslaved Africans were brought surreptitiously to the island for years afterward (Murray 322).[13] The institution of slavery in Cuba, however, was not abolished until 1886, more than a generation after most Spanish-speaking nations of the Americas had outlawed the practice. As a result, the African presence remained constant and strong throughout most areas of the island, influencing and enriching not only the population, but also the language, the literature, religious practices (e.g., *santería, ñañiguismo*), and many other aspects of Cuban culture and society. Understandably, black and brown faces were certainly common sights not only in the capital but throughout the different regions of the island. During the protracted struggle against Spanish domination, which began with the Ten Years War (1868–78) and ended with the Cuban-Spanish-American War (1895–98), Cubans of African descent became a significant force.[14] Notwithstanding the prejudice and discrimination that Afro-Cubans faced throughout these years and after independence, the recognition accorded by José Martí and other white leaders to such distinguished military and civilian Afro-Cuban leaders as Antonio Maceo (1845–96), Juan Gualberto Gómez (1854–1933), and Martín Morúa Delgado (1856–1910) may serve as an indication of the inexorable and crucial involvement of blacks in Cuban affairs (Masferrer and Mesa-Lago 351).

The harshness and prolongation of plantation slavery in Cuba also stimulated the creation of a sizeable body and noteworthy tradition of antislavery literature, which further helped to center black Cuban life and problems within the general struggle for national independence from Spain and to place them on a strong footing with other literary themes (Olivera 150, 151).[15] Whether inspired by the horrors of African bondage or by fear of the growing black presence on the island, many white poets and novelists, such as Domingo del Monte, Félix Tanco y Bosmeniel, Anselmo Suárez, Cirilo Villaverde, Gertrudis Gómez de Avellaneda, José Jacinto Milanés, and Gerónimo Sanz exposed and denounced the evils of slavery in moving verses and stirring prose that reached audiences throughout the Hispanic world and beyond.[16]

Clearly, slavery had a sustained and widespread impact on Cuban society, culture, and literature. Encouragement and manumission of slaves of African descent who demonstrated literary talent was, if not common, at least not unheard of. Spanish suppression of black and mulatto conspiracies—real or imagined—that sought an end to white rule served to dramatize throughout much of the Western world the sufferings of Afro-Cuban people and, by creating martyrs, further publicized the writings of Plácido and others who condemned tyranny and slavery. Finally, antislavery writings by white Creole intellectuals were also widely disseminated in Spain and Spanish America. This had the effect of exposing the inhumanity and atrocities of African bondage, furthering the intimate relationship between literature and slavery in Cuba, and enhancing the representation of the island as a primary site of black struggle in Spanish America. By extension, this helped to maintain Afro-Cubans as a major focus of Cuba's intellectual and literary concerns. All of these factors contributed to the creation in Cuba of a tradition of writing both by and about blacks that later poets and writers—especially those of African descent—could call upon proudly while also attempting to find expression for their own individual voices.

Colombia

While slavery was on the rise in Cuba, it was declining in most other lands of the Americas (Knight, "Slavery" 221), including Colombia. The decreased importation of slaves, the financial inability of owners to acquire more slave labor, and other economic factors contributed to this decline (Jaramillo Uribe, *Ensayos* 71–77). Moreover, unlike Cuba, Colombia did not have an intensive monoculture economy that required thousands of laborers. Rather, as pointed out in chapter 1, slave labor was quite diversified, although most of the bondmen were concentrated in the mining zones of the Chocó and the greater Cauca region. Despite the heavy involvement of slaves in many different activities, with the coming of the new spirit of Enlightenment New Granada was not so dependent upon slave labor that "creole antislavery leaders could not prepare society to sacrifice the institution upon the altar of democratic idealism" (J. King 314). Later, during the War of Independence (1810–21), both the patriot and Spanish armies enlisted slaves in their cause under the promise of freedom, which further weakened the institution.

Between 1778 and 1852, the year of final abolition, the majority of slaves were still located in the gold-mining provinces of the Colombian south and southwest, fairly distant from the major urban and cultural centers of Bogotá and Popayán. In fact, as one student of Colombian slavery has noted, African bondage in Colombia was unique in that only there were Africans "consistently used in large numbers during a long period of time as the chief source of labor in the [gold] mines" (J. King 296). (It is not surprising that the best-known popular song of black resistance, "A la mina no voy" [To the mine I will not go], is directed against forced labor in mining, whereas in Cuba the intensive plantation labor of the sugar harvest season [the *zafra*] provoked protest songs.) In sum, as historian James Ferguson King points out, the importance of slavery "as a source of labor in the mining of gold and its wide distribution in small settlements . . . were in contrast to the primarily agricultural character and denser, more even distribution of slavery in Cuba, Puerto Rico, and other regions" (307).[17]

While the total black population of Colombia never exceeded the white, in many of the western mining areas, such as Barbacoas and the Chocó, blacks and mulattoes often outnumbered whites (Hamnett 297, 303; Sharp, "Manumission" 93–94).[18] Although working conditions were often harsh and arduous and led to rebellions and flight, in the Chocó, at least, the lack of weapons, the possibility of increased personal comforts, and the incentive of manumission through individual initiative effectively kept the slaves in subjection (Sharp, "Manumission" 106–07; J. King 311). Those same conditions seem to have worked simultaneously against the growth of a strong spirit of group solidarity and action among many slaves and freemen, and probably fostered a concentration of efforts on gaining individual liberty rather than on undertaking collective acts of resistance conducive to freedom and black empowerment.

Understandably, upon becoming free many ex-slaves preferred an isolated existence in the jungles and forests to coexistence with whites. The paucity of schools, the lack of financial resources among the ex-slaves, and the existence of discriminatory policies, however, meant that formal educational and cultural opportunities for these descendants of Africans were virtually nonexistent (see Velásquez, "Apuntes socio-económicos" 189; Sharp, "Manumission" 98–99).[19] Obviously, such circumstances were not conducive to the pursuit or acquisition of European models of culture and standards of learning, nor to the writing and publishing of literary works. This would explain to a great extent the absence of known black writers from the Negroid areas of western Colombia prior to the late nineteenth century.

On the Atlantic coast of Colombia, where people of African descent had long constituted a significant proportion of the population and where opportunity for economic and social advancement was greater, slavery, as mentioned above, was less important to the economy. Consequently, manumission was common and blacks and their descendants were more peacefully integrated into coastal society. Subdued racial conflict, combined with a high degree of interracial mixing, permitted a greater proportion of persons of African descent in the Atlantic coastal region to gain entry or access to the ranks of the culturally and educationally privileged. Significantly, Cartagena, the largest urban center on the coast throughout the colonial period (Grahn, "Cartagena and its Hinterland" 180), contrasted with Havana, in that in Cartagena, "men of obscure origin managed to redefine their status through militia office" and Spanish officers, exhibiting a flexibility not found in the Cuban capital, were known to protect their black soldiers against local justice (Kuethe, "Havana in the Eighteenth Century" 32).

As a consequence of these conditions, one might expect to encounter occasionally the name of a poet or writer who stood out if only because of African ancestry. Such, however, is not the case, and this raises several conjectures: first, that there were no authors of African descent in the early decades of the 1800s; second, that the racial identity of a person—especially if educated—was considered irrelevant or insignificant and therefore not worthy of mention; or, third, that African ancestry was in some way concealed or downgraded. The first conjecture, as I will show shortly, can be readily discounted. Regarding the second, there is no evidence to show that racial identity had ceased to be irrelevant, even in social, cultural, and educational circles. More convincing is the third conjecture. If in slave societies, as Frederick P. Bowser claims, "free blacks and mulattoes were anxious most of all to forget their racial origins or at least to whiten themselves as much as possible" (56), it is likely that mixed-race persons of African descent who had achieved some measure of social status and respect would be even less willing to embrace blackness and champion the African heritage.

The example of Juan José Nieto (1804–66) of Cartagena would seem to confirm the custom of minimizing or understating Negroid ancestry. Of mixed racial ancestry and "of humble birth"—which often was a veiled allusion to nonwhite racial origins—Nieto rose militarily and politically to become an army general, the governor of Cartagena, the president (or caudillo) of the state of Bolívar, and a leader of the Liberal Party. He even occupied for a brief time in 1861 the presidency of the young republic (Fals Borda 146B, 156A–57A). By virtue of having published in 1844 and 1845 two historical novels, Nieto enjoys the distinction of being Colombia's first novelist (Curcio Altamar 64).[20] Although coastal sources have identified Nieto as a "a lean, tall and proud scion of the vanquished race" and "a noble exponent of the colored race" (Vega 76; *Geografía económica de Colombia* 205),[21] until recently national biographical sources have tended to avoid mention of Nieto's racial heritage (e.g., Ospina 3:90–91). On the surface, such practice might indeed suggest that racial concerns in Colombia have been insignificant or minimal. A more plausible explanation, however, is that since African ancestry carried the stigma of slave origins, and Nieto's attainments had clearly elevated his social status, separating him from the colored masses, it would be inappropriate and insulting to call attention to his racial background—and even more so during his lifetime.[22] Indeed, Nieto, who had been exiled from Colombia during the early years of the new republic, was not a man to be trifled with.[23] For those unfamiliar with Nieto, the official silence surrounding his racial background served to accord him "quasi-white"—or at least nonblack—identity, thereby in effect erasing, or rather excluding, his name from the ranks of recognized and self-identified writers of African origin.

The problem of identity in early Afro-Colombian writers is probably no better exemplified than in the life and writings of the poet Candelario Obeso. Also a native of the Atlantic coast region, Obeso is best known for his *Cantos populares de mi tierra* (1877), the first book of poetry—or prose for that matter—by an Afro-Colombian author that focuses directly and primarily on black people of Colombia.[24] Written in the first person and employing the vernacular speech of the coastal inhabitants, the *Cantos populares* express the voices of the anonymous Negroid boatmen, peasants, and fishermen of the Atlantic littoral and the lower Magdalena River Valley. This work, as well as other writings by Obeso, offers a black, nonelitist perspective on Colombian society and provides a glimpse of the difficulties and dilemmas Obeso faced as a poor but talented and intelligent black coastal man in a racially conscious yet genteel, European-oriented culture. Two prose pieces by Obeso are especially illustrative. The first, a public letter to Santiago Pérez, then president of Colombia and a recognized dramatist, was a retort to an article that took issue with an earlier criticism Obeso had leveled against the Pérez administration. The anonymous author of the article, who signed himself "Uno que no es Obeso," stated that "the writer Obeso must have arrived a short time ago from Asia or Africa, since he is unaware of the distinctive character of Mr. Pérez" ("Lo que suena"). In his letter Obeso asked,

> And . . . how did Your Excellency find out that I come from Africa? It seems to me that Your Excellency employs the free time which the dramatic art leaves you in studying something of more usefulness and honor, anthropology, for example, because only in that way could Your Excellency hit upon the strange discovery that my ancestors were animals of that zoological region, inasmuch as I cannot present the characteristic type of the race, by virtue of mediating mixtures, and because my predecessors, having settled a long time ago in a cold rather than warm country, little by little lost their skin pigment up to the point that I am now a *mulatto*, and not a Negro, as Your Excellency mistakenly thinks. ("Palabras al aire"; original emphasis.)[25]

Assuming it was a sincere expression of his feelings (and not an example of "*mamagallismo costeño*," i.e., coastal jesting), Obeso's statement evinces the delicate sensitivity of educated Afro-Colombians to societal emphasis on family origins and to racial stereotype and innuendo. It is important to note that Obeso was a member of the first generation of postemancipation, educated Afro-Colombians, which, on the one hand, was seeking admittance to the privileged ranks of the modern, European-oriented society of Colombia, dominated by the white and mestizo Creole elite. On the other hand, these Afro-Colombian individuals still had strong emotional and familial ties—and even regional loyalties—to the people, culture, and values that informed, maintained, and characterized traditional black life. As a member of this generation, Obeso no doubt found himself in a tenuous, and at times uncomfortable and psychically demanding, position: attempting to reconcile his proud provincial background and his identity as a humble yet intelligent, black *costeño* with the Euro-ethnocentric culture of the privileged, white-mestizo elite of Bogotá. Such a position or dilemma corresponds to what Lawrence W. Levine has called "a culturally marginal situation." This "marginality," as Levine explains, is "a more obviously bi-cultural or multi-cultural situation in which a group, poised to some extent between two worlds, finds its desire to absorb and emulate the culture of a dominant group, in an attempt to attain and enjoy the latter's privileges and status, in tension with its urge to continue to identify with many of its own central cultural traditions" (138).

To Obeso's credit, however, he succeeded in coming to terms with his black identity and rejected the cult of whiteness so prevalent in his country. In a later prose piece published in 1878 he asserted:

The tradition of some is horrible, dark like their souls. Their aim is to be white and *pretty.* . . . As for me I am honored to be black and my ugliness delights me. When ugliness polished pleases, it is for real. Human regeneration is in my race. (*Lectura para ti* 5)[26]

While many readers today may appreciate and admire Obeso's proud affirmation of black identity, such remarks seem to have only earned him a reputation as a *negro acomplejado*—that is, a black man ashamed of his race—as comments by Uribe (2:109) and A. J. Restrepo (*Sombras chinescas* 214) show.[27] For in Obeso's time, and even since then, the notion of racial harmony and equality permeated Colombian literature and society and was the more credible when contrasted with the situation of blacks and mulattoes in countries such as Cuba or the United States (see J. M. Samper, *Ensayo* 91; Cordovez Moure, *De la vida de antaño* 80; and chap. 1:31 above).[28] It was generally claimed—if not believed—that with independence from Spain and the subsequent abolition of slavery, all Colombians came to enjoy the same legal rights and privileges. Indeed, as mentioned earlier, in Colombia—and particularly on the Atlantic coast—a less severe and less overt form of discrimination tended to give the impression of a more open and just society. Even Obeso contributed to this notion. In his poem "Epresión re mi amitá" [Expression of My Friendship] the three primary racial groups that compose Colombia's population—African, European, and Amerindian—are described as enjoying equality of citizenship. One can also discern, however, in the poem's brief comparison of the situation of the Afro-Cuban and the

Afro-Colombian, Obeso's awareness and critique of the condition of people of African descent in his own homeland. As the narrator of the poem recalls,

> . . . when I was a sailor,
> as bad luck would have it,
> I went to Havana, and damned
> If I ran into a happy zambo
> They being treated as an ass more than here . . .
> Not for one single moment could I
> Enjoy my free will.

> . . . cuando fui marino,
> Poc malo re mi pecaos,
> Tuve en la Habana, y mardito
> Si topé un zambo richoso
> Siendo má que aquí un pollino . . .
> Ni pure un solo momento
> Hocgarme re mi albedrío! . . . (*Cantos populares* [1877] 27)[29]

The subtle yet telling metaphorical allusion to the Afro-Colombian (*zambo*) as a beast of burden (*pollino*) suggests that even if Obeso truly believed that legal equality existed for the different racial groups in Colombia, he did not fail to apprehend the socioeconomic inequalities and ethnic considerations that prevented persons of African descent, like himself, from achieving full acceptance and self-actualization.

Nevertheless, there did not exist in Colombia the same overt hostility, discrimination, and flagrant forms of oppression against people of color as existed in Cuba—a situation that, as we have seen, made it advisable and necessary for Afro-Cubans to band together and establish self-help organizations and institutions of a racial character. Moreover, such groupings and activities probably would have been interpreted by Colombian political elites as a threat to the incipient spirit and sentiment of national solidarity and, doubtless, would have been discouraged, if not stifled.[30] It is also significant that after slavery finally ended in Colombia in 1852, the white authorities saw no need for social and economic assistance programs geared specifically to the ex-slaves and their families. It is likely that the incidence of interracial marriage and the presence of noteworthy descendants of Africans who had risen to high positions in the military and in regional and national politics, both before and after 1852, served to blunt or discredit any black discourse critical of the racial status quo.[31]

All available evidence indicates, then, that on the whole, Afro-Colombians, unlike their Cuban counterparts, did not form racially based institutions separate from those of mainstream Colombian society.[32] Rather, it seems that they were more intent on either living freely and independently of former masters or claiming a legitimate space and place in Colombian mainstream society. In any case, they were determined to erase or forget the stigma of slavery. As early as 1832 one foreign traveler in the new republic noted that ex-slaves did not wish to be reminded of their former status, preferring to put both physical and psychological distance between their position as free persons and that of their enslaved forebears (Empson 56). If they were not white and well-off, at least they could enjoy and take pride in being—even if only theoretically—free and equal members of the new society.

The possibility of an individual's improvement of his social standing and economic condition, or that of his progeny, through good connections (*palanca*), education, wealth, intermarriage, or miscegenation, may well have served to weaken among many Afro-Colombian communities—except in times of crisis or extreme duress—the potential or perceived need for group solidarity and action based on racial identification.[33] Separated from one another by geography, diverse slavery experiences, and racial mixing; not subject generally to any overt or direct policy of racial discrimination as in Cuba; and lacking an adversarial catalyst (internal or external) that might stimulate group action, Afro-Colombians, like others who belonged to or more or less identified with the dominant Hispanic group, tended to relate as much to their region, their class, and their political affiliation as to their race or African heritage—if not more so.[34] Moreover, as historian Germán Carrera Damas has stated,

> In societies where Blacks [*sic*] were few or very dispersed, abolition was the final blow to resistance to deculturation, even though this might seem to contradict the deculturing nature of slavery. In fact, the last possibilities of resistance vanished as soon as direct coercion ceased, as soon as Blacks were faced with the problem of becoming incorporated into a discriminatory society without even the support of a viable cultural identity. (36)

In addition, the desire, need, or ability to distance themselves from slavery and to remove the shame associated with the institution probably led many Afro-Colombians to seek assimilation via cultural and even biological amalgamation. Consequently, Afro-Colombians who wanted or envisioned for themselves and their progeny greater opportunities for social, economic, and political advancement were inclined to blend into the society as much as possible, ridding themselves of any aspects of blackness or vestiges of slavery that could be detrimental to social acceptance and improvement. Understandably, those who enjoyed the advantages of a European-oriented education or possessed literary talent and aspirations consistent with the mainstream culture necessarily tended to imitate the models established or followed by the dominant Creole elite. By demonstrating mastery of the prevailing literary forms and themes to a predominantly white and privileged audience, these Afro-Colombian authors might reinforce their public image as cultural and intellectual equals of whites, prove the legitimacy of their association with the Hispanic Creole group, and perhaps solidify their own feelings of adequacy, capability, and Colombianness.

Black and mulatto authors were probably alienated even further from identifying with and expressing concern for black populations by the often unflattering portrayal of people of color in literature as savage, uncultured, backward inhabitants of the uncivilized wilderness, or as simple, contented, childlike elements within a picturesque and paternalistic setting. Moreover, as I have suggested above, the abolition of slavery in the mid-nineteenth-century enhanced the image of Colombia as a burgeoning democratic nation free of racially biased institutions, and no doubt gave the impression to the citizenry that racial problems or racially motivated matters affecting black people were finally laid to rest. Such a view, naïve at best, failed of course to take into account the cultural, social, and intellectual impact of slavery, whose centuries of degradation and privilege could not help but affect the thinking and behavior of Colombians of all shades and racial backgrounds.

Ironically, Afro-Colombians, such as Obeso, who insinuated that racial bias against dark-skinned citizens remained firmly entrenched, ran the risk of being labeled social misfits. On the other hand, those who might dare to espouse black unity and solidarity as a strategy risked being accused of promoting racial division and societal unrest. Therefore, if many of Obeso's white contemporaries found his *Cantos populares* to be not merely novel but even exotic, his revaluation and affirmation of black identity must have seemed ludicrous, and his censure of color prejudice and the cult of whiteness unfounded and full of resentment. Because of his remarks, it will be remembered, some of Obeso's friends assumed that he suffered from feelings of racial inferiority, of having a racial chip on his shoulder. That may have reflected—and even reinforced—a belief in Colombia that assertion of black pride and indictment of white racial attitudes indicated the existence of a problem not in society but rather in an individual who, as one commentator implied of Obeso, had to be either a malcontent or maladjusted (Illidge 154–55).

Considering, too, the widely accepted rumor of Obeso's romantic but inglorious death as a suicide, allegedly caused by his unrequited love for a white woman of Bogotá society (which contrasts sharply with Plácido's heroic martyrdom),[35] it is not strange that no other Afro-Colombian writer would embrace and express blackness as forcefully and resolutely as Obeso did until nearly fifty years later. Moreover, Obeso's use of the black coastal dialect may have been too reminiscent of the speech of illiterate slaves, and his foregrounding of the lives of "uncultured" Negroid masses too embarrassing to set well with those Afro-Colombian poets, writers, and intellectuals determined to prove themselves in accordance with dominant Eurocentric standards of culture.[36]

Seeking accommodation rather than conflict with the dominant culture, Afro-Colombian authors who emerged during the four decades following Obeso's death tended to eschew mention of sensitive matters of race that might call adverse attention to their color or heritage. Moreover, it is likely that they, like other Colombian intellectuals and writers, were often motivated in their behavior and writings as much—if not more—by political and regional sentiments as by racial ideology. To that extent, then, they wanted to be judged by the same criteria supposedly used for nonblack writers: that is, by their talents, abilities, originality, and ideas—and not by their race.

Unlike Cuba, Colombia produced very little imaginative literature directly inspired by the slavery issue (Jaramillo Uribe, *Ensayos* 263). Although there were many obdurate opponents of abolition—including some who cited Biblical scripture to justify black slavery—black bondage never provoked a large outpouring of literary texts. In fact, it appears that most Colombian literature related to slavery was produced after emancipation.[37] Both literary and nonliterary factors appear to have been at work here. Inasmuch as the gold-mining provinces were distant from the major urban cultural centers (e.g., Bogotá, Tunja, Popayán), the cruel realities of slavery, the drama of black life, and the richness of Afro-Colombian culture were neither readily visible, nor of interest, to Colombian men of letters, who generally looked to Europe for literary direction and inspiration. Indeed, as Jonathan C. Brown states, "During the last century, the Colombian displayed his erudition in order to set himself apart from the common man. . . . Culture thus became the deliberate monopoly of the aristocracy—a monopoly sustained, like the elite itself, by a combination of Colombia's economic growth and Bogotá's isolation" (450). Considering, too, that "the outstanding characteristics of Colombian poets in this era were their denial of the environment and their preoccupation with subjects unrelated to national life" (Brown 455), the paucity of Colombian works dealing with slavery is readily understandable.

In sum, the different patterns of slavery and their consequences, as discussed above, were important for promoting in Cuba and hindering in Colombia the emergence of writers of African descent. In the case of the former, several interrelated factors stand out: the prolongation of the Atlantic slave trade and the lengthy duration of slavery resulting, in part, from the dependence on labor-intensive sugar plantations; the dense concentration of Africans (slave and free) on the island; the support, publication, and emancipation of slave poets who exhibited literary talent; the political interests and struggles of Creoles; and the racially discriminatory policies and restrictions of the Spanish authorities. All of these facilitated or fostered the appearance of authors of African descent whose names or works, or both, are part of an undeniably rich and continuous tradition of Afro-Cuban writing.

In addition, the outpouring of antislavery literature and, by extension, of literature on blacks, served to publicize widely the conditions and hardships of black Cubans, in general, and the literary talents of several Afro-Cuban authors, in particular. Dissemination of writings by and about Afro-Cubans also helped to establish and promote Cuban authors as the standard-bearers of Spanish-American literature by and about blacks. With the growing interest in *negrismo* during the early twentieth century, Cuban writers could easily evoke this dual literary heritage to demonstrate the precedence and primacy of their country within the new literary tendency.

In the case of Colombia, however, other factors held sway. These included a more diverse economy without a monoculture dependent on slave labor; a sharp decrease in the importation of Africans into the territory; the frequent practice of manumission and the opportunity for self-purchase; the decline of slavery and its relatively early abolition; the dispersion of ex-slaves into remote and isolated regions of the Pacific coast without the benefit of schools; the absence of overt, racially restrictive, and discriminatory policies; and the incorporation of Negroid peoples into the socioeconomic structure of the more developed Atlantic coast. All of these factors served to inhibit the emergence of racially assertive Afro-Colombian authors and to hinder among Afro-Colombian communities nationwide the development of a collective and combative sense of racial identity and a strong need for group solidarity. This, in turn, tended to impede the creation of black-based institutions that could foster strong racial consciousness, aggressive or uplifting pride in the African heritage, and a recognized tradition of black literary expression.

Thus, while the African element became an integral part of Cuban literature, to the extent that it even produced Cuba's twentieth-century national poet, Nicolás Guillén, in Colombia it failed to become fully recognized and integrated into the national image and cultural consciousness. It is not surprising, therefore, that during the *negrismo* period, when black and white intellectuals in such racially divergent countries as Cuba and Uruguay published anthologies of *poesía negra* (e.g., Ballagas, *Antología;* Guirao, *Orbita;* Pereda Valdés, *Raza negra* and *Antología*) and founded associations and periodicals devoted to the study and dissemination of their nations' African heritage (see Jackson, *Black Writers* 93–111; Lewis, *Afro-Hispanic Poetry*

8–45), Colombian intellectuals failed to do anything comparable. In fact, as I will show in the next section, the racial discourse of leading Colombian social scientists often condemned the black and Indian masses as barbarous and lazy, imputing to them the cause of much of the nation's cultural backwardness. At the same time, however, they devoted little attention to the study of the conditions of black populations per se.

Significantly, through his poetry, prose writings, lectures, and recital tours, Jorge Artel would seek to correct that degrading image and to bring about full recognition and revaluation of the African heritage and the incorporation of Afro-Colombia into the "national" culture. For Afro-Colombian authors both before and after Artel, however, the nature of race relations and the problems of publishing in Colombia would continue to blunt a more assertive racial posture and a more pronounced literary profile.

RACE RELATIONS IN TWENTIETH-CENTURY CUBA AND COLOMBIA

Slavery was finally abolished in Cuba in 1886, some thirty-four years after all slaves had been emancipated in Colombia, and the island finally gained its independence from Spain as a result of the Cuban-Spanish-American War of 1895–98. Despite these momentous events, the situation of Afro-Cubans did not change significantly and racial conflicts continued (Masferrer and Mesa-Lago 360; Fernández Robaina 21). Not only did a small group of white Cubans (the Creoles) come to exercise control and refuse to share power with the blacks and mulattoes, but economic and educational opportunities for people of color were also slow in coming.[38] Economically, Afro-Cubans continued to occupy the lower wage sectors in disproportionate numbers, holding menial jobs and performing work that required much heavy or intensive physical labor.

The persistence of subtle forms of discrimination customarily directed against Afro-Cubans and the presence of disparities stemming from "the economic inequalities of a developing nation" (Masferrer and Mesa-Lago 351) also prevented Cuban people of color from making significant socioeconomic inroads. Furthermore, the strong U.S. presence (i.e., its occupation of the island) at the end of the war and its frequent intervention in the internal affairs of the new nation, legally permitted under the Platt Amendment, no doubt heightened racial discrimination and increased racial tensions.[39]

Consequences of these conditions were a more militant and aggressive attitude of resistance on the part of Afro-Cuban intellectuals and writers and the establishment of organizations devoted to securing the rights of Afro-Cubans. Even before independence was won, Afro-Cuban journalists and intellectuals had long been condemning racial injustice, urging the union of blacks and mulattoes, supporting education for Afro-Cubans, and struggling to overturn discriminatory policies (Deschamps Chapeaux 13–17). From the pages of his newspapers *La Fraternidad* (1879–90) and *La Igualdad* (1892–95), both of Havana, Juan Gualberto Gómez denounced deprecatory remarks directed against black women, promoted unity of Cubans irrespective of color, and forcefully articulated the concerns and interests of Cubans of African descent (Fernández Robaina 25–26; Deschamps Chapeaux 52–63, 75–80).

At the end of the nineteenth century and during the early years of the twentieth century, black Cubans established various organizations of mutual assistance and collective action, such as the Central Directory of Societies of the Colored Race and the Committee of Veterans and Societies of the Colored Race (Fernández Robaina 23–24, 38–39). In 1907 several Afro-Cubans, committed to gaining power and obtaining benefits for the black and mulatto population and disgruntled with white political leaders' failure to address their concerns and to include them in the governance of the nation, organized their own political party, the *Partido Independiente de Color,* which attracted many followers. When their efforts for change were ignored and their leaders imprisoned, members of the party rose up in revolt in 1912. The "little war of 1912," as it was called, resulted in the deaths of more than three thousand black and mulatto Cubans and effectively blocked Afro-Cuban influence in national politics (Rout 304).[40] Although Afro-Cubans continued to be largely excluded from political affairs and other areas of society, they ceased neither their intellectual struggle nor their literary productivity.

Evidence of this perseverance is provided by Carlos M. Trelles, who in 1927 published an impressive "Bibliografía de autores de la raza de color de Cuba" [Bibliography of Authors of the Colored Race of Cuba], the first such compilation of its kind on the island and possibly too for Spanish-America. Trelles's work recorded 402 publications written by Cubans of African descent between the years 1815 and 1926. Careful scrutiny of the list, however, reveals that not every work was published (e.g., some were lectures) and not every author was a native-born Cuban (e.g., the Puerto Rican Francisco Gonzalo Marín). Moreover, as Trelles himself acknowledeged, not every publication belonged to the realm of the belles lettres; included were letters (e.g., by military leader Antonio Maceo), medical writings, and bills for laws presented by congressional representatives. Nevertheless, the overwhelming number of Afro-Cubans in the listing demonstrates the constancy of their intellectual and literary efforts over more than a century. The fact that Trelles could compile such a work also exemplifies the unceasing attention given to racial matters in Cuba and suggests the staunch determination and pride with which Cubans of African descent endeavored to express their racial self and to inscribe themselves into Cuban history, culture, and society.

Continuing that tradition, in November of 1928 journalist Gustavo Urrutia (1881–1958) began publishing in the Sunday edition of the Havana
newspaper *Diario de la Marina* "a page dedicated to divulging and analyzing
the sociocultural problems of the Cuban Negro," titled "Ideales de una Raza"
[Ideals of a Race] (Fernández Robaina 125). Creation of the page stemmed
from the success of Urrutia's column of the same title, initiated earlier in the
year. From its inception until 1931, when it ceased to appear, the page offered
a forum to Cuban writers and intellectuals of all colors for the discussion of
racial matters. It also served as a vehicle for the publication of literary works,
most notably the "Motivos de Son" of Nicolás Guillén.

As a section of *Diario de la Marina,* Cuba's largest and principal newspaper,
"Ideales" benefited from the publication's wide circulation. Guillén himself
acknowledged the significant role the page played in opening the racial
question and related concerns of Afro-Cubans to public deliberation and
scrutiny, and in shaping his own poetic voice:

> it encouraged a very important debate in a very broad medium, the
> broadest that there had been up to then, and to whose enthusiasm came
> forth several important names of Cuba's black population. I have no
> objection to acknowledging it and proclaiming that the formation of my
> poetic personality owes much to Urrutia's page and to Urrutia personally.
> (Morejón 44)

It is also important to keep in mind that "Ideales" appeared at a fortuitous
moment: when interest in "things Negro" in Cuba and in many other areas
of the world was uniquely intense. As Guillén recalled in the same interview:

> Do not forget . . . that "Ideales de una raza" [*sic*] comes into being at
> the moment black art and culture had its greatest force in the world, a
> fact vividly reflected in Cuba where the historical conditions of social
> integration were very favorable. (Morejón 44)

Earlier in the century ethnologist Fernando Ortiz (1881–1969) had laid
much of the intellectual groundwork for modern studies of the African
presence in Cuban society and culture, stimulating widespread interest in
the subject (see, e.g., *Hampa afro-cubana. Los negros brujos* [1906]; *Hampa
afro- cubana. Los negros esclavos* [1916]). Notwithstanding the racist orientation of his early writings, Ortiz later championed a fair and unbiased
appreciation of black contributions to Cuba's cultural and social heritage.
In addition to founding the Sociedad de Estudios Afro-Cubanos [Society
of Afro-Cuban Studies], he also promoted the study and dissemination of
information related to blacks in Cuba via the society's journal, *Estudios
Afro-Cubanos* (1937–46). Ortiz's writings gained both international respect

and wide dissemination, and his invaluable work promoting awareness of Africa's contribution to Cuban culture and society was acknowledged by many, including Nicolás Guillén.

With Ortiz setting the example for a cadre of researchers of Afro-Cuban history, music, folklore, religion, and literature, Cuba quickly took the lead among Spanish American nations in the reevaluation of the African presence in those republics. Similarly, Afro-Cuban writing of the late 1920s and the 1930s, created by white as well as black and mixed-race authors, would set the standard for the growing production of Spanish-American literary texts dealing with peoples and cultures of African descent. José Z. Tallet, Ramón Guirao, Lino Novás Calvo, Alejo Carpentier, Emilio Ballagas, Marcelino Arozarena, Regino Pedroso, and, of course, Nicolás Guillén are among the better-known Cuban poets and prose writers commonly associated with that trend.

The Gerardo Machado regime (1925–33) and the Fulgencio Batista-dominated period of Cuban life (1933–58) also served to bring blacks and progressive whites closer together. Upon championing the rights and denouncing the exploitation of the working classes—which included, of course, most Afro-Cubans—the Communist Party showed again that the interests of the common people were synonymous with those of the Negro citizens and that politics and black struggle were often united (see Fernández Robaina 146–47, 176–77). Guillén, who became a member of Cuba's Communist Party in 1937, would often use his poetic art to assail imperialism, class exploitation, political tyranny, and racial injustice.[41]

Although institutional forms of racial discrimination had been outlawed by the new republic, racist practices against Afro-Cubans continued systematically "in exclusive social associations and in those places (i.e., fashionable hotels, restaurants, and night clubs) frequented" by the Cuban upper class and American tourists (Masferrer and Mesa-Lago 351, 371). African-American poet and writer Langston Hughes experienced such discrimination during his visit to Cuba in 1931 (*I Wonder as I Wander* 10–15). And almost a quarter of a century later the Afro-Colombian poet Jorge Artel would express poetically his sorrow and indignation upon witnessing in 1951 the segregation of blacks and whites on Cuba's Varadero Beach (see chapter 7). Meanwhile, successful Afro-Cubans, undeterred and following previous custom, formed their own associations, such as "the sophisticated Club Atenas" (Masferrer and Mesa-Lago 371), which Hughes described as "the leading club of color" (*I Wonder as I Wander* 8).

While Afro-Colombians did not fare much better economically and politically than did their Cuban counterparts, generally they did not face the more overt, systematic forms of violence, racial segregation, and discriminatory practices to which Afro-Cubans were subjected. Certainly, laws aimed at limiting political participation to the literate and the landholders directly affected the masses of poor and unschooled Afro-Colombians; the latter, however, were not alone in their plight and did not necessarily ascribe their situation to race alone. Consequently, they did not resort, for the most part, to establishing separate social and political organizations based on race as a means of improving their conditions. (Of course, where local or regional identity coincided with black majority population, as in the Chocó and in settlements and townships of the Cauca, Nariño, and Bolívar, social and political entities often reflected racial group sentiments and concerns.) With the two-party system of Liberals and Conservatives remaining strong, blacks, in general, continued throughout the period of Conservative domination (1885–1930) to support the Liberal Party, which had abolished slavery in 1851. As the words of one popular *copla* declare,

A black conservative
is music that doesn't ring true,
it is a patch on the hamstring
when the pain is in the tooth. (A. J. Restrepo, *El Cancionero de Antioquia* 245)[42]

The Atlantic coast weekly *Rojas Garrido,* named in honor of the distinguished Liberal politician and orator José María Rojas Garrido (1824–83), may well exemplify the approach of the educated—but by no means privileged—black *costeño* to politics and race. Founded in Lorica (Bolívar) in 1917 by Antonio María Zapata [Vásquez] (1898–1968), who was also editor and an occasional contributor of poems, *Rojas Garrido* was unswervingly committed to the Liberal cause, as the opening sentence of Zapata's statement of purpose, published in the premier issue, shows: "We are liberal and as such we only want the triumph of the principles that embody the liberal idea" ("Nuestras ideas" 1).

No mention of race, however, appears in Zapata's declaration. On the other hand, racial awareness is evident in a later article signed by (Gen.) Jesús M. Lugo, a friend of Zapata's and a veteran of the nation's last declared civil war. Lugo argues that Colombian blacks, as descendants of the African slaves, especially should support the erection of a monument to General José Hilario López, the ex-president widely hailed as the liberator of the slaves (Lugo 1). Still another article, published in the newspaper's sixth issue, pays homage to the late Afro-Colombian statesman, Liberal politician, and orator Luis A. Robles, whom the Bogotá intellectual elite called "the Colombian [Frederick] Douglass" (Ceyte 2). Clearly, though, such expressions of racial sentiment and pride do not approach the aggressive group criticism of national policies or match the vindicatory tone of demands for justice and equality that characterized many contemporary Afro-Cuban publications.[43] Given the general assumption and veneer of racial equality and the relatively low level of interracial conflict, most Afro-Colombians probably had little reason or incentive to adopt a militant posture.

Three events occurring at the end of the nineteenth century and the beginning of the twentieth century perhaps best reveal the problem of a lack of national black leadership and the continuance of Afro-Colombians in the lower socioeconomic ranks of society. In September of 1899, Luis A. Robles, the most prominent Afro-Colombian political figure and statesman of the last quarter of the nineteenth century, died in Bogotá. Although Robles did not present himself as a leader of the black population of Colombia, nor did his voice articulate the specific needs and aspirations of Afro-Colombians, his death at the age of fifty effectively left black Colombians bereft of any significant visibility on the national political scene.[44] Moreover, until the return to power of the Liberal Party in 1930 and the removal of legal restrictions on voting, Afro-Colombians were not a factor in national politics (Rout 242).

The year 1899 also marked the beginning of another bloody, protracted civil war, which lasted about three years. The War of a Thousand Days (1899–1902), as it was called, again pitted Colombians, including those of color, against one another. Nevertheless, unlike in Cuba's war of independence, waged only a short time before, no important black political or military leader akin to Cuba's Maceo or Gómez emerged from the conflict.[45] In any case, at least none is mentioned or easily recognizable in the nation's history books.

Finally, in 1903, as a kind of ironic and bitter culmination of the war, the state of Panama, supported by the threat of armed intervention from the United States, declared its independence from Colombia. In addition to the geographical dismemberment and the blow to Colombia's political sovereignty and national honor that this move entailed, the separation of Panama—one of the republic's heavily Negroid coastal states—also meant the immediate loss of a potentially significant source of black writing. At the least it occasioned a serious setback to the salience of Afro-Colombian authors and to black literary expression in Colombia. The Isthmus had already produced the poet and writer Federico Escobar, and in the first decade of the new century the poet Gaspar Octavio Hernández (1893–1918) would make his appearance. Writings by other talented writers of African descent, such as Emilio Echévez and Demetrio Herrera Sevillano (1902–50), would also later enrich the belles lettres of the young republic.

During the early decades of the twentieth century, race as a factor of national development became a major topic of discussion and debate among social scientists and intellectuals in Latin America. Influenced by Positivist ideas, essayists such as Octavio Bunge (1875–1918) of Argentina, Francisco García Calderón (1883–1953) of Peru, and others unashamedly maligned African peoples as a deleterious element that corrupted indigenous and European blood and hindered Latin America's social, economic, and political development. Colombia, too, had its share of learned men who questioned the ability of Afro-Colombians and indigenous peoples to handle the tasks that modernization entailed (Jiménez López et al. 47, 192, 234).[46] Luis López de Mesa (1884–1967), Colombia's preeminent psychologist, and other contemporaries concerned about the alleged physical and moral degeneration of the Colombian people urged the immigration of white Europeans to offset the perceived deficiencies of the colored masses and to provide a more competent workforce (Jiménez López et al. 74–75, 130 and passim).[47] In 1922 the national congress did pass a law encouraging immigration from Europe with a view to improving the genetic component of the country's population (Uribe Celis 31).

Contemporary race relations in Colombia have largely followed the same patterns as those of the last century and earlier periods. Serious, open racial conflict has usually been absent. Unlike Cuba or the United States, Colombia has not experienced de jure racial segregation. As we have seen, however, the geo-ethno-racial configurations of the country have resulted in a de facto separation of large concentrations of Negroid populations from the predominant white Hispanic and mestizo populations. This does not deny, of course, the expression of deeply ingrained racial prejudices among nonblack persons who are natives or residents of heavily Negroid areas (see Naranjo M.).

Moreover, although racial discrimination exists in Colombia, in general it continues to be unacknowledged by those in power, unless it is directed against the indigenous populations. In fact, when Afro-Colombians have charged the existence and practice of racial discrimination, their claims have usually been met with denial and counteraccusations of discrimination from official and institutional quarters. Those who defend Colombia as racially fair and tranquil have been quick at times to point to the United States to support their claims, although they could probably have mentioned Cuba just as easily. Indeed, a cursory comparison of the three countries with respect to peaceful race relations during the nineteenth and twentieth centuries would place Colombia ahead of the others. Certainly in the face of Jim Crow legislation, brutal lynchings, and the segregation of schools and other facilities, which defined much of U.S. society until at least 1954, white and colored Colombians could almost take for granted—and with pride—that racial discrimination against Afro-Colombians was virtually nonexistent.[48]

The absence of antidiscrimination laws in Colombia might also support the notion that such behavior has been nonexistent. In reality, however, as Solaún and Kronus have shown, Colombia maintains "discrimination without violence," or "low levels of race conflict accompanied by the presence of racial discrimination" (1).[49] As a consequence of this societal pattern, it is not easy to prove the intentional practice of racial discrimination, and it is even more difficult to mount a struggle against it. For visitors from abroad who manage to see only the deceptive surface of Colombian life, black citizens often appear to be "happy and free Negroes" (Dolinger) who lead carefree lives of equality, merriment, and fiestas. Indeed, as Rout has wryly observed, "Colombia is . . . presented as a nation where the diverse races have become one big, happy family" (244).

Until recently, in the absence of groundbreaking fieldwork and archival research, this image has remained fairly intact. Unlike Cuba, Colombia shows no strong tradition of scholarly concern for its populations of African descent. Although one can find scattered throughout the historical and scientific literature occasional writings on blacks, mulattoes, and zambos, study of Afro-Colombian communities has been neither systematic nor sustained. At the base of this problem appears to lie an almost reflexive censure of research on racial, or rather, black-related, topics—research that, to many, smacks of unfair distinction. As one Colombian educator admits, "We do not know how many blacks there are now in Colombia, in part because of the difficulty of distinguishing their mixtures, in part because of the horror which we all feel toward racial discriminations" (Arango Bueno 159).[50]

Thus, even questions of race have been eliminated from Colombia's census. According to sociologist T. Lynn Smith, the 1912 and 1918 censuses failed to make racial classifications and grouped all mixed-bloods together, effectively exasperating efforts to determine the precise racial composition of Colombia (63). Subsequent surveys also have omitted racial references. Rout has suggested that regional or national officials may have intentionally committed such omissions in order "to minimize the number of blacks and mulattoes in the country" (243). In that way they could represent Colombia as a predominantly white nation.[51]

All of the events, ideas, and conditions discussed in this chapter help to explain the low visibility of Colombia's population of African descent in national affairs and culture, especially when compared with Cuba. They also elucidate the equally low profile of Colombian writers of African descent, and illuminate Jorge Artel's poetry and thought, which, like Obeso's decades earlier, would mirror the racial climate, geographical separation, and cultural distinctions that characterize their homeland. These factors alone, however, do not fully explain the complex and difficult situation that has impeded the aspirations and efforts of Afro-Colombians to become published and respected authors. Thus, before turning specifically to Jorge Artel and his work, it is necessary to discuss briefly the inveterate problems of the book publishing industry in Colombia.

Geographical barriers, regionalism, slavery, and the paternalistic nature of race relations are not the only important factors that have hindered the development of black literary expression and a more prominent profile for writers of African descent in Colombia. Another major stumbling block has been the underdevelopment of the nation's publishing enterprise, which has presented for lower- and middle-class writers generally no little difficulty in getting their works published, publicized, and distributed.

In his study of the book trade in Colombia, Tito Livio Caldas declared that the state of the country's publishing industry was precarious and disadvantageous owing to a lack of prestigious commercial publishing houses "that have at their disposal international channels of distribution" (29). Caldas explained that the publisher usually is the person who finances the publication. If the publisher is unable—or refuses—to underwrite the work because financial success is not guaranteed, then the author must accept an edition smaller than desired, or he himself must defray the costs of publication by going directly to a (job) printer. Failure to pay for the printing or to sell the work results in confiscation by the printer, who might offer the remaining copies to the public as part of a special sale or promotion.[52]

Undoubtedly, many Afro-Colombian authors, from Obeso's time to the present, have been obliged to resort to direct dealings with a printer in order to get their works published. As persons largely from families occupying the lower rungs of the socioeconomic ladder and often lacking advanced educational training, would-be Afro-Colombian authors no doubt have been hard-pressed to obtain the funds necessary to publish their works—especially the first ones. The art of writing and publishing, like higher education, it must be remembered, has traditionally been the province and pursuit of the privileged classes. Throughout the nineteenth century, as Jonathan Brown reminds us, most Colombian writers who published books belonged to the (white) aristocracy. For members of that privileged group, literary production, although important, was not a professional activity from which they derived their primary income. Rather, they "depended upon the inherited wealth of their families or upon their professions in law or medicine" (449–50). Generally lacking such resources and the educational opportunities and social connections that would enable them to improve their lot substantially, Afro-Colombians have had to struggle continuously to surmount invisible walls of economic disadvantage, cultural exclusivity, and class bias in order to obtain an education, to gain the power of writing, and thus to puncture the silence to which they would otherwise be condemned.

In light of the prohibitive costs of a private university education and the centralism of Colombian society, Afro-Colombians who wished to pursue higher education or obtain certain professional degrees had to gain admission to a public institution in their region or to the National University in Bogotá. For coastal citizens like Obeso and Artel, who did the latter, that path not only meant a long, arduous trip into the high mountainous interior, but also a confrontation with an environment and culture very different from their own. Cultural and environmental differences often were compounded by racial prejudice, as the writings of Obeso (*Lectura para ti* 54) and Zapata Olivella (*¡Levántate, mulato!* 177–80, 183–86) confirm. In addition to these challenges, the economic handicaps under which many black students labored often made it difficult for them to meet the ordinary demands of college studies and to fulfill the basic necessities of life.[53]

When educated Afro-Colombian writers of little means have been able to publish, the size of their first works often have matched their humble economic condition. That is, the publications frequently have been modest efforts—small books, opuscles, and pamphlets, rather than large or "full-length" volumes. Obeso's *Cantos populares* consists of only forty-five pages on 20 cm. x 12 cm. sheets. His novel, *Las cosas del mundo. La familia Pygmalion* (1871) is only nineteen pages in length. Taken together these two books amount to just sixty-four pages. Similarly, Antioqueño author Manuel Baena's first opus, *Aventuras de un estudiante* [Adventures of a Student] (1914), published when he was barely out of school, contains only thirty-seven pages. And *Sal y lluvia* [Salt and Rain] (1948), the first poetry collection by Hugo Salazar Valdés (1926–97), a native of the Chocó, is a pamphlet of merely eight pages containing eleven compositions. Poet Marco Realpe Borja's first book, *Un canto civil a Whitman y otros poemas* [A Civil Song to Whitman and Other Poems] (1959), consists of thirty-nine pages, while Alfredo Vanín Romero's *Alegando que vivo* [Alleging I Live] (1974) numbers just eighteen. As Obeso's poems attest, however, a work's size is not necessarily indicative of its quality—even though first works frequently lack the maturity of style and language of later ones. Nevertheless, it is likely that a slim volume can be overlooked, dismissed, or even lost more easily than a large one.

For financial reasons, too, first works like those mentioned above must have had very small editions, probably of no more than five hundred or one thousand copies, if that many.[54] Consequently, the likelihood of their reaching a large readership was reduced. Artel's long-awaited volume, *Tambores en la noche* (1940), was unusual in that it had an edition of fifteen hundred copies. Even this quantity, however, would be insufficient to reach a large audience within Colombia, much less outside of it.[55] Obviously, publications of this number are aimed at a local market or, at best, a limited national readership.

Unless the author takes it upon himself to see that the book circulates abroad, there is little chance for readers in distant lands to get to know it.

In fact, literary works that appear under such conditions often do not have much of a market. Without a publisher to promote and distribute the work, the book does not reach a wide reading public. Understandably, then, scholars and critics of other countries, and even Colombians unaffiliated with the city or department where the work is printed, might not learn about the new book—much less obtain it—before it disappears from sight. That would explain why in 1946, six years after the publication of Artel's *Tambores en la noche,* the Cuban poet and anthologist Emilio Ballagas was still unaware of its existence (*Mapa* 218). Likewise, poet Lino Antonio Sevillano Quiñones's first effort, *Costa Azul* [Azure Coast], published in Pasto in 1949, apparently did not circulate much beyond the Department of Nariño and possibly a few other areas of the Pacific coast. Héctor Orjuela duly records the book in his bibliography of Colombian poetry, but also notes that he was unable to locate it (414).

Often the author has had to be his own promoter, either personally taking or sending his work to book dealers and thus running the risk of delayed reimbursement for his creative efforts, or distributing his work gratuitously to friends and influential persons and perhaps ending up with no copy of his own.[56] If one of these happens to be a newspaper columnist or magazine editor whose job it is to comment upon literature and to take note of new publications of interest, the work might begin to receive attention, circulate more, and gain its author some critical attention. Nevertheless, the more distant from major cultural centers (e.g., Bogotá, Medellín, Cali) an author is, the less likely it is that his or her work will be sufficiently publicized, circulated, and read, not only beyond the local site of publication, but also beyond the nation's borders. Certainly many books and literary magazines of the "provinces," as the regions beyond the capital used to be called, do not appear in national bibliographical compilations, despite the law requiring that two copies of all works published in Colombia be sent to the National Library. Understandably, then, many aspiring authors from the provincial "margins" endeavor to have their works published in the nation's cultural and political center, where it is more likely that they will be noticed, read, and evaluated. Even with the increased circulation and publicity that editing works in Bogotá offers, however, there is no certainty that the literary establishment there will give them an impartial and constructive critical review.[57]

Indeed, another related factor that has hampered a sharper profile of the Afro-Colombian author has been the difficulty of gaining access to the major print media concerned with cultural promotion. According to the late short-story writer Carlos Arturo Truque (1927–1970), the editors of newspapers and journals exercise considerable censorship and control, severely restricting the writer's freedom and effectively determining which works will appear in their publications ("La vocación y el medio").[58] In an interview published in 1960, Truque asserted that if a writer is not "the begging appendage of a party, it becomes impossible for him to gain access to the publishing media, which is the only way *to get out of anonymity* in our environment which lacks a well oriented publishing industry" (Alvarez D'Orsonville 352; emphasis added).

Besides the impediments mentioned above, certain fundamental problems within Colombian society, posing severe obstructions to book consumption in general, have also hampered the emergence of many an Afro-Colombian author and a general familiarity with black writing. Ironically, illiteracy, a major problem even in the late twentieth century, often has prevented the writer of African descent from reaching either his own racial and regional confreres or the masses of Colombian citizens. Furthermore, many Colombians cannot afford the luxury of buying books, especially those publications that do not serve a practical, instructional purpose in their lives or that are written by little-known authors. As José Nieto rightly questioned, "[How can one] oblige the people to buy if they don't know their authors, if the latter are estranged from all publicity, and if, moreover, it is so expensive to publish a book?" ("Problema de la Actualidad Permanente" 2).[59]

Referring specifically to the lack of stimulus by the public and the indifference of the state in this matter, critic Juan Alvarez Garzón succinctly described the situation of the Colombian writer as a tragedy. In his review of Sevillano's first book, Alvarez Garzón declared: "to write a book is a work of sacrifice, of dedication, of giving of oneself and, in most instances, of running aground against a hard rock of incomprehension" (147).

Political disturbances and natural disasters have also jeopardized at times the incipient careers of young Afro-Colombian writers. Novelist Arnoldo Palacios lost a major part of the manuscript of his first novel, *Las estrellas son negras,* in the conflagration arising from the popular violence, known as the *bogotazo,* that followed the assassination of Liberal leader Jorge Eliécer Gaitán in the capital on April 9, 1948 (see "Las Estrellas son Negras"). Fortunately, Palacios was able to reconstruct the sections that had been destroyed, and published the novel the following year.

Although no such calamity befell Tumaco poet Sevillano's *Costa Azul,* which appeared in the same year, today that book of poems is nowhere to be found. According to one bibliographical source, a copy of the work was located in the library of the University of Nariño, in Pasto (Acosta Hoyos 153). Upon requesting a photocopy of the book in 1974, however, I was informed by the library's director that it was one of several volumes destroyed in a fire. Because the Pacific region, which is home to many small, technologically disadvantaged Negroid communities, has been especially vulnerable to fires, earthquakes, and floods, it is possible that other, unpublished literary creations written by less formally educated inhabitants of that area have been lost forever.[60]

In bygone years, all of the circumstances just described no doubt conspired to prevent many would-be authors from realizing a long-held dream of publishing a work of literature that would be well received by an appreciative audience and read by future generations. In newspapers of the 1940s and 1950s one can read announcements of forthcoming books and notices of manuscripts received by publishing houses that, in the end, have never appeared in print.[61] In an interview conducted in 1943—that is, in the midst of World War II—Artel, who admitted having several books ready for publication, lamented that there was "no paper nor money, nor easy publishers" ("El Poeta Jorge Artel"). Years later the situation had not changed. Writer José Guerra complained in 1950 about the high import taxes on paper, ink, modern equipment, and other items essential to a healthy publishing industry, and about the ease with which foreign books were allowed to enter the country ("El problema editorial" 408).

In sum, it appears that working- and middle-class individuals—of all colors and ethnicities—who have dedicated themselves to the belles lettres have had to face many problems both economic, ideological, and—in the case of those of African descent—racial that have hobbled their aspirations. It thus becomes understandable why titles of works of Afro-Colombian authors frequently have included the word "struggle" (*lucha*) or have intimated an effort to overcome adversity. Examples that can be cited are Obeso's *Lucha de la vida* [Life's Struggle] (1882), Baena's *Cómo se hace ingeniero un negro en Colombia* [How a Black Becomes an Engineer in Colombia] (1929), Francisco Botero's *Fruto de lucha* [Fruit of Struggle] (1931), and Zapata Olivella's *¡Levántate, mulato!* [Rise Up, Mulatto!] (1990).

Notwithstanding the disappointments and setbacks inherent in the struggle to get into print, many talented Afro-Colombian writers have succeeded in doing just that. It is important to mention that the early works of several Afro-Colombian authors who began to gain prominence in the late 1940s and early 1950s—namely, Manuel Zapata Olivella, Arnoldo Palacios, Eugenio Darío, Hugo Salazar Valdés, Miguel A. Caicedo M., Carlos A. Truque, and Rogerio Velásquez—were published by the Editorial Iqueima, whose owner was the Spanish exile Clemente Airó.[62] It is also worth noting that these writers not only knew and interacted with each other, but also assisted one another and gave mutual support. For example, Zapata Olivella encouraged Palacios to rewrite the part of his manuscript that had been destroyed and, later, as head of the Alianza de Escritores Colombianos, also supported the publication of Velásquez's *Las memorias del odio* [The Memoirs of Hatred] (1953). Palacios, in turn, was praising the work of fellow Chocoano Velásquez years before the anthropologist gained national stature ("Sangre Nueva"). Years later, Darío, who had been introduced to the Cartagena reading public by Juan Zapata Olivella, dedicated poems to Palacios and to Natanael Díaz (see *Caminante sin sitio* 38–42; 70–73).

Appearing more than a decade before those authors, Jorge Artel did not enjoy the supportive comradeship of such a diverse and talented group of black contemporaries. Neither did he suffer, however, the lonely isolation and economic disadvantages of earlier writers such as Obeso and Botero.[63] Rooted in Spanish- American postmodernism and receptive to the currents of his day, Artel had the good fortune to reach maturity in the midst of the avant-garde turmoil and the widespread literary vogue of blackness. These trends would impact his thinking and poetry profoundly. Standing at a pivotal point in the development of black literary expression in Colombia and armed with an acute sense of racial identity, *costeño* pride, and personal dignity, Artel was able to move Afro-Colombian writing almost single-handedly into a more spiritual and more profound dimension of racial and historical consciousness than it had experienced before. In so doing he united the best of a modest and intermittent Afro-Colombian literary discourse with contemporary artistic currents and sociocultural concerns without sacrificing either its uniqueness or his own originality. How Artel accomplished that, particularly in the face of both external and internal handicaps like the ones discussed previously, and also influenced the artistic thought of younger writers is the subject of the remaining chapters of this book.

3

$\mathcal{J}$ORGE ARTEL (1909–94):

A Literary Life

> I began by making romantic verses, Alexandrine sonnets wherein swooning princesses and ridiculous deities pined away. Later I realized that all this was absurd. I sensed man, I became aware of the Negro's problem, and I devoted myself sincerely and passionately to serve it, through my poetry.
>
> Jorge Artel (1959)

Colombia, as the previous chapter shows, has produced many authors of African descent, who have published numerous works of poetry, prose fiction, drama, and essays. In recent years a few of these texts have begun to be rediscovered and reread, revealing a significant if uneven body of Afro-Colombian writing. For reasons discussed in the foregoing chapters, however, the majority of the works have seen but one edition, usually in small issues, thus limiting their readership both within and outside of Colombia. Likewise, relatively little up-to-date information on the lives of the authors and the literary context of their works has been readily available through the mainstream sources of Colombian biography and bibliography. Often, as in the case of Obeso (*Lectura para ti*), Juan Coronel (1868–1904) (*Un peregrino*), Baena (*Aventuras de un estudiante, Cómo se hace ingeniero un negro en Colombia*), and Zapata Olivella (*Pasión vagabunda, He visto la noche, ¡Levántate, mulato!*), authors of prose works have provided significant and illuminating data about themselves and their hardships. As members of nonprivileged, slave-descended groups, they may well have felt the necessity and importance of affirming their human existence and documenting their creative efforts. For the most part, however, the absence of such self-referential texts has left the lives and accomplishments of many Afro-Colombian writers (e.g., Francisco Botero, Eugenio Darío, Natanael Díaz, Teresa Martínez de Varela Restrepo) undocumented, shrouded in ignorance, and subject to speculation and innuendo.

In general, Jorge Artel has fared better literarily than his Afro-Colombian predecessors, managing not only to publish several books (some of which were republished during his lifetime), but also to live to see a new generation of readers take interest in his poetry, his ideas, and his cultural activities. Nevertheless, with his passing in 1994, it is evident just how little collected information exists about his life, his literary and cultural undertakings, and his myriad writings. Indeed, the absence of a biography of Artel, one which provides accurate and reliable details about the poet's family and educational background, literary beginnings, journalistic endeavors, professional and cultural activities, and various travel experiences (particularly between 1929 and 1959), severely handicaps the ability of the literary critic or historian to gain an overall, contextualized view of the poet's labors.

While some biographical data on Artel can usually be found in general reference works (e.g., Sánchez López 81), in writings on Cartagena (e.g., Esquivia Vásquez, *Lienzos locales*), and in some anthologies of poetry, too often these sources repeat the same recycled information. Occasionally, the few apparently new and current "facts" they appear to offer are actually outdated at the time of publication or are even incorrect. Regrettably, Artel's own published books offer little concrete information about his life; and, as far as we know, he did not write an autobiography. The lack, too, of a bibliographical compilation of criticism of his works no doubt has further hindered a more comprehensive examination of the poet's creative writing and a closer analysis of his significance within both Colombian literature and Afro-Hispanic literature.[1]

Clearly, information necessary to a full appreciation of the interwoven dimensions of Artel the poet, the man, and the promoter of *costeño* and Afro-Colombian culture has been sorely lacking. It is no wonder, then, that Artel has generally been regarded as an isolated figure within Colombian literature, disconnected from the principal literary currents of Spanish America and separated from the generational and artistic contexts that nourished his poetic vocation and outlook—so much so that he is not even mentioned in contemporary studies and general histories of Colombian poetry.[2] Too often the occasional Colombian critic who does cite Artel views his work as merely derivative of the *negrista* or Afro-Antillean verse that was in vogue when Artel came to prominence, or as an extension of the *Piedra y Cielo* group that emerged in the 1930s (e.g., Ortega Torres 595; Toruño, *Poesía y poetas de América* 73; Lagos 261). On the one hand, these omissions and misconceptions reinforce Artel's separation and isolation from Colombian literature in general or continue to disseminate misinformation about his position in Colombian poetry. On the other hand, they tend to diminish peremptorily the significance of the poet's contributions or to deny them any transcendence. In effect, such oversights and misapprehensions often serve to perpetuate the genteel tradition of ignoring the autochthonous and popular, and to reinscribe the customary underrepresentation—and even dismissal—of the African presence inherent in Colombian society and culture.

This chapter will address these oversights and lacunae by providing a general summary of the major events, experiences, and activities of Artel's life, presented within the historical, social, and cultural context of the nation and times in which he lived and wrote. The chapter does not pretend to be biographically or bibliographically exhaustive. Rather, its purpose is to document and clarify Artel's literary production while also demonstrating his participation in the literary, social, and cultural happenings of Colombia and America, and illuminating the difficulties and challenges he faced as a Colombian poet and intellectual of African descent, particularly during the momentous decades of the 1920s, 1930s, and 1940s. Much of the data incorporated here has been obtained from various interviews conducted with the poet—both published and unpublished—as well as from several newspaper columns he himself wrote during the late 1950s and early 1960s in Panama. These sources contain an abundance of useful particulars relevant to many aspects of Artel's life and long career. Collected and assembled, they afford ample information for constructing the concise and detailed bio-bibliographical sketch that follows.

Jorge Artel was born on April 27, 1909, to Miguel de Arco and Aurora Coneo de de Arco in the historic, walled, coastal city of Cartagena, which, as stated earlier, had been one of the chief ports of entry for enslaved Africans in the seventeenth and eighteenth centuries. His given name was Julio Agapito de Arco. Raised in the historically black working-class barrio of Gethsemani by two paternal aunts, Doña Carmen and Doña Severina de Arco—the former a respected midwife and the latter an educator—Artel received his primary school education under his aunt's tutelage. He completed secondary school studies at the University of Cartagena and the Instituto Politécnico de Martínez Olier in 1929.

Having served an apprenticeship as a typographer with the hometown newspaper *Diario de la Costa* (Artel, "Cuestión de Minutos"), by 1928 Artel was publishing, under his legally adopted nom de plume (Jorge Artel), articles, stories, and original poems in *La Patria,* also of Cartagena, and elsewhere.[3] Thus, by the end of 1930, when he went to Bogotá to study law at the National University, Artel had already earned favorable distinction on the coast as a promising young poet and intellectual of the new generations ("Un cronista cartagenero").

Artel's adolescent years, transpiring in the decade of the 1920s, coincided with a pivotal period of transformation in Colombian history. As Carlos

Uribe Celis points out, the 1920s marked a decisive step toward the modernization of the country (20). Modernization and change, much of it brought about by external forces operative in the wake of World War I, permeated all areas of national life—economic, political, social, and cultural. For example, with the construction of new roads, the extension of railroad lines, and the introduction in 1919 of air service between Barranquilla and the interior (Uribe Celis 24; Bushnell 165–66), transportation and communication in the country improved. Travel between the coast and the interior, however, was still carried out primarily via steamboat on the Magdalena River. Thus Artel made his first trip from Cartagena to the capital in 1930 via steamship, railroad, and automobile, an experience he recounted in lyrical prose soon after his arrival ("De Cartagena a Bogotá").

The close of the 1920s also witnessed the end of the long period of Conservative political rule of Colombia, begun in 1884. In 1930, the very year that Artel went to Bogotá, Liberal candidate Enrique Olaya Herrera was elected president of Colombia. During that same period Marxist and other leftist ideas, spread by the triumph of the Russian Revolution and the successes of the Mexican Revolution, began to take hold in the country, particularly among Liberal youth.[4] All of these changes could not help but affect—to a greater or lesser degree—Artel's own social and political views, which, to a certain extent, would be manifested in his poetry. As the son of an Indian countrywoman (*campesina*) of the Sinú Valley and a black brickmason who had fought there on the Liberal side in the Thousand Days War, Artel identified closely with the Liberal cause. At the same time, however, like other young intellectuals and students of the time, he was also attracted to the committed and idealistic vision of the new nonmainstream Left. Commenting in 1932 on the political situation in his native Department of Bolívar, Artel lauded the "veritable leftist crusade" headed by a handful of youths who "seek and try to bring to politics a purified atmosphere of whole renewal, impressing upon those concerns an appealing physiognomy of struggle and intensity which is making Cartagena experience days of great expectation" ("En Bolívar se presencia un movimiento de renovación").[5]

Intellectual and artistic currents as well as new inventions from abroad paralleled political change, exercising a direct impact on Colombian cultural life and a decisive influence on Artel's poetic development. Postwar disillusionment with the West's emphasis on the rational nature of man and disenchantment with the destructive use of Western industrial and technological advances fostered among European artists and intellectuals a search for primitive, unspoiled humanity and stimulated a new sense of daring creativity in art and literature. Various artistic and literary avant-garde movements (e.g., Cubism, Expressionism, Dadaism, Futurism, Surrealism) emerged and flourished—usually briefly—spreading throughout

Europe and the Americas their revolutionary manifestos and iconoclastic spirit. Federico García Lorca's neopopularist *Romancero gitano* (1928), also composed during this period, demonstrated the rich poetic values inherent in cultures of nonindustrialized peoples, who were usually regarded as inferior and treated as pariahs. The popularity of Lorca's ballads spawned in Colombia innumerable poems and prose pieces related to gypsies (e.g., García Borrero; León; Salgar Pérez). One of Artel's own early poems, "Gitana," published in Barranquilla in December of 1929, certainly seems to fall within this body of gypsy-inspired writings.[6] Indeed, years later, recalling this period of poetic and artistic ferment, Artel stated:

> We who made poetry in the year 1930 found an America shaken by the echo of the new schools. The contours of the continent were populated with daring voices, filled with a lyrical accent impregnated with obscure suggestions, and there was—let us say—duty-free admittance for all values, a green light for all kinds of emotions. . . . Lorca, [Pablo] Neruda, [Pedro] Salinas, [Rafael] Alberti, presided over the banquet. . . . But as one would say then—and thus it has turned out in reality—that was a quest, a labor of trial and error that was leading us towards immanent beauty, towards the sole and eternal poetry. ("El poeta colombiano Jorge Artel habla para el *Panamá-América*")[7]

With the introduction of radio (in 1921), the phonograph, and the expanding popularization of the cinema, the music, excitement, and gaiety of the jazz band and the music hall entered Colombia, ushering in a new cultural age. In large measure this period was characterized by a frenzied, almost worldwide interest in things Negro, from African art, dance, and folklore to Afro-American theater, music, and literatures. Two U.S. artists closely identified with this music were African-American dancer and chanteuse Josephine Baker (1906–75) and Euro-American bandleader Paul Whiteman (1890–1967). Baker, who had taken Paris by storm with her exotic and risqué dances invoking images of a primitive Africa, was the rage of Europe (Linares, "Josefina Baker; Quijano Mantilla").[8] Carrying her exciting music and erotic movements to South America in 1929, she attracted throngs to her performances, overshadowing the learned lectures given by philosopher Count Keyserling ("La 'Venus Negra' en Buenos Aires"; Barrera Parra). In effect, the music and culture that Baker embodied appeared to lend support to Oswald Spengler's theory that Western civilization was on the decline.

During those same years, Whiteman and his orchestra, recently signed with the Columbia Phonograph Company and publicized as "the most notable Jazz orchestra in the United States," were spreading jazz music and new dances such as the Charleston and the fox-trot via phonograph records and film.[9] Other artists, such as the Black Stars dancing troupe, gave additional impetus to the popularity of the music via personal appearances in Colombia (see "La Gran Compañía de Artistas Negros"). Several of Artel's poems of the early 1930s reflect the frenzied hurly-burly of the jazz band craze, and one in particular, "Dancing," first published in 1932, pays tribute to the international prominence of both Baker and Whiteman. (For a discussion of jazz in Artel's poetry, see chapter 5).

In the Hispanic lands—and especially the Antilles region—the new interest in black life and culture, known as *negrismo,* took the form of musical and artistic compositions; research on Afro-Hispanic subjects by Fernando Ortiz, Ildefonso Pereda Valdés, and other scholars; and an outpouring of poetry and fiction by Pereda Valdés, Ramón Guirao, José Z. Tallet, Nicolás Guillén, Luis Palés Matos, Emilio Ballagas, Alejo Carpentier, Manuel del Cabral, Lino Novás Calvo, and others. In Colombia, too, *negrismo* found a fertile and receptive milieu. From the late 1920s through the 1930s, newspapers, literary journals, and popular magazines carried essays and reviews by European and American writers (Anglo as well as Latin) on jazz music in Paris (Guillenar; Linares, "Charleston - City"), cultural life in New York's Harlem (Ocampo), race relations in the United States ("Un negro linchado y después quemado vivo"; Guglielmini), and more. They also reproduced articles, poems, and artwork by or about such foreign notables as Nicolás Guillén ("Pequeña oda a Kid Chocolate," "Yambambó"), Palés Matos ("Danza negra"), Langston Hughes (Morillo, "Una evocación"), Josephine Baker (Ruiz Herazo; Labarca), Claude McKay (Salazar), Miguel Covarrubias (see illustration in Francés), and Mario Carreño (see illustration in Martín). During this period many Colombian writers, poets, and artists, stimulated by the happenings and examples abroad, turned their attention to the black presence in Colombia and elsewhere. Their productions focused on native dances (Amaya González), legendary military heroes (Arciniegas, "El Negro Infante"), popular types in religious traditions (Valencia), and the music of the jazz band (Mateus), among other themes.

Captivated by the innovative spirit reflected in the new music, arts, and literatures, and admittedly not a good student ("Artel visto por Artel"), Artel apparently spent less time on his law studies than on his literary interests. In the capital he soon became active in prominent literary circles, participating in café *tertulias* with both established and other young writers, poets, and artists, such as Ricardo Rendón (1894–1931), Federico Rivas Aldana (Fray Lejón) (1902–82), Arturo Regueros Peralta (?–1941), and Juan Roca Lemus (1908–83). Although Artel specifically credits Jaime Barrera Parra— then editor of "Lecturas Dominicales," the literary supplement of Bogotá's *El Tiempo* newspaper—with introducing him to the national readership (Moreno Blanco), Valerio Grato's article " 'Jorge Artel,' el poeta negro," may have been the first to imprint his visage and poetry on the pages of the Bogotá press.[10] While Grato remarked favorably that the young costeño was "an agile and sincere writer . . . and a poet who makes delightful juggling acts with the rich arsenal of words," he also seemed to suggest, as others had done previously with Obeso, that Artel's tall, robust, black physique was inconsistent with the sensibilities of literary pursuit:

> Physically, Jorge Artel is a tall lad, with squared shoulders and strong arms like those of a boxer, completely black on the outside; he looks like he was bathed in Stafford ink.

> The day that the poet Ruiz Herazo introduced him to me, I thought that I was dealing not with a writer but with one of those ebony bruisers who become masters of the ring by the force of their fists. He stood squarely before me and extended his hand and I got the terrible impression of the knockout.

> Looking carefully at his figure—agile and black like that of all those who belong to Josephine Baker's race—, at times one is tempted to make a big drum beat and to hit the cymbals to see him dance jazz.

While Grato was not the first to imply that Artel's racial identity appeared to be at odds with his poetic vocation (see Mendoza P., "Jorge Artel"; and Ruiz Herazo, "El hombre que parecía un bull-dog"), his remarks reinforced the notion that poetry was apparently incompatible with blackness and that it was virtually the exclusive province of white people. Therefore—and despite a general insistence on the neutrality and even endearing connotations of the epithet *"negro"* when applied to black people- -the designation of Artel as *"poeta negro"* [black poet] bore a certain ironic or ambivalent quality, not entirely free of pejorative or discriminatory innuendo.[11] Nevertheless, as we shall see in subsequent chapters, Artel would embrace and bear the title proudly, infusing it with positive meaning and thereby subverting its derogatory implications.

Although the jazz craze and the interest in *lo negro* no doubt helped to facilitate Artel's entry into literary and artistic circles of the capital, like Obeso before him he faced an often skeptical, ignorant, and prejudiced intellectual climate in tradition-bound Bogotá—one that probably required him to overcome doubts and biases through demonstration of his poetic talent, intellect, and ability. It is no wonder, then, that Artel, like Obeso, seemed to establish closer friendships with poets and writers from other "provinces" than with those from the nation's center. Understandably, as a *costeño* and a member of the younger generation of poets and writers who supported a more equitable and inclusive approach to Colombian culture and national government, Artel could identify with the call for "literary federalism" propounded by various contemporaries (D. Samper; Caballero Escovar).

Encouraged by the cordial companionship he enjoyed and more attuned to the literary and artistic trends from abroad, Artel's writing matured and developed significantly and steadily. His poetry, already displaying influences of the European avant-garde (most notably Futurism), moved further away from its Spanish-American postmodernist origins. Freeing himself from the constraints of the sonnet and the traditional metrics in which he had composed much of his early poetry, Artel chose to write almost exclusively in free verse. Abandoning, too, the escapism, aristocratic pose, and mannered elegance of his juvenile verses, and nostalgic, no doubt, for the bright warmth, ocean breezes, and colorful landscape of his coastal homeland, Artel turned his attention to the everyday reality of the northern littoral. He soon gained national attention when his poetry, evoking intimate scenes of the Atlantic ports and recreating images, emotions, and rhythms of black coastal people, began appearing in "Lecturas Dominicales." The publication in late 1931 of "La cumbia," a poem celebrating a coastal dance of African and indigenous origins, marked a milestone in Artel's self-assertion as a poet of the Colombian coast and of Afro-Colombian identity and cultural heritage. For the first time since the late nineteenth century, Colombia had a black poet who, artistically, unashamedly, and in a dignified manner sang a black song. During the next few years other compositions (e.g., "Playa," "Tamboriles en la noche," "Barrio abajo," "Dancing," "Cartagena 3 a.m.," "Evocación de la tierra nativa") projecting coastal images and extolling Afro-Colombian life and culture appeared.

Between 1932 and 1937, Artel, having suspended his law studies, devoted himself fully to journalism and literature, working in Bogotá as an editor with both *El Nuevo Tiempo* and publications of the Liberal Party (*Unión Liberal, Acción Liberal*), collaborating in *El Tiempo*, writing columns for *El Diario Nacional*, and contributing poems and occasional literary articles to various reviews and newspapers of the interior and the coast.[12] During this period there appeared in *El Tiempo* two prose writings signed by Artel that are crucial to an understanding of his artistic attitude and racial poetics. The first, "un manifiesto de los ultra jóvenes" [A Manifesto of the Ultra Youths] (see "el pleito de las generaciones"), was written in October of 1931 by Artel and twenty-seven other members of the group of writers and poets who became known as "los Post-Nuevos." The signataries of the unusual manifesto—printed entirely in lowercase letters and perhaps the only avant-garde document of its kind to come out of Colombia—declared their inconformity with the literary status quo and asserted their separation from their immediate generational predecessors, the "Centenaristas" and

"Los Nuevos." Dismissing the former as "situated in comfortable postures of magnates and university presidents" and criticizing the latter as a generation "that looked to the classics for the formulae of their inner enrichment," the "young Turks" saw themselves as representatives of

> the intolerant affirmation of principles and doctrines, the revolution of the whole literary and social organism and, rather than tranquillity— a petit bourgeois affection—intranquillity, restlessness, imponderable vigilance, daring struggle against everyone and everything. ("el pleito de las generaciones")

As a cosigner of the manifesto, Artel clearly identified himself—and likewise was regarded—as a member of the youthful avant-garde group that, like others in Spanish America, sought to break with the past and to incorporate new concepts, visions, and styles into the national literature.

Less than a year after the appearance of the historic but apparently innocuous document, Artel published under the title "La Literatura negra en la Costa" [Black Literature on the Coast] an open letter addressed to his friend, journalist Gregorio Espinosa of Cartagena. Prompted by certain ingenuous and unfounded remarks on black coastal literature made by a novice writer of the region, Artel asserted that "the accidental fact that an individual belongs to a certain race does not mean that that person is its intellectual or artistic expression." Neither, Artel added, does "having read four poems by Luis Palés Matos or Nicolás Guillén, and naïvely proclaiming oneself to be black in a literary article or lecture" qualify a person to be "a racial writer or to erect a professorial chair from which one can expect to have disciples follow us." Rather, as the poet explained, quoting from a commentary on his work written by journalist and friend José Morillo (" 'Tamboriles en la noche' "),

> To be a black poet, writer, or artist, one needs to carry within his soul—and know how to imprint an eloquence on—all those "ancestral emotions," "the complex of pains, hopes, dreams stirred up in a people, which make their appearance condensed in certain minds."

While Artel did not unequivocally disallow that nonblack persons could write black literature, clearly he emphasized the necessity of a strong, spiritual quality and commitment that, it seems safe to say, would more likely be found in persons of African descent. More precisely, Artel believed in and was committed to a black literary expression that arose from the emotional wellsprings of Afro-American experiences and that addressed the deeper, spiritual aspects of black life and culture. Therefore, he argued, it was necessary for those who would seek to articulate such expression, for those truly concerned with the spiritual and intellectual movement of black people and eager to affiliate with it, to enrich their cultural background with relevant works by authors such as Waldo Frank, Count Keyserling, and Paul Valery, who—in Artel's opinion—had contributed significantly to the abundant bibliography dealing with Afro-American artistic trends.

Furthermore, Artel stated, it was equally important to read the novels of René Maran and Claude McKay, and to be familiar with the poetry of Langston Hughes and Paul Laurence Dunbar, in whose works "the true image of the race and its unmistakable voice" began to be found. By linking Afro-North American poets and Anglo- and Francophone Caribbean writers with the implicit search for an authentic expression of blackness, Artel revealed his own identification with these authors. At the same time, however, by describing their works as an initial phase of this expression, Artel was also reserving or opening a space wherein he could make an original and valuable contribution to the development of black literature, particularly in Colombia.

Unlike many middle-class *costeños* of African descent, who, the poet remarked, "hid their skin like a curse, not only in literature but also in politics," Artel exhibited his blackness proudly, accepting and delighting in the critics' judgment that he was "the only faithful interpreter of my race in Colombia." More important, by likening his poetry to a drum "wherein vibrate the unknown voices of my race," Artel not only reaffirmed the African heritage and the little-known and unappreciated black presence in Colombia, but also provided, as we will see later, a clue to his own artistry and ethnic affirmation. In short, Artel's letter—to which we will have occasion to return—is an important document, one essential to a full understanding of the motivations behind his poetic craft and of the orientation of his racial thought.

As Artel's reputation grew, he received invitations to recite his poems in different locales. At possibly one of his earliest recitals, which took place on November 30, 1933, in the city of Honda, writer and playwright Salvador Mesa Nicholls introduced the young poet as a leading member of Colombia's poetic vanguard. Via such recitals Artel was able to expand his audience beyond the reading public and to broaden his reputation as an important voice of the new generation.

While Artel, of course, was more than qualified to convey the meaning, emotion, and music inherent in his poetry, he could well have benefited from having his work recited by either of the two most celebrated *declamadoras* (poetry performers) of the time, Berta Singermann of Argentina and Eusebia Cosme of Cuba. The role of these professional performers in disseminating the work and enhancing the reputation of given authors cannot and should not be underestimated. Singermann's numerous recital tours of Spanish America during the 1930s and 1940s served to publicize and engrave in the public mind various poems by select authors and thus helped to solidify or advance their reputations. Although she made several appearances in Colombia, often devoting a section of her repertoire to *poesía negra,* there is no evidence that any of Artel's poems were ever included in her performances.[13] Neither apparently did his poems find their way into Cosme's programs. It is quite possible, however, that the Cuban performer's familiarity with Artel's poetry dates only from the early 1950s, when both were in New York City. In any case, Cosme's recitals in her native Cuba, Puerto Rico, and New York City—not to mention her commercial recordings—did much to spread and popularize the poetry of Guillén, Palés Matos, Ballagas, and others connected with literary *negrismo.* The fact that several Cuban poets wrote poems specifically dedicated to Cosme may suggest their high regard for her talents and, possibly, their acknowledgement of her real or potential impact.[14]

Also during the decade of the 1930s Artel married Zoila Esquivia Vásquez of Cartagena, the sister of his friend and local chronicler Aníbal Esquivia Vásquez (1906–86?). With Zoila, his first wife, the poet traveled frequently—usually by air—between Bogotá and Cartagena, often receiving enthusiastic welcomes in the local press. Several of Artel's compositions of the early 1930s, such as "Breve Canción para Zoila," testify to the poet's intimate feelings for his spouse and reveal less known yet more romantic aspects of his poetic inspiration.

In February of 1937 Artel resigned his position as editor-reporter of the newspaper *La Razón* of Bogotá, owned by Juan Lozano y Lozano, and left the capital to take up residence on the coast. Settling in Cartagena, he founded in May the literary review *Costa,* subtitled "La Revista del Litoral Atlántico." According to the editorial in the inaugural number, the pages of *Costa*

> will be dedicated exclusively to furthering the fraternal rapprochement of the cities of the coast, to gathering their diverse manifestations in order to show them to the eyes of the entire country and to fight to make Cartagena a real center of interest, since historically, culturally and commercially it is equipped to exercise an essential role in the nation's life. ("Editorial")

While much of Artel's poetry was concerned with reevaluating the concept of blackness in Colombia, his literary review had a more regional orientation. As Artel stated in the initial editorial, he believed firmly in "the existence of valuable mental, ethnic and geographical elements capable of contributing factors of extraordinary worth to the formation of a port culture." Consequently, he envisioned *Costa* as "a home of the intellectual youths who wave their concerns over the sea ports of the Atlantic. . . ."

True to its aims, *Costa* featured essays, poems, and fictional excerpts on coastal themes, as well as articles by and about Atlantic coast writers such as José Morillo, Fernando de la Vega, Pedro Bustillo, and, of course, Artel himself. At the same time, much of the content did have a racial focus. For example, one issue included a prose version of Artel's poem "La cumbia," accompanied by a drawing of a black female dancer. Another issue carried an article titled "Un héroe oscuro" [A dark hero], about a black railroad engineer who gave his life in the performance of his duty.

Notwithstanding his literary achievements and personal success, Artel remained both mindful and critical of the negative and stereotypical representations of Africans and African-Americans in Colombia. Thus he inveighed vigorously against an article written by a Barranquilla newspaper correspondent that labeled as nonintellectual, African, and uncouth a group of youths who protested the arrival in Cartagena of the representative of Franco's Spain. In a note titled "Carne de Africa contra los negros" [Flesh of Africa against the Blacks], published in the November 1937 issue of *Costa*, Artel retorted:

> We accuse all those who may rise up against their own homeland, against Spain tatooed with blood, hunger, treason. We accuse Hitler of expelling from the homeland its sages and its free men, and of tearing from the people's breast the cross of Christ, the first democrat of the universal milennia. We accuse Mussolini of assault on Abyssinia, a land of blacks, our race, and surely that of the correspondent. . . .

Regrettably, Artel's review had a brief existence, publishing its last issue in 1938. Nevertheless, *Costa*—one of only a handful of known Afro-Colombian literary periodicals published since the abolition of slavery—performed an important cultural service in promoting the coastal (and thus African) presence and foregrounding black literary expression in Colombia. In so doing, it strengthened Artel's reputation as a committed black writer and enhanced his standing as a leader of the intellectual and literary movement of the Atlantic coast during the late 1930s and 1940s. In the words of one contemporary commentator,

> *Costa* is not even a commercial enterprise, but merely a monumental effort in favor of our literary values. Its pages have brought to the fore a restless and jovial group of youths who otherwise would have remained waiting in an anteroom. . . . By saying that it is published only every month, we have indicated that its commercial radius is limited. But it carries a beautiful banner on the highest pole of its masts. And the fact is that its pages from beginning to end are dedicated to exalting the intellectual concerns of the Atlantic littoral, to showing the country an autochthonous culture, to creating a geographical and racial consciousness, as corresponds to this shore of our national homeland. ("Día a día. Jorge Artel")

After the demise of his review, Artel obtained a professorship by examination ("cátedra por oposición") at the University of Cartagena, teaching the course on universal literature ("El poeta Jorge Artel huésped de nuestro país" 4; "Artel visto por Artel").[15] In November of 1938 he was nominated as a candidate for the Departmental Assembly of Bolívar ("Un grupo de intelectuales y universitarios lanzará candidato a Jorge Artel"), but apparently later withdrew his candidacy ("Jorge Artel renuncia"). By this time a few of Artel's poems had begun to be known outside of Colombia, thanks, in part, to their inclusion in a few Colombian anthologies. In El Salvador critic Juan Felipe Toruño devoted a section of his book *Los desterrados* (1938) to the poet, situating him within the poetic avant-garde movement of Spanish America. The following year (1939) "La cumbia" appeared in the noted journal *Repertorio Americano* of San José, Costa Rica, and a Portuguese version of "Danza, mulata!" was published in Brazil ("Dansa, Mulata!").[16] Also in 1939 Artel became affiliated with the literary group "Viernes" of Caracas, Venezuela, and made his first trip to Panama to visit relatives (Artel, "Visiones: Panamá").[17]

In early 1940 Artel published in Cartagena his first book, the long-awaited volume of poetry titled *Tambores en la noche,* which included as introductions or prologues three earlier written critical commentaries by Juan Lozano y Lozano (1902–79), Carlos Vesga Duarte (1910–81?), and Adolfo Martá [Adolfo Támara], 1899/1903–?). While the dates on the title page indicate that the poems were written between 1931 and 1934, it is certain that some were composed later.[18] As early as 1932, however, there had been mention of the book's appearance (Morillo, " 'Tamboriles en la noche' "),[19] but for various reasons Artel was unable—or unwilling—to bring it out.

The financial hardships that faced most aspiring Colombian authors—particularly those of African descent (see chapter 2)—may have been a factor. The poet's own former bohemian lifestyle, however, marked by an uninhibited enjoyment of literary creativity and youthful merriment, also seems to have contributed to delaying publication of the book.[20] In addition, writings by friends suggest that the poet did not feel he had a corpus of finished poems sufficient to compose the book he envisioned. In his brief commentary on the publication of *Tambores en la noche,* journalist and fellow *costeño* Gregorio Espinosa recalled that after Artel had returned to the coast with his manuscript of verses, there followed a period of revision characterized by an eagerness to surpass the written texts and an awareness of their originality and autochthonous quality ("Palmerín"). Similarly, Antonio Bruges Carmona states that Artel was reluctant to publish his compositions and that friends convinced him to collect and put them in a book ("Poetas jóvenes de la Costa. Jorge Artel"; "Algo sobre poesía negra").[21]

Despite its delayed appearance, *Tambores en la noche* was enthusiastically received by much of the literary establishment of both the coast and the interior. The *Revista de las Indias,* one of the nation's most important and prestigious periodicals, stated that Artel's book "reaffirms its author's lofty poetic quality and marks the presence of a new force in poetry, not just Colombian but American" (Rev. of *Tambores en la noche*). A local newspaper, *El Fígaro,* called the book's publication "an authentic literary happening for Cartagena" ("El libro de Jorge Artel"), while *El Liberal* of Bogotá declared that "Mr. Artel's verses deserve a long, enthusiastic and popular reception," and added that "almost all of them could be the words of exquisite songs" (Rev. of *Tambores en la noche*).

Like the majority of new Colombian authors who did not form part of the economic and cultural elite, Artel himself was largely responsible for ensuring that his volume reached the attention of the mass media in Colombia and elsewhere. With an edition of only 1,500 copies, however, *Tambores en la noche* most likely was not intended to be commercially profitable nor destined for many markets outside of Colombia. Although the publisher, Editora Bolívar, was a respectable and professional local press (see "Notas breves. *Tambores en la noche*"), it was not a publishing house. That is, it enjoyed limited nationwide trade and had little or no access to international markets. Also, the fact that the book was published in the coastal city of Cartagena—located within one of the so-called provinces—and not in the national center of Bogotá further reduced the likelihood of widespread publicity and reading. As a consequence, systematic promotion and distribution of Artel's book both within and without Colombia was probably limited or nonexistent.[22] For that reason, no doubt, and as pointed out in chapter 2, Cuban critic and anthologist Emilio Ballagas was unaware of the book even six years after its publication.

Such ignorance of the work of contemporary Colombia's principal poet of black expression and leading Afro-Colombian author certainly was lamentable. More than that, however, it was detrimental—to Artel, in particular, and to a more prominent profile for Afro-Colombian writing, in general. The lack of an established, well-organized network of publishing houses in Colombia capable of promoting and distributing publications systematically and efficiently both within the country and beyond its borders lessened the possibility that noted literary critics and historians would learn of the book's existence. For this reason both Artel and Colombia were relegated to the margins of literary *negrismo* and thus kept in the shadows of Afro-Hispanic literature. Also, by denying critics and historians—"creators," to a great degree, of the Spanish-American literary canon—full access to the extensive and varied body of Artel's work, Colombia's weak publishing enterprise left them with only a partial and decontextualized view of the poet's works—often those poems most similar to Afro-Antillean compositions. Limited in their ability to discern and appreciate the originality and distinctive features of Artel's verses, literary critics and historians such as Luis Alberto Sánchez tended to regard Artel as a mere epigone of the more famous Afro-Antillean poets. In short, the failure of *Tambores en la noche* to circulate widely and systematically within the Hispanic world and, thereby, to receive a fair "hearing," worked against a proper consideration of Artel's writing within literary *negrismo* and Spanish-American poetry and precluded his receiving much-deserved recognition for his contribution to the development of black writing in Colombia.

These same editorial shortcomings also circumscribed Colombia's literary presence within the Afro-Hispanic world. Artel's absence from canon-forming anthologies of *poesía negra* gave the impression that after Obeso, Colombia had contributed little or nothing to this modality.[23] Simultaneously, however, even nonblack Colombian poets who had written on black themes or within the *negrista* style (e.g., Gregorio Castañeda Aragón, Arturo Camacho Ramírez, and Darío Samper) were usually overlooked. From this void a reader might infer that the South American republic had little or no population or culture of African origin worthy of attention; or, what is worse, that Afro-Colombians, despite being a significant proportion of the country's population, did not contribute to their nation's literary production and cultural development. Indeed, when compared, for example, with the number and poetic output of Afro-Uruguayan authors—made known primarily by Pereda Valdés' 1936 anthology and other efforts—, Afro-Colombian authors are woefully inconspicuous. Similarly, when contrasted with Cuba, Colombia's representation in anthologies of black-inspired poetry pales considerably.

Lack of commercial promotion and distribution probably was not the only factor that influenced the low international awareness and reception of Artel's book. The fact that it appeared when the *negrista* tendency was waning may also have occasioned a certain disregard outside of Colombia.[24] Although Artel neither envisioned his poetry as a fashion ("una moda") nor considered it circumstantial, the publication of *Tambores en la noche* did occur after the zenith of black-inspired, or *negrista,* literature. During the decade of the 1930s those poets considered initiators or leading practitioners of poetic *negrismo*—Palés Matos, Pereda Valdés, Guillén, Ballagas, Manuel Del Cabral, Manuel Rodríguez Cárdenas—already had published one or more collections.[25] Even poets known for just one or two *negrista* compositions— e.g., Ramón Guirao, Vicente Gómez Kemp—had managed to bring out a pamphlet or small book of verses.[26] By 1940, with World War II well under way and new directions in poetry emerging, *negrismo* had fallen under more severe reevaluation and had begun to decline in interest. Coming when it did, then, *Tambores en la noche* probably caused little sensation among the

Spanish-American reading public, possibly stirring less interest than if it had been published a few years earlier.[27]

Other factors operative in Colombia also hampered Artel's efforts to foster the creation of a genuine black literature in his country. Although, as stated above, the Colombian press generally reacted favorably to the appearance of *Tambores en la noche,* acceptance of the racial import of Artel's poetry and evaluation of his poetic ability were by no means unanimous. Ambivalent, lukewarm comments and even negative appraisals of the book, especially by members of the critical establishment, revealed a strong undercurrent of sentiments adverse to the very notion of black poetry. For example, *El Liberal* scoffed at what it considered a vain and useless attempt to divide poetry into Aryan and Negro components. A reviewer in nearby Panama, also rejecting the concept of black poetry, asserted, "The insistence on songs characterized as black is disturbing and adds nothing to the intrinsic poetic value" (Ruiz Vernacci).

Given that in Colombia—and in Spanish America, generally—the dominant groups refused to recognize black citizens as a legitimate ethnic group and to acknowledge the continuing existence of harmful racial distinctions, such remarks are not at all surprising. Nevertheless, by negating the existence or questioning the validity of black poetry—that is, of poetry written by people of African descent that addresses and communicates their unique experiences, human concerns, and cultural heritage—these remarks served to undermine the legitimacy, acceptance, and viability of black literary expression in Colombia. Furthermore, such comments strengthened the perception that a genuine black literature, that is, one that dignified black life and culture, reevaluated slavery and race relations, and questioned—even implicitly— the social and economic status of people of African descent, posed a threat to national unity and artistic integrity, or the oneness of human creativity, by engendering racial tensions and reviving old rifts. In a sense, then, the potentially liberating implications of Artel's work went largely ignored.

Ironically, the critical commentaries placed at the beginning of the book and no doubt intended to provide supportive appraisal of the author's work may also have been less helpful than expected. Although each critic was a well-known literary and intellectual figure within various regions of Colombia, only Lozano y Lozano could really be considered a writer of national prominence. Certainly none of the three enjoyed an international reputation similar to that, say, of the distinguished Spanish writer Miguel de Unamuno (1864–1936), whose 1932 letter to Nicolás Guillén served to enhance and circulate the Cuban poet's name throughout the Spanish-speaking world.[28]

It is doubtful, then, that the three commentaries placed in Artel's book had any significant impact on Artel's career or served to advance public understanding of Afro-Colombian literary expression either within or without the nation. In fact, Lozano y Lozano's self-confessed inability to appreciate "the harmony of poems not written in the traditional meters of expression" would seem to have undermined much of his generally complimentary appraisal of Artel's avant-garde verse. A conservative poet of classical formation from the interior city of Ibagué, Lozano y Lozano believed that "Poetry's charm consists precisely in accommodating the poetic thought to literary formulae" (Lozano y Lozano 6). Understandably, Artel's avant-garde spirit and use of free verse clashed with the critic's lyrical sensibility, rendering him, perhaps, less capable of appreciating the merits and originality of Artel's poetic art or of recognizing its sociocultural value and implications for Colombia.[29]

Given the shortcomings of the three prefatory essays, as well as an earlier charge that Artel failed to display an intense racial pride like Langston Hughes (Roca Lemus), and Luis Alberto Sánchez's dubious description of the poet as the Colombian Guillén, Artel may well have felt the need to clarify his work and put it in a broader and proper perspective. About the same time that *Tambores en la noche* appeared, the poet gave a public address at the first Feria del Libro in Cartagena. Happily, the text of Artel's remarks, unlike that of many other speeches and lectures he gave throughout his career, was published under the title "Modalidades artísticas de la raza negra" [Artistic Modalities of the Negro Race].

Like his open letter "La literatura negra en la Costa," written almost eight years earlier, "Modalidades" is an important document that illuminates Artel's vision of his own poetry and reveals his perceptive insights into black poetry in Colombia, Cuba, and the United States. Noting significant differences in the three nations, Artel seems to have used the occasion to answer those critics who faulted his poetry for failing to imitate the peculiar rhythms of the Afro-Cuban mode or the racial protest of the North American poets. As I will discuss later in greater detail (chapter 5), Artel distinguished his Colombian racial poetry from that of the North American and Cuban varieties, citing historical, cultural, and social factors. In fact, he asserted, in Colombia one could not really speak of black poetry but rather of "mulatto reactions" (*reacciones mulatas*), as he described his own song-poems, precisely because Afro-Colombians had experienced centuries of miscegenation with both indigenous and European peoples, which had diluted the purity of the African ancestral emotion.

As in his 1932 letter, Artel expressed here, too, his admiration for Langston Hughes. He referred to his African-American confrere as "the first . . . of Negro poets of North America" (16) and read a Spanish version (possibly his own translation) of Hughes's famous poem "I, Too." Undoubtedly, Artel was moved and inspired by Hughes's literary and spiritual example and identified with his racial message. Simultaneously, however, he also noted that black poetry in the United States offered a deep rebellious tone, "a very special tonality, since it reflects the difficult situation of the Negro in that country" (17).

On the other hand, he believed that Afro-Cuban poetry, with its attention to "noises, sensual and sensualizing dances" and its exploitative emphasis on onomatopoeia and alliteration, failed to convey "black feeling in an integral manner." As Artel insisted, "The onomatopoeic words give a partial emotion of blackness, but surely do not show us the very heart of the race, it does not show us its anguish nor its deep great sorrow" (17).

As these excerpts demonstrate, "Modalidades artísticas de la raza negra" represents another facet of Artel's efforts to promote and legitimize a unique Colombian version of black literary expression. Unlike the 1932 text, however, "Modalidades" is not so much a personal statement of Artel's *poética*, or poetics, but rather a fairly erudite lecture explaining characteristics of music, poetry, art, and theatre of African and African-American peoples. Like his recitals, the lecture also provided a medium for Artel to take his ideas, his teachings, his particular message, to the common people, who often relied more on oral communication than on written forms. In that way Artel was carrying out the important mission of the black poet that he himself had assumed and that he outlined in his remarks. Declaring that the aesthetic characteristic of the black race is anguish and not the drum, Artel insisted that Africans had brought to America

a profound human pain, which must be rendered faithfully by the poet who today wishes to serve as an emotional and historical bridge between our deceased slave forebears and the present-day humanity. And we must make a parenthesis to say that this is the poet's lofty social mission.

Artel realized that Colombians (and perhaps particularly *costeños*, as evidenced by the audience's snickering at his suggestion that enslaved Africans could have been royalty) lacked knowledge of and respect for the African background and presence in Colombia, and in the Americas, in general. All of this underscores both the dearth of scholarly attention to this aspect of the nation's identity and Artel's almost single-handed endeavors to disabuse and educate his fellow citizens. Regrettably, it appears that this lecture did not circulate much beyond coastal Colombia and a few foreign subscribers to the journal *Muros*. In any case it is not mentioned in any of the contemporary sources on Artel. Consequently, its content and significance seem to have gone largely unnoticed by literary critics and historians. Nevertheless, as an opportune complement to the publication of *Tambores en la noche,* the "Modalidades" lecture reinforced in the eyes of northern *costeños* Artel's position as the poetic standard-bearer of Afro-Colombian culture and the literary and cultural leader of a younger generation of Cartagena poets, writers, and intellectuals.[30] As one writer pointed out in April of 1940, "Nationally, Artel is established as one of the new minds of literature and among us he is the most outstanding notable in poetry" (Fernández, "Artel y nosotros").

During the following five years (1941–45) Artel continued to live and work in Cartagena. Motivated by a desire to help destitute delinquents ("Artel visto por Artel"), he completed his law studies at the University of Cartagena in 1945, specializing in criminal law. His thesis, "Defensa Preventiva del Estado o El Derecho Penal frente a los Problemas de la Cultura Popular en Colombia" (Preventative Defense of the State or Penal Law in the Face of the Problems of Popular Culture in Colombia), was recommended by the doctoral committee as "worthy of being accorded honors" ("digna de ser laureada"). He held a number of posts in municipal and departmental governments, including *Defensor de Oficio* (public defender) and press chief in the controller's office of the Department of Bolívar.

Artel also remained active literarily, writing and occasionally publishing poems and articles, engaging in polemics on poetry, and traveling and promoting his work and that of coastal writers within and beyond Colombia. In 1941 he briefly visited neighboring Panama, home to some relatives of his, where he established important contacts with the literary and intellectual community.[31] Also that year Artel won an essay contest sponsored by the University of Cartagena with his entry "Hacia una interpretación de Santander" [Toward an Interpretation of Santander], which was published in 1942. In that year and again in 1943 he made an artistic tour of Barranquilla, Medellín, Manizales, Cali, Puerto Tejada, and Bogotá, giving a series of in-person and broadcast poetry recitals in libraries, halls, and radio studios. These tours generated a spate of local interviews, which provided the poet with numerous opportunities to elucidate his poetry, to expound upon his ideas regarding black poetry in Colombia, and to discuss various works in preparation. The press coverage may have also stimulated professional reciters such as Stella Balcázar of Barranquilla and Andrés Olías of Cuba to incorporate Artel's poetry into their repertoire ("Noticiero Cultural. Recital"; "El primer intérprete").

In January of 1944, as a representative of the Bogotá Liberal-backed weekly *Sábado*, Artel returned to Panama, where he was eagerly awaited and warmly received. He performed there a much-appreciated service of cultural exchange and promotion, lecturing on contemporary Colombian literature, giving recitals of his own poetry, and writing prologues for books and literary criticism in local periodicals. The weekly newspaper *Calle 6*, which had moved from Colón to Panama City, also featured a section edited by Artel titled "Página Itinerario Cultural," which he continued even after leaving the Isthmus.[32]

Artel remained in Panama for about seven months, moving on to Costa Rica at the end of July. In San José, the capital, he continued to maintain a busy schedule of activities, including recitals, lectures, interviews, and collaboration in the local press. In September he traveled to Mexico City, where he became affiliated with the Comité Mexicano Contra el Racismo [Mexican Committee Against Racism] and apparently also gave recitals. In its journal, *Fraternidad,* the Committee acknowledged Artel's collaboration ("Actividades del Comité") and also published his poem "Velorio del Boga Adolescente." Artel returned to Cartagena in November of 1944.

As a result of all these activities, Artel's reputation broadened considerably beyond the "corralito de piedras" [little stone corral], as writer Daniel Lemaitre dubbed Cartagena. Equally important, he also widened his own poetic vision and strengthened his awareness of Spanish-American reality. He recorded some of his experiences and observations in articles published between the years 1944 and 1946 in various periodicals such as *Calle 6, Voces de America,* and *Vida.*

In May of 1946 Cuban poet Nicolás Guillén visited Colombia, meeting with enthusiastic receptions throughout the country. Abandoning Bogotá to become acquainted with the Atlantic coast, Guillén was met by Artel at the airport in Cartagena. Throughout Guillén's stay Artel acted as his unofficial host and guide, showing the internationally famous poet around Cartagena and Barranquilla and introducing the Cuban at the latter's poetry reading in Artel's hometown (Guillén, "Recuerdos colombianos" 21; Artel, "Presentación de Nicolás Guillén").[33] The two poets posed for a studio photograph, which later appeared in Guillén's memoir of his Colombian visit and more recently in Artel's 1986 collection *Antología poética.*

At the end of 1946 Artel returned to Panama briefly, for health reasons (Esplandián, "Aquí está Jorge Artel"). Throughout the following year (1947) he continued to produce poems and to give lectures. In September his "Soneto del hielo" [Sonnet of the Ice] appeared in *El Panamá-América,* with a dedication to Federico Tuñón, a Panamanian critic who had defended Artel and the concept of black poetry a few years earlier ("Acerca de la poesía negra"). During that same month at the Departmental Library in Barranquilla, Artel gave a lecture titled "Insistencia en América" [Insistence on America], in which he emphasized, like Obeso before him, the contribution of the popular element to American culture and called for the creation of an autochthonous literature based on the geographical, cultural, and social realities of American life. The ideas expounded here formed the basis of several talks he would give years later during his sojourns in Venezuela, the Antilles, the United States, Mexico, and Central America.[34]

Although the year 1948 began rather tranquilly, finding the poet once again in Panama (Esplandián, "Por aquí anda Jorge Artel"), it would mark a turning point in Artel's life and career. Several pivotal events took place that precipitated the poet's twenty-three-year period of self-exile from Colombia. On April 9 the Liberal leader Jorge Eliécer Gaitán was assassinated on a main street in Bogotá. His death brought about an immediate and violent popular reaction or uprising, known as the *bogotazo*, and marked the sharp escalation of the undeclared civil war between Liberals and Conservatives that had been smoldering for months before and that came to be called *La violencia* [The Violence]. Artel, who sympathized with the left wing of the Liberal Party, and other outraged citizens were detained by the authorities in Cartagena when they marched upon the naval base. After less than a month of detention Artel and his companions were released ("Jorge Artel y Alfonso Castro están en libertad desde ayer"), but Artel continued to denounce political conditions in Cartagena ("Jorge Artel habla en Bogotá"; "Desgobierno en Cartagena"). Shortly thereafter, doña Carmen de Arco, the aunt who had raised him and to whom he had dedicated the poem "La voz de los ancestros," died. Artel returned to practicing law and also received encouragement that *Tambores en la noche* might be staged in the capital. The killing of his friend Braulio Henao Blanco by a policeman in Cartagena on June 21, however, may have been interpreted by Artel as a final omen of political storms to come. It was about that time that he wrote "Canción del hombre sin retorno" [Song of the Man without Return], a poem that seems to pay homage to fallen comrades and to anticipate Artel's own eventual departure from Colombia.

In July Artel undertook another recital tour, accompanied by the Barranquilla folksinger Esthercita Forero, eventually reaching Bogotá in September to discuss the staging of his work with government officials. The prospect that authentic aspects of coastal life and culture would be presented on the boards in the national capital excited members of Cartagena's literary and intellectual community. Writing in *El Universal*, to which he had been recently introduced by novelist Manuel Zapata Olivella, the young Gabriel García Márquez predicted optimistically: "In his voice the Bogotá public is going to know the sea—the one that Artel likes 'because it has waves voluble like females; and because it belongs to no one'—through the staging of *Tambores en la noche*." Unfortunately, bureaucratic opposition to the theatrical project prevented its realization ("Lo exótico frente a lo autóctono").

By October 1948 Artel had moved on to Cúcuta, the site of his final recital. Not long afterward he crossed the border into Venezuela, where he went on to lecture at the University of Zulia; in 1949 he joined the Maracaibo newspaper *Panorama*, as head of the editorial staff (*jefe de redacción*). In addition to conducting interviews and writing articles for the newspaper, Artel also maintained, under the pseudonym "Lucas Fabers," a regular column titled "Glosario Dominical" [Sunday Glossary] and a later editorial section titled "Hoy. Desde el Mirador" [Today. From the Watchtower]. He used these columns to publicize, promote, and criticize cultural events in Venezuela and Colombia, and to present challenging—and sometimes controversial—ideas and opinions on a wide range of topics, including classical and folkoric music; the cinema; racial matters; and "poesía negroide" [*negrista* poetry] as interpreted by professional *declamadores*. Toward the end of 1949 Artel journeyed to Caracas, where he spent the final months of the year giving interviews, recitals, and lectures.

In January of 1950 Artel flew to the Dominican Republic, where he remained until the end of February. As usual he was well received, being interviewed often by the local press and invited to give lectures and to recite his poems. From the capital of Santo Domingo (then called Ciudad Trujillo) Artel traveled to Puerto Rico, where he sojourned for several months. While there he met poet Luis Palés Matos and the Afro-Puerto Rican song artist, Rafael Hernández. To both men he dedicated the poem "El itinerario jubiloso," which forms part of his unpublished book, *Un marinero canta en proa*.[35] At the University of Puerto Rico the renowned author of *Tuntún de pasa y grifería* introduced Artel to the audience gathered to hear the Colombian lecture and read his poetry. As Artel relates in a brief sketch, Palés Matos was an inseparable companion during his stay on the island ("Carboncillo de Luis Palés Matos").

By November of 1950 Artel had moved on to Cuba, where, apparently, he had been expected for some time (Baquero; "Jorge Artel"). At the University of Havana he gave his lecture on "Insistencia en América," identifying himself as an "Indo-mulatto poet" (*poeta indomulato*) and deftly establishing the African and Amerindian heritages as inextricable and integral elements of Latin American identity. In doing so, he was clearly combatting the hegemonic Eurocentrism of Latin America and calling for peoples of the Americas to face and embrace their entire geo-ethno-racial reality—past and present. His own poetry, he is reported to have stated,

> is American in the expression of that ancestral anguish, of that Indo-mulatto sensitivity; it is not a folkloric black poetry in the commonly held sense of onomatopoeic or falsely popular—that is, cheap—which characterizes the false black poetry. (Arroyo)

In Cuba Artel also reestablished contact with Nicolás Guillén and spent several months visiting various areas of the island, especially Oriente Province (Artel, "En mi concepto"), and familiarizing himself with its culture.

In October of 1951 Artel traveled to New York City, where he had been invited to lecture at the Casa Hispánica of Columbia University. The local Spanish-language press took immediate note of Artel's presence, reprinting critical commentary on his poetry and reporting on his various activities.

Having spent almost two years experiencing and becoming acquainted with the people, culture, and rhythms of the Hispanic Antilles, Artel was able to speak with greater confidence and authority on Afro-Antillean poetry. In an interview with a local reporter conducted shortly after his arrival he debunked stereotypical representations of black life and culture; criticized the simple, facile, mocking verse that was presumed to be black poetry; rejected commonly held, essentialist notions of black dance, laughter, and speech as uniquely sensual, declaring them common to all peoples; and called for poetic expression that goes down deep to the ancestral roots (Portela).

On November 19 Artel gave his lecture at Columbia University, where he was introduced by Federico de Onís, director of the Casa Hispánica. In his remarks Onís said of the speaker, "In his book *Tambores en la noche* and in other poems which he has published, the American sentiment finds a new expression" (qtd. in Artel, *Tambores en la noche* 1955: 6). Speaking on his favorite theme, "Insistencia en América," Artel reiterated and elaborated upon statements he had made on previous occasions, with some alterations. According to one write-up, Artel asserted:

> To understand the mysteries of the Negro's ancestral pain, it is necessary to belong to that race. One cannot use onomatopoeic phrases or colorful scenes, assuming certain movements of the black woman in order to describe her, since all women feel, think and dance equally, no matter what the color of their skin. ("Jorge Artel, Poeta de América")

Furthermore, as the newspaper report continues, Artel affirmed the mestizo, or mixed-race, quality of American culture, declaring (in words reminiscent of Obeso's preface to his *Cantos populares*) that

> by abandoning the imitation in his writings and poems [which] until a short while ago the American held vis-à-vis Europe, he has forged recently an original literature and his songs are songs of America— of that new breed of mixed-race peoples formed by the conquistador, himself a mixed-race person of many strong strains in which the Iberian predominated.

By way of conclusion and as an illustration of his remarks, Artel read several of his poems, including "Good Evening, Colón," "Velorio del boga adolescente," and "La cumbia."

Taking advantage of his stay in New York, Artel journeyed to Harlem, where he was able to meet poet Langston Hughes, whom he had long admired. Harlem's "poet laureate" had become aware of Artel years earlier through Manuel Zapata Olivella, who in the late 1940s had traveled to the United

States and spent considerable time in New York City. The following February (1952) Hughes honored his Colombian colleague with "a splendid party" at his Harlem home ("Noticiero Cultural. Homenaje"; Rampersad 2:197).

On April 26 of 1952, the day before Artel's forty-third birthday, the Círculo de Escritores y Poetas Iberoamericanos of New York sponsored a public lecture by the Colombian titled "Importancia del Folklore [Americano]," which appears to have been a version of his previous lectures on "Insistencia en América." Coming between exhuberantly acclaimed recitals of Afro-Antillean poetry ("*poesía afro-antillana*") by the ever popular Eusebia Cosme (at Town Hall) and by Eulogio Perlaza (El "Rapsoda Cubano"), Artel's lecture—which Cosme and Perlaza attended—provoked a storm of controversy, prompting at least two letters to local newspapers (Franco; Benítez). As he had done before at the Casa Hispánica lecture and on other occasions, Artel assailed the so-called *poesía negroide,* which, in his opinion, tended to denigrate black people through derisive verses, disparaging and reductive representations of black women, and exaggeratedly defective speech. To help clear up matters, the newspaper *La Prensa* asked Artel to write a summary of his lecture. Under the title "Importancia del folkore," Artel's lengthy and cogent synopsis was published on Sunday, May 18, 1952.

If *La Prensa* had not requested the summary from Artel, it is likely that there would not be a published text of his remarks. Happily, however, that it is not the case. Like previously mentioned writings of Artel on black poetry, this essay is another important document of his literary career, one that sheds light on Artel's developing poetic vision and his perceptive insights on what some critics have described as *negrista* poetry's period of decline along humoristic and sentimental paths (Fernández de la Vega and Pamies 12). Pointing out the error of both Eurocentric and exclusivist Americanist thinking, he debunked the tendency of many poets to ascribe sensuality solely to African peoples and criticized the all too common and stereotypical depiction of black folk as clowns. As we will show later, these and other ideas would become manifest in poems inspired by Artel's travels and experiences during these years.

Artel remained in New York until 1953, where, as he wrote years later, he worked successively as a laborer, translator, and writer ("Artel visto por Artel"). For a time he was employed as a writer in the Latin American Division of Radio at the United Nations. During this period he also contributed articles to the Spanish edition of *Reader's Digest* and lectured at Princeton University. Upon leaving New York for Mexico he traveled through the southern United States, where he was able to observe firsthand the separate and unequal facilities, the unjust treatment, and the racial insults suffered by African-American citizens living under legal segregation. These images and experiences were seared into the poet's memory and soul and would inform several of the poems that were to become the nucleus of a new edition of *Tambores en la noche.*

In Mexico Artel held teaching posts at the University of Nuevo León in Monterrey and later at the University of Guanajuato in Guanajuato, all the while continuing to publish prose and poetry, to give public readings of his poetry, and to lecture on Afro-American themes. In 1955 he brought out the second, revised edition of *Tambores en la noche,* published by the University of Guanajuato. (The several major changes in this edition that distinguish it from the original 1940 book are discussed in chapter 7.) Persevering in his poetic mission to be an emotional and historical bridge between the African past and the African-American present, Artel traveled around Mexico promoting his book through lectures and poetry recitals. Wherever he went he was well received, although he did encounter one incident of racial discrimination in early 1957 ("Eminente Conferencista Discriminado"). Meanwhile, efforts to sell his book in Colombia met with some resistance, and in Venezuela a reviewer who lauded Artel's work erroneously stated that the new book was a republication of the first edition ("Una Librería"; "Meridiano Cultural").

After residing in Mexico approximately four years, Artel traveled through Central America and finally to Panama, where in 1959 he joined the staff of the daily newspaper *El País.* He remained in Panama for about twelve years, collaborating in all the major newspapers of the capital and frequently in *El Espectador* of Bogotá. On several occasions his journalistic articles were honored with awards from the Sindicato de Periodistas de Panamá [Union of Panamanian Journalists] (see, for example, "*La Hora* se anotó dos . . ."). During these years Artel held the posts of director of the Office of Information and Publications and secretary of publicity of the University of Panama. In that capacity he returned to Colombia briefly in 1966 to attend a public relations conference in Medellín. Coming after a hiatus of eighteen years, his month-long visit prompted numerous interviews and culminated in a poetry recital at the Biblioteca Luis-Angel Arango in Bogotá.

The following year Sonolux issued a recording of Artel reading from *Tambores en la noche* (Castro); and his play "De rigurosa etiqueta," a one-act monologue that had been cited as the best work of 1965, was performed in Panama ("'De Rigurosa Etiqueta'"). In 1968 Artel made a brief visit to Ecuador, where he gave lectures and met with Antonio Preciado and other Afro–Ecuadorian poets ("Meridiano de la Cultura"). While living in Panama he met and married Ligia Alcázar, a Costa Rican–born poet residing in the Isthmus, with whom he had two sons, Jorge Nazim and Miguel. Forced for political reasons to abandon Panama, in 1971 Artel and his family moved to Barranquilla. There he taught literature at the Universidad del Atlántico, which also published in 1972 two new volumes of his poetry, *Poemas con botas y banderas* [Poems with Boots and Banners], a collection of politically and socially inspired poems, and *Sinú, riberas de asombro jubiloso* [Sinú, Banks of Jubilant Wonder], a long elegiac poem to the people, landscape, and culture of his mother's homeland.

In 1974 the family moved to Medellín, where Artel held a teaching post at the University of Antioquia (and other schools) and wrote a column called "Señales de humo" [Smoke Signals] for the newspaper *El Colombiano.* The first Congreso de Cultura Negra de las Américas, which convened in Cali in September 1977 under the leadership of Colombian novelist and folklorist Manuel Zapata Olivella and Brazilian writer and politician Abdias do Nascimento, honored Artel and fellow Afro–Colombian poet Helcías Martán Góngora (1920–84) for their significant contributions to black culture. In 1979 two more books by Artel appeared: a collection of previously published poems titled *Antología poética* [Poetic Anthology], which contains most of the new compositions from his 1955 book; and a novel, *No es la muerte, es el morir* [It's not the Death, It's the Dying], which deals with guerrillas in Colombia.[36] By this time Artel had received appointment as police inspector at Santa Elena, a small town located on a mountain overlooking Medellín. Removed unceremoniously—and, some say, unjustly—from his post in early 1981 and generally dissatisfied with Colombia, Artel returned abruptly with his family to Panama in December of that year. His sudden disappearance prompted a rumor that the poet had died, which resulted in premature eulogies and commentaries in various newspapers (García Ochoa; "Murió el poeta Jorge Artel").

Resurrected, Artel was one of several national poets invited by President Belisario Betancur in 1983 to participate in a series of recitals at the national palace, Casa de Nariño. From his recital of July 14 came the volume *Cantos y poemas* [Songs and Poems], a selection of thirty-three poems published by the Office of the President. Besides a brief biographical note, the eighty-page book also included "Some Opinions on the Poetry of Jorge Artel," which are the same excerpted commentaries by critics and fellow poets that preface the 1955 edition of *Tambores en la noche.* Moved by Artel's economic hardships and historic recital, the national government provided the poet, then seventy-four years old and suffering from arthritis and heart trouble, with a house in a suburb of Barranquilla. Later, Artel was appointed librarian at the Universidad Simón Bolívar there, a position he held for life. On occasion he also served as acting rector, presiding over graduation ceremonies and performing other duties.

Fully repatriated, Artel began to receive some overdue but well deserved appreciation for his unique work in Colombian letters. In 1985 the University of Antioquia awarded Artel the National Prize for Poetry in recognition of his outstanding, lifelong contributions to Colombian poetry (López, "Jorge

Artel"). The award included the publication of a new collection of his poetry under the title *Antología poética*. With the monetary portion of the prize, Artel also was able to realize another long-held ambition: to bring out a third edition of *Tambores en la noche*. Published in 1986, the volume contains all of the poems of the two earlier editions. About a year later a new Colombian journal of Latin American literature published Artel's vitriolic "Al oído de Reagan," which may be the last poem by Artel to have appeared during his lifetime.

In September 1992 the international Colloquium [on the] African Contribution to the Culture of the Americas, held in Bogotá, paid homage to Artel during its final session.[37] The following year Artel visited for the first time the island of San Andrés, where he discovered he had relatives. Almost a year later, on August 19, 1994, Jorge Artel died of heart failure, at the age of eighty-five, in a Barranquilla hospital. Colombian journalists rendered impressive tributes to the nation's poet of Negritude (e.g., Guarín and Cantillo; "Un Jorge Artel Continental"). Although the announcement of Artel's passing was carried internationally ("Necrológicas"),[38] news of his death does not appear to have reached English-language North American newspapers.

Although Artel managed to edit several collections of poems during his lifetime, all of his published poetry has yet to be collected, much less studied. Conspicuously absent from Artel's books are a handful of poems of his youth, written in the late 1920s and published in newspapers and magazines of the coast and Bogotá. Although forgotten or disparaged by their author, these compositions reveal much about Artel's early aesthetic orientation and provide valuable insights into the development of his poetic art. The following chapter offers a brief examination of some of these poems for the purpose of demonstrating, as far as possible, the origins of Artel's poetry, and situating him within a broader artistic and literary context. In this way, the chapter serves as a useful—and, indeed, necessary—introduction both to Artel's progression toward a poetics of blackness and to a study of the poems of *Tambores en la noche*.

4

ℱROM *POSTMODERNISMO* TO *VANGUARDISMO*:

Literary and Aesthetic Foundations of the Poetry of Jorge Artel

> We younger Negro artists who create now intend to express our
> individual dark-skinned selves without fear or shame. . . . We
> build our temples for tomorrow, strong as we know how, and we
> stand on top of the mountain, free within ourselves.
>
> Langston Hughes (1926)

> we are an affirmative generation that brings to the country a
> breeze of fundamental reforms that are acclimated in the zone of
> our constant restlessness and of our firm orientation to national
> themes. we want a republic exalted by intelligence and action.
>
> Jorge Artel et al. (1931)

Jorge Artel is recognized primarily as the author of *Tambores en la noche*. With this book, as Javier Arango Ferrer has stated, the
poet earned for Colombia legitimate recognition and standing within the
realm of Afro-Hispanic literature (*La literatura de Colombia* 152). It is not
strange, then, that the literary critics and historians who have written on
Artel have tended to focus on the the racial poems of Artel's first book,
even though other themes and concerns, such as nostalgia for the coastal
homeland, recollections of the seaport, and the joys and pains of romantic
love, figure prominently in his work.[1] Indeed, as Antonio del Real Torres
once observed, "Jorge Artel, with all his poetry of blackness, is showing
in his lustful language, that he saw the world from a port" ("La influencia
geográfica"). Clearly, however, Artel's book—and I am referring here to the
Cartagena edition—with its foregrounding of African heritage and Atlantic
coastal culture, constituted and still remains a unique chord within the
contemporary lyric of Colombia.

Paradoxically, however, the almost exclusive critical emphasis on the
poems of *Tambores en la noche* and the designation of Artel as the "poeta
negro" of Colombia have also contributed to his perception as an isolated
figure within Colombian literature, disconnected from the principal literary
currents of Spanish America and separated from the generational and literary
contexts that nourished his poetic vocation and outlook.[2] Notwithstanding—
and perhaps because of—Artel's unique place in Colombia's literary history

and his singular contribution to Colombian belles lettres, much of his poetry, especially that written before his arrival in Bogotá in 1930, remains unexamined by critics and largely unknown to the general public. Although forgotten or even dismissed by the poet himself, several little-known poetic texts (together with other writings in prose) provide useful information about Artel's literary origins and thus help to situate him within the principal artistic currents of his era. In addition, they offer valuable insights into the early poetic orientation and creative processes of Artel's muse—i.e., motifs, language, verse forms, etc.—thereby permitting a greater appreciation of his evolution toward a poetry of black expression. On the other hand, ignorance of Artel's early compositions or failure to take them into account when assessing Artel's later poetry often has led, I believe, to a limited understanding, narrow appreciation, and even faulty interpretation of the poet's work.

Theorist and critic Carlos Bousoño offers an approach to the study of literary history that corroborates the relevance and usefulness of a discussion of Artel's early poetry. In his book *Teoría de la expresión poética* Bousoño suggests that

> the history of literature evolves as [it is] pushed by the fusion of two very different impulses which give it mobility. One is the state of society at the time in question, with which the literature is to correspond in a certain manner; the other consists of the state of the preceding literature, to which the present literature is partially opposed. According to this scheme, the literature of a determined moment is the offspring of the society, on the one hand, and of the preceding literature, on the other. (523)

The new literature arises always respecting what Bousoño calls "the law of continuity and contradiction" (524). That is, the present-day artistic moment does not come to oppose all the elements of the previous moment, but only some. At the same time, as Bousoño points out, the former

> carries on in a different way, perhaps with a slight change in intensity, other [elements] which still maintain value because they serve to express that new conception of the world which the social structure of the present day imposes. From that it is clear that we cannot understand what may be an artistic moment if we do not have in view, in one way or another, the whole process in which art is born and within which, like a dialectical member of a series, [it] acquires the fullness of its meaning. (523)

Bousoño's observations are especially applicable to Artel's situation. As we have already stated, critics of Artel's work customarily have dealt with the poems of *Tambores en la noche*, written after 1930. Usually they have compared them, without detailed study, to Obeso's poetry or they have examined them in relation to the *poesía negrista* of other societies, frequently situating them within the Afro-Antillean orbit without any consideration for their antecedents (e.g., Bruges Carmona, "Algo sobre poesía negra"; Carranza, "La poesía negra de Jorge Artel").[3] Since this first book of Artel's does not contain all of his previously published poetry, by studying only the poems contained therein we come away with an incomplete idea of his work and a false or partial notion regarding his exact location within the literary panorama of Spanish America and his full participation in the development of Colombian poetry.

Excluded from Artel's collected poetry are several poems written at the end of the decade of the twenties. In my opinion these poems are important for at least two reasons. First, they permit us to discern the possible forces and aesthetic currents that influenced the poet during his formative years; and second, they reveal elements that would lay the groundwork for Artel's later, more mature work—specifically, the poems of *Tambores en la noche*. A brief examination of some of these early poems will reveal the poet's transition from a Spanish-American postmodernist stance to an avant-garde position. It will also show with more exactness how Artel fits within the generation and era in which he lived and wrote. Finally, insofar as possible, it will evince some changes and constants in the development of his poetic art. In this way we will arrive at a better appreciation both of Artel's lyrical and cultural evolution toward the poems of *Tambores en la noche* and of his contribution to the development of black literary expression in Colombia.

As pointed out in the previous chapter, Artel's formative years coincided with the postwar decade, which in Spanish-American literature corresponds to the expiration of Modernism and the expanding influence of a new artistic spirit. Federico de Onís groups into two principal modes or divisions the multiple and contradictory poetic tendencies that developed out of the decline of Rubén Darío's Modernism. Onís characterizes the first one, *"post-modernismo,"* as "an attempt to react against Modernism, by restraining its excesses." A conservative reaction, this attitude left little room for individual creativity; the poet who adopted it "takes refuge in the enjoyment of the good that has been attained." The second tendency, which Onís labels *"ultra-modernismo,"* and which today is generally known as *vanguardismo,* or avant-gardism, carries Modernism's "fervor of innovation and freedom" even further (xviii) and "ends in a series of bold and original attempts at the creation of a totally new poetry" (xix). While Modernism's influence stretched well into the twentieth century, in Colombia, where traditions die slowly, it seemed to linger with more persistence than in other places (Henríquez Ureña, *Breve historia del modernismo* 326–31; Corvalán 13, 92). As a consequence, the avant-garde impact there was not as strong as in other countries.

ARTEL AND *POSTMODERNISMO*

Several youthful compositions of Artel reflect—almost simultaneously—features of the two divisions noted by Onís. An example of the persistence of the Modernist aesthetic is found in the Alexandrine sonnet "Siglo XV" [Fifteenth Century], written in 1928. Beginning with the very title, which evokes the medieval period, several features of the end-of-the-century movement—such as escapism to the age of chivalry through fantasy; identification with classical Greek culture; and a noble, almost aristocratic attitude—are evident in the first quatrain:

Yo soy un caballero de una corte galante
de princesas helénicas y príncipes dioscuros,
donde los besos premian el acero triunfante
y tienen las miradas románticos conjuros.

[I am a chevalier of a gallant court / of Hellenic princesses and Dioscuri princes, / where kisses reward the triumphant blade / and glances have romantic spells.]

The elegance and refinement so characteristic of the poetry of Rubén Darío, together with the delight in the luminous and a subtle synaesthesia are also present, but restrained, in "el pañuelo bordado," "los encajes ligeros," "los marcos de carey," and the "suave tono blanco," as well as in the words connoting light that appear throughout the rest of the poem:

Yo recojo el bordado pañuelo que a la hermosa
se desliza por entre los encajes ligeros . . .
y terciada la capa que el rostro medio-emboza,
defiendo mi trofeo contra los altaneros.

Cuando la luna pone sobre la encrucijada,
de suave tono blanco su leve pincelada,
plateando en las ojivas los marcos de carey

bajo el plúmeo [*sic*] chambergo yo cruzo los portales,
dispuesto a dar cien vidas entre los pedregales
por mi Dios y mi dama, por mi patria y mi rey!

[I gather up the embroidered handkerchief that from the belle / slips along the delicate laces . . . / and with my cloak drawn across to half-hide my face, / I defend my trophy against the haughty.

When the moon sets on the crossroads / its light stroke of soft white tone, / silvercoating the tortoise shell frames on the ogives

beneath my broad-brimmed hat I cross the portals, / ready to give one hundred lives on the stony ground / for my God and my lady, for my country and my king!]

In two other sonnets titled "Careta trágica" [Tragic Mask] and "Carnavales" [Carnivals], not only do we find Modernist reminiscences again in the allusions to Edgar Allan Poe and Pallas, and to Pierrot and Columbine,[4] but also a turning back toward Romanticism in the subjective expression of disillusionment in the face of a world indifferent to personal suffering and tedium. Published in 1929 when Artel turned twenty years of age, "Careta trágica" seems to capture a moment of crisis or an awakening of consciousness when one realizes that in order to be able to get along with others, it is necessary to adopt before the world an attitude or a behavior different from one's natural manner, even though this turns out to be a less sincere, less open, and less genuine expression of one's feelings:

Pero llegó el momento de ocultar a la Vida
los dolores y el tedio, con sonrisa fingida,
entre frívoles goces, tras alegre careta . . .

[But the moment arrived of hiding from life / the pains and the boredom, with faked smile, / amidst frivolous joys, behind a cheerful face . . .]

The second tercet summarizes admirably the personal implications of the conflict:

Y entonces fui festivo mostrándome contento
escondiéndole a todos mi propio sentimiento,
como una mezcla trágica de payaso y poeta!

[And then I became festive showing myself happy / concealing from everyone my own feeling, / like a tragic mélange of clown and poet!]

"Carnavales," written in March of 1930, is another variation on this theme of indifference and disillusionment, which further highlights an idea insinuated by Darío in his stories "El rey burgués" and "El sátiro sordo": namely, that those who love, those who maintain a poetic attitude toward life, are seen as clowns, entertainers, buffoons for the rest. Indeed, Artel seems to be lamenting the inability of the bourgeois to accept individual differences and to respect personal dreams and inclinations. Whereas "Careta trágica" refers to the moment when the poet hides his face from life, "Carnavales" presents the context of that concealment.

> Fué en una hermosa noche de alegre Carnaval,
> entre un mar de confettis y vivas serpentinas,
> cuando sentíme enfermo del incurable mal
> de amar eternamente las bellas Colombinas.
>
> Y la locura humana, que gusta de lo irreal,
> enharinó mi rostro, y al són de mandolinas
> me puso a flor de labios—Pierrot sentimental—
> las más dulces estrofas de viejas sonatinas. . . .

[It was on a beautiful night of gay Carnival, / among a sea of confetti and bright streamers, / when I felt sick with the incurable ill / of loving eternally the fair Columbines.

And human folly, which enjoys the unreal, / smeared my face with flour, and to the sound of mandolins / made me—a sentimental Pierrot—/ sing the sweetest stanzas of old sonatinas.]

Oblivious to, or disdainful of, the individual's outlook of idealism and love, the pleasure-driven, unrefined, less sensitive elements of society impose upon the poet their own less serious pose or less transcendental outlook, one consonant with limited, transitory, mass-oriented values and tastes. The description of the music favored by this element—"las más dulces estrofas de viejas sonatinas"—suggests nostalgic, sterile, hoary airs that are passé or outmoded. The poet's own voice (or vision)—new, sober, yet sincere and thus unpopular—is overlooked, repressed, in preference for the old, for that which evokes the past, emphasizes acquiescence, and poses no threat. (Implicit in this idea is a denial of the new person or artist within the young poet whose notes and chords sound strange to those enamored of or bound by empty, meaningless, temporal sounds and gestures of the past.) In that respect, the poem seems to anticipate a new, independent spirit developing in Artel. As Spanish philosopher-critic José Ortega y Gasset observed of the young, iconoclastic artists and writers of the avant-garde, in his essay *La deshumanización del arte* [The Dehumanization of Art]:

> they are endowed with a perfectly clear, coherent, and rational sense of art. Far from being a whim, their way of feeling represents the inevitable and fruitful result of all the previous artistic achievement. Whimsical,

arbitrary, and, consequently unprofitable it would be to set oneself against the new style and obstinately remain shut up in old forms that are exhausted and the worse for wear. (12)[5]

Understandably, the imposition and repression implied in "Carnavales" lead not to cheerfulness and fulfillment, but to sadness and disillusion and to an awareness that life, too, is carnival—that is, deceptive fantasy. Artel also reiterates the idea that those who love, searching for a higher ideal, are merely poets playing the part of dreamers—that is, clowns (Pierrot):

> Al terminar la farsa sentí que la congoja
> de la amargada vida, que es otro Carnaval
> oscurecía mi alma. . . . —Qué triste paradoja!—

> Y convencíme entonces ante mi propio Yo
> que todos los que amamos, buscando un ideal
> no más somos poetas que hacemos el Pierrot. . . .

[When the farce ended, I felt the anguish / of embittered life, which is another Carnival[,] / darkening my soul. . . . —What a sad paradox!—

And I became convinced then before my own Self / that all of us who love, searching for an ideal / are only poets who play the part of Pierrot. . . .]

Although the image of the tragic, smiling mask and the evocation of Pierrot, the dreamer with a sad, whitened face, are not at all new in Spanish-American poetry, they take on a certain freshness and originality in the work of the young coastal poet, who deftly combines them with the carnival tradition of his native Cartagena. On a general level, use of the carnival context and allusions to disguise underscore the common human error of confusing superficial forms with a deeper, genuine reality.[6] On a geo-cultural level, these elements call attention to the failure of many Colombians to see beyond the facile, mirthful visage and occasionally brusque manner of the *costeño*.[7] On yet a more personal and artistic level, use of the carnival motif exposes the (perhaps perennial) conflict between the old and the new, between mass-oriented art and the individualistic, poetic currents that were seducing Artel and many others.[8]

That is, "Careta trágica" and "Carnavales" evince a determination to maintain artistic independence and integrity in the face of pressure to conform to a trendy, more popular art of mass appeal. This determination would guide Artel's creative spirit and inform much of the poetry of *Tambores en la noche*. Artel would reject the frivolous, carnival-like manipulation of black peoples and their culture (especially music, dance, and speech) carried out by many of the practitioners of *poesía negrista,* who, too often, like minstrels with faces darkened with burnt cork, merely put on a Negro mask and imitated black language. Rather, Artel would create and adhere to a more dignified, uplifting poetic approach to the African experience in America, one that did not rely on sound and sight devices such as onomatopoeia, jitanjáfora, and alliteration to gain attention and acceptance.

At the same time, within the implied contrast of appearance and reality, one cannot help but see also an extraordinary parallel between these poems by Artel and "We Wear the Mask" by African-American poet Paul Laurence Dunbar. Although the latter composition is related to a racial context while Artel's sonnets deal with an existential or individual situation, in both cases the paradoxical adoption of the mask—a false face—as a means of dissimulating unappreciated feelings and as a way of maintaining one's personal integrity in the face of a fraudulent reality and a hostile or indifferent world is striking.[9]

Just as these early poems suggest life situations that necessitate concealing one's true self behind a mask, so too will the poems of *Tambores en la noche* suggest another dimension or reality behind the outward gaiety and sensuality of black dance and song. Like Langston Hughes, who conveyed in "Minstrel Man" and other poems the tragic irony behind black laughter and entertainment in the United States, Artel would seek to unmask and affirm the forgotten and disdained presence and heritage of Africa in Colombia.

Use of the conventional sonnet can also be seen as an indication of the traditional orientation of Artel's poetic beginnings and of the persistence of Modernism in Colombia. According to Rudolf Baehr, with the triumph of Modernism the sonnet once again became a favorite form among Spanish-American poets and continues to be so in contemporary poetry (398–400). In fact, Artel's sonnet, "Carnavales," offers an example of the crossed arrangement ("disposición cruzada") in the quatrains (ABAB ABAB), which, according to Baehr, was an innovation of the Modernists. Moreover, the practical experience that the poet gained upon submitting himself to the rigorous discipline of condensation and concentration demanded by the sonnet would be confirmed years later in the creation of other sonnets, such as "Soneto del hielo" [Sonnet of the Ice] and, most notably, "Soneto más negro" [Blacker Sonnet].

ARTEL AND THE AVANT-GARDE

With respect to the other poetic mode noted by Onís, *vanguardismo,* or avant-gardism—with its conscious and implacable negation of the past, its rebellion against the traditional demand of beauty, its violation of the logical and grammatical functions of language, its unclear associations and obscure images, its audacious typographical arrangements, and so on,—it is clear that neither Artel nor the great majority of Colombian poets of the period embraced it fully. Even the members of "Los Nuevos," the most important literary group of the 1920s, "were cautious in walking along those labryinths" (Arango Ferrer, *Dos horas de literatura colombiana* 147).[10] Nevertheless, in Artel's poems and prose writings of this early period one senses occasionally a certain approximation to the avant-garde spirit that liberates the poet from the imitative subjection to Modernist tradition and lays the groundwork for his poetic explorations of black culture and identity.

Artel seems to have been drawn, in particular, to some aspects of Futurism.[11] As articulated in various manifestos by its founder, F. T. Marinetti, and his adherents, Futurism affirmed a new aesthetic: the beauty of speed and dynamic, aggressive movement, as embodied in the automobile, steamships, locomotives, and airplanes, especially in the context of struggle. Seeking to bring about a renovation of all artistic expressions, the Futurists assailed the veneration of the old and the past, exalted every kind of originality, and rebelled against the tyranny of the terms *harmony* and *good taste*.

Two poems by Artel seem to reflect the widespread lure of the subversive movement. In "Signos" [Signs] (1929), a composition dedicated "A una estenógrafa" [To a stenographer] and written in polymetric, or irregular, verses (primarily of seven and fourteen syllables), Artel takes as a device to express his romantic attraction the technique of stenographic or speed writing, with its "Círculos, / líneas rectas y curvas . . . / Trazos cortos y largos mudamente habladores / que se enfilan correctos y sintetizadores" [Circles, / straight lines and curves . . . / Mutely speaking strokes short and long / that align themselves correctly and synthesizingly]. Here one perceives an attempt on the part of the poet to capture something of the rapid and dynamic nature or character of stenography without actually reproducing or imitating it—as many avant-garde poets attempted to do in their verse. As we will see in the drum poems of *Tambores en la noche*, Artel, unlike many *negrista* poets, names the art or skill of drumming but usually does not attempt to (re-)create or (re-)produce it visually or phonetically.

At the heart of "Signos," as the remaining verses show, what the poet is actually concerned about is not the technical skill of the stenographer per se, but rather the underlying emotion or passion that she evokes in the poet. Note the immediate moving of attention from the circles and lines of the writing to the hands of the writer in the first stanza:

Círculos,

líneas curvas y rectas . . .

Elocuentes figuras por tus manos trazadas,

agilísimas manos que, para el signo aladas,
van poniendo ligeras
en la intensa negrura
del sencillo tablero
con rasgos hechiceros
la embrujada escritura.

[Circles, / lines curved and straight . . . / Eloquent figures by your hands drawn, / most agile hands that, with wings for the sign, / go nimbly putting / with magic strokes / the bewitched writing / upon the intense blackness of the simple board.]

The poet's amazement at and appreciation for the enigmatic art of speed writing is linked to and exceeded only by his passionate feelings for the stenographer. Ironically, while he acknowledges his ignorance of the various enigmatic signs and lines, she is unaware of his personal secret and unspoken desires. This simultaneous or parallel ignorance is cleverly conveyed or heightened by the ambiguity of wordplay with "clave" [key; type key] and "signo" [sign].

Círculos,
líneas mixtas y oblicuas . . .
Absurdos caracteres cuyos significados
ante mi vista torpe se quedan ignorados,
así como tú ignoras
que soy la clave humana
de una ansia inexpresada
y soy un triste signo
que aún no diciendo nada
para tí encierra un himno! . . .

[Circles, / lines mixed and oblique . . . / Absurd characters whose meanings / remain unknown to my dull sight, / just as you do not know / that I am the human key / of an unexpressed yearning / and I am a sad sign / that while saying nothing / for you holds a hymn! . . .]

Significantly, the self-description ("soy la clave humana / de una ansia inexpresada") enunciated in the above lines anticipates later verses of Artel's, wherein he identifies himself as the voice of Afro-Colombia ("Negro soy desde hace muchos siglos. / Poeta de mi raza, heredé su dolor") (*Tambores*

[1940] 31), or assumes the burden of the slave past ("yo—Jorge Artel / galeote de un ansia suprema") (*Tambores* [1940] 37).

Where one most discerns the presence of the avant-garde spirit—particularly that of Futurism—in Artel's early poetry, however, is in the poem "Exodo" [Exodus]. Published in January 1930, "Exodo" transmits the emotional experience of departure and travel by locomotive. Sensibly yet significantly, the poem opens at the train station, which, according to Ramón Gómez de la Serna, was the abode of the Futurists' divinity (123):

> Las manos tienen
> una como ansia
> desconocida
> de apretar otras tantas
> manos amigas.
>
> Sonrisas de los ojos.
> Por sobre la colmena,
> la humana colmena
> de la Estación,
> un murmullo se escurre inquietante
> y se mete adentro;
> sigiloso apache . . .

[The hands have / something like an unfamiliar / longing / to squeeze other equally friendly hands.

Smiles from the eyes. / Above the beehive, / the human hive of the Station, / a murmur oozes disturbingly / and slips inside; / a silent bandit . . .]

Particularly evident in the poem are the zeal for innovation; the surprising interplay of images, perspectives, and time; and the broadening of poetic themes through the incorporation of machines:

> La campanada,
> intangible puñal que rasga el aire,
> pone a mover la fiera
> que me llevará en su seno
> para después vomitarme.
>
> Crujen las paralelas

que infinitamente se alargan. . . .

Atrás se queda la mañana.
Los montes van de prisa.
Todo corre
como huyendo
del gran cíclope gigante
que promete,
en la furia conque avanza,
como romper el alma
de la selvática distancia!

El tiempo va de caza
y las flechas de las horas
lanza
sobre el lomo formidable;
se oye el grito herido
de la férrea
bestia
negra
que se traga los kilómetros.

Mientras,
siento que los ojos
—ventanas de mi alma—
se abren para que pase
todo el añil de los cielos
y el verde limón de la montaña.

[The ringing of the bell, / intangible dagger that rips the air, / sets in motion the beast / that will bear me within its bosom / in order to disgorge me later.

The parallel bars that extend infinitely clatter. . . .

Morning remains behind. / The mountains go by quickly. /
Everything runs / like fleeing from the great giant Cyclops / that promises, / in the fury with which it advances,/ to break through the heart / of the wild distance!

Time goes hunting / and launches / the arrows of the hours / on the formidable back; / the wounded cry is heard / of the black / iron / beast / that swallows up the miles.

Meanwhile, / I feel my eyes / —windows of my soul— / open to let pass / all the indigo of the heavens / and the lemon green of the mountain.]

The avant-garde notion also reveals itself in the bolder metaphors ("La campanada, / intangible puñal que rasga el aire"; "del gran cíclope gigante"; "las flechas de las horas"); in the more provocative kinetic, visual, and auditory images ("la fiera / que me llevará en su seno / para después vomitarme"; "Los montes van de prisa"; "la férrea / bestia/ negra/ que se traga los kilómetros"); and in the dynamic verbs ("corre," "huyendo," "avanza," "romper," "lanza"), almost all of which are charged with energy, suggesting an inexorable movement forward that manifests the powerful force of the locomotive and the implacable passage of time.

As in the previous poem "Signos," the language of "Exodo" also marks a significant departure from the Modernist aesthetic. Instead of recondite vocabulary evoking refinement and elegance or exotic escapism, Artel uses common, everyday words to poeticize ordinary situations and events, although the usage and arrangement of the words result in highly lyrical, uncommon effects. Moreover, unlike the earlier sonnets, these poems and others that Artel composed during the years 1929–30 (e.g., "Gitana," "Elegía de los veinte años," "Canción pierrotesca en gris y blanco") are written exclusively in free verse ("verso libre")—that is, in verses without regularity or fixity of syllable, stanza, or rhyme—considered "the new metrics with which one attempted to reach the most extreme ranges of the poetic word" (López Estrada 103). Thus Artel's search for and affirmation of a greater freedom of expression coincides with and finds a ready vehicle in the avant-garde assertions of a new, more flexible verse.

Still, Artel's poetic participation in the avant-garde does not reach the extremes that some more radical—and usually older—avant-garde poets (e.g., Vicente Huidobro, César Vallejo, Pablo Neruda, León De Greiff) achieved. For example, he does not resort to radical alterations of syntax or employ innovative typographical arrangements to reflect simultaneously the theme or content of the poem. Nor does he seem to have been interested in the rebellion against language that seeks to "deprive words of their meaning and to use them as material for the creation of a completely autonomous poetic reality" (Fernández Moreno 73).[12] This may help explain, from a stylistic point of view, why the later poems of *Tambores en la noche* do not exhibit the jitanjáforas and onomatopoeias so characteristic of poetic *negrismo*. Artel's poetry approaches more the "impure poetry" of a Pablo Neruda than the "pure poetry" of a Mariano Brull. The semantic value and import of the word, the communicative function of the poem, always matters to him.[13]

Similarly, Artel's poetry does not share that attitude of the avant-garde that "conceives [of] art as a non-transcendental, sport-like, trivial thing, as a game" (Fernández Moreno 61).[14] Rather, it is more consonant with the tendency that, according to César Fernández Moreno, accentuates poetry as a means of knowledge and affirms "life in itself, inclusively and principally in those . . . least explored and exploited strata" (57, 61). It is also probably accurate to say that until the advent of the avant-garde, accompanied by a growing interest in African and Afro-American cultures, black life and problems constituted one of those least explored and exploited strata.

Artel's poetry does reflect, however, other aspects of the avant-garde noted by Ortega y Gasset and others. One of these is the antipopular attitude of the *vanguardista* literature:

> Modern art . . . *will always have the masses against it.* It is essentially unpopular; moreover, it is antipopular. . . . On the other hand, the new art also helps the elite *to recognize themselves and one another in the drab mass of society* and to learn their mission which consists in being few and *holding their own against the many.* (Ortega y Gasset, *Dehumanization of Art* 5, 7; emphasis added)[15]

It should be understood, of course, that "antipopular" as used here does not mean an elitist or condescending attitude toward the folk (*pueblo*) or the literature inspired in the folk, but rather a reaction against mass culture. As Guillermo de Torre explains in *Minorías y masas en la cultura y el arte contemporáneos:*

> That exaggerated culture of the masses has nothing to do—or very scant points of contact—with our old familiar and congenial popular culture. Its content and its intentions are strictly different, since it is well known that the people is one thing, the sum of individualities, and the mass something radically opposed: its disintegration and annihilation. (13)[16]

Indeed, as we noted previously in our discussion of "Carnavales," Artel's "antipopular" *vanguardismo* implies an opposition to that mass culture that would annihilate individual creativity and perspectives. Shortly after the publication of these early compositions, as Artel began writing the racial poems that would constitute the first section of *Tambores en la noche,* he would distinguish himself (and other select authors) from the mass of poets and would-be poets for whom black literary expression apparently consisted in facile, formulaic writing, involving little more than imitation of Afro-Antillean poets and self-declaration as a black poet. On the other hand, as

I have pointed out in chapter 3, Artel would adopt a scrupulous, selective, and committed minority point of view toward the creation of black literature in Colombia, a view undoubtedly shaped—at least in part—by avant-garde experiences and values and that would place him in the forefront of Afro-Colombian writing.

In this respect, too, it is worthwhile mentioning again Artel's participation in the creation and issuance of the unique, albeit barely noticed, "manifiesto de los ultrajóvenes," published in Bogotá in October 1931. Although the manifesto does not seem to have had any far-reaching or lasting impact on Colombian literature in general, it does provide evidence of the existence of a nascent avant-garde consciousness in Artel and other poets and writers of the "Post-Nuevos" group, and confirms Artel's copartnership in the historically significant document. Undoubtedly, ever increasing contact with new ideas and modes of artistic expression implicit in the avant-garde, and closer ties with other men of letters sensitive to new and unusual ways of thinking and creating,[17] contributed to Artel's intellectual and literary growth and, in turn, to a spiritual awakening that led to greater linguistic possibilities, deeper ethnic concerns, and wider aesthetic horizons. Precisely, it is during these early years in Bogotá (circa 1931–34) that Artel, far removed from his beloved coastal clime, surrounded by the Andean mountain mists, and submerged in the culture of the highlands, loses his shout (*grito*)—"the wide shout / that the open horizons of my coast / taught me to give like a note" ("Meridiano de Bogotá")—and discovers his voice, the voice through which he would express his own individual emotions as well as the collective, historical experience and spiritual legacy of Afro-Colombia. That is to say, the physical and cultural distance from the coast stimulates Artel to (re-) discover and explore his racial and ethnic heritage, not unlike Candelario Obeso's earlier poetic expression of racial identity and black coastal life. Artel initiates an internal journey of consciousness and undertakes a poetic odyssey that will result in an affirmation of black identity and of the important yet often forgotten presence of coastal Colombia. As I will show later, all of these elements contribute to and are manifest in the first edition of *Tambores en la noche* (1940) and in other poems.

As in other countries where the new artistic spirit had begun to penetrate, the efforts of Artel and his fellow poets to incorporate the avant-garde spirit into Colombian letters and to challenge traditional approaches to poetry met with much resistance. In Bogotá, older, conservative poets, either unwilling or unable to countenance the anarchistic posture of their younger counterparts, defended established norms and traditions and impugned the violation of conventional harmony and order occasioned by the use of free verse and obscure symbolism. Ismael Enrique Arciniegas, an untiring and unrelenting Romantic for whom emotion and harmony were indispensable elements of poetry, rebuked the callow rebels in his perfectly rhymed "Canto a la rima," which begins:

> ¿Decís que la rima ya ha muerto, y que es ruido,
> De compás monótono, muy fuerte al oído,
> Y que rotos ritmos son música interna
> Para los arcanos del alma moderna?
>
> ¿Música? ¿Mas cuándo lo que no es eufónico
> Por suerte ha dejado de ser inarmónico?[18]

[You say that rhyme has now died, and that it is noise, / of a monotonous beat, very strong to the ear, / and that broken rhythms are inner music / for the arcana of the modern soul?

Music? But when has that which is not euphonic / by chance stopped being unharmonious?]

Other defenders of the status quo (e.g., Pérez y Soto) were soon contributing their own barbed rhymes to the satirical counterattack on the unorthodox poetic forms.

The new poetry, however, was not the only manifestation of the avant-garde artistic spirit in Colombia to come under attack by the defenders of tradition. The contagion of jazz-band music and dance, or *jazz-bandismo,* as the Spanish writer Ramón Gómez de la Serna called it (178–97), was also condemned. For this leading exponent of the experimental and iconoclastic movements, the rebellious, black-based or black-inspired jazz music defined "the anarchistic mixture" of the new age, and thus paralleled the inconformity and freedom of the new poetry (179). Jazz became "the music of the present, hornblowing, thrashing, scintillating" (189), while the jazz bands themselves were "the laughter in the beards of the seriousness of the past, that remains in the present and refuses to become aware (191).[19]

Not everyone, however, shared the Spanish critic's enthusiasm and optimistic opinion. That the imaginativeness, improvisation, and spontaneity of jazz-band music reflected and was intimately connected to the revolutionary spirit of the new age (and thus to the poetry), probably sufficed for many self-appointed guardians of tradition to denounce it as decadent.[20] Equally detestable—if not more so—were the jazz band's Negro and popular origins and musicians. For those more shocked than excited by the growing interest in African peoples and cultures, jazz-band music and dance probably conjured up uncomfortable, tumultuous images of uncivilized and shameless African natives cavorting in the jungle. It is not surprising, therefore, that some would consider it a threat to European classical music in the same way that Arciniegas and other conventional poets viewed avant-garde verse as a menace to "classical" poetry.

In *El Mercurio* of Cartagena, for example, one Hector de Villaselva sounded an alarm against the infiltration of jazz-band music in Colombia. Warning that classical music was being rapidly displaced in several American republics by the merchandising of Afro-American "plebeian airs" as played by jazz bands, Villaselva noted that Colombians, too, were becoming involved in "producing Negro music." Outraged by jazz band's "gross music," which, he declared, "calls into doubt the virtue of the decent woman," the writer cited recent measures by German authorities to suppress that music considered offensive to good taste and manners. He ended his caution by urging Cartagena officials to take heed of the German example "for the good of our historic town and above all for the feminine sex which, with those extravagant airs is losing one hundred per cent of [its] decency."[21]

A direct linking of *jazz-bandismo* and poetic *vanguardismo* is patently evident in an announcement of the publication of a collection of poems by Eduardo López of the Cauca Valley. Appropriately and tellingly titled *Cosas viejas* [Old Things] (1931) and prologued by the venerable Antonio José Restrepo, López's book contained a direct message for the avant-garde poets, as the writer of the announcement was quick to point out:

> For those who claim to scorn this volume because it has no suggestions of jazz-band, a stanza that stood out . . . is worth copying:
>
> > Versos sin metro y sin rima
> > son versos? Son novedad.
> > Unos lo hacen por capricho
> > y otros por necesidad.
>
> [Verses without meter and without rhyme / are verses? They are novelty. / Some do it as a whim / and others out of necessity.] ("Bibliografía")

Resistance in Colombia to the penetration and dissemination of the poetic avant-garde was not restricted, of course, to the capital. In Cartagena, too, as one might well expect, the youthful challenge to poetic tradition met with opposition and criticism, eventually giving rise to a spirited polemic. To foster a more productive discussion of the issue, José Morillo, then editor of *El Mercurio*, invited the city's intellectual community to participate in a literary poll precisely on "the suitability of introducing into our literature the currents called avant-garde" (Del Real Torres, "El Vanguardismo"). Most of the responses were equanimous, like that of cronista Antonio del

Real Torres, who asserted: " 'Avant-gardism' has come to be in the present tormented youth something like the compendium of a morbid aspiration to innovate, which in every age has had its revelatory standardization" ("El Vanguardismo"). Del Real Torres dismissed the avant-garde thrust largely as "the same old song," with only a change in the label and a slight variation in the disposition of the matter.

Less tolerant and charitable, however, was one Julio García Rovira, whose caustic animadversions upon the avant-garde ("Arrancando Postillas") appeared in the newspaper's "Criticism Section" in September 1932, several months after the close of the poll. Exasperated and bemused by the nonconformist poetry of Artel and other young poets of Cartagena, García Rovira considered the "vanguardista" label to be simply a "refuge of ignoramuses and novices, as if avant-gardism consisted in making typographical pirouettes." Claiming that "The poet who does not shape his work, who does not castigate the style and image that first comes to mind, in the end turns out mediocre and becomes, in course of time, ordinary," García Rovira declared that the false notion of spontaneity, which he viewed as puerility, had caused a great deal of havoc.

Turning his attention specifically to "el vanguardista Jorge Artel," García Rovira censured as "strings of prosaic nonsense layed out in a line" the following excerpt from the poet's "Versos para zarpar un día" [Verses for Getting a Day Under Way], which had been published two months earlier:

Y la pálida
voz de la luna
caerá sobre el mar
con su honda
sonata
de silencio . . .

[And the pale / voice of the moon / will fall on the sea / with its deep sonata of silence . . .]

Failing to recognize or accept the Modernist legacy of synesthesia, the critic questioned Artel's "capricious" use of the modifier *pálida* with the noun *voz*. Furthermore, he rejected the alliterative paradox "sonata de silencio," observing that "Sonata is music, and it cannot be silence," and concluded: "It is simply a contradiction, an absurdity."[22] In short, García Rovira could not appreciate the illogic and inventiveness that give poetry its character and appeal.

Unrelenting in his criticism, García Rovira reproached Artel's imaginative license in the metaphorical lines "Hacia otras tierras / emproará mi alma sus quimeras" [Toward other lands / my soul will steer forward its illusions], taken from the same poem. Not content with mere censure, however, the commentator added insult to his ignorance by resorting to an inexcusable affront to the poet's person.[23] While expressing a liking for the poem "Tamboriles en la noche," the critic also took exception to Artel's use of the verb *"plasmar"* in the lines "plasmando en sus pupilas / un confuso motivo de rutas perdidas" [molding in their pupils / a confused motif of lost routes], protesting that

> "Plasmar" in good speech means to make a figure or form in clay; in the case in question the use even in the figurative sense does not fit well, because any object or thing can be drawn, reflected, portrayed, but molded? . . . Nonsense!

Although García Rovira did concede that Artel was an intelligent lad ("mozo inteligente") who possessed ability to write good verse, he took issue with his delight in "twisting the figure of speech and using similes at dissonance with verisimilitude and correct diction as they related to the application of words." This so-called "dissonance with verisimilitude," however, is exactly what Ortega y Gasset had referred to as "dehumanization of art," that is, a moving away from rendering in art an exact copy of reality. Apparently García Rovira was unaware of, or took exception to, the following analogy made by the noted Spanish philosopher with respect to the new art and the new poetry:

> Far from going more or less clumsily toward reality, the artist is seen going against it. He is brazenly set on deforming it, shattering its human aspect, dehumanizing it . . . [We are thus compelled] to improvise other forms of intercourse completely distinct from our ordinary ways with things. We must invent unheard-of-gestures to fit those singular figures. . . . The weapon of poetry turns against natural things and wounds or murders them. (20, 32)

In sum, García Rovira matches perfectly Ortega y Gasset's description of the person who is unable to comprehend the new art: "when his dislike is due to his failure to understand, he feels vaguely humiliated and this rankling sense of inferiority must be counterbalanced by indignant self-assertion (*Dehumanization of Art* 6).

Although Artel may have given consideration at some time to Garcia Rovira's criticism,[24] during this period of tumult and dissension he seems to have been less preoccupied with promoting the artistic avant-garde per se, and more concerned with developing an original poetics—one that simultaneously incorporated aspects of the geographical and spiritual realities of both his native coastal homeland and of Afro-Colombian life and culture.

Certainly, by then, Artel already viewed his poetry as "essentially racial" in character (see "Actualidades"). Furthermore, as we have already shown, the poet's missive on black literature on the coast, written in July of 1932, demonstrates his growing attention to the spiritual and intellectual movement of black peoples and his pride in being acclaimed the only faithful interpreter of the race in Colombia.

While Artel did not embrace the European "isms" slavishly or wholeheartedy, they would act for him as a stimulus to question the past; as an impulse to revaluate African contributions to Colombia; and as a point of departure for rectifying, poetically, the false, distorted, and incomplete history of Colombia—a history that had contributed to a contempt for and neglect of the coastal regions, to the ignorance and concealment of the African presence and heritage, and to the rejection of black identity. Artel recognized the need to advance Afro-Colombian literature beyond the valiant and admirable but limited efforts of Candelario Obeso, as well as beyond the stereotypical, unflattering representations of black people created by other Colombian poets and writers. In addition, he realized that if Colombia was to create an authentic black literature, it was necessary to eschew or go beyond the derivative verse of contemporary authors who too often merely imitated the Afro-Antillean *negrista* poets, and to nurture a national tradition rooted in the autochthonous culture.

Adopting an eclectic approach to the avant-garde, Artel incorporated into his poetry aspects of Futurism, Surrealism, *jazz-bandismo,* and *negrismo* that harmonized with his artistic tastes, personal sentiments, and poetic purposes. Futurism seems to have liberated him from conventional verse to engage in poetic experimentation and innovation, and to have brought him face to face with the demands, possibilities, and new sensibilities of the twentieth century. Quite possibly, *jazz-bandismo* would exercise a strong, subliminal influence on Artel, stimulating him to discover in the modern, frenetic expression of black jazz-band instrumentalists and in the traditional expression of the no less skilled folk musicians of his native Cartagena a common ancestral origin. Indeed, as we shall see in the following chapter, elements of the jazz band inform several poems in *Tambores en la noche.*

With its emphasis on exploring the subconscience and searching for the deep, unseen forces of the mind and human existence, Surrealism (e.g., via García Lorca) may well have inspired Artel to explore the collective unconscious of Afro-Colombia and to examine the reality and meaning that lay behind the music, dances, and songs of the coast. Certainly, as various allusions he made to that movement suggest, Artel was well aware of the influence that it exerted upon artists and writers. At the same time, however, he did not give himself to it entirely.

With respect to *negrismo*, it is fair to say, as pointed out earlier, that although Artel was familiar with poems by Palés Matos, Cuba's Guillén, and others of the Afro-Antillean school, he felt a greater kinship with writers of the Harlem Renaissance, such as Langston Hughes and Claude McKay, and of the Francophone Caribbean, such as René Maran. That affinity probably sharpened Artel's awareness of the inner magnitude of Afro-American culture and experience and may well have encouraged his disposition to confront the slave past. On the other hand, Artel was not averse to writing poems that paralleled themes and images widely associated with the practitioners of poetic *negrismo*, such as black dance, music, and female sensuality. As chapter 5 will show, however, *negrismo* in Artel was tempered by a strong consciousness of racial mixture, a respect for maintaining the dignity of the black persona, the constant presence of the sea, and the poet's proud identity as a citizen of the coast.

Although the poetic art itself (i.e., the creative element) may not have been within the reach or power of all to realize and appreciate, the message it communicated was aimed not solely at a select group of poets, artists, and critics, but also at the people, in whose cultural forms and manifestations much of Artel's work was inspired. Artel's position as a "minority" artist, therefore, relates more to his attitude of self-differentiation vis-à-vis those readers and would-be "black" poets who conceived of black literature and art as a fairly easy creation involving the use of certain formulaic elements—e.g., onomatopoeia, jitanjáfora ("nonsense word"), and "black" speech.

Contrary to the (European) avant-garde artists described by Ortega y Gasset, Artel—no doubt cognizant of his identity as a black man in a Euro-centric society and as a marginalized coastal native in a country dominated by the views, values, and interests of the interior highland center—must have realized and accepted at some point that his poetic work was not merely an individual effort, but one that had broader, collective implications. That is, his poetry bore a certain potential and responsibility to bring to the forefront of the national culture and consciousness the very real and profound presence of black and coastal peoples and their culture. Consequently, his poetic voice also entailed a mission of teaching, of consciousness-raising, with respect to uncovering the psychic dimension of Africa in America and correcting the representation of black peoples in Colombian and Spanish-American poetry. Specifically, as we will also show in the following chapter, through *Tambores en la noche* Artel rediscovered and reaffirmed black identity and the African heritage in Colombia, and in so doing, advanced significantly and almost single-handedly the development of black literary expression therein.

5

SPIRIT-VOICES:

(Re)Claiming Black Identity and Ancestral Heritages in

Tambores en la noche (1940)

> I think that the past is all that makes the present coherent, and
> further, that the past will remain horrible for as long as we refuse
> to assess it honestly.
>
> James Baldwin

> If we kill off the *sound* of our ancestors, the major portion of us,
> all that is past, that is history, that is human being is lost, and we
> become historically and spiritually thin, a mere shadow of who
> we were, on the earth.
>
> Alice Walker

In the preface to his study of the Nation of Islam entitled
Black Nationalism: A Search for an Identity in America, Nigerian scholar E. E.
Essien-Udom stated:

> The tragedy of the Negro in America is that he has rejected his origins—the
> essentially human meaning implicit in the heritage of slavery, prolonged
> suffering, and social rejection. By rejecting this unique group experience
> and favoring assimilation and even biological amalgamation, he thus
> denies himself the creative possibilities inherent in it and in his folk
> culture. (9)

Although Essien-Udom was referring specifically to the United States of
America, his words are also applicable to the historical situation of black
people in Spanish America and, particularly, in Colombia. There, too, as I
have shown, the values and prerogatives associated with fair skin, Caucasian
features, and European culture were predominant. Traditionally, whiteness
was identified with culture, upper-class status, wealth, and authority while
blackness (or Africanness) was synonymous with slave ancestry, lower-class
status, barbarism, and other negative characteristics. It should not be surprising, then, that many persons of African descent, harboring deep-seated feelings of inferiority and self-hatred, and despising the negative representations
of black identity and culture that existed and were widely disseminated, would

resent being identified as black (*negro*). Nor is it surprising that they would seek to erase or escape the painful stigma of blackness by elevating themselves on the racial color scale (as Obeso once did), by eschewing attention to African ancestry and by mastering the artistic, literary, linguistic, social, and cultural forms associated with the dominant group.

In literature, too, white aesthetics and European models provided the direction and tone of much of Spanish-American literature. For example, in their affirmation of, or search for, national identity, many writers, consciously or unsconsciously, tended to glorify the European background and contribution to America while simultaneously idealizing or diminishing the Indian presence and either ignoring, simplifying, or negating the African heritage. Even the few poets and writers of African descent who appeared in Colombia after Obeso and before the 1930s (e.g., Coronel, Cano, Botero) seem to have followed the example set by their nonblack contemporaries. That is, they failed to explore and project in their writings an overt, self-consciously black experience—collective or individual.

Indeed, it was not until the late 1920s and the 1930s that Spanish-American writers, in general, turned their attention to the rich and diverse cultural traditions and experiences of peoples of African descent in America. As mentioned earlier (chapters 3 and 4), in the Hispanic lands this new interest in the Negro was labeled *negrismo*. It had its origins in the disenchantment of European intellectuals and artists with Western civlization, the concomitant European "discovery" of African and Oceanic art and oral literature, the spreading popularity of jazz and other musical forms of African origin, and the influence of writers of the Harlem Renaissance. While Langston Hughes and other black writers of the United States sought to "grasp the meanings and rhythms of jazz" and other aspects of black life and culture, and to "change through the force of [their] art that old whispering 'I want to be white,' . . . to 'Why should I want to be white? I am a Negro—and beautiful!' " (Hughes, "The Negro Artist and the Racial Mountain" 171), many followers of *negrismo* exploited these same aspects for the picturesque qualities and heightened poetic effects that they could render. Ignorant of, or indifferent to, the spiritual and psychological content of black identity, these poets and writers—mainly white or mestizo—produced a literature that in many ways served to perpetuate the superficial and stereotypical images of blacks that had been developed earlier.

Since at least the 1930s, various scholars have noted and discussed the principal stylistic and thematic features of this modality (e.g., F. Ortiz; Valdés-Cruz; Mansour; Leslie N. Wilson). When one considers the high concentration and cultural predominance of peoples of African descent in the Caribbean islands, the general recognition of the Hispanic Caribbean as the birthplace of Spanish-American *negrismo,* and the widely acknowledged preeminence within *negrista* poetry of Luis Palés Matos, Nicolás Guillén, and Emilio Ballagas (Valdés-Cruz 133),[1] it is not surprising that these features largely reflect the realities, concerns, and literary traditions of the Hispanic Antilles and the perspectives of its leading poets, artists, and thinkers. In fact, it would appear that the Afro-Antillean poetry created by the aforementioned poets and other lyricists writing in the 1920s and 1930s established the norms for modern Spanish-American poetry dealing with black people (Prescott, *Candelario Obeso* 41–42; Mullen).

Thematically speaking, that poetry often pictured the merriment and excitement of black dance (e.g., the rumba), paying particular attention to the body movements of the female dancer. It exalted the sensual and seductive beauty of the mulatto woman, exposed tensions and conflicts between blacks and mulattoes, and evoked religious rituals of African origin (e.g., Santería) and magic incantations against fantastic entities and mythic animals. In addition, it criticized the often deplorable and unequal status of blacks and mulattoes within society and protested against foreign economic exploitation and home-grown political oppression. The convergence in Cuba, Puerto Rico, and the Dominican Republic of social, economic, political, and cultural circumstances intimately related to and affecting the lives of millions of peoples of African descent, as well as the long-term literary depiction of these realities and the widespread dissemination of writings by Hispanic Antillean authors, strengthened the identification of the region as the center of Afro-Hispanic literary discourse.[2]

Regarding stylistic features, for our purposes we need only mention here that many poets sought to give their verse a genuine black flavor by approximating popular Negro speech and reproducing sounds and rhythms of black music and dance such as the *son*, the rumba, and the cumbia. To achieve this effect, poets resorted to imitating musical instruments, such as maracas, drums, bongos, and güiros, through various poetic devices, including onomatopoeia, alliteration, *jitanjáfora*, verses with masculine rhyme (*versos agudos*), and African toponyms or words that "sounded African." The following excerpts from Cuban poet José Z. Tallet's "La rumba" and Palés Matos's "Danza negra" may serve as illustrations:

Zamba, mamá, la rumba y tambó,
mambimba, mabomba, mabomba y bombó.

. . . .

Chaqui, chaqui, chaqui, charaqui.

Calabó y bambú.
Bambú y calabó.

El Gran Cocoroco dice: tu-cu-tú.

La Gran Cocoroca dice: to-co-tó. (Ballagas, *Antología*

158–59; 147)

For the poets who imitated the "sonorous Africanisms" of Palés Matos (E. Williams 5), the equally resonant verses and the Negroid idiom of the early Guillén (e.g., "Yambambó," *Motivos de son*), or "the sensuality and musical jocularity of the Negro" as projected by Ballagas (de la Torre 90), the essence or worth of Africa in America seemed to be rhythmic music, orgiastic dance, quaint speech, and exotic, superstitious ritual.[3]

Furthermore, within such poetry Negroid physical features were often compared to those of animals—*belfos* and *bemba* in place of lips; *grupa* in place of hips or buttocks. White teeth were frequently contrasted with dark skin, as in "Anzaemba," a "Micro-Poema" (1938) by Gregorio Castañeda Aragón of Santa Marta, Colombia. The swaying hips of black female dancers suggested the heat of uncontrolled passion, as in Ballagas' "Comparsa habanera" (*Antología* 50).

Non-Antillean poets, such as José Ignacio Bustamante (1906) of Popayán, seem to have found in this imagery of ardent, dusky, dancing women a model worthy of imitation, as his "La negra Antonia" shows:

La negra Antonia enciende sus caderas
y se quema en el són del currulao.

. . . .

La negra Antonia ríe y canta y danza
y se hunde en la noche de su carne.
Es un carbón ardiente que se apaga
en el claro marfil de su sonrisa. (99)

[Black Antonia fires up her hips, / and burns in the sound of the currulao.

. . . .

Black Antonia laughs and sings and dances / and sinks into her nocturnal flesh. / She is a burning coal that extinguishes itself / in the clear ivory of her smile.]

Occasionally a poet gave an instrument more than musical significance, as in Guillén's "Canción del bongó," where the two-headed drum represents the mulatto spirit of Cuba, and in Palés Matos's poem "Tambores," where the drums serve to express the power of the "primitive" over the "civilized." A more profound symbolism, however, does not seem to have been especially common or well developed in *negrista* poetry.

Indeed, few poets of the period—and even afterward—attempted to go beyond the surface of music and color, to explore the deep-seated sentiments that inform the black soul. Jorge Artel, however, did—and continued to do so long after the heyday of *negrismo*. Regrettably, just as literary historians and critics have ignored or been unaware of Artel's early poetry, which situates him within the postmodernist and avant-garde trends, they have also failed to examine closely the better-known poems of *Tambores en la noche* and the contexts in which they were created. As a consequence, Artel's poetry has generally been classified under the general rubric of *negrismo* or *afroantillanismo*, and too often he has been regarded as a mere epigone of the more famous *negrista* poets. After Luis Alberto Sánchez, Emilio Ballagas may be responsible, on a continental level, for characterizing Artel's poetry as an imitation or extension of Afro-Antillean verse. In an essay published in 1951, Ballagas noted in Artel's "Bullerengue" the same "easy musicality" that distinguishes some of Guillén's poems, and he incorporated the Colombian poet under the Afro-Cuban banner ("La poesía afro-cubana" 86).[4] More recently, Mónica Mansour, grouping the diverse currents of modern black-inspired poetry under the generalized label of *poesía negrista*, has observed in two of Artel's compositions ("La cumbia" and "Negro soy") themes and techniques also found in the works of other poets of the period (148–50, 204–05, 207–08, 237). This suffices for her to justify inclusion of Artel under the broad *negrista* heading.

Taking issue with such all-inclusive approaches, René Depestre cites the failure of critics and anthologists such as Mansour to establish clearly "the different (and at times divergent) lines of force which dominate the magnetic field of Latin American *negrismo*" (*Buenos días y adiós* 32).[5] Depestre makes a distinction between *negrismo* and what he calls "literature of identification" (28). Whereas the former, created largely by white artists and writers, became "the Antillean or Cuban version 'of Ibero-American indigenism and worldwide populism'" (30), the latter, as exemplified primarily in the works of artists and writers of African descent, completely renewed "the images of the descendants of African slaves in the respective national contexts of the literatures of their countries" (28). Despite his concession to "national contexts," Depestre still regards Artel as another "autonomous slant of Antillean negrismo" (32).

Although the *negrismo* tendency undoubtedly provided some impetus for Artel, writers and poets beyond the Spanish-speaking world, as I have shown, also stimulated or influenced Artel's racial outlook and thinking. Thus, while it would be erroneous to say that Artel's poetry has nothing in common with *negrismo* or does not manifest some of the features of the Afro-Antillean verse characterized by Palés Matos, Guillén, and others, it is also incorrect to regard Artel as just one more imitator of the more celebrated *negrista* poets.

Furthermore, by taking the Hispanic Antilles as the criterion or exemplar of Spanish-American black poetry (i.e., *poesía negra*), members of the Latin American critical establishment have overlooked the individual situation of non-Antillean poets, such as Artel, and the particular national context in which they wrote. Unaware of or lacking access to Artel's book, they have tended to make certain assumptions about him and his work on the basis of a few poems and the more obvious *negrista*-like or -inspired features therein, without further interrogating the texts.

By regarding Artel as only an offshoot or imitation of the Antillean *negrista* poets, critics such as Ballagas, Mansour, and Depestre—notwithstanding remarks to the contrary—overlook the uniqueness and very real significance of his poetry within his native land and Spanish America. Moreover, by constructing or continuing an Antillean-based canon of Afro-Hispanic poetry and centering it in Cuba, they evade, or excuse themselves from, serious examination and consideration of the work of other poets, such as Artel, and thereby effectively condemn them to the margins of Afro-Spanish-American poetry. In this way, too, they deprive themselves—and other potential readers—of an opportunity to explore, discover, and appreciate the particular challenges and contributions of black literary expression as realized in other lands, such as Colombia.

Ironically, another Antillean author and critic, Edward K. Brathwaite of Barbados, offers a more useful framework for initiating a discussion of Artel's *Tambores en la noche,* especially as it pertains to the African heritage. (The fact that he, like McKay and Hughes, is Anglophone, may have some bearing on his particular perspective and insights.) Although Brathwaite's article, "The African Presence in Caribbean Literature,"[6] addresses that regional literature exclusively and never mentions Artel, it does furnish insights that are especially relevant and helpful to an appreciation of the Colombian's poetry and to an understanding of the role that he has played in developing black literature in his homeland and in Spanish America.

Brathwaite theorizes that "There are four kinds of written African literature in the Caribbean" (112). The first, which he calls "rhetorical," is characterized by the writer's use of "Africa as a mask, signal, or *nomen.*" Although the writer reflects a deep desire to make a connection with the continent, he is not necessarily informed about Africa. While he may be saying the word "Africa" or invoking an African river in a dream, "he is not necessarily celebrating or activating the African presence." Brathwaite notes, however, that elements of this first category are also found in the other three.

Brathwaite calls his second category "the literature of African survival." This literature, he states, "deals quite consciously with African survivals in Caribbean society, but without necessarily making any attempt to interpret or reconnect them with the great tradition of Africa." The third category, "the literature of African expression," is rooted in the folk and "attempts to adapt or transform folk material into literary experiment."

Brathwaite's fourth and final category is called "the literature of reconnection." This is literature "written by Caribbean (and New World) writers [of the 1930s and 1940s] who have lived in Africa and are attempting to relate that experience to the New World, *or who are consciously reaching out to rebridge the gap with the spiritual heartland*" (emphasis added). To appreciate Artel's rightful inclusion within this select group of discriminating poets and writers who were seeking to "rebridge the gap" with Africa, one need only recall his assertion that the lofty social mission of the black poet is to serve as an emotional and historical *bridge between the deceased, slave ancestors and their living descendants* and to render fully the deep human pain that informs the souls of black folk in the Americas (see chapter 3).

To carry out that mission, Artel embraced and proclaimed within his poetry a positive black identity rooted in the reclamation of the African heritage in America: a legacy of slavery, resistance, survival, and creativity. This endeavor, I submit, was no mean feat for a "black" poet of mixed racial ancestry born and raised in a predominantly mestizo nation whose white, Eurocentric elite maintained the image of a racial democracy precisely by promulgating the mixed-race character of its citizens, promoting the folkloric aspects of its diverse cultures, and persistently purporting the absence of racial barriers. The occasional publication in major newspapers and periodicals of collaborations and submissions by Afro-Colombian intellectuals and nascent writers undoubtedly reinforced the impression of racial fairness and openness. Also, the triumph in 1930 of the Liberal Party—traditional stronghold and refuge of working classes and Negroid masses—no doubt augmented the promise or hope of change and improvement in the lot of the average black citizen. Consequently, an overtly militant poetic stance, one that raised questions about black social inequality and racial discrimination, seemed neither appropriate nor justifiable at that time, and would most likely have been met with ridicule, silence, or hostility—even in some black quarters. Moreover, Artel's own individual inclination to separate art from politics, that is, to eschew the political in poetry—possibly a Modernist legacy—led him to place greater emphasis on spiritual and intellectual values and to give less attention to material concerns.

Keenly aware of the Negrophobia, or inveterate disdain for black identity and culture, that many of his mulatto countrymen held, and cognizant of the general rejection and widespread misrepresentation of the historical experience of slavery, Artel envisaged and realized a poetry that would confront this injurious self-loathing and fear as well as challenge the distortions and misunderstanding of black cultural expression in Colombia. His commitment to revindicating black identity and the African roots of

Colombia was not exclusive, however. That is, it did not prevent him from calling attention also to the indigenous presence within himself and his society. In fact, the almost indivisible and virtually inseparable cultural and biological melding (*mestizaje*) that characterized the poet's land and his own background would seem to require that he do so. Whereas Nicolás Guillén in his self-described "mulatto verses" was concerned with bringing about an awareness and acceptance among Cubans of the biracial (i.e., African-European, black-white) character of their Caribbean nation, Artel, facing a more complex reality (i.e., Caribbean and Andean) and embodying a triethnic racial heritage (African, Amerindian, and European), sought to encourage his fellow citizens to embrace not just one disparaged ancestry, but two; that is, two cultural and spiritual identities that were regarded and treated with contempt and aversion, or with condescension and paternalism.

Furthermore, the attractively facile verse of much of the pervasive and popular Afro-Antillean mode of black poetry made it difficult at times for readers and critics to discern and accept new and different modes of black literary expression, especially when presented within the familiar contexts of black dance and Negroid speech. In sum, the above-mentioned social, ethnic, literary, and cultural realities that Artel faced complicated and muddled the embryonic sense of literary blackness in Colombia, thereby rendering Artel's sustained and committed poetry more subject to misunderstanding, misinterpretation, and unfair, misguided criticism. Paradoxically, however, those same realities also make apparent and underscore—at least, for this reader—the daring originality and courageous independence of Artel's art.

As I have been suggesting, Artel's poetry differs significantly from that of his *negrista* and Afro-Antillean contemporaries—and intentionally so. Artel is not concerned primarily with imitating the superficial sights and sounds of black music and dance. Nor does he exploit and caricature the black persona as Palés Matos does. Neither do the poems of the first *Tambores en la noche* take on political and economic issues in the manner of Guillén's verses. Rather, Artel seeks to penetrate the external and deceptive manifestations of black life and culture in order to discern and commune with the remote, ancestral voices that dwell within them. His poetry plumbs the depths of the Afro-American soul to reveal the spiritual content of black cultural expression, so often concealed from the eyes and ears of the outsider and casual observer. Focusing primarily on several key poems from the first edition of *Tambores en la noche,* the remainder of this chapter will demonstrate Artel's efforts to reclaim black identity in Colombia, to rediscover and reconnect for his fellow Colombians the deep spiritual roots of the African presence and heritage, and to give voice to the silent and disparaged ethnicities of Colombian society and culture.

(Re)Affirming Black Identity

> I am a Negro:
> Black as the night is black,
> Black like the depths of my Africa.
> Langston Hughes

"Negro soy," the third poem in Artel's 1940 book, offers the most obvious and outspoken example of the poet's affirmation of black identity. Consisting of only twelve verses arranged in three stanzas, it is at once a bold and succinct declaration of the poet's racial self and an insistence on a continuity of ethnic consciousness and solidarity. As the first verse shows, the poet proudly places himself within that tradition:

Negro soy desde hace muchos siglos. (31)

[I have been black for many centuries.]

The reference to a centuries-old identity indicates the poet's strong and inexorable identification with generations of peoples of African descent and may also be a subtle, yet sharp, rebuke of the artificial, *negrista*-inspired poets who wrote as if blackness were something new and as if the creation of formulaic verses sufficed to convey the essence of African-descended peoples and thus constituted real "black poetry." As the second verse of the poem reveals, Artel sees himself as a poet of a race whose historical experience in the New World is marked by a deep and prolonged suffering to which he, by virtue of membership in and commitment to the group, is heir:

Poeta de mi raza, heredé su dolor.

[Poet of my race, I inherited its pain.]

Cognizant of the racial mixture, acculturation, and passage of time that have diluted African blood, transformed African traditions, and weakened the sound of ancestral voices, Artel seeks to rediscover and tap into the original, clear, and true emotions that informed the songs, the shouts, the music, and the dances of the ancient and enslaved Africans:

Y la emoción que digo ha de ser pura
en el bronco son del grito
y el monorrítmico tambor. (31)

[And the emotion that I convey must be pure / in the rough sound of the shout / and the monorhythmic drum.]

The third stanza enunciates the poet's unashamed acknowledgment and acceptance of the disparaged African ancestry evoked by the sound of the drum:

> El hondo, estremecido acento
> en que trisca la voz de los ancestros,
> es mi voz. (32)

[The deep, tremulous tone / in which the voice of the ancestors gambol, / is my voice.]

From the poet's own inner drum-voice and through his coastal speech emerge the remote, perturbed voices of African peoples, violently deracinated from their cultural homelands and forced to labor as bond servants throughout the Americas. The anguish caused by and emanating from that unique experience—and which is the profound spiritual legacy of the descendants of the enslaved Africans—can almost be said to be sacrosanct, inviolable. Consequently, for Artel, poetry that makes use of the African experience and heritage in America deserves respect, even reverence, and should be expressed with dignity. Within the beats of the drums and behind the shouting and gaiety of black singing voices is an inheritance of suffering and pain, largely concealed from passing poetic tourists and other casual interlopers, for whom the presentation of black music and dance is often reduced to spectacle. For that reason, as Artel concludes in "Negro soy,"

> La angustia humana que exalto
> no es decorativa joya
> para turistas.
> Yo no canto un dolor de exportación. (32)

[The human anguish that I exalt / is not a decorative jewel / for tourists. / I do not sing a pain of exportation.]

Clearly, Artel differentiates himself from the legion of poets and improvisers whose ventures into literary blackness lack a strong and intimate connection with the African heritage in America and, it must be said, seem to harken back to nineteenth-century minstrelsy. In doing so, Artel also distinguishes his poetics of black identity and consciousness from verse that entertains more than it enlightens, and that more often exploits or appropriates black speech and cultural forms without appreciating the spiritual values and emotional sources that inform them.

The Shout: Vocal Marker of *Costeño* Culture

One of the major symbols or motifs of black expression that appears in "Negro soy" and throughout *Tambores en la noche* is the *grito*, or shout. Loud, vigorous, unrestrained, the *grito* encompasses a wide range of contexts and references. In a general sense, it may refer to the fairly widespread tendency of coastal people within the greater Caribbean area—including Colombia's Atlantic littoral—to speak vociferously, in shouts, especially when animated. Noted by scholars and writers familiar with the region (e.g., Alba 27; Zapata Olivella, "Genio y figura"), this common cultural phenomenon is a vital component of the poet's verse, as the initial lines of "Mi canción" [My Song]—Artel's personal ars poética—show:

> Un tono cálido
> amasado de gritos y de sol. (227)

[A warm tone / kneaded with shouts and sun.]

and as the following verses from "Canción para ser cantada desde un mástil" [Song to be Sung from a Mast] also demonstrate:

> Ah, las velas erguidas de mi nave,
> alegrada de gritos
> que nadie y sólo yo sabe decir! (128)

[Ah, the erect sails of my ship, / enlivened with shouts / which no one and only I know how to express!]

Consequently, when the poet refers specifically to "mi grito" (as in "Meridiano de Bogotá" [Bogotá Midday] and "Canción en el extremo de un retorno" [Song at the End of a Return]), he is also testifying to his *costeño* identity:

> He perdido mi grito,
> el grito ancho
> que me enseñaron a dar como una nota
> los horizontes abiertos de mi costa. (111)
>
> . . . .
>
> Serpentina de altanería,
> mi grito irá ciñendo sombras en la noche
> para hacerlas bailar como mujeres. (136)

[I have lost my shout, / the full shout / which the open horizons of my coast / taught me to give like a note.

. . . .
A soaring streamer, / my shout will go encircling shadows in the night /
to make them dance like women.]

So distinctive of Artel's verse is the *grito* that it may also exemplify the
desired blooming of the poetic unknown or ineffable song, as in "La canción
imposible" [The Impossible Song]:

> Si acaso floreciera—tal vez alguna noche—
> como un grito desnudo sediento de horizontes,
> aquella canción enigmática
> que mi corazón desconoce,
> la escribiría con sangre. (247)

[If perhaps it were to blossom—maybe some night— / like a clear shout
eager for horizons, / that enigmatic song / which my heart does not know,
/ I would write it with blood.]

Besides these meanings and connotations, the shout also symbolizes in
Artel's poetry the freedom, joy, spontaneity, and uninhibitedness associated
with black dance, jazz music, and the rebellious avant-garde. This facet is
evident both in "La cumbia" [The Cumbia], where

> El humano anillo apretado
> es un carrusel de carne y hueso,
> confuso de gritos ebrios
> y sudor de marineros. (26)

[The tight human ring / is a carrousel of flesh and bone, / mixed with
drunken shouts / and sailors' sweat.]

and in the following lines from "Los turistas" [The Tourists]:

> Gritería de la marinería
> en cuya voz palpita
> la tormentosa urgencia del *jazz-band*. (170)

[Shouting of the sailors / in whose voice throbs / the tumultuous urgency
of the jazz band.]

At times the *grito* may simply give testimony to inspired nights of seafaring
men engaged in carousal, song, and drink, as in "Cartagena, 3 a.m." and
"Puerto" [Port]:

Zambra de bogas borrachos
por sobre el Puente de Heredia,
gritos de juerga y charanga
que vienen de Mamonal! (155)

[Uproar of bibacious boatmen / along the Heredia Bridge, / shouts of carousing and dancing / that issue from Mamonal!]

. . . .

Y del confuso cafetín cercano,
—gritos, ron, oscuridad—
saca el viento un murmullo
para ahogarlo en el mar. (190)

[And from the small crowded coffee shop nearby, / —shouts, rum, darkness— / the wind draws out a murmur / only to drown it in the sea.]

Occasionally, the word *grito* (and its related forms) is replaced by a synonym, such as *algarabía,* which also translates effectively the roisterous merriment accompanying jazz-band music and dance or inspired by nocturnal sprees of singing and drinking:

Retumban
las bombas
de la algarabía! ("Dancing" 74)

[The bass drums / rumble / with the din!][7]

Turning again to Gómez de la Serna, we find—to little surprise—a remarkably similar corroboration of the *grito* symbolism in the Spanish writer's discussion of *jazz-bandismo:*

In the jazz-band are set free and given license those *shouts* which before had to take advantage of the great tumults or the noise of the great machines in order to be uttered. (190; emphasis added.)[8]

The clamor and freedom of the jazz band would seem to coincide and even harmonize with the often loud, unrestrained, yet lyrical manner of speaking of Atlantic coastal people, but also, especially, with the intensity, movement, and gaiety of Cartagena's independence holiday celebrations. In fact, it is likely that the first areas of Colombia where jazz-band music gained a foothold were the port cities of the northern coast, naturally open to the influx of new products and advanced ideas and spiritually disposed to Afro-American beats. It is understandable, then, that some coastal intellectuals viewed life on the oceanic "margins" of Colombia as possessing a natural "avant-garde temperament" (Fernández, "Artel y nosotros")[9] and that Artel's poetry would manifest a strong affinity for the music of the jazz band.

Within Artel's poetry, however, shouts are not just revelry or vociferous speech. They also communicate a more profound, more earnest dimension of black identity, one that harkens back to African origins and evokes the painful tragedy of slavery. As the poet sings in his "Canto nuevo para loar a Barranquilla" [New Song to Praise Barranquilla], the penetrating and tense sound of the shout

> puede ser lamento
> y ser altivo reto
> de un recóndito ancestral ardor. (237)

> [can be lament / and be proud challenge / of a recondite ancestral fervor.]

In "La voz de los ancestros" [The Voice of the Ancestors], the *"gritos ancestrales"* [ancestral screams] (35) that emboss the winds from the sea—winds that propelled the sails of the slave vessels toward Cartagena and other ports—are the voices of the captive African forebears. And in the electric gestures of the *cumbia*—"black dance, dance of my land!"—an entire race cries out ["Toda una raza grita"] (27).

Elsewhere, the *grito* is a vocal sign of popular resistance and struggle, as exemplified by the poem "El líder negro" [The Black Leader], addressed to Diego Luis Córdoba (1907–64), congressman and nationally recognized politician from the Chocó:

> Tú erej *eggrito* y la sangre
> de locque ettamoj abajo,
> de locque tenemoj hambre
> y no tenemoj trabajo,
> de locque en la huegga sufren
> la bayoneta calá,
> de locque en laj eleccionej
> son locque luchan má,
> pa que despuéj loj obbiden
> y ni trabajo ni ná. (86–87; emphasis added)

[You are the shout and the blood / of us the underdogs, / of us who hunger / and do not have work, / of those who on strike suffer / the fixed bayonet, / of those who at elections / are the ones who struggle most, / so that afterward they are forgotten / and have no job, no nothing.]

Thus, as already pointed out in "Negro soy," the *grito* is not only a manifestation of coastal identity but also, particularly, of black identity.[10]

The freedom and ability to "pegar un grito," that is, to let out a shout, is essential to the costeño's expression of self.[11] As presented in Artel's "Meridiano de Bogotá," loss or repression of the *grito* is a poignant revelation of the poet's physical separation from the warm, bright environment of the coast and his sense of alienation upon being immersed in the chilly, cloudy, and damp monotony of the mountainous Bogotá clime and culture.

> He perdido mi grito,
> el grito ancho
> que me enseñaron a dar como una nota
> los horizontes abiertos de mi costa.
>
> Gira la ciudad bajo la lluvia
> como un desnivelado carrusel,
> la ciudad neurasténica
> que cubre las horas
> con bufandas de nubes. (111)

[I have lost my shout, / the full shout / which the open horizons of my coast / taught me to give like a note.

The city whirls beneath the rain / like an unbalanced carrousel, / the neurasthenic city / that covers up the hours / with mufflers of clouds.]

Like his predecessor Candelario Obeso, who, in "Arió" [Farewell], rejected the lugubrious, somber, melancholy character of life in the high Andes, Artel also feels and communicates something of the stifling of the costeño's natural or customary exuberance, brought on by the dull, monotonous ambience of the interior, highlands capital.[12]

> Aquí la carcajada
> se fue no sé por cuáles
> caminos de tristeza.

Y la alegría la ha borrado
un pañuelo de niebla.

Gira la ciudad bajo la lluvia,
finos hilos que surcen el tedio
largo y amargo de los días.
Una monotonía
está enredada en la ciudad. ("Meridiano de Bogotá" 112)

[Here the outburst of laughter / departed along who knows what roads of sadness. / And joy has been erased by a neckerchief of mist.

The city whirls beneath the rain, / fine threads which weave / the long and bitter tedium of the days. / A monotony is tangled up in the city.]

Artel's poem also exhibits a close intertextuality with Langston Hughes's poem "Our Land" (Locke 144). Each composition expresses, in its own way, a dissatisfaction or disappointment with the existing circumstances and a longing for a new or more familiar and life-affirming environment. In both poems there is an overt or implied contrast of lands or regions; and the mention or insinuation of natural elements parallels the human emotions, which reflect, and are affected by, the environment. Hughes's poem speaks of a desire for "a land of sun, / of gorgeous sun, / And a land of fragrant water," and of a yearning for "a land of trees, / Of tall thick trees, / Bowed down with chattering parrots / Brilliant as the day." Simultaneously, it rejects "this land / Where life is cold" and "where birds are gray."

In "Meridiano de Bogotá" the contrast is less direct but no less evident in the references to "mi costa" and "la ciudad" and in the absence of "la carcajada" and "la alegría." Exuding "una tácita nostalgia de sol!" [a tacit nostalgia for sun] (113), Artel's poem also conveys a longing to escape to warmer, salutary climes, more consonant with the poet's intrinsic marine or coastal nature: "Un íntegro deseo de viajar / se ha clavado en mi puerto interior / como un ancla . . ." [A complete desire to travel / has become stuck in my inner port / like an anchor . . .] (112).

A major difference, however, also sets the two poems apart. In Artel's poem the explicit loss of the *grito* is intimately tied to the speaker's separation from the distant coastal homeland, which, despite the hegemony of the interior center, is an integral and recognized part of the poet's beloved nation. In Hughes's verses, however, the implicit absence of a more hospitable land of brilliant sun, fragrant water, tall thick trees, and chattering birds evokes a nostalgic image of a pristine, ancestral homeland (Africa) or an unspoiled tropical refuge, where the persecuted descendants of enslaved Africans in the United States could lead a life "Of love and joy and wine and song." Inherent in "Meridiano de Bogotá" is a desire on the part of the poet to return to that invigorating region of Colombia which is his by birth. Implicit in "Our Land" is a desire to get away from the native soil of repression and denial ("where joy is wrong"), or to transform that nation where the poet's forefathers have lived, worked, suffered, and died without enjoying even the appearance of full and equal citizenship or acceptance. Whereas a cultural and spiritual void emanating from regional distinctions within a national context is at the heart of Artel's poem, in Hughes's composition the phrase "this land" suggests a wholly national dilemma based not on geo-cultural diversity but on arbitrary evaluations of human differences.[13]

NOCTURNAL DRUMS, ANCESTRAL VOICES

> It is not always enough to hear music or to pay attention only to its formal features. One must also evaluate it in terms of the other meanings associated with it.
>
> J. H. Kwabena Nketia (153)

Until fairly recently, commentators on Artel's poetry made relatively little reference to the African presence therein. Early critics of *Tambores en la noche* usually related the book to Africa in a vague, oblique, or superficial manner, either alluding occasionally (in highly rhetorical prose but in general or fairly simple terms) to Artel's racial inspiration or origins, or else acknowledging his use of the ancestral drum. José Morillo, for example, described some of Artel's verses as written "with the soul saturated with race, hearing the distant call, the indefinable moan of the African drums in the silent dawns of the dark Coast, just as one hears a lament which comes from the depths of the past" (" 'Tamboriles en la noche' "). An anonymous reviewer of Artel's book maintained that "Through the verses of Jorge Artel the spirit of a race speaks, with all its nostalgia" (Review, *Revista*); and Humberto Jaramillo Arango asserted that Artel "heard from deep within himself, from his blood, the ancestors gathering, with their drums of Africa, at the sweet celebration of the song and the return."

Without a doubt, Artel identifies himself as a poet of African descent. It is also true that the drum is the primary musical element in Artel's poetry and signals an ongoing African presence. To say this, however, merely touches the surface of his work. Indeed, by failing to investigate and explore more deeply, for example, the significance and function of this percussion instrument within an African cultural context, critics have sorely overlooked or simplified its function and importance within Artel's poetry. An examination of the role and significance of the drum, therefore, is in order.

The very title of Artel's collection, *Tambores en la noche* [Drums in the Night], alerts the reader immediately to the poet's attachment and commitment to the African presence. Although the title may call to mind the exotic sounds of jungle drumming as reproduced by many *negrista* poets, or evoke nocturnal jungle images of dancing native Africans as popularized in Hollywood films,[14] attentive reading soon makes it clear that Artel's drum-poems emit a much more profound and solemn tone and perform a more important function.

It is well known that the drum *(el tambor)* is the principal musical instrument in many traditional African societies.[15] Its function, however, is not just musical. The "legendary talking drums" have long been used as a vehicle for communication among African peoples, just as writing has served Western cultures.[16] Beyond its secular use, the drum also serves in rituals and ceremonies and as the medium for communication with the spirit world. Thus, as John S. Mbiti notes, certain drums "are regarded as sacred so that they are played only on certain occasions or to announce important messages, and are kept in sacred houses" (242; cf. Zárate 40, 41).

Sensible to the sacred nature and function of the drum, Artel has made of his poetry a metaphorical drum in which "vibrate the unknown voices of [his] race" (Artel, "La literatura negra") and whose purpose is to reestablish and strengthen the broken or loosened bonds that link the exiled African forebears, their descendants in the New World, and the ancestral homeland. Just as the music of the drums brings the living beings in touch with the spirit of the forefathers, so too the poems or drum messages of *Tambores en la noche* serve to remind us, the current generations, of those living-dead who suffered, resisted, and survived. In order to hear and apprehend those vocal vibrations, one must listen intently, not only with the outer ears but also with the ears of the soul:

> Los tambores en la noche
> son como un grito humano.
> Trémulos de música les he oído gemir,
> cuando esos hombres que llevan
> la emoción en las manos
> les arrancan la angustia de una oscura saudade,
> de una íntima añoranza,
> donde vigila el alma dulcemente salvaje
> de mi vibrante raza,
> con sus siglos mojados en quejumbres de gaitas. (20)

[The drums in the night / are like a human shout. / Trembling with music
I have heard them groan, / when those men who bear / emotion in their
hands / wrench from them the anguish of a dark nostalgia, / of an intimate
yearning, / wherein keeps watch the sweetly savage soul / of my vibrant
race, / with its centuries dampened in moans of *gaitas*.]

Here, the anguished sound emanating from the drums communicates a
mysterious and intimate longing that dwells in the soul of the race. Gradually
the poet is able to perceive in the music of the drums a talking voice whose
vibrations move inward to touch his own soul:

Los tambores en la noche, hablan.

Y es su voz una llamada

tan honda, tan fuerte y clara,

que parece como si fueran sonándonos en el alma! (21)

[The drums in the night, speak. / And their voice is a call / so deep, so
strong and clear, / that it seems as if they were resounding in our soul!]

Thus "Tambores en la noche," both the lead and title poem of Artel's
collection, evinces the poet's awareness and pious representation of the
phenomenon of the "talking" drums of Africa (Alakija 251; Harris 17; H. C.
Davidson 3:126.). It is also important to note, though, that Artel has not
resorted to onomatopoeic and alliterative devices—common to *negrista*
verse—to achieve a sonorous effect. These devices would only impede or
distort the communication of the immanent music of the drums. Indeed,
one senses in this absence of faddish imitation a desire to attend to the
deeper, inner music of the drum, a concern too often overshadowed in other
poets by a transitory interest in the external and the technical. On the other
hand, Artel's technique is no less effective for his purposes.

Specifically, Artel employs precise, emotionally laden verbs (e.g., *suenan, gemir, arrancan, vigila, resuenan, sonando*), nouns (*rutas, banderas,
mástiles, proas, grito, angustia, saudade, añoranza, quejumbres, golpe, voz,
alma*), and modifiers (*fatigados, sombríos, perdidas, dulcemente salvaje, mis-
teriosos, honda, fuerte, clara*), as well as personification (*Los tambores en la
noche, hablan*) and simile (*Los tambores en la noche / son como un grito
humano*) to create potent, moving auditory and visual images. Images reminiscent of lost, faraway African communities, of the anguish of the slave trade
and the Middle Passage, of the severance and dilution of ancestral ties. Other
times the poet merely allows the connotative powers of the word-symbol
(*tambor*) to convey sound and meaning.

That the drum is the repository of the race is made clear in the first stanza
of another frequently anthologized poem, "Danza, mulata!":

Dánza, mulata, dánza,
mientras canta
en el tambor de los abuelos
el són languidecente de la raza. (41)

[Dance, mulatto woman, dance, / while sings / in the forefathers' drum / the languishing sound of the race.]

For Artel, then, the drum (*tambor*) is a leitmotif of remembrance and functions as a vital link between the past and the present, between the Afro-American and the African forebears. Such recollection is indispensable to African peoples, for by keeping alive the memory of the departed, who, according to Mbiti, are "the guardians of family affairs, traditions, ethics and activities" (108), those who remain are able to carry on with a firm sense of self and identity. In effect, to the extent that the African remembers and reveres the living-dead and maintains contact with the spirits of the forefathers; to the extent that the men and women of the community remain faithful to their traditions and values, they are also participating in the perpetuation of their culture and, by extension, of themselves. In the same way, then, as Afro-Colombians remain true to the spirit of the enslaved Africans by remembering them with pride and not with shame, by keeping alive the dances and traditions, and by being aware of the real history and legacy of Africa; they, too, maintain and fortify the cultural and spiritual linkages with the maternal homeland and develop a more positive self-image.

If Artel's book is analogous to the African (and Afro-American) drum, then he, the poet, is, by extension, the drummer, a role and position that entails serious responsibility and requires skillful execution. In African societies, he who plays the drum has been carefully chosen and meticulously trained to carry out an important function in the life of the community. According to Janheinz Jahn, "In Africa the official drummer was not simply a conveyor of information: he presented on ceremonial occasions news of the ancestors, most sacred Nommo, the Epics of the past" (189). Like the African drummer who, as Eugene B. Redmond notes, was required to learn "not only drumming techniques but the legends, the myths, the meanings and symbols of which the drum was derivative" (20), Artel, too, prepared himself to be the bearer of "the voice of the race" in Colombia. He understood that to accomplish this, to be an authentic black poet, it was necessary to become familiar with fundamental aspects of African religion and culture. That understanding is evident in the statement quoted earlier (chapter 3) from Artel's 1932 open letter to his friend Gregorio Espinosa, in which he urged those concerned with the intellectual and spiritual movement of the black race to strengthen their knowledge by reading pertinent writings of

Waldo Frank, Count Keyserling, and Paul Valery, as well as creative works by
noted black authors.

Other small, yet significant actions point to Artel's conscientious dedication to a respectful rendering of the African heritage. For example, the change
he made in the title of his book—from *Tamboriles en la noche* to *Tambores
en la noche*— indicates not only a close attention to sound and meaning, but
also a conscious effort to maintain the African orientation of his poetry.[17]
The dedication Artel placed in the book also demonstrates his respect for the
memory of the deceased ancestors:

> Al marinero que hubiera sido yo. Al corazón grumete que canta en mí
> como en un puerto solitario. *A mis abuelos, los negros.* (16; emphasis
> added)

> [To the sailor that I might have been. To the cabin-boy heart that sings in
> me as in a solitary port. *To my forebears, the blacks.*]

Previously cited excerpts from Artel's 1940 public address, "Modalidades
artísticas de la raza negra," demonstrate how closely Artel's self-defined role
as a black poet approximates that of certain African "specialists." According
to Mbiti, African "specialists," such as medicine men, mediums, and diviners,
are not only "the repositories in knowledge, practice and, symbolically, of
the religious life of their communities," but "the symbolic points of contact
between the historical and spiritual worlds" (252). Particularly noteworthy
here are the mediums because their main duty is "to link the human beings
with the living dead and the spirits" (224). Clearly, Artel's own vision of
himself as a connection or "bridge" between the past and the present parallels
that of the African mediums: that is, he sees himself as an artist who, faithful
and attuned to the spirit of Africa in America, is morally bound to help
the living to actualize themselves in the here and now by incorporating into
their present (known as the Sasa period in some African religions) the full
measure of their past (called the Zamani period).[18] By facing rather than
fearing their past, by discovering rather than disdaining the African heritage,
Afro-Colombians can begin to achieve a greater sense of self and dignity,
which, in turn, can lead to the spiritual enrichment and intellectual liberation
so necessary for cultural viability and integrity.

African Heritage and Natural Phenomena

Artel's poetic efforts to reclaim and revaluate the African
heritage in Colombia also find expression through other forms rooted in
Old World belief systems. For some African peoples, one of the ways in

which God and the spirits are perceived or manifested is through natural phenomena, such as wind, fire, water, rain, sun, sky, and air (Mbiti 42, 44, 46). Senegalese poet Birago Diop (1906) expressed this aspect of African religious beliefs in his celebrated poem "Souffles," variously translated into English as "Spirits," "Breaths," and "Forefathers" (see, respectively, Kennedy 152–54; Drachler 94–96; and Miller, O'Neal, and McDonnell 105–06, whose abbreviated version, which I use here, is based on Langston Hughes's *An African Treasury* [1960]). As the first stanza shows, fire, water, and the sound of the wind in the trees communicate the presence of the living-dead:

> Listen more often to things rather than beings.
> Hear the fire's voice,
> Hear the voice of the water.
> In the wind hear the sobbing of the trees,
> It is our forefathers breathing. (105)

Artel reveals a strikingly similar awareness in his poem "La voz de los ancestros" [The Voice of the Ancestors]. In fact, the corresponding use of a verb of audition (*oír*) and its specific application to the winds of the port suggest an almost direct response to the challenge presented in Diop's message:

> Oigo galopar los vientos
> bajo la sombra musical del puerto.
> Los vientos, mil caminos ebrios y sedientos,
> repujados de gritos ancestrales,
> se lanzan al mar.
> Voces en ellos hablan
> de una antigua tortura,
> voces claras para el alma
> turbia de sed y de ebriedad. (35)[19]

[I hear the galloping of winds / beneath the musical shadow of the port. / The winds, a thousand drunk and thirsty roads, / embossed with ancestral screams, / throw themselves into the sea. / Voices within them speak / of an ancient torture, / voices clear for the soul / troubled from thirst and inebriety.]

For Artel, black poet of the New World, the voices in the wind are not merely breathing but also echoes from the past.[20] The mysterious voices and vague recollections enunciated in "Tambores en la noche" have become clear understanding in "La voz de los ancestros," communicating to the poet "an ancient torture," a mournful message of human suffering and longing. The reference to ancestral screams and the image of the winds throwing themselves into the sea evoke the violence, torment, and terrible human toll exacted by the slave trade. This idea is reinforced and clarified by the poem's third stanza, in which the winds bring the poet closer to his anguished history:

> Mi pensamiento vuela
> sobre el ala mas fuerte
> de esos vientos ruidosos del puerto,
> y miro las naves dolorosas
> donde acaso vinieron
> los que pudieron ser nuestros abuelos.
> —Padres de la raza morena!—
> Contemplo en sus pupilas caminos de nostalgias,
> rutas de dulzura,
> temblores de cadena y rebelion. (36)

[My thought flies / on the strongest wing / of those noisy winds of the port, / and I look upon the pitiful ships / on which perhaps came / those who could have been our grandparents. / —Fathers of the dark race!—/ I contemplate in their pupils roads of nostalgia, / routes of sweetness, / tremblings of chain and rebellion.]

Whether Artel's poem appeared before Diop's is uncertain. What is clear again, however, is that Artel's poetry exhibits a learned understanding of— or, at least, a sensitive appreciation for—even the most subtle aspects of the religious heritage of Africa. In light of the above, what Eugene B. Redmond says of the black poet in the United States is also true of Artel: he embodies the tradition of the griot-singer-poet who has "the job of unraveling the complex of his past and present-future worlds" (18) for the benefit of the community.[21]

BLACK DANCE AND RHYTHMIC MOVEMENT

Another salient feature of the African heritage that is an important part of Artel's poetry is dance and rhythmic movement. In traditional African societies, dancing is intimately bound up with all aspects of life, including religious rites and activities (e.g., initiation and puberty, marriage, burial) and secular events. Dancing is laden with meaning and can also be an intrinsic aspect of music making (O. Wilson 10). Moreover, as one scholar has stated, "the dance was the channel through which the African immersed himself in the very force of his being. In the dance he became one with the powers of divinity and the ancestors; in the dance he became immortal" (Barrett 211).

Among Colombian dances, and especially those of African origin, the *cumbia* is the most widely known and practiced. It is accompanied by drums, reed instruments, maracas, and other instruments, which reflect, in part, its mixed racial heritage (Abadía Morales 205).[22] Although it may be impossible to determine the original meaning or function of the *cumbia*, the movements of the male and female dancers suggest that it may be related to fertility or marriage dances. In any case, for Artel, the *cumbia* exhibits those characteristics of African dance noted above and serves as a vivid reminder of the living, dynamic presence of Africa in Colombia. While the poem's delight in revelry and its descriptions of "agile hips of sensual females" and "drunken shouts and sweat of sailors" ["las caderas ágiles de las sensuales hembras"; "gritos ebrios y sudor de marineros"] approximate it to *negrista* dance poetry, the movements of the dancers suggest the expression of something more profound whose original meaning has been hidden or diluted by blood and time. Within the dance, as the poet senses,

> Trota una añoranza de selvas
> y de hogueras encendidas,
> que trae de los tiempos muertos
> un coro de voces vivas.
>
> Late un recuerdo aborigen,
> una africana aspereza,
> sobre el cuero curtido donde los tamborileros,
> —sonámbulos dioses nuevos que repican alegría—
> aprendieron a hacer el trueno
> con sus manos nudosas,
> todopoderosas para la algarabía.
>
> ¡Cumbia! Mis abuelos bailaron
> la música sensual. Viejos vagabundos
> que eran negros, terror de pendencieros
> y de cumbiamberos
> en otras cumbias lejanas,
> a la orilla del mar . . . (28)

[A longing for jungles / and lighted bonfires trots, / which brings from times dead / a chorus of living voices.

An aboriginal remembrance, / an African roughness throbs, / on the hardened leather where the drummers, / —new sleepwalking gods who sound out joy— / learned to make thunder / with their knotted hands, / all powerful for the uproar.

Cumbia! My forefathers danced / the sensual music. / Old vagabonds / who were black, terror of fighters / and cumbia dancers / in other distant cumbias, / on the edge of the sea.]

Artel's presentation of the dance and music of his beloved coastal homeland goes beyond spectacle and empty movements. It is celebration of the African cultural heritage of Colombia, for the *cumbia* is a direct and moving reminder of the endurance of the vital ancestral spirit of Africa in America.

Among certain African groups women dance more often than men (Ames 112). Close association of women with dancing is also evident in the mediums, usually women, whose training involves dancing (Mbiti 226, 227). In some Afro-American ceremonies it is a woman who leads the dance (Barrett 196). A female dancer of mixed ancestry is the focus of "Danza, mulata!", one of Artel's most famous poems. Here the poetic voice celebrates, against a background of drumming, the physical beauty, vibrant energy, and rhythmic movement of the dancer and encourages her kinetic expression.

> Danza, mulata, danza,
> mientras canta
> en el tambor de los abuelos
> el son languidecente de la raza.
>
> Alza tus manos ágiles
> para apresar el aire,
> envuélvete en tu cuerpo
> de rugiente deseo,
> donde late la queja de las gaitas
> bajo el ardor de tu broncínea carne. (41)

[Dance, mulatto woman, dance, / while sings / in the forefathers' drum / the languishing sound of the race.

Raise your agile hands / to seize the air, / wrap yourself in your body / of roaring desire, / wherein beats the gaitas' moan / beneath the ardor of your bronzelike flesh.]

Critic Ann Venture Young has suggested that Artel's description of the mulatto dancer is "inspired by an obsession with her physical attributes and with the movement of her body as she dances" (*The Image of Black Women* 34). Indeed, the multiple, sensual references to the woman's anatomy—agile hands, body of roaring desire, bronzelike flesh, disquieting flanks, breasts, lubricous hips—suggest the pervasive influence of male-oriented or male-dominated discourse in *negrista* poetic imagery, which often reduced the black or mulatto woman to "a sexually uninhibited amoral animal full of sensual jungle rhythm, oozing sex through animal eyes, sensual voice, and inviting flesh" (Jackson, *The Black Image* 46).[23] Such reductionism, however, does not seem to be at the heart of Artel's poem. Rather, the attention that the poet first gives to the hands and, later, to other parts of the body—sides, breasts, waist, legs, hips—may also be said to exemplify what Paul Bohannan and others have noted with respect to much of African dancing:

> The point of African dancing in many parts of the continent, at least, is for various parts of the body to accompany one of the rhythms in the orchestra so that the polyrhythms in the orchestra are reproduced by the dancer's body. The head moves in one rhythm, the shoulders in another; the arms in still a third, the trunk in another, and the feet in still another. . . . African dancing both demands great precision and allows great freedom of expression to the dancers. (142–43)

It is also important to remember, as ethnomusicologist Esi Sylvia Kinney points out, that

> Rhythm is the most striking aspect of African music, with drumming displaying it in its most complex form. African dance responds to this rhythm and makes visible its complexities. The body of the dancer or group of dancers incorporates both the subtleties and the more direct dynamics of expression, translating them into movement which corresponds to the music. One dancer can metaphrase—that is, duplicate exactly—all the rhythms of an entire drum ensemble *by using the several parts of the body simultaneously.* (51; emphasis added)

This is not to say that Artel was fully aware of this aspect of African dance and that he self-consciously or intentionally tried to emulate it in his poetry. We may recall that upon describing his poems as "mulatto reactions," Artel himself acknowledged the dearth or weakness of African traditions in Colombia, especially when compared with Cuba, Brazil, or even the United States. Rather, this feature of African dance, like other "rhythmic complexities" that were carried over to the Americas, is present in many Afro-American styles of dance and seems to be reflected, perhaps unintentionally, in the poem. While the poem may fall within the *negrista* pattern of emphasis on black or mulatto female dancers, and the representation of the female body may not "subvert or critique images of female sexuality which were part of the cultural apparatus of 19th-century racism," neither does it perpetuate wild animalistic sexuality or lust (hooks, *Black Looks* 62, 67). Instead, it exhibits an admiration for and encouragement of a certain graceful, dynamic, rhythmic freedom of movement that seems to challenge "assumptions that the black body, its skin color and shape, is a mark of shame" (hooks 63). Emotions of pride and joy in aesthetically pleasing, elastic, graceful, physical movement also are central here. Unlike much of *negrista* and Afro-Antillean verse, which brazenly compared the excitement of black women dancing to female animals in heat, or which described them as hot-blooded, seductive temptresses, eagerly predisposed to sexual liaison (Prescott, "Negras, morenas, zambas y mulatas"; Young, "The Black Woman in Afro-Caribbean Poetry"), "Danza, mulata!"—notwithstanding its sensually descriptive adjectives (*rugiente, inquietantes, atormentado, lúbricas*)—initially and ultimately is concerned with the spiritual and ancestral component of black music and dance, which unites and affirms, in the final stanza, both the mulatto dancer and the mulatto poetic voice.

> Dánza, mulata, dánza!
> Tú y yo sentimos en la sangre
> galopar el incendio de una misma nostalgia. . . . (42)

[Dance, mulatto woman, dance! / In our blood you and I feel / galloping the passion of a same nostalgia. . . .]

In addition, it is also important to note that the use of the verb in the imperative mode ("Danza, mulata!") coincides with the communal nature of African dance. That is, the poetic male gaze, rather than reducing the dancer's movements to "mere spectacle" or inviting mutilation of her body (hooks, *Black Looks* 62, 64), identifies with the dancer and encourages her movements. In that way, the poem conforms to a common characteristic feature of African dance observed by Judith Lynn Hanna:

> When both dancers and spectators are present, there is strong mutual identification based on kinesthetic and psychological empathy. The individual spectator may encourage an admired performer with a gesture, cheer, or word of praise. ("What is African Dance?" 314)[24]

Remembering, too, Artel's conception of his poetry as a metaphorical drum, the poem may be said to serve as accompaniment to the dancer's movements. As the authors of a study on the drum explain, in certain African cultures "the musician follows the dancers. The dancers move, and the musician finds the corresponding sounds. It is a dialogue. Visible waves of body movement speak and are answered by audible waves of music. . . . The musican is evaluated on the basis of his ability to follow movements and gestures spontaneously" (Diallo and Hall 98). The words of Artel's poetry would seem to be analogous to the "audible waves of music."

It is safe to say, then, that not every representation of black dance or black dancers is exploitative or "tends to reinscribe prevailing stereotypes" (hooks, *Black Looks* 72) by virtue of describing the activity or drawing attention to the body. Indeed, as conscientious and fair critics concerned with challenging demeaning, stereotypical representations of blackness, we must also be careful to avoid denying aspects of the African cultural background that are regarded by the people themselves as positive hallmarks of a rich and valued legacy. This is a legacy that colonialist and racist thinking, on the one hand, often has perverted to mean savagery and backwardness, and that self-righteous moralists and revisionists, on the other hand, have condemned as immoral lust and animal sensuality. As Gerald Moore acutely observes, "There is a real dilemma for the black writer who genuinely believes that his people are more spontaneous and life-loving than their white fellows, since he daren't say so without being accused of exoticism" (69)—that is, of reiterating and reinforcing primitivist, essentialist, and pejorative distortions of black identity and culture. Similarly, novelist and essayist Alice Walker's comment on the use of black language in literature offers some insight into the controversial matter of representation that is relevant to our discussion. As she states in *Living by the Word*,

> it is not by suppressing our own language that we counter other people's racist stereotypes of us, but by having the conviction that if we present the words in the context that is or was natural to them, we do not perpetuate those stereotypes, but, rather, expose them. And, more important, we help the ancestors in ourselves and others continue to exist. (58)[25]

Artel's vision and representation of black dance and dancers certainly seems to prefigure, if not confirm, the opinion of the noted African-American author.

"Danza, mulata!" also brings to mind two other compositions focusing on a black female dancer or on a dance of African origin: Claude McKay's "The Harlem Dancer" and Langston Hughes's "Danse Africaine." A brief comparison of the three poems will serve to further corroborate our previous remarks. Significantly, the poetic voice of McKay's sonnet observes not only the woman as she dances, but especially the devouring, "eager, passionate gaze" of "wine-flushed, bold-eyed [white?] boys" and "young prostitutes" who "watched her perfect, half-clothed body sway" (*Selected Poems* 61). This dual or metaperspective reveals an ironic conflict or contradiction between what the youths see and feel and what the dancer senses and interprets. Despite the reference to "blended flutes / Blown by black players," the context seems to be deliberately ambiguous; it is not clear where the dancer is (e.g., in Harlem or elsewhere); whether she is dancing for the youths or merely before them; whether her movements are meant to delight and entertain, or whether they reflect a deeper, more personal, possibly spiritual orientation with little or no attention to the audience. As in Artel's poem, the final verses of McKay's poem offer an all-important key to a meaning beyond that of the act of dancing itself:

> But, looking at her falsely-smiling face
> I knew herself was not in that strange place.

These verses show the dancer to be both aware and in command of her situation; her mind is on something or someone else, suggesting an aloofness or possibly even a trancelike, ecstatic state that transports her far from the stares and cheers of the onlookers. Similarly, the mulatto woman of "Danza, mulata!," apparently absorbed in her dancing, shows no awareness of the speaker.

Hughes's "Danse Africaine" offers a different perspective on black dance (*Selected Poems* 7); nonetheless, it parallels "Danza, mulata!" in the evocation of the African presence and heritage. At the same time, it also exhibits other, perhaps more fundamental, similarities. In both poems the drum stands out, although the onomatopoeic quality of the English word "tom-tom" conveys a more immediate and direct musical sound than the descriptive verses "mientras canta / en el tambor de los abuelos / el son languidescente de la raza" of Artel's poem.[26] Similarly, we note the use of the verb in the imperative form("Dance!"). The lone reference to the dancer in Hughes's poem—"A night-veiled girl" who "Whirls softly into a / Circle of light. / Whirls softly . . . slowly, / Like a wisp of smoke around the fire"—connotes that she, too, is of African descent. Her movements, however, not unlike those evoked in "La cumbia," are soft and slow instead of fast and sudden; and the reference to "smoke around the fire" suggests a nocturnal setting in the African bush similar to that of Artel's poem ("Trota una añoranza de selvas / y de hogueras encendidas").

The major point of intertextuality between Artel's poem and that of Hughes, however, lies in the connection that both poets make between the dancing inspired by the drum music and the ancestral memories carried in the blood. In the one, "the low beating of the tom-toms / Stirs your blood." In the other, the poetic voice, psychologically engaged with the mulatto woman in dance, reminds her that they both feel "galloping in the blood / the passion of a same nostalgia" ("en la sangre / galopar el incendio de una misma nostalgia)—that is, a common ancestral heritage.

In short, what this brief comparison shows us is that Artel, like his North American and Jamaican counterparts, also can appreciate the physical beauty and grace of the woman of African descent and rejoice in the excitement of black dance.[27] Simultaneously, he remains proudly aware of the remote, ancestral spirit that is their life force. As a poet firmly rooted in the Latin American cultural tradition, Artel, as we have shown, participates in and identifies with the literary legacy of earlier generations; but he is also receptive and committed to artistic change and innovation. Thus, while his dance poems may reflect the probably unavoidable impact of *negrismo,* they also maintain and exude a sincere respect for black womanhood and a constant assertion of the African presence, not unlike works of the Harlem Renaissance poets whom he admired. Artel's celebration of black dance and dancers is not voyeuristic spectacle or touristic entertainment, but participatory event, remembering, evoking, and renewing the spiritual content of African musical and ritual traditions.

"Dancing," another of Artel's poems related to the theme of dance, exhibits less of the overt African rhythmic spirit than "Danza, mulata!" or "La cumbia." On the other hand, it reflects more of the avant-garde interest in primitivism and the jazz-band music craze as well as the *negrista* technique of onomatopoeic percussive instrumentation.

Maraca y timbal!
Marimba y tambor!
La noche empapada
en sudor de jazz-band!

Confusión:
la religión del día!
Un pedazo de selva
cayó en el salón!

Retumban
las bombas
de la algarabía!

Maraca y timbal!
Marimba y tambor!

Aullidos de cobre:
la jungla africana!
Broncíneas caderas
se quiebran al ritmo
que marca el trombón!

. . . .

. . . .

Josefina Baker,
negro lucero del Siglo,
tus piernas jugando
con la civilización!

Paul Whiteman,
brujo señor del Fox,
el mundo es de los dos!

Los hombres de ébano
cantan el són.
Maraca y timbal!
Marimba y tambor!

Confusión:
Ya los blancos aprenden
a bailar charlestón.

[Maraca and timbal! / Marimba and drum! / The night soaked in sweat of jazz-band!

Confusion: / the religion of the day! / A piece of the jungle / fell into the ballroom!

The bass drums / rumble / with the din! / Maraca and timbal! / Marimba and drum!

Howls of brasses: / the African jungle! / Bronzelike hips / bend to the rhythm / marked by the trombone!

. . . .

. . . .

Josephine Baker, / black morning star of the age, / your legs playing / with civilization!

Paul Whiteman, / master wizard of the fox-trot, / the world belongs to you both!

Men of ebony / sing the song. / Maraca and timbal! / Marimba and drum!

Confusion: / Now whites are learning / to dance Charleston.]

Nevertheless, the omnipresent drum and the specific reference to the jungle in contradistinction to the ballroom, suggest that within jazz-band music and dances there dwells a still vital, albeit distant, African presence that exercises a powerful, magnetic attraction even upon members of white civilization.[28] Clearly, Artel's inclusion of the phrase "the African jungle," by no means derogatory, sought to capture and express in poetry—just as Paul Whiteman was doing in music and Josephine Baker in dance—the exciting, irresistible interest in the so-called primitive cultures and its joyous, liberatory effect.[29] At the same time, the image of a sudden intrusion of "a piece of the jungle" into the ballroom graphically captures the powerful impact of African-based music upon Euro-American cultures (cf. "El mundo está dominado por Africa"). It also echoes Gómez de la Serna's questionably worded observations that jazz music "Appears at every moment [to be] a mixture of the jungle and the modern" (181), and that "In jazz we feel the embrace of two civilizations, the Negro one of the era in which we were water-soaked toads and the era of the Grand Avenues and the surprising show windows" (182).

WORK SONG

One final aspect of the African heritage that stands out in the first edition of *Tambores en la noche* and deserves at least brief mention is the custom of uniting song with work. Perhaps the best example of this is the poem "Barrio abajo" [Low District], in which the poetic voice addresses a black woman who pounds kernels of corn:

Al son de viejos pilones,
chisporroteados de cantos,

meces tu talle de bronce
sobre el afán inclinado. (45)[30]

[To the sound of old mortars, / sparked with songs, / you rock your bronze
figure / bent over the task.]

Although travelers and scholars have long seen this practice as a means
of lightening and quickening the work, German Africanist Janheinz Jahn
attributes it to Nommo, the magic power that carries the word. "The song,"
he insists, "is not an aid to the work, but the work an aid to the song" (224).
Be that as it may, it is certain, as Olly Wilson observes, that "physical activity is
part of the music-making process," and that music and movement in African
cultures are inextricably associated (17). The third strophe of Artel's poem
further reflects this practice:

Pones música al trabajo
para burlarte del sol
y lo amasas bajo el día
con el maíz y el afrecho
que pilas en tu pilón. (46)

[You put music to your work / to mock the sun / and you knead it beneath
the day / with the corn and the bran / that you crush in your mortar.]

BLACK IDENTITY AND *MESTIZAJE*

In an earlier section of this chapter I stated that Artel's
espousal and assertion of a positive black identity rooted in the reclamation of
the African heritage in America was no mean feat for a "black" poet of mixed
racial ancestry living in a multiracial, multicultural, and yet predominantly
mestizo society whose white, Eurocentric elite perpetuated an image of a
racial democracy. I also stated that Artel's commitment to revindicating black
identity and the African roots of Colombia did not prevent him from calling
attention also to the indigenous presence within himself and his society. Of
this first edition of *Tambores en la noche*, three poems in particular—"Ahora
hablo de gaitas," "Mi canción," and "La canción imposible"—confirm these
ideas, offering insights into both the complexity and difficulties of black
literary expression in Colombia and the poet's own creative, resourceful
efforts to come to voice with a multiracial perspective.

From the outset of his book, Artel insists on the multiethnic nature of
coastal—and, by extension, Colombian—society and culture. In the title

poem, "Tambores en la noche," which accentuates the African heritage via the drum, one also discerns in the lines "mi vibrante raza, / con sus siglos mojados en quejumbres de gaitas" (20) [my vibrant race, / with its centuries dampened in moans of gaitas] an allusion to another heritage. The reference to the *gaita*, a wooden, flutelike instrument of indigenous origin, poetically affirms the indivisible cultural melding that characterizes Colombia's Atlantic coast and the poet's own ancestry.[31] Mention of the *gaita* occurs frequently throughout Artel's poetry. In "Bullerengue" (the title refers to a popular dance of the coast) the poetic voice desires to become a *gaita* to play only for his black beloved (50). Playing the *gaita* "in the cumbias of Marbella" was one of the artistic talents of the dead young boatman of "Velorio del boga adolescente" [Wake of the Adolescent Boatman] (69).

Often presented in a context of moans, laments, and tears, the whining of the *gaita* evokes the sadness and mourning occasioned by the violence of the conquest and the subsequent upheavals and ruptures suffered by native peoples. Thus in "La cumbia" we hear a weeping of *gaitas* ["llanto de gaitas"] and in "Romance mulato" [Mulatto Ballad] we read that the instrument cried its ancestral laments ["lloraba la gaita / sus quejumbres ancestrales"]. It is in "Ahora hablo de gaitas" [Now I Speak of Gaitas], however, where the woodwind achieves individual prominence in order to fully convey its symbolic significance and to pay homage to the Native American presence of Colombia's Atlantic coast and of the poet's own background. Dedicated to Artel's lifelong friend, journalist and writer José Morillo, the poem opens with verses of affirmation and interrogation, which are quickly answered:

> Gaitas lejanas la noche
> nos ha metido en el alma.
> Vienen sus voces de adentro
> o de allá de la distancia?
>
> —De adentro y de la distancia,
> porque aquí entre nosotros
> cada cual lleva su gaita
> en los repliegues del alma! (57)

[Distant gaitas the night / has inserted in our souls. / Do their voices come from within / or from the distance afar?

—From within and from the distance, / because here among us / each one carries his gaita / in the folds of his soul!]

145

Significantly, the guitar, a well-known European instrument brought over to the New World by the Spaniards and which is identified with Hispanic cultures, is made to yield here to the indigenous flute, of which there are male and female forms.

> —Compadre Carlos Arturo,
> no toque más su guitarra:
> oigamos mejor las gaitas
> que suenan dentro del alma! (58)

> [—Compadre Carlos Arturo, / don't play your guitar anymore: / rather let us hear the gaitas / that sound within our souls!]

In this way Artel gently but effectively urges greater recognition and acceptance of the Native American patrimony, which, like the African, constitutes a fundamental element of Colombia's triethnic culture, but that, like the latter, too often has been disowned, derided, and maligned.[32] Such chronic alienation and scorn, together with the inordinate interest in extraneous airs, have fostered ignorance and repudiation of the autochthonous culture, to the detriment of national pride and identity. The poet, therefore, encourages his compatriots,

> aquellos [sic] que no comprenden
> la voz que suena en sus almas
> y apagan sus propios ecos
> con las músicas extrañas,
> que se sienten en la tierra
> para que escuchen lo dulce
> que han de sonar sus gaitas. (59)[33]

> [those who do not understand / the voice that rings in their souls / and who extinguish their own echoes / with foreign strains, / to sit down on the earth / so that they may listen to the sweetness / which their *gaitas* are to emit.]

As the poem suggests, however, it would be a mistake to limit the relevance of the *gaitas* solely to indigenous ancestry. Centuries of *mestizaje* have resulted in an inextricable and rich syncretism of diverse ethnic elements. These wind instruments, then, also imply cultural union and harmony, in the same way that Artel's poetry seeks and reflects transcendence of racial and cultural boundaries. As the poet informs us in "Las gaitas," an uncollected poem that pays homage to the instrument and that was published in the same year as his book, the *gaitas* "Speak / in a language trembling with water / to tell the anguish of all the ancestors" ["Hablan / en un lenguaje trémulo de agua / para decir la angustia de todos los ancestros"].[34]

The second poem to which we turn our attention for a more penetrating understanding of Artel's efforts to come to voice is "Mi canción" [My Song], which occupies the antepenultimate position in the book. As mentioned earlier, "Mi canción" is a kind of ars poética, or personal statement of his lyric inspirations and poetic orientation. The first stanza gathers together several essential elements of Artel's book that were discussed earlier: shouts; a warm, sunny climate; a black verse characterized by a blending of the indigenous and the African:

> Un tono cálido
> amasado de gritos y de sol.
> Una estrofa negra
> borracha de gaitas vagabundas
> y golpes dementes de tambor. (227)[35]

[A warm tone / kneaded with shouts and sun. / A black stanza drunk with nomadic gaitas / and violent beats of drums.]

A reference to waves and beach in the second strophe introduces another major element of Artel's poetry—the sea, which permeates much of the second section of *Tambores en la noche*. Although hardly mentioned in this study to this point, it is an obvious and indispensable factor of the port and of coastal reality. Also implied here, however—and no less important—is the sea's special relevance to Afro-Colombians, for through its paths captive Africans were transported to Cartagena and other ports to labor as slaves in the New World.

> Un oleaje frenético
> erizado de calor.
> Una playa foetada
> como espaldas morenas,
> por las fustas ardientes,
> y un pedazo de mar—hermano mayor
> que me enseñó a ser rebelde—,
> me dieron la canción. (227–28)

[A frenetic wave bristled with heat. / A beach lashed / like brown backs, / by the red hot boats, / and a piece of sea—older brother / who taught me to be a rebel—, / gave me the song.]

The skillful double entendre ("Una playa foetada / como espaldas morenas, / por las fustas ardientes") creates a simultaneous image of the beach as covered with fiery red boats (vedettes) and as brown backs beaten by burning whips. In this way Artel is able to convey both the beautiful, quotidian reality of the marine coast and the painful, historical experience of the slave trade and slavery.[36] The insubordinate, indomitable nature of the sea— ruled by no one—also shaped the poet's own love of freedom, his rebellious (avant-garde?) character and poetic attitude. As he confesses in "Canción para ser cantada desde un mástil" [Song to be Sung from a Mast],

> (Amo el mar porque es atrabiliario y loco,
>
> porque tiene olas volubles como hembras
>
> *y porque no es de nadie!*) (127; emphasis added)

[(I love the sea because it is irritable and mad, / because it has waves voluble like females / *and because it belongs to no one!*)]

Besides the obvious marine allusions, references to other elements of Artel's poetry, such as the jazz band, sailors, and the port-city (e.g., light-house, night lights) are also present in "Mi canción," suggesting an intimate connection with the environment. In fact, so intertwined is the poet's artistic creativity with the ordinary activities and entities of coastal and harbor life, so natural, unaffected, and unobtrusive his song, that he imagines both drunk seamen and toiling fishermen—the common people—identifying with it and embracing it, as if it were their own:

> Alta, mi canción se irguió en los mástiles
>
> y los marinos ebrios
>
> creyeron que era suya.
>
> Suya, la creyó el pescador,
>
> porque en las redes blancas de los pescadores
>
> como un pez de bronce se escondió. (228)

[Aloft, my song raised itself on the masts / and the drunken sailors / believed it was theirs. / His, the fisherman believed it to be, / because in the white nets of the fishermen / it hid like a fish of bronze.]

Finally, other components of the coastal landscape, such as the swaying palm trees, the unruly waves, and the odor of the land itself, imbue the poet's song with a sensuous mélange of sounds, sights, and smells. Movement and smell also connote the strong and constant force of that fecund, symbolic presence—the wind.

> Para mí fue la música
> de las palmeras cimbreantes.
> Las olas despeinadas
> me mostraron su voz.
> Su olor de brea mi tierra puso en mi canción,
> y en las cuatro rutas de la bahía,
> sonámbula, mi canción, se desnudó. (229)

[For me it was the music / of the swaying palm trees. / The unruly waves / showed me their voice. / My land put its odor of pitch in my song, / and in the four routes of the bay, / my song, somnambulant, revealed itself.]

Deceptively simple in title and form, "Mi canción" succinctly harmonizes and displays, all at once, the inseparable union within Artel's verse of several fundamental motifs or elements, rooted in a reverential remembrance of the African and indigenous ancestors and in a secure, psychic mooring to the poet's beloved coast.

"La canción imposible" [The Impossible Song] is the third composition related to Artel's effort to articulate a poetics of blackness within the context of *mestizaje*. The final poem of *Tambores en la noche*, it concludes the volume by affirming the poet's quest for an unknown song that speaks to the many and sundry sources of inspiration that dwell within and without him. Paradoxically, it translates the difficulty and frustration of the poet's inability to bring forth the ineffable song that might capture the multiple ethnic voices—African, Amerindian, European—that compose his racial and cultural identity.

> Hace tiempo que traigo, extrangulada [*sic*],
> la canción imposible
> que enmudece mis labios,
> y la siento ulular por todo el alma. (245)

[For some time I have been carrying, stifled, / the impossible song / that silences my lips, / and I feel it wailing through my entire soul.]

The last line of the preceding strophe—"y la siento ulular por todo el alma"—poignantly captures the mournfully evasive and mysterious quality of the

149

soulful song. A melancholy wind resounds eerily through the onomatopoeic quality of the aptly chosen verb *ulular*. Nevertheless, as the succeeding strophe shows, by verbally representing his personal and unsuccessful struggle to intone that which eludes him, Artel succeeds, paradoxically, in giving us some semblance of the song.

> Poeta sin palabras,
> marinero sin cantos,
> yo entoné mi silencio.
> La voz de mi espíritu dejó extraviar su eco
> en el puerto expectante de mi insomne tristeza.
> Un alcatraz de sombras picoteó insaciable
> los peces de colores de mi ensueño. (245)]

[Poet without words, / sailor without songs, / I intoned my silence. / My spirit's voice let its echo wander / in the expectant port of my sleepless sadness. / A gannet of shadows pecked insatiably / the colorful fish of my reverie.]

As the poet admits to frustration and ignorance about which of the multiple voices and experiences within him (black, white, Indian; *costeño,* valley, highland) will surface, he also indirectly evinces the triethnic origins of his coastal self and affirms as well the diversity of his personal experiences within a geographically and culturally varied Colombia.

> Ignoro aún si es negra o blanca,
> si ha de cantar en ella
> el índio adormecido que llora en mis entrañas [*sic*]
> o el pendenciero ancestro del abuelo
> que me dejó su ardiente
> y sensual sangre mulata.
> Si ha de llevar sabor de agua salada
> o tambores al fondo
> o claridades de sol de la mañana
> o nebulosos fríos de montaña. (246)

[I still do not know if it is black or white, / whether singing in it will be / the dormant Indian who weeps in my heart / or the passionate ancestor of the grandfather / who left me his fiery / and sensual mulatto blood. / Whether it will have the taste of saltwater / or drums in the background / or brilliances of sun in the morning / or misty mountain chills.]

Thus "La canción imposible" poeticizes the contradiction of giving voice to the poet's inability to express himself. It transmits the lyrical frustration of the attempts to raise the subconscious to a conscious level, to verbalize that which, at bottom, is ineffable. Implicit in the poem is the dilemma of expressing blackness when one is more than black; the quandary of asserting—within a mixed-race society that pretends to be free of racial prejudice and discrimination, but that frowns upon any assertion of ethnicity that goes beyond the folkloric—an authentic voice, one that speaks to the African heritage in the individual and the national culture, without disdaining or seeming to disdain the other ethnic components of individuals and society.

Evidently, this dilemma poses serious obstacles for the committed Afro-Colombian author who, eschewing the commonplace and stereotype, chooses to confront the history of Africans in America and dares to explore the inner dimensions of black identity. When that poet or writer, moreover, undertakes a personal mission, as Artel did, to revaluate African ancestry and affirm blackness in order to exorcise the fear of slavery, to remove the shame of slave ancestry, and to eliminate the hatred of black skin, he is challenging, in effect, those attitudes, practices, and beliefs that perpetuate ignorance and self-loathing and serve to uphold the dominant social, cultural, and political order. Indeed, as we suggested in an earlier chapter, the mere fact that Artel was a talented and accomplished poet challenged assumptions in Colombia about the art of poetry. Moreover, as Lozano y Lozano's commentary reveals, Artel's avant-garde approach signified a subversion of the traditional, centrist conception and practice of poetry in Colombia.

Artel's poetic challenge, however, remained largely on the spiritual, cultural, and intellectual plane, with little overt concern for the material or political. It was in the former arena that he felt most comfortable and where he believed the aesthetic essence of poetry could make a difference. As he explained in 1943:

> —Es que yo soy espiritualista . . . El arte conduce a la belleza ideal, la única perdurable, la que no muere y deleita. Por los caminos del espíritu se llega a todas las cosas, especialmente a Dios. (Nieto, "Los Poetas Colombianos)

> [The fact is I am a spiritualist . . . Art leads to ideal beauty, the only lasting one, the one which does not die and pleases. By the paths of the spirit one reaches all things, especially God.]

It is on the spiritual level, too, however, that all and sundry Colombians, particularly those of the denigrated colored masses, were obliged to struggle—both individually and collectively—to acquire greater consciousness, and to bring about progressive change.

Realizing that Colombia differed significantly from countries such as Cuba and the United States with regard to race and politics, Artel considered illogical and inconsonant with national reality a poetics of blackness that reflected acute racial tensions where there were none, or a political approach that created further social divisions. As he is reported to have said in a 1944 interview with Jorge Moreno Clavijo:

> La situación del negro en Colombia es completamente igual a la de los demás ciudadanos de la república. Entre nosotros no hay esos crudos antagonismos de razas que existen en otros países, como en Estados Unidos, el Brasil o Cuba. Y es porque el colombiano, consciente o sub-conscientemente, *se sabe fundamentalmente mestizo,* y nadie que no sea un ignorante, puede creer aquí en la superioridad de un determinado tipo racial sobre otros. (Moreno Clavijo; emphasis added.)

> [The situation of the Negro in Colombia is completely equal to that of the rest of the citizens of the republic. Among us there are none of those crude antagonisms of race that exist in other countries, as in the United States, Brazil, or Cuba. And it is because the Colombian, consciously or subconsciously, *knows himself to be fundamentally mestizo,* and no one unless he is an ignoramus, can believe here in the superiority of one particular racial type over others.]

That realization did not prevent him from appreciating, however, the rebellious tone of black poetry in the United States. He recognized that the Civil War there had "tinged with blood a boundary between the white man and the black man" and separated the minds (*los espíritus*) of that citizenry. For Artel, that fact explained why both the pain and laughter of black people in the United States are more intensely expressed. That "very special tone" existed, he concluded, because Afro-American poetry of the United States mirrored the difficult situation of black people there ("Modalidades" 17).

On the other hand, Artel asserted, at least on Colombia's Atlantic Coast the man of color lacked any inferiority complex and enjoyed—to the extent that his learning and upbringing allowed—all the privileges that respect confers. Therefore, he opined:

> Me parece a mí fuera de lugar e inmotivado crear una atmósfera de forcejeo nacional entre los negros y los que no lo son. Entre otras razones porque los que no lo son no están hostilizando ni persiguiendo a los negros, no están desconociéndoles ninguno de sus derechos. De manera que esa pugna racial sería encaminada a conquistar qué?[37] (Moreno Clavijo)

> [It seems to me out of place and ungrounded to create an atmosphere of national opposition between blacks and nonblacks. Among other reasons

because those who are not black are not antagonizing nor persecuting the blacks, they are not denying them any of their rights. So that that racial conflict would be directed to achieve what?]

In light of the fact that Colombia's racial problems were deemed nonexistent—that is to say, they were largely ignored, denied, and brushed away—it is understandable that Artel himself might adopt a more circumspect position on matters of race. Indeed, it would be difficult to call attention to and promote solidarity around a wrong or condition whose existence others cannot or refuse to acknowledge. By contrast, overt discriminatory policies and practices directed at people of African descent in Cuba and in the United States, and the blatantly racist and oppressive conditions under which they were often forced to live, had long necessitated and stimulated a tradition of organized struggle and resistance at many levels of society and also within the cultural realm. (As I pointed out in chapter 2, blacks and mulattoes in Cuba often joined forces out of mutual need and interest. The grouping together of black and mulatto authors—e.g., Plácido, Manzano, Guillén—in Calcagno's study and Trelles's bibliography might attest further to the palpable climate of race consciousness and racial cleavage that existed on the island.) Clearly, the expression of a militant literature of blackness would be more likely to appear in a society where peoples of color are diametrically opposed to whites than in a society where the ethos and reality of *mestizaje* is believed to preclude or obviate hard and fixed racial barriers.

For Artel, a self-acknowledged person of African, indigenous, and European bloodlines and of a similarly mixed cultural heritage, it was necessary and important to honor, as Zapata Olivella notes, "all of the ancestors" ("Jorge Artel, marinero de un mar mulato"), especially the more despised and hated ones, and to do so in a way which does not exacerbate existing hatreds and fears, but, rather, alleviates them. Certainly, in speaking of black literary expression, Artel was quick to avoid (or dispel) the suggestion of an art of exclusivity; that is, of a poetics of black racial superiority and dominance.[38] By revealing the spiritual wealth and contributions of the cultures of enslaved Africans and affirming the creative harmony and fecundity of *mestizaje,* Artel sought to promote a true national culture, to empower Afro-Colombians with a sense of ethnic pride and wholeness, and to disabuse Colombians and others of the fallacious ideas of racial purity and superiority that could only weaken their identity as a people and as human beings. Artel's poetry, then, may be said to lead toward the articulation of a discourse of synthesis that harmoniously reconciles black identity and *mestizaje* rather than subordinating one to the other. Given this understanding, it is not surprising that the first edition of *Tambores en la noche* contains no expressions of racial animosity or scenes of unequivocal violence. In fact, Artel assumes a nonthreatening stance in his book. For example, the three specific references to white people represent them as eager to learn black dance, envious of black sensual beauty, and respectful of strong, honorable black leadership—all actions that redound favorably upon black people and black culture.

Nevertheless, just as some Colombian critics could not appreciate Artel's avant-garde style, others failed to recognize the achievements of his poetry and to appreciate the challenges that he confronted—and posed—in attempting to create a genuine poetics of blackness in Colombia, one that took into account the nation's racial, ethnic, social, and political realities. By no means unanimous or consistent, critical opinions about Artel's poetry and his identification as a black poet often raised serious questions about the propriety, meaning, worth, and viability in Colombia of a written literary tradition by and about people of African descent. Even though Artel does not seem to have been unduly affected by the criticism, it may not be unfair to view the second edition of *Tambores en la noche,* at least in part, as a response to those critics who questioned or denied his role as a legitimate voice of Afro-America. Therefore, before discussing the 1955 book, it is important and useful to consider some of the remarks on Artel, his work, and black poetry, written by critics in Colombia and other lands that the poet visited during the fifteen years separating the publication of the two editions of *Tambores en la noche.*

6

$\mathcal{A}$FFIRMATION AND DENIAL:

Critical Responses to *Tambores en la noche* and the

Implications for Black Poetry in Colombia

> To write black poetry is an act of survival, of regeneration, of love. . . . To assert blackness in America is to be "militant," to be dangerous, to be subversive, to be revolutionary. . . .
>
> Stephen Henderson

> Critics create not only the values by which art is judged and understood, but they embody in writing those processes and actual conditions in the *present* by means of which art and writing bear significance.
>
> Edward W. Said

From the moment Artel began publishing the poems that would become *Tambores en la noche*, critical opinion about his writing and his position as a black poet varied. Stimulated perhaps by the uniqueness, daring, and rich promise of his poems, many of Artel's early commentators— themselves *costeños* and no doubt filled with pride and great expectation— were very supportive of their countryman's efforts to project within the national literary panorama a lyrical celebration of coastal life and culture that was neither caricature nor counterfeit. Writing in 1931, Cartagena journalist José Morillo referred to Artel as "the Langston Hughes who left this port city with his lips wet with the salt of the sea and his soul full of its mysterious rumors" ("Artel"). In Morillo's estimation, Artel's poems uniquely confronted the racial aspect of Cartagena's art, that which "has not yet been tried, and which must encompass all that soul of the Dark Continent, transplanted in the days of secular martyrdom, in the holds of the slave ships." Although Colombia had produced other black poets, for Morillo they were never

> so typical of their race and so permeated with their ethnic ego and their Afro-American temperament as this one who begins to proclaim himself to us and who fulfills the imperatives of his racial temperament, choosing for his motifs those capable of producing an aesthetic emotion unnoticed by the majority.

Equally enthusiastic, the ill-fated poet Oscar Delgado (1910–37) of Santa Ana, Magdalena, placed Artel among a new generation of coastal poets who "without pretensions of monopolizing the high temperature, [had] begun to define the tropical dimension of Colombia's new literature." While Delgado criticized "the chord of vacillating strains" that he discerned in Artel's poetry, he also expressed the hope that once this had been removed,

> the tropics will mature in his verses and in the prose of those of us who are feeling songs violently ours, like our breeze, our music, our stars, our rivers, and our trees.

For Aníbal Esquivia Vásquez, too, Artel's verses embodied the scandalously romantic soul of the coastal motifs and offered literary studies of port life. He urged Artel, however, to never forget that he was a black man and reiterated advice given the poet by writer Arturo Regueros Peralta of Santander:

> "You must be more black. Don't put rice powder on your race, because you will kill it. You need to make a school, and your future is in the jazz band. The violin is a utensil of the novel." (Qtd. in "Artel, poeta porteño")

Writing about the same time as Esquivia Vázquez, the politically minded Juan Roca Lemus (1908–83), also of Santander, was more direct and less laudatory in his appraisal. While he discerned in Artel the potential to be "the singer of his race" in Colombia, precisely because he "carries within his soul the poetic 'shout' endowed by his race . . . a shout that is anguish of a proud and Latin race," he also perceived within the poet a struggle between repression (or inhibition) and the subconscious, by which the former deflected the poet at times from his intended purpose. Because of that, the critic objected, "there is in his poetry the shout which we mentioned, shaded with white emotions, foreign to his race. He is the black poet who paints white sensations."

Touching specifically upon "Danza mulata" [sic], Roca Lemus adjudged the poem lacking in "all the intensity that should correspond to the pride or to the protest against the oppression of his brothers and sisters." For contrast, he cited the poem "I, Too," by Langston Hughes, whose more racially outspoken approach he urged Artel to emulate. Finally, after accusing Artel of not showing with sincerity the race to which he belonged, Roca Lemus chided him for what he considered the defect of most Colombian avant-garde poets: namely, the failure to make their art the instrument of an ideological expression. As he stated somewhat categorically at the end of his critique:

Programmatic poetry, whatever its ideological order may be, establishes a following and excites like a political proclamation: moreover, it leads the masses! Art for art's sake, sound for the sake of sound, words for the sake of themselves, only create auditory emotions, of an exasperating monotony and mulattoish social results.

No doubt well-intentioned, Roca Lemus—to whom Artel had earlier dedicated his poem "Añoranza de la tierra nativa" [Longing for the Native Land]—seems to have wanted his friend to avoid the *negrista* poetic pattern that had become so popular. Apparently, however, he was either unaware of or dubious about Artel's 1932 statement on black coastal literature, in which the poet himself affirmed the example of Hughes's poetry while minimizing that of the acknowledged leaders of the Afro-Antillean mode. By admonishing Artel for not putting his poetry at the service of a political program and by separating human sentiments into distinct racial (i.e., black and white) categories, Roca Lemus was denying Artel the right and the freedom to express himself, his identity, and his perspectives in his own way, and also limiting his humanity. Furthermore, by seeking to push Artel to create a form of black poetry that was both inconsistent with Colombian history and reality as Artel knew and lived it and inharmonious with his own current poetic outlook, Roca Lemus was actually urging Artel to create a work that, in essence, would have been spurious.

Sensing a discrepancy in Artel's poetry similar to that noted by Roca Lemus, Salvadoran critic Juan Felipe Toruño also suggested that Artel's poetry did not match his color. All of it, Toruño declared in a penetrating essay, "has that deep bitterness of not feeling itself in its ethnic element" ("Artel" 28). More lenient and psychological in his evaluation and lacking any overt political motive, Toruño implied that Artel's verses were possibly influenced by his mixed-race ancestry. He opined that the poet "detaches himself from the individual in order to try to live in the past and the present." Artel, the critic noted, eschews divisions in men and in ideas; he "loves the [human] community in a strange way, feeling himself in all and all in him" (27). For Toruño, the tension or dichotomy discerned in Artel's verses involved a reconciliation of the past and the present, of the spiritual and the corporeal. In short, the poems reflected the poet's internal struggle to find his own soul, "to discover the frame for his vital landscape" (29).

Toruño's critique appears to have had little or no impact upon Colombian views of Artel's writing. Years after the appearance of the first edition of *Tambores en la noche,* Colombian critics continued to fault Artel's poetry for failing to match the aggressively racial tone or socially militant stance of verse written by black and mulatto poets elsewhere in the Americas. In a commentary written on the occasion of Nicolás Guillén's visit to Barranquilla

157

in 1946 and just six years after the publication of Artel's book, local *cronista* Lorenzo Ortega, writing under his pseudonym "Dr. Argos," maintained that from the racial point of view, Artel's poems were "colorless":

> In none of them is seen the true and authentic consciousness of blackness because blackness, even though it may seem paradoxical, is not in the color, is not in the features and not even of [*sic*] the expressions of those who emit it. Blackness in poetry must be a pure thought; it must be the pride of feeling black and reclaiming the origin and tradition of our ancestors. ("Breve incursión")

For this critic, Artel's poetry, when compared to that of his Cuban counterpart Guillén or to that of black North American poets, would seem to lack the purity of thought and proud racial sentiment that he mentions. Ironically, however (and as we have shown in the previous chapter), Artel does assert in his self-defining "Negro soy"—a poem that Dr. Argos seems to have overlooked—something similar to this critic's own call for purity: "la emoción ha de ser pura / en el bronco son del grito / y el monorrítmico tambor." Indeed, it is apparent in these lines that the poet acknowledges not a shortcoming of his poetry but the problematical situation of the African heritage and experience in Colombia—ignored, disdained, relatively unstudied—which prompted sensitive and race-conscious Afro-Colombians like Artel, Natanael Díaz, and Manuel Zapata Olivella to set about (re)discovering, reclaiming, and reasserting black identity and the forgotten, discarded, and diluted presence of Africa in their land. In that respect, the poetry of Artel can be understood and appreciated both as longing or yearning and as quest to uncover the hidden, submerged spiritual dimensions of Afro-Colombia.

Regrettably, "Dr. Argos," like Roca Lemus, seemed to want Artel to do and to be more than Colombian reality of that time warranted or might even tolerate; that is, to adopt a position which, given the nature of Colombian society and culture, was probably untenable and might even have been detrimental to the development of an authentic Afro-Colombian literary tradition. The adoption of an aggressive, racially combative voice, I maintain, did not match Artel's poetic posture and would have been out of step with the social and political state of Afro-Colombia as he knew it. The following remark, which Artel made about Colombian politics in mid-1943, seems to parallel his particular racial poetics and to support my interpretation:

> Nothing of bourgeois individualisms nor Creole bolshevikisms. The only mirror in which an evolutionist party should look at itself is in the mirror of national reality. The rest is theories and intellectual gymnastics. (Nieto, "Los Poetas Colombianos")

With the publication of *Tambores en la noche* there began an intermittent and almost decades-long, undeclared debate on the existence of *poesía negra* in Colombia and the correctness of labeling Artel a "black poet." Those who took an opposing view offered several reasons for their position. The author of the book review published in *El Liberal* seems to have been the first to raise the issue upon inquiring rhetorically, "Is his poetry, then, as Mr. Artel himself says, Negro poetry?" For this reviewer, whose words recall Ballagas's 1937 article "Poesía negra liberada" [Black Poetry Liberated], reprinted in Colombia less than a year after its original appearance, Artel's work was poetry pure and simple. The addition of a distinctive marker that circumscribed it to certain boundaries, the reviewer concluded, in no way proved that there was a black poetry as opposed to an Aryan one.

Other critics, like poet and fellow *costeño* José Nieto flatly refused to accept the designation of Artel's poetry as black and rejected the notion of Artel as poetic standard-bearer for Afro-Colombia. In a 1942 interview Nieto declared:

> I have never been in agreement with the critics who say that Jorge Artel is the poet of the black race. Artel is a poet like any poet. The fact that he exploits the Negroid theme in his poetry does not justify calling his poetry black. . . . Poetry is one and unique. (Nieto, "Entrevista")

For Nieto, Ballagas, and others, what distinguished so-called black poetry was the presence (and treatment) of black people and culture as theme, which outweighed any considerations of the racial background or ethnic identity of a given author.

Echoing Nieto's opinion, writer and journalist Bernardo Restrepo Maya held that Artel was not so much a race singer ["cantor de raza"] as a climate singer ["cantor de clima"]. Anticipating "Dr. Argos'" 1946 critique, Restrepo Maya maintained that Artel's poetry exuded "no social meaning nor insistence on redemptions." It was constructed, he stated, "more on the emotion than on the problem" ("Poetas del Litoral Atlántico"). By denying Artel the position of artistic representative or emblem of Afro-Colombia, and negating the existence of a poetry that addressed the spiritual and cultural experiences of black Colombians, these critics, in effect, were also denying their darker countrymen not only a rightful space within the cultural and literary map of the nation, but also due recognition as a legitimate ethnic or racial group. Tending to ignore or overlook the tacit equating of colorless art with whiteness, exponents of the above views reflected and perpetuated— albeit unintentionally—the historical suppression or inveterate diminishment of blackness, a complexion largely associated with lower-class status and suggestive of a lack of culture. Indeed, as writer José Gers pointed out, in

Colombia blackness and the gentle art of poetry were traditionally regarded as mutually exclusive or incompatible (see Micromegas [pseud]).

Like the well-entrenched Colombian aversion to research on racial topics (see chapter 2), the reluctance to consider the existence of a black-produced poetic art also seemed to stem from a covert desire to avoid any racial expression that arbitrarily separated the art of poetry, gave the impression of discrimination, or contradicted the ethos of *mestizaje*. (Occurring as it did in the midst of the Allied struggle against fascism, the question of an ethnic or racial expression in literature and politics probably raised more than a few apprehensions about possible racial conflict in Colombia.) At times, acting out of a sense of repulsion for even the slightest hint of racial separatism or literary Balkanization, critics seemed intent upon averting any serious and sincere artistic effort by Afro-Colombians to express their African cultural heritage and historical experience, unless it was on their terms—through folkloric music and dance, for example. In a nation that considered itself to be above and beyond problems of color, any expression—especially by blacks—that suggested racial cleavage was to be repressed. On other occasions, however, possibly acting out of a need to feel fully within the Latin American literary mainstream, critics did call attention to racial problems, provided that these lay beyond the national boundaries. Both attitudes or approaches had the effect of determining the content and criteria for ethnic and literary expression by black Colombians, thereby undermining the emergence of a racially assertive discourse that might challenge the nation's centrist and mestizo-white (Hispanic) hierarchy.

Of course the aforementioned views did not represent the entire spectrum of critical opinion. Other, more insightful commentators such as Gustavo Ibarra, Jaime Angulo Bossa, and Esaú Becerra y Córdoba affirmed that Artel was indeed the poetic voice of the black race in Colombia. Emphasizing the spiritual quality and inward direction of Artel's poetry and understanding the significance of the various motifs that informed it, Ibarra and Angulo Bossa, both northern *costeños,* averred the uniqueness and authenticity of Artel's lyrical expression of black suffering and nostalgia. Becerra y Córdoba, an Afro-Colombian of the Chocó and thus, perhaps, more sensitive to the cultural needs of that minority group, showed a particular appreciation of the demands placed upon Artel's writing. While he fully acknowledged that the black presence in *Tambores en la noche* was not actuated by social concerns or racial protest, he dismissed the notion that black poetry always had to deal with struggle and faithfully reflect conflicts, bloody clashes, and liberation yearnings.[1] In Artel's songs, he pointed out, the Afro-Colombian community had found the vigorous reflection of their feelings. For that reason, he considered Artel to be "the clearest, purest and most appealing voice" of black people and the "proudest expression of Colombian black poetry." Despite such earnest and cogent analyses and eloquent testimonials, the question of whether Artel's work qualified as black poetry—and he as a "black" poet—persisted.

Inconsistency regarding Artel's racial identity seems to have been another factor influencing the perception and reception of his poetry. While it was common for critics to refer to Artel as a *negro* (i.e., Negro, black man), some emphasized his mixed-race background or called attention to his coastal origins in order to explain the thematic variations of his poetry or to insist upon the nonexistence of black poetry in Colombia (e.g., Camacho Carreño; Nieto, "Los poetas colombianos: Jorge Artel"). Of course, emphasis on mixed-race identity, like the recourse to racial euphemism, could also be a way of "improving the race"—that is, of whitening the poet by minimizing the longstanding stigma attached to black skin and Negroid features and lessening the shame traditionally associated with slave ancestry. It must also be remembered, however, that in certain contexts the word *negro* could be used as an epithet (cf. "black" or "nigger" in English) to insult or degrade a person of African ancestry. Ironically, even though Artel openly and proudly proclaimed his "negritude" within his mestizo or "tri-racial" identity, that did not shield him from being the target of such racial denigration (see, for example, "El negro Artel").

Without exactly denying the racial dimension of Artel's poetry or his identity as a black poet, other critics unwittingly complicated matters further by implicitly classifying his poems either as "black" (i.e., racial) or as "universal." This tacit categorization gave the impression that poetry dealing with race—and with black ethnicity in particular—was, like the poets identified with blackness, narrow in scope and limited in significance, whereas poetic expression that supposedly was "colorless" or race-neutral (i.e., "white") was unlimited in its appeal and value. In 1943, for example, the young writer Otto Morales Benítez, of Caldas, wrote of Artel's work:

> One part of his poems is not essentially black poetry. It has a universal air, of human emotions cordial to all racial conglomerates, wherein a love without nostalgia makes itself felt, and a full ecumenical shiver begins to traverse the vision of the city: the song to the universal matters which arrest the heart. ("La poesía de Jorge Artel")

Although well-meaning, these and similar remarks by other critics seem to suggest that *lo negro* is somehow divorced from the "pure," "universal" concerns or values that all human beings are believed to share.[2] It is clear, too, however, that what passed as black poetry was largely of momentary interest, even considered insular, marginal, or separate from the mainstream poetic discourse of Spanish America, which, presumably, had a broader and more generic base and supposedly was devoid of any ethnic considerations or free from racial constraints. Black poetry (*poesía negra*), it would appear, did not address the realities of Americans in the fullest sense of the word, nor did it speak or relate to the broad mass of humanity in general. Rather, critics seemed to imply, by dealing overtly with black and mulatto peoples and cultures black poetry was confined to feelings, experiences, aspirations, and needs of those groups, as if their feelings, aspirations, and needs could have no transcendental meaning, no far-reaching implications for, or relevance to, other peoples and individuals. To argue the contrary, however, that writing about black experiences does have relevance to nonblacks, is not to deny, by any means, the unique historical circumstances of African-American peoples or the importance and necessity of a literature that would speak to the complexity and full range of their past and contemporary existence. Rather, the raising of the question of universality suggests a certain confusion or obfuscation of black poetry and black literature in general, insofar as meaning and scope are concerned. It also demonstrates, as George Kent eloquently states, that "Literature is one instrument by which a dominant class or race asserts its interests, preserves its heritage and values, and preempts for them the category of the universal" (165).[3]

On a related note, it is strangely ironic and yet perhaps illustrative of the confusion and complexity of racial matters in Colombia that the term *racista* ("racist") was frequently applied to literature—and, especially, to poetry—written by persons of African descent and that affirmed black identity and expressed pride in African heritage. For example, speaking of Artel's verse, *costeño* poet and novelist Rafael Caneva Palomino (1914–86), himself of African ancestry, wrote in 1939: "The poet of the blacks also has words to lullaby the soul. His poetics ceases to be only *racist* in order to extend placidly along the unlimited territories of lyric poetry" (*1 y 9 poemas* 61; emphasis added). This peculiar usage of the words *racista* and *racismo* paralleled the terms *indigenista* and *indigenismo,* which were applied to literature—usually written by nonindigenous authors—that exposed the exploitation and suffering of the Amerindian masses and championed their rights and recognition. The usage was still current in the 1940s, as commentaries on other Afro-Colombian poets show. For example, speaking of fellow Caucano Natanael Díaz's production, Guillermo Payán Archer wrote in 1946: "In spite of repeated demonstrations of faith and racist lyric poetry . . . Natanael Díaz—our admired and admirable poet of color—offers us on this occasion a poetry oriented into the purest and finest channels of 'white poetry'" ("Breve nota").

Although this application of "*racista*" does not appear to have been limited to Colombia,[4] it is not difficult to imagine the possibility of confusion with the word's more familiar reference to the doctrine of racial superiority and the institutionalized policy of hatred of racial groups.[5] In fact, only several months after Payán Archer wrote his words, writer Manuel Zapata Olivella—who had recently returned to Colombia after three years of travels—was using *"racista"* in the latter sense to describe the censorship exercised by Creole elites against black cultural expression ("El porro conquista a Bogotá" 8). The likelihood, then, of ascribing to black poetry characteristics and intentions it did not have would certainly seem to have been greater as a result of this ambivalent usage.[6]

With the emergence of younger Afro-Colombian poets (viz., N. Díaz, Hugo Salazar Valdés, Eugenio Darío of Cartagena) and the approach of the centennial of Candelario Obeso's birth (1949), the debate about Artel's work and the issue of black poetry in Colombia gained additional stimulus.[7] In a commentary on Salazar Valdés, Helcías Martán Góngora of the Cauca, who was quickly establishing himself as a leading poet of the Pacific region, continued to deny Artel full standing as a black poet, asserting:

In Colombia no one responds to the Afro-American invitation. . . . Jorge Artel? No. His work of indubitable racial intention, is oriented along different channels and the blackness in it is fleeting accident but never the essence.[8] ("Presentación")

Shortly thereafter, in a review of Darío's collection of love poems, *Mi hacha y tu cántaro* [My Hatchet and Your Pitcher] (1948), critic Antonio Cardona Jaramillo acknowledged the black poet to be a living, creative entity, but rejected and assailed the notion of black poetry by reiterating a common argument: "Poetry is simply poetry. Because of its qualities and mysteries it is certainly equal in the white and the mestizo and the black" ("Notas de humo"). That opinion did not prevent the reviewer, however, from criticizing Darío for failing to confront life and "losing himself in a voice of hysteria"; that is, for not writing poetry that exhibited an obvious identification with blackness.

Ironically, Darío, in a response to such criticisms, also objected to the idea of *poesía negra,* retorting that in poetry, "there are not, there cannot be considerations of color nor of races" ("De mi otra agenda"). Viewing black poetic or artistic expressions in the same light as Surrealist, Symbolist, Romantic, Costumbristic, and other poetic "-isms," he offered the term *"poesía negrista"* as the logical and appropriate designation for the kind of poetry under discussion. In doing so, he agreed that Artel, Palés Matos, Guillén, Obeso, and others had written *"poesía negrista."*

Although the controversy over "black poetry" lingered on, apparently little or nothing was resolved. If the debate accomplished anything, however, it seems to have weakened rather than strengthened the possibility of the creation of a poetics of blackness in Colombia aimed at exploring the historical and contemporary dimensions of peoples of African descent. It is likely that Ballagas's writings on the matter were influential. In his essay "Situación de la poesía afro-americana," which formed the basis of the prologue to his 1946 anthology, *Mapa de la poesía negra americana,* the respected Cuban critic insisted that a legitimate poet of color who does not write "in a black way" may well be an example or reflection of *universal* human and artistic preoccupation (57; emphasis added). The equating of nonracial poetic expression with a higher, universal poetics may have been too great an appeal for many Colombian writers and intellectuals to resist. That thinking, along with *negrismo*'s preoccupation with sensualizing black dance and music, probably encouraged many a black poet to turn his attention to matters not concerned with or limited by race.

Artel's own frequent attempts to explain his poetry and to clarify the matter of color and identity in literature also complicated the debate on black poetry and reveal again how thorny and sensitive the question of race and writing in Colombia was. In response to one interviewer's query about whether he was "exclusively a black poet or, rather, a poet of blackness," Artel, reiterating remarks made in his "Modalidades" speech, explained:

I only know that I am a poet. *What the critics have been bent on calling the Negro poetry of Jorge Artel is a simple reaction of my mulatto temperament in the face of my external world.* At one point I explained that I was not a black poet in the sense of those race singers who have been an anguished reflection of all its sufferings in other places of America. And it is because in Colombia the Negro does not live a social exile, nor is persecuted, beaten down, or scorned, so that his poet, which the critics have said I am, turns out to be in an independent and calm position that shows its emotion before the world in an entirely anti-racial way. *For me the black element or the mulatto element are scarcely instruments of aesthetic order.* In my work there can be neither the justified social rebelliousness of Guillén nor the poetic crusade of separation of Langston Hughes. (Qtd. in Moreno Blanco; emphasis added)[9]

Throughout the 1940s Artel found himself facing the same questions and repeating the same answers, at times with slight, but revealing modifications. In his introduction of Guillén, however, Artel took the initiative. Recapitulating statements he had made in his "Modalidades" lecture, Artel agreed with the Cuban that in [Latin] America there was no black poetry (*poesía negra*), but a mulatto or mixed-race poetry (*poesía mulata* or *poesía mestiza*) that expressed "the ancestral voice of the different ethnic constituents that make up our mixture" ("Presentación" 388–89). Expounding upon his remarks, Artel offered:

And the fact is that if we were to admit the presence of a black American poetry, it would be like agreeing to a racial inequality, to an ethnological discrimination, given that in these mixed-race lands there are no whites or blacks; we are all the product of two racial groups, Africans and Europeans, mingled here with the native element. (389)

Two years later (1948), in another interview conducted in the wake of the comments by Martán Góngora and Eugenio Darío, and several months after the tragic assassination of Liberal leader Gaitán, Artel informed his two interlocutors:

I believe that black poetry does not exist in Colombia; there is, yes, mulatto poetry. I, for example, sing mulatto reactions. To try to write here black poetry is to create a false poetry. Moreover, black poetry is folkloric and had its origins in the United States, in the cotton fields where a real slavery was experienced. The different social milieus have differentiated also the poetry. . . . In Colombia the opposite occurs. The factors that imply a black culture do not exist. Here we all can lodge in the same hotels, we can enjoy the same government positions and get an education in the same universities. We are, rather, the contribution to Fernando González's great mulatto; without us America cannot present its great type. We are the humanity of the future. (Qtd. in Rey)[10]

As these statements show, when it came to originating a poetics of blackness that emanated from Afro-American peoples whose cultural ties to the African heritage remained strong, and who lived under iniquitously unfair conditions because of their racial background or identity, Artel readily deferred to the United States and Cuba. Clearly the racial horizons of Artel's poetic vision reflected the limitations of his circumstances. Although he was aware of the abhorrent injustices, social problems, and economic hardships that blacks in the United States, Cuba, and Brazil faced as a result of blatant racial discrimination; and while he even empathized with his fellow Afro-Americans, no doubt he felt far removed from the everyday, degrading experiences that marked their lives and that, fortunately, he did not share. Therefore, if from Artel's perspective, "pure" or true black poetry was that written by poets such as North America's Langston Hughes and Cuba's Nicolás Guillén, and which reflected the reactions and emotions of black people enduring and struggling against the harsh, inhumane conditions of legalized segregation, racial discrimination, and political persecution, then his poetry could not qualify as "black." Moreover, as he stated in 1940 and would repeat on other occasions, centuries of *mestizaje* had diluted the emotional purity of the African heritage in Colombia, leaving isolated traces of racial memory.

During his sojourns in Venezuela and the Dominican Republic, Artel continued to insist that to create in Colombia a poetry that raised the question of racial antagonism or denounced discrimination would be an act of dishonesty, a betrayal of the reality he knew and lived. Such poetry, emerging from neither his internal nor his external reality, would necessarily be false. As he explained to Venezuelan poet Vicente Gerbasi:

I have never believed in black poetry in Colombia, for a simple reason of cultural order . . . in Colombia there are only vestiges of a black race and few are the places—such as Puerto Tejada in the Cauca and Palenque in Bolívar—where authentic black conglomerates exist. We are a true indo-mulatto nucleus, for which reason *to speak among us of a purely black poetic attitude would be false.* (Gerbasi; emphasis added)

The aesthetic value of his poetry, Artel pointed out later, consisted in having achieved a highly racial note in a region of Colombia lacking a heavy African artistic heritage ("El poeta colombiano Jorge Artel opina sobre la poesía negroide").

ARTEL AND GUILLÉN

Our struggle is also a struggle of memory against forgetting.
(*Freedom Charter;* qtd. in hooks, *Yearning* 147)

Of the poets of black expression to whom Artel was compared, the one most often mentioned was Nicolás Guillén. Influenced, no doubt, by Luis Alberto Sánchez's remark casting Artel as a Colombian version of the Cuban poet, some Colombian critics were quick to mention Guillén when discussing Artel's work (Dr. Argos, "Apuntes literarios"; Burgos Ojeda; Jaramillo Arango; Martán Góngora; Auqué Lara). Although some comparisons were intended to clarify, and others to praise, the mere fact that Artel's countrymen often viewed his poetry through the prism of Afro-Antilleanism or Afro-Cubanism suggests not only the widespread fame and preeminence of the Hispanic Caribbean poets, but also a continuing tendency on the part of many Colombian intellectuals to look to models outside of their country for legitimation, justification, or improvement of their own values. Capitivated, perhaps, by Guillén's lyrical prowess and international renown, and ignoring the many significant factors differentiating the conditions of blacks in Cuba and Colombia and that could illuminate divergent literary traditions of the two societies, Colombian critics, as shown above, argued for years whether Artel was indeed a black poet and whether his poems could rightly be called "black poetry." Ironically, the criticism that would have a more visible impact upon Artel's poetic evolution and would be a more direct catalyst for the changes that distinguish the second edition of *Tambores en la noche* from the first one came not from fellow Colombians but from Guillén. In the brief but pithy article written on the occasion of Artel's arrival in Havana in late 1950 and published in Venezuela a short time later ("Nota sobre Jorge Artel"), Guillén made several pointed observations about Artel's 1940 book that would move the poet to respond.

Specifically, Guillén contended that the dominant note in Artel's poetry was not blackness but the sea. He based this assertion on the three-part dedication of Artel's book and on the numerical preponderance of poems dealing with the sea or the seaport of Cartagena. Dismissing black poetry once again as discrimination, Guillén declared that Artel's poems were "popular poetry" (*"poesía popular"*), in the best sense of the word, and associated Artel with his Colombian compatriot Obeso and with his own work. Inasmuch as Guillén enjoyed a highly regarded international reputation both as a distinguished poet and—his remonstrances to the contrary notwithstanding—as the foremost "black" poet of Spanish America, his views and judgments no doubt carried considerable weight. (In fact, the opinion by Guillén placed in the "Noticia" section of the second edition of Artel's book is taken from the article under discussion.) Artel, however, may well have interpreted the words of his Cuban contemporary as a challenge to, if not a denial of, his standing as a legitimate, bona fide representative of literary blackness. Despite his own occasional concession to the primacy of *mestizaje* over group ethnicity and the unassuming description of his verses as "mulatto reactions," it is certain that Artel preferred to define himself rather than be defined, especially by another poet of *negrismo*—Cuban at that—whom Colombians had often represented as a rival and whose own *son*-based work, according to critics, had set or become the standard for black poetry in Spanish-speaking America (see, for example, "Recital poético"). Moreover, given the warm comradeship that resulted from their first meeting in Cartagena in 1946 and Artel's encomiastic presentation of Guillén, he may well have expected Guillén to be more receptive, perceptive, and appreciative of his own verse.

For his part, Guillén had long before embarked on a more intensely social and political course in poetry—one consonant with his experiences in Cuba and Spain—and seems to have expected his Colombian confrere to do likewise. As he stated rather broadly in his note:

> Art always reflects the age in which it is produced and even the social class to which the artist belongs, although he at times does not even suspect it . . . the great task of every creative person consists precisely in expressing the conflict of his time, in "propagating it," in delivering to the future the profile of the days which it fell to his lot to live. To do so in such a way

that life does not betray beauty, but nourishes it with its blood and bones. Artel is on that path.[11]

In light, however, of the different backgrounds—social, political, cultural, and personal—of these two gifted poets, and the manner in which critics such as Sánchez, "Dr. Argos," and Auqúe Lara had compared Artel to Guillén, it is understandable that the two individual artists might not share a similar outlook on poetry and politics. Clearly, as we have seen, the historical reality of Colombia differed from that of Cuba; and the sociopolitical situation of Afro-Colombians, unencumbered by open racial conflict and segregated facilities, did not match that of Afro-Cubans. Moreover, as pointed out earlier, the temporal, cultural, and psychological separation of Afro-Colombians from their enslaved African forebears, and their continuing amalgamation with both indigenous and European peoples, precluded a strong sense of ethnic awareness and racial pride in the African inheritance—at least one comparable to that among Afro-Cubans. Furthermore, it must be remembered, unlike his Cuban counterpart, Artel did not live in a country whose leading artists and enlightened intellectuals claimed it to be a mixture of "Africa and Spain," but rather in a nation exhibiting a more complicated blending of Amerindian, European, and African elements, and whose combinations and recombinations defied a simple biracial national identity and discourse.[12] Therefore, as already shown, Artel saw the need to bridge the historical-cultural gap that prevented Colombians from recognizing the fruitful, expansive, and often hidden imprint of Africa, and to reconnect alienated, marginalized black Colombians with their ancestral origins.

Inherent in Artel's poetry is the premise that a people (in this case African-Americans) needed to rediscover and reclaim their history in order to reaffirm and forge anew, on the basis of that awareness, an identity free of shame, fear, and self-hatred. Consequently, a fundamental aspect of Artel's poetic style, as we have seen, is the constant presence of nouns that evoke the past and suggest the poignancy of absence, separation, loss: *nostalgia, añoranza, tiempos muertos, recuerdo, saudade, eco*. Likewise, as in the poem "La voz de los ancestros," we encounter modifiers denoting a similar retrospection or sense of deprivation: *antiguo, perdidos, ignoto, remoto*. Together these words suggest or embody a longing, a struggle, to find and become (re)familiar with the ancestral spirit that informs and stimulates the memories and nostalgias inherent in black music, song, and dance. They serve, I repeat, as emotional bridges that the poet constructs in order to reestablish the nexus between the past and the present, between the ancestors and himself; a nexus stretched thin by time and diluted by the mixture of bloods. As Artel would assert in "Poema sin odios ni temores" [Poem Without Hatreds or Fears], which culminates the second edition of *Tambores en la noche:*

Nuestra voz está unida, por su esencia,
a la voz del pasado,
trasunto de ecos
donde sonoros abismos
pusieron su profundidad, y el tiempo
sus distancias. (1955: 145)

[Our voice is united, by its essence, / to the voice of the past, / a reflection
of echoes / where resonant abysses / placed their depth, and time / its
distances.]

Although Guillén confronted the African heritage and slave past in such
poems as "Balada de los dos abuelos," "El abuelo," and "Sudor y látigo," his
poetry was more concerned with bringing about a new Cuban consciousness
(in the less than half-century-old republic) by increasing his countrymen's
awareness of their nation as a thoroughly biracial entity. As he wrote in the
prologue to *Sóngoro cosongo:* "Some day one will say: 'Cuban color.' These
poems wish to hasten that day" (*Summa poética* 75). Furthermore, it must
be remembered, throughout the history of Cuban literature a nationalistic
tradition combining racial struggle with political struggle (witness Plácido
and José Martí) prevailed. Guillén's poetry continued in that vein—battling
both North American imperialism (e.g., "Caña," "Yanqui con soldado") and
home-grown despotism and oppression (e.g., "No sé por qué piensas tú,"
"Soldado libre," "Mi patria es dulce por fuera"), clearly, again, in order to
help create a new consciousness among Cubans that would lead to total and
lasting liberation.

Paradoxically, then, while Artel's pre-1940 poems do not contain as many
elements of conspicuous African origin—e.g., sonorous and magical words,
allusions to African peoples and religions—as are found in Guillén's work (for
example, the words *congo, yoruba, mandinga, carabalí, Changó,* in the poems
"Sensemayá," "Balada de los dos abuelos," "Balada del güije," "Son número
6"), they do exude, as Artel himself claimed, more racial spirit—"aliento
racial" ("Modalidades artísticas" 17–18). That is, they reveal a deeper sense
of atavistic longing, a greater preoccupation with rediscovering African roots
and reaffirming black identity, without excluding, of course, concern for the
indigenous lineage or awareness of the European background.[13] Perhaps that
is why Guillén, before actually meeting Artel, imagined him as a tall, dark-
skinned Negro and was surprised "to find a solidly built mulatto man, of short
stature . . . and overflowing with cordiality," as he described the Colombian
two years after his trip to South America ("Recuerdos colombianos" 21).
Indeed, for Artel, a person of mixed ancestry who suffered discrimination as

a black man, it was imperative to acknowledge, to take pride in, and to pay homage to the blood that bore the painful and unfair mark of inferiority. He knew that in Colombia and other parts of America many descendants of black people, ashamed of their ancestry, concealed their color as if it were a curse. Therefore, Artel, unlike Guillén, embraced the title of black poet ("poeta negro") in order to affirm black identity and to revaluate the socially and culturally despised African heritage ("Habla un gran lirida cartagenero"; cf. Guillén's remarks in Fuenmayor).

As I will show in the next chapter, the second edition of *Tambores en la noche* evinces a not so subtle response to Guillén's (and other critics') negation of Artel as a black poet and to the Cuban's apparent failure to understand and appreciate Artel's aesthetics; that is, his cultural, spiritualist, nonideological approach to black culture and identity (see Artel's comments in the interview "El Dr. Alfonso López"). This new edition, however, confronts much more than Guillén's opinions and his difficulty in appreciating Artel's artistry and circumstances. Just as Artel had expressed concern about the penetration—and perhaps even displacement—of native coastal Colombian music by such celebrated Cuban musical forms as the *son* and the *rumba* ("Modalidades artísticas" 19; "Instantáneas antillanas"),[14] he also realized the necessity and importance of demonstrating that the more popular and well-known Afro-Cuban or Afro-Antillean mode of black poetry was neither the sole approach to, nor necessarily the best expression of, the conditions and concerns of black peoples in the Americas.[15]

In short, Artel refused to allow the Afro-Cuban mode or perspective, symbolized by the *son,* to dictate the terms of black literary expression for all Spanish America. Furthermore, he was mindful of the degeneration of poetic *negrismo* into monotonous imitation of the external sounds of black music, excessive exploitation of "Negro dialect," and comic ridicule of the black persona (see Arroyo, "Notas hispanoamericanas"; Portela, "Lo afroantillano"; and "Jorge Artel, Poeta de América"). In fact, several of Artel's journalistic writings and interview statements of the period 1949–54 take issue with the false black poetry that, in the artful voice and theatrical manner of many professional *declamadores,* too often projected mere caricatures of Afro-American emotion and culture, thereby perpetuating mocking, detrimental stereotypes of black peoples (Artel, "Desde el Mirador. Declamador," "Importancia del folklore"; Portela).[16]

Although Artel steadfastly avoided political ideology in his racial lyric, his poetic vision and racial understanding broadened and deepened considerably as a result of the seven-year odyssey that took him from Colombia to Venezuela, the Dominican Republic, Puerto Rico, Cuba, the United States, and Mexico, and brought him into direct contact with various writers, poets, intellectuals, musicians and artists, including Miguel Otero Silva,

Vicente Gerbasi, Guillermo Morón, Luis Palés Matos, Rafael Hernández, Isabel Cuchí Coll, José Z. Tallet, Langston Hughes, Eusebia Cosme, and Pedro Vargas. More important, these journeys—as much psychological as physical—enabled Artel to observe and experience firsthand the commonplace conditions, activities, and expressions of Afro-American life on a much wider and deeper scale than life in his native Colombia afforded. Everywhere he heard the spirit-voices confirming the universal and transcendental meanings of black identity: music through pain, creativity in the face of bondage, perseverance of the spiritual and cultural inheritance of Africa, struggle and exaltation of freedom. Face to face with the absurd racist practices of mestizo Cuba and the infamous violence, degradation, and injustice perpetrated against Afro-Americans in the United States, Artel overcame the circumstantial barriers of history, geography, regionalism, nationality, and ethnicity that had limited his poetic vision and impeded an unqualified identification with a broader African-American experience. As the next chapter will show, the new poems of the second edition of *Tambores en la noche* vibrate with a more assertive, vigorous tone, and several of them evince a more overtly social and militant stance without sacrificing, however, the lyricism and aesthetic qualities that characterize Artel's earlier work.

7

ℬREAKING THE *SON* BARRIER:

Jorge Artel's Poetic Odyssey of the Afro-American Soul

(*Tambores en la noche* [1955])

> The recognition of an ancestral relationship with a folk or aborig-
> inal culture, whether African or Amerindian, involves the artist
> in "a journey into the past and hinterland which is at the same
> time a movement of possession into the present and future."
> Ashcroft, Griffiths, and Tiffin 147 (quoting E. Brathwaite)

Some twenty years ago, on the occasion of the thirty-fifth anniversary of the publication of *Tambores en la noche* and the sixty-sixth birthday of Jorge Artel, I pointed out that literary critics and historians who have dealt with Artel's black poetry have tended to ignore the 1955 edition of *Tambores en la noche,* basing their remarks primarily on the earlier book, which, as we have seen, corresponds to the *negrismo* era (Prescott, "Aniversario"). While numerous articles and reviews on the poems comprising the first edition have appeared since the early 1930s, there are few secondary sources—none from Colombia—that make reference to the poems of the second edition of the University of Guanajuato in Mexico.[1]

Indeed, since 1970 only three other critics, Wilfred G. Cartey, Richard L. Jackson, and Marvin A. Lewis—all working in North America—have examined and commented upon various poems of the Guanajuato edition. None, however, has studied the work as a whole—either within the wider context of Artel's poetic production or within that of Colombian literature, society, and culture. This state of affairs certainly begs the question: What accounts for the lack of critical attention to this second work by Colombia's preeminent black poet? How might we explain the silence surrounding this collection of Artel's work, published forty years ago?

There appear to be three principal reasons for the dearth of critical study on the book. First, as already noted, by 1940 the *negrismo* tendency was waning in the centers where it had flourished prominently (i.e., Cuba and Puerto

Rico), and those regarded as the leading practitioners (Guillén, Ballagas, Palés Matos) were already exploring other dimensions and concerns. (Ballagas, of course, had died the previous year.) As Fernández de la Vega and Pamies point out, much of the so-called *poesía negra, negroide,* or *negrista* that continued to be written had taken a sentimental and humoristic course, separate from a more social, proletarian-oriented approach ("Ebano y Canela" 12). In short, Spanish-American poetry was taking new directions and *poesía negra* no longer enjoyed the wide popularity and interest it had in previous years.[2]

The second reason for the absence of commentary on Artel's book is the general ignorance of its existence. Between mid-1956, approximately six months after the book's publication, and 1970, the year Cartey's *Black Images* appeared, few, if any, literary pundits in Colombia seem to have been aware of the volume. In any case, I know of no study of Colombian poetry and literature, published during that period, that mentions the work. Even Héctor Orjuela fails to record it in his comprehensive *Bibliografía de la poesía colombiana* [Bibliography of Colombian Poetry], which came out in 1971. Beyond Colombia, mention of *Tambores en la noche* during the 1950s seems to have been confined largely to newspaper write-ups of the author's lectures and recitals in Mexico and Central America, although an article on the book did appear in a Spanish-language newspaper in Florida (see Negroni).

Assuming, however, that Colombian critics were aware of the edition and interested in examining it, they may have encountered considerable difficulty in locating the book—which is the third reason why it has been sorely overlooked. While Artel had copies sent to institutions where he had lectured or recited, circulation and promotion of the book does not appear to have been systematic or widespread. Moreover, at least one book dealer in Colombia is reported to have refused to sell the work ("Una librería que se niega a vender la obra"). Although Artel informed me that some two thousand copies of the volume were printed, outside of Mexico it appears to have been available in only a handful of public libraries. Significantly, as late as 1984 only one of the several public libraries of Colombia visited for this study—the Biblioteca Departamental del Atlántico in Barranquilla—possessed a copy.[3] In the United States, on the other hand, at least two copies of the 1955 edition are known to exist: at Columbia University and at Princeton University.

Cartey, who studied and taught at Columbia, may have been the first person to cite the second edition since the 1950s. His remarks touch on nine poems: "Tambores en la noche," "Extramuros," "Ese muchacho negro," "Mi canción," "Noche del Chocó," "Encuentro," "Barlovento," "Alto Congo," and "La ruta dolorosa" (48–50). The first four of these poems appear in versions slightly different from those published in 1940. Inasmuch as Cartey's aim was to examine "some of the ways in which the black man has been portrayed in poetry, tracing his literary evolution from the image of slave to one of human distinction" (xi), with particular attention given to the poetry of Ballagas, Palés Matos, and Guillén, he devotes little more than two pages to Artel's poetry.[4]

Richard Jackson also uses the 1955 edition for his study *The Black Image in Latin American Literature* (1976), and includes two of the new poems ("Poema sin odios ni temores" and "El mismo hierro") in his discussion (116–19). Although Jackson cites the book's imprint in his text, oddly enough he does not record it in the selected bibliography at the end of his study. Rather, he lists only the 1940 edition (155), which he also mentions in the text (116). This inconsistency may illustrate another factor behind the failure of critics to discuss Artel's work in depth: namely, the assumption that the 1955 book is merely a "reissue" or a "reprint" of the 1940 edition (Jackson, *Black Image* 116; Jackson, *The Afro-Spanish American Author* 51). That assumption might easily lead a reader to ignore one or the other edition, resulting in only a partial awareness of the poet's production.

Unlike Cartey and Jackson, Marvin Lewis, in his book *Afro- Hispanic Poetry, 1940–1980* (1983) examines many of Artel's poems, using the 1940 edition of *Tambores en la noche* and the 1979 *Antología poética*. Although the latter collection contains most of the new poems of the second *Tambores en la noche,* it makes no reference to this book. Neither, for that matter, does Lewis, who was under the impression that Artel had published up to that time only "three volumes of poetry" (133): *Tambores en la noche, Poemas con botas y banderas,* and the *Antología.*

The new poems from the 1955 edition of *Tambores* that are included in the *Antología* form part of the second and third sections of this volume, and are interspersed with poems of the 1940 edition and other compositions not previously published in book form. According to Juvenal Herrera Torres, the author of the prologue to the *Antología,* the collection was "organized by Artel himself" (xiv), although Artel suggested to me otherwise. Be that as it may, since this arrangement does not reproduce the order of the poems as originally presented in either of the editions of *Tambores en la noche,* and as the poems bear no dates, the volume can be misleading for the critic or reader who seeks a clear understanding of the relationship between text and context, but is unfamiliar either with the origins of the poems or with where they fit within the poet's literary production. Thus, for example, Lewis unwittingly states that eight of the poems in the third and last section of the collection "are new material" (155). In actuality, however, all—with one possible exception ("Aprende a comer mierda")—were published or written between the decades of the 1930s and the 1960s. In fact, three of the poems ("Cartagena 3 a.m.," "Canción en el extremo de un retorno," and "Versos para zarpar un día") appear in the 1940 edition.

More problematic than the anthology's arrangement, perhaps, are the numerous printing errors, which do not merely disrupt the reading, but actually mar the meaning of the texts. The most conspicuous—and presumably unintentional—of these errors is the alteration of the title of "Poema sin odios ni temores" [Poem without Hatreds or Fears] to "Poema sin odios ni tambores" [Poem without Hatreds or Drums] (63).[5] In light of my previous (and following) discussions of the drum in Artel's poetry, this deplorable and egregious error, or intentional modification, undermines the poem's message (and intent) and subverts Artel's poetics. Other, less noticeable, violations of the texts can be found in the poems "Superstición" (48); "El lenguaje misterioso" (59); "Barlovento" (60–61); and "Yanga" (135).[6] Although it is unfairly demanding to expect a perfect, unblemished printing of any book, the errors in the *Antología* suggest a certain carelessness that could well have been avoided.

Clearly, a study of the second edition of *Tambores en la noche*, one that takes into consideration the biographical, literary, and sociocultural contexts in which they were written and their relationship to the previous edition, is in order and long overdue. While knowledge of the contextual origins of Artel's poems may not be a requirement for some critical approaches, as the above-mentioned studies show, I believe that it is essential for a more penetrating analysis of the body of Artel's work, for a more insightful understanding of the role his poetry plays in the development of black literary expression in Colombia, and for a deeper appreciation of Artel's unique contribution to black writing in Spanish America.

TAMBORES EN LA NOCHE (1955)

In view of these introductory remarks, it is fitting to begin discussion of the 1955 edition with a brief description of the volume itself and a statement of the major formal changes that distinguish it from the earlier edition. An explanation of the possible motives for the changes follows, which may lead to a better appreciation of the revisions and the influences that shaped them. Starting with the cover of the book, we find below the title and near the bottom a small illustration. The drawing depicts the black hands of an ex-slave—whose wrists still bear the remains of shackles and broken chains—beating an African-style drum. Effective yet unobtrusive, the illustration offers a pictorial representation of the salient thematic concerns and dominant symbolism inherent in Artel's work: music through sorrow and pain, creativity in the face of bondage, perseverance of the spiritual and cultural heritage of Africa in America, exaltation of freedom. Noticeably absent from the book is the famous charcoal sketch of the poet by artist Ramón Barba, which follows the title page of the 1940 edition.

With respect to the contents of the volume, we note that it consists of forty-three poems, whereas the first edition contains forty-six. Owing, however, to the use of individual sheets for the title of each poem, the 1940 edition numbers 247 pages—excluding the table of contents—while the 1955 edition has 146 numbered pages. In addition to the table of contents and a page listing previous and projected publications of the author, the latter volume also includes a glossary ("*Vocabulario*") of various proper and common nouns that appear in the poems (147–49). As many of these words relate to different geographical regions and various cultural manifestations of hemispheric Afro-America that Artel encountered in his travels and readings, they may be unfamiliar to many native Spanish-speakers, not to mention non-Hispanic readers. Thus the glossary facilitates understanding of many references to dances, songs, and folklore whose meaning or significance might otherwise not be apprehended.

For this revised edition Artel dispensed with the three long commentaries that preface the earlier book. Instead, the brief "*Noticia*" (5–8) that introduces the author to the reader also contains excerpts of opinions on the poet and his work, written by six established, if not entirely well known, critics and poets, most of whom Artel had met during the period 1950–54. They include Federico de Onís, who had presented Artel at the latter's lecture and poetry reading at Columbia University; Federico Berrueto Ramón, the author of an article on the poet published in the year prior to the book's appearance; Luis Palés Matos, who had introduced the poet at several recitals in Puerto Rico; Adolfo Martá, whose 1938 article had previously graced the Cartagena edition of *Tambores en la noche;* Nicolás Guillén, who had welcomed the poet to Havana; and José Antonio Portuondo, also of Cuba, whom Artel may have met in Mexico or New York. Their critical remarks and encomia confirm Artel's stature as a poet of merit and situate him and his work well within the geographical, historical, ethnic, and literary parameters of Spanish-American poetry.

If the above modifications in the second edition seem to be of relatively little importance and even external to an understanding of the texts them-selves, other changes that Artel made indicate a more substantive revision of—and departure from—the first edition of *Tambores en la noche,* one that evinces a more decidedly racial orientation. Significantly, Artel shortened the original dedication to read simply "A mis abuelos, los negros" ["To my forebears, the blacks"].[7] He also eliminated twenty-four of the original thirty-one compositions forming the section "Otros poemas" [Other Poems]. Since these compositions expressed nostalgia for the coastal homeland, romantic sentiment for the absent love, and an ambivalent black voice (e.g., in "La canción imposible"), Artel may well have considered them as weakening or detracting from the strong racial profile he sought to project within the new book. Conversely, he added twenty-one new poems translating the experiences and emotions, the encounters and discoveries of his odyssey around the Americas. Some of the twenty-two other poems remaining from the 1940 edition underwent slight yet meaningful alterations. For example, "Ese muchacho" [That Boy] became "Ese muchacho negro" [That Black Boy]. Accordingly, the first line was changed from "Ese muchacho porteño" [That boy of the port] (1940: 193) to "Ese muchacho negro" (71).

Here and there other words were also changed, further intensifying the emphasis on black identity and African heritage previously noted in the 1940 book. For example, the adjective "*alegres*" (happy) in the first line of the poem "El minuto en que vuelven" [The Minute in Which They Return] was replaced with "*oscuros*" (dark), leaving as the new line: "Los oscuros marinos de mi barrio" [The dark seamen of my district] (65). That Artel considered it necessary or advantageous to specify the color or racial identity of the sailors suggests a common problem of black and other "minority" literatures. When racial identity is not specified and the context is unfamiliar or does not provide unequivocal information or intimations, readers might automatically assume that the people referred to are white. While the subject of Artel's poem "Juan el holandés" [John the Dutchman] may be presumed to be Caucasian by virtue of national origin, theoretically one would not expect the same presumption to hold for citizens of multiracial nations or societies. Given the dictates of white Eurocentric hegemony, however, outside of sub-Saharan African nations and certain Caribbean islands, black citizens are generally not considered to be emblematic or representative of the national image or voice of their particular country.

Evidently, for the new edition of his book, Artel felt the need to clarify or insist upon the color—that is, blackness—of the sailors in his poem. It no longer sufficed—if it ever had—that in the 1940 edition the poem "El minuto en que vuelven" follows "Rincón de mar" [Sea Corner], which specifically describes the fishermen as black:

> Y sin embargo,
> no es éste el mar que anhelo,
> no es el mar que yo canto . . . :
> el de los bogas rudos
> y los pescadores negros
> y el denso vaho amargo. (1940: 177–78)

[And nevertheless, / this is not the sea that I long for, / it is not the sea which I sing . . . : / that of the coarse boatmen / and the Negro fishermen / and the dense, bitter vapor.]

The juxtaposition of the two poems in the first edition, however, would seem to suggest the likelihood of a probable, tacit connection: namely, that the people in both poems are, in the main, of African descent. Furthermore, it is well known that the *bogas*, who could also fit the broad classification of sailors (*marineros*), were largely of black ancestry. It must be remembered, too, that Artel, who viewed himself as a direct descendant of these hardy boatmen, identified them as black. The last lines of a self-portrait by Artel, which Esquivia Vásquez reproduced in his article "Artel, poeta porteño," confirm this fact: "The full, sensual lips, precede the hard chin which contrasts astonishingly with the rough nose which *my ancestors the bogas, who were black,* passed on to me" (emphasis added)."[8]

A change analogous to that of "El minuto en que vuelven" also occurs in the poem "Puerto" [Port]. The second strophe, which originally reads:

Acordeón:
lento bostezo de música.
Están abriendo un canal de sones ebrios
sobre el negro silencio del puerto.
Las frías agujas del sueño
comienzan a coser los párpados
de los hoscos marineros. (1940: 189–90)

[Accordion: / slow yawn of music. / They are opening a canal of drunken sounds / over the black silence of the port. / The cold needles of sleep / begin to sew the eyelids / of the dark sailors.]

becomes in the second edition:

Acordeón:
lento bostezo de música.
Están abriendo un canal de sones ebrios
sobre el hosco silencio del puerto.
Las frías agujas del sueño
comienzan a coser los párpados
de los negros marineros. (57–58)

[Accordion: / slow yawn of music. / They are opening a canal of drunken sounds / over the dark silence of the port. / The cold needles of sleep / begin to sew the eyelids / of the black sailors.]

Artel shifts the position of the adjectives "*negro*" and "*hoscos,*" thereby removing any ambiguity about the racial identity of the seafarers. In this case, however, the process of alteration seems to sacrifice some of the poetic nuance (i.e., connotative power or musicality) of the less common word "*hosco*"—which can also mean "gloomy" or "arrogant"—and to lose the synaesthetic quality of the port's black stillness, in exchange for the clarity of the more familiar word "*negro.*"

On the other hand, the changes Artel made in "Extramuros" [Beyond the Walls], originally dedicated to his friend and brother-in-law Aníbal Esquivia Vásquez, have the opposite effect. In the 1940 book the third strophe of the poem reads:

Por la boca de los negros
principia a trotar una canción,
—acaso el brote oscuro
de un dormido ímpetu ancestral—. (1940: 223)

[Through the mouths of the blacks / begin to trot a song, / —perhaps the dark emergence / of a dormant, ancestral impetus—.]

In the 1955 edition those verses appear altered as follow:

Por la boca de los negros
principia a trotar una canción,
acaso el *humming* oscuro
de un dormido ímpetu ritual. (67; original italics)

[Through the mouths of the blacks / begin to trot a song, / —perhaps the dark *humming* / of a dormant, ritual impetus— .]

The substitution of the English noun *humming*—a word and activity that Artel no doubt heard during his years in New York—for the Spanish *brote*, augments the musical immediacy or expressiveness of the lines, allowing the reader to imaginatively hear the song. Likewise, the replacement of *ancestral* with *ritual* adds a new, richer dimension to the black fishermen's song, imbuing it and the poem with a subtle religious tone and quality (which, as we will see, also permeates a few of the new poems).[9] In this way, Artel moves beyond the more general, nondescript meaning of "ancestral" and reconnects black Colombian musical expression, directly and more explicitly, to the African spiritual heritage that, as we have seen, is not always readily apparent or recognized, but often lies buried, or dormant, deep in the collective unconscious of the descendants of the African ancestors.

Another important change evident in this edition occurs in the order of the poems. Whereas the 1940 edition opens with the title poem ("Tambores en la noche"), the second edition begins with the self-assertive "Negro soy" and continues with "La voz de los ancestros," "Danza, mulata!," "La cumbia," and then "Tambores en la noche." Clearly, Artel was leaving no doubt about the racial identity he sought to project and the ethnic perspective he was emphasizing in his poetry. Undoubtedly, he wanted to imprint upon this edition an unquestionably and profoundly black stamp. The emphasis on blackness, however, did not imply a lessening of or conflict with the poet's identity as an American or as a person of mixed racial ancestry. Rather, it confirmed the black presence as an integral part and vital, creative force of Indo-Mulatto—that is, mixed-race—America. As Artel makes plain in the poem "Playa de Varadero" [Varadero Beach], his voice, too, is American, and it is the black side of America that sings within him: "mi voz americana, / desde mi lado de negro / —que es el lado que en mí canta" [my American voice, / from my black side / —which is the side that in me sings] (133–34).[10]

The new edition of *Tambores en la noche* also finds Artel returning to poetic forms he had pursued earlier in his career. "Soneto más negro" [Blacker Sonnet], for example, manifests the poet's continued attachment to the sonnet and his unfaltering ability to subordinate traditional form to modern black expression. Similarly, "Canción en tiempo de porro" [Song in Porro Time], as well as other poems, reflect Artel's continued mastery of patterned rhyme schemes. A few other minor changes in punctuation, phraseology, and orthography round out the significant formal differences that individualize the two editions. Concerning punctuation, one especially noticeable change occurs in the final line of "Negro soy" [I Am Black], which in the second edition ends not with a period but an exclamation point: "Yo no canto un dolor de exportación!" (14) [I do not sing a pain of exportation!]. The visual and phonic emphasis that the subtle alteration confers supports the more vigorously assertive tone implicit in the reordering of the poems. Examples of modifications in phrasing are evident in various poems: "me devuelven un eco" [they return to me an echo] (16) versus "siembran en mí un eco" [they sow in me an echo] (1940: 36) from "La voz de los ancestros" [The Voice of the Ancestors]; "Nunca podré olvidar / su rostro contra el sol" [Never will I be able to forget / his face against the sun] (70) versus "Mas no podré olvidar / —fue en un país de sol—" [But I will not be able to forget / —it was in a land of sun—](1940: 53–54) from "La canción"; and "que nos cuentan su nostalgia!" [that tell us their nostalgia!] (32) versus "que suenan dentro del alma!" [that resound within the soul!] (1940: 58) from "Ahora hablo de gaitas" [Now I Speak of Gaitas].

All of these tranformations and permutations—be they subtle or obvious—expand and intensify the emphasis on black identity and tend to sharpen the poetic language and image of the African presence set forth in the 1940 book. As a consequence, blackness moves from being one of three major themes—along with the seaport and romantic love—in the first edition, to the almost exclusive—but by no means monotonous—concern of the second edition. As previously stated and as we shall show below, many of these modifications are a direct result of the new experiences and awarenesses gained by the poet during his years (1948–55) of travels, sojourns, lectures, and readings in his native Colombia and in other American republics. At the same time they reflect Artel's determination to demonstrate more openly and unequivocally his literary identity as a genuine, unqualifiedly black singer of Afro-America, and his unfailing commitment to a liberatory poetics of black expression. This determination, I submit, was also motivated, in part, by the critical reaction to the poems of the 1940 edition—and especially by the comments of Nicolás Guillén—discussed in the previous chapter.

Doubtless, the 1955 edition diverges considerably from the 1940 edition, both thematically and stylistically. At the same time, however, the book continues and, at times, amplifies themes, motifs, symbols, and stylistic elements either overtly presented or subtly and indirectly suggested in the earlier book and in later writings, while also exploring new concerns of topical importance. The remainder of this chapter will examine the major concerns, motifs, and elements of the new poems and show how they relate to previously considered elements of the earlier edition, to Artel's travel experiences, and to his untiring efforts to probe the deep, emotional wellspring of black life and culture in order to discover and render artistically the spiritual dimension of the African heritage in America—a dimension that other Latin American poets often failed to perceive and appreciate.

(Re)Affirming Black Identity and the African Heritage

(Re)affirmation of black identity and the African heritage in the second *Tambores en la noche* is immediately noticeable in Artel's placement of his signature poem "Negro soy" at the outset of the book. Although less explicit than "Negro soy," several of the new poems also emphasize the poet's determination to project, without apology or animus, without apprehension or acrimony, a decidedly racial perspective. It is fitting that the section of new compositions testifying to Artel's long odyssey opens with the poem "Noche del Chocó" [Night of the Chocó]. Occupying the northwestern part of Colombia's Pacific coast, the Chocó has long been an area noted for its vast mineral wealth, its heavy rains, and its overwhelmingly Negroid population. At the same time, it has been one of Colombia's most isolated and neglected areas, cut off from much of the rest of the nation by high mountains, thick jungle, and a lack of good roads. Quibdó, the capital of the department (which was an *intendencia* until the 1940s), was one of the last cities Artel visited before departing Colombia in 1948 (see Lozano Garcés). Though brief, his stay there no doubt enhanced and sharpened his awareness of Africa's legacy in Colombia. "Noche del Chocó" evokes the emotional impressions of his journey, allowing Artel to convey some of the beauty and grandeur as well as afflictions and suffering that characterize the region and its people.[11]

Although recollection of Africa has also faded in the memory of the black people of the Chocó, their musical and popular traditions (*currulaos, velorios, cortejos fluviales*), perhaps even more than the African-inspired traditions of the Atlantic coast, attest to the continuation of the vital African cultural heritage of Colombia. With words reminiscent of earlier poems, Artel affirms this presence in the first stanza of the poem:

> En tus currulaos,
> tus velorios y tus cortejos fluviales,
> se prolongan los ritos,
> como voces perdidas,
> que hablan a mi raza
> del primitivo espanto frente a la eternidad. (77)

[In your currulaos [dances], / your wakes and your fluvial processions, / the rites are extended, / like lost voices, / that speak to my race / of the primitive fright in the face of eternity.]

Writing from without his country and emboldened with a deeper knowledge of Afro-Colombia and a more acute yet unobtrusive social consciousness, Artel does not fail to note the perennial abandonment and deafening desolation that the Chocó, forgotten by much of the nation, suffers. Even the surrounding jungle or thick forest seems to act as an accomplice to underdevelopment, restricting the range of human aspiration, vision, and hope. Indeed, in the Chocó nature and human life are intimately and inextricably joined, as Artel discovered:

> El ensueño limita con la selva,
> la mirada limita con la selva,
> la esperanza limita con la selva,
> cuyos árboles nacen en la sangre
> y aferran sus raíces a la vida del hombre. (78)

[Dream is bounded by the jungle,/ vision is bounded by the jungle, / hope is bounded by the jungle, / whose trees are born in the blood and anchor their roots to human life.]

Deftly and cogently Artel captures this union of nature and humanity in the Chocó by giving the region's principal river a somber human face ("rostro sombrío"):

> Tus horas son profundas y remotas
> como el rostro sombrío del Quidbó,
> constantemente flagelado
> por el azote de la lluvia,
> electrizada de resplandores dramáticos. (78)

[Your hours are deep and remote / like the somber face of the Quibdó, / constantly scourged / by the lash of the rain, / electrified with dramatic flashes.]

With this subtle personification Artel simultaneously insinuates the gloomy, dismal abandonment of the Chocó, on the one hand, and the dark color of the region's inhabitants, on the other. Furthermore, the metaphor of the rain as a whip on the river's face not only suggests the cruelty of nature—i.e., the pluvious conditions of the Chocó—but may also be seen as a subtle allusion to the harshness of slavery days and of contemporary life. This metaphorical process recalls the simultaneous description of the boat-ridden coast and the whiplashed brown backs in "Mi canción" (see chapter 5).

As one might surmise from the titles "Noche del Chocó" and *Tambores en la noche,* and from references in other poems, night is an especially significant and alluring time within the poet's lyrical vision. While tradition often associates the obscurity of night with the mysterious and the frightful, in Artel's poems it acts more as a means of reaffirming the faces of African-American peoples and the presence of sacred, ancestral spirits. The vastness and depth of the Chocó night symbolically darkens and mirrors, at the same time, the blackness of the inhabitants, strengthening their union with the cosmos:

> Noche del Chocó, maestra de estrellas y silencios!
>
> .   .   .   .
>
> sobre la piel del habitante
> extiendes tu sombra,
> impregnada de misterios. (78–79)

[Night of the Chocó, teacher of stars and silences! /

. . . .

on the skin of the inhabitant / you extend your shadow, / saturated with mysteries.]

Artel also employs this imagistic process of racial identification in the initial lines of another poem, "Encuentro" [Encounter]:

> La sombra de los tiempos
> calca, en taciturnos ébanos, tu rostro,
> hombre oscuro del Sur. (117)

[The shadow of the ages / traces, / in taciturn ebonies, / your face, / dark man of the South.]

Use of the shadow metaphor enables the poet to project and emphasize human blackness in a subtle yet admirably artistic manner that confirms a profound poetic quality.

In "Soneto más negro" [Blacker Sonnet] Artel also affirms and revaluates blackness in a highly original way. As a European-created verse form of the learned and privileged classes, the sonnet may be regarded as emblematic of Eurocentric (white) culture and tastes, inscribed in the nonpopular poetic tradition. Indeed, for many the sonnet is a model of poetic competence (Marchese and Forradellas 390). Mastery of the form, therefore, attests to a poet's consummate skill and talent, especially with respect to intense concentration (Baehr 390). While Artel's poem clearly demonstrates such mastery, it also transgresses traditional boundaries of thought by subverting the longstanding, stereotypical association of blackness with ugliness, the uninspiring, the benighted, as the two quatrains show:

> Tambor, lágrima errante, a la deriva!
> conjuro voduísta del Caribe,
> tu alma torturada y sensitiva
> se pierde en el silencio que la inhibe.
>
> Desde el transfondo oceánico, intuitiva,
> mi dársena sonora te percibe
> y me llega tu luz mucho más viva
> y es más negro el soneto que se escribe. (99)

[Drum, wandering teardrop, adrift! / voodooistic conjuration of the Caribbean, / your tortured and sensitive soul / is lost in the silence that inhibits it.

From the oceanic background, intuitive, / my resonant inner harbor perceives you / and your light reaches me much brighter / and the sonnet that is written is blacker.]

As the light emanating from the drum—symbol of African culture—reaches the poet's inner self, it becomes brighter; paradoxically, the sonnet created around the African instrument is darker. That is, the illuminating presence of the drum and the clear message it emits grow more intense as the poet's own soul becomes attuned to the instrument's sound and significance. Like the earth that gave life to the tree from which the tambour emerged, the spiritual immanence of the drum makes the poem psychically richer, fuller, and darker. By encasing a decidedly African experience (the Atlantic slave trade and American slavery) within a traditionally European frame; that is, by using a "white" poetic form to project in a positive manner a unique, defining circumstance of blackness in America, Artel also seems to suggest the existence of a vital, submerged black presence within outwardly white cultural expressions. The following verses from "Poema sin odios ni temores" certainly seem to support this idea:

Aunque muchos te ignoren
yo sé que vives, y despierto
cantas aún las tonadas nativas,
ocultas en los ritmos disfrazados de blanco. (141)

[Although many may not know you / I know that you live, and awake / you sing still the native airs, / hidden in the rhythms disguised as white.]

In this way, too, Artel subtly represents the inexorable, omnipresent reality of *mestizaje* in New World culture, and the African presence that dwells within it.[12]

The African Presence and Heritage in America

Song

> They that walked in darkness sang songs in the olden
> days—Sorrow Songs—for they were weary at heart.
> W. E. B. Du Bois

As in the earlier edition of *Tambores en la noche,* manifestations of the presence and heritage of Africa in America (e.g., song, dance, music) inform many of the poems of the 1955 book. In the latter, however, such manifestations are overtly and unambiguously linked with the

African cultural inheritance. By virtue of numerous references, song occupies a central place in the poems and plays a significant role in Artel's work.[13] According to two scholars of African-American history, song was the "most frequently used musical form" of traditional African societies (Franklin and Moss 22). This black song, however, is not loud, empty, rhythmic utterance, but rather an unrestrained expression—at times joyous, at times sad—of a people's ancient and proud cultural identity. In Artel, song, like dance, is clearly tied to African origins, as the tercets of "Soneto más negro" show:

> Febril impulso tu hontanar eleva,
> en proceloso vértigo me lleva
> hacia pueblos hundidos en la sombra,
>
> donde vierten los cánticos su oscura
> emanación de hechizo y de locura
> sobre una voz remota que me nombra.

[Febrile impulse your wellspring raises, / in tempestuous vertigo it carries me / toward villages sunk in the shadow,

where the songs pour their dark / emanation of magic and madness / on a distant voice that names me.]

Song, therefore, serves as an identifying trait of peoples of African descent in the Americas. In "Encuentro" Artel reminds his U.S. African-American brethren that "Nuestros corazones arden / en las brasas del canto" [Our hearts burn / in the coals of song] (117).

Song in Artel's poems further signifies free, spontaneous, and uninhibited expression of the black self. This is particularly evident in the composition "Yanga," a paean to the maroon chieftain of seventeenth-century Mexico who led his people to freedom. For Artel, whose own happy and rewarding experiences in Mexico seem to permeate the sentiments of the poem, the rebel slave embodies those qualities of character that made successful the maroons' enterprise of resistance and restored to them their voice:

> Varón insobornable,
> por quien los tristes y perseguidos
> de tu raza recuperaron el sol y las canciones,
> y pusieron a crecer la historia, como un árbol. (136)

[Incorruptible man, / through whom the sad and persecuted / of your race recovered the sun and the songs, / and set history to grow, like a tree.]

In this context the songs symbolize the traditions, values, and mores linking the uprooted Africans to their native lands and ancestral cultures. Although they are unable to return to their maternal homelands, recovery of voice and reproduction of song enable the self-liberated Africans to maintain and express a significant measure of their culture and to inscribe themselves as authentic, self-determined agents in humanity's struggle for freedom:

> Tu nombre, oh, Yanga,
> siempre recordará que somos libres!

> [Your name, oh Yanga, / will always be a reminder that we are free!] (136)

Of course the mention of sun and song in "Yanga" also recalls the earlier discussion of Artel's "Meridiano de Bogotá" and Hughes's "Our Land" (chapter 5). Here, too, the absence of sun and song, symbolically implicit in the gloomy and repressive ordeal of slavery, connotes deprivation of warmth, protection, and life; separation of the Africans from the joyfulness of family and home and the sacredness of their land.

For enslaved Africans, as lines from the poem "La ruta dolorosa" [The Painful Route] state, "destiny united / the song with the whip" ["unió el destino / la canción con el látigo"] (101). Similarly, in "Canción en tiempo de porro" [Song in Porro Time] we also find sorrow and music intimately joined:

> Oigo llegar en el viento,
> salpicado de rumores,
> una mezcla de lamento
> con resonar de tambores. (88)

> [I hear arriving in the wind, / sprinkled with murmurs, / a mixture of lament / with resounding of drums.]

In the face of untold hardship and suffering, the element of song in *Tambores en la noche* also appears as a creative, spiritual act through which enslaved Africans and their descendants have endured oppression and voiced their pain. As critic bell hooks observes,

> Cultural production and artistic expressiveness were also ways for displaced persons to maintain connections with the past. Art was necessary to bring delight, pleasure and beauty into lives that were hard, that were materially deprived. It mediated the harsh conditions of poverty and servitude. (*Yearning* 105).

The following verses from "La voz de los ancestros," one of the key poems in the 1940 edition, also bear this out:

Una doliente humanidad se refugiaba
en su música oscura de vibrátiles fibras. . . .
—Anclados a su dolor anciano
iban cantando por la herida . . . — (1940: 37)

[A suffering humanity took refuge/ in their dark music of vibratile fibers. . . . /—Anchored to their ancient pain / they went singing through the hurt . . . —]

Indeed, suffering amidst work and song, as Artel discovered during his visit to Barlovento (Venezuela), often defined the Afro-American's life: "El negro vive su vida. / Pesca. Sufre. Canta" [The Negro lives his life. / He fishes. He suffers. He sings] (82). Even for black people in the great metropolis of North America, as Artel recalls in "Palabras a la ciudad de Nueva York" [Words to the City of New York], song afforded refuge:

Te hablo, Nueva York

. . . .

desde cualquier rincón de Harlem,
la orgullosa humanidad que espera y canta
refugiada en sus blues de sarcástica tristeza (120–21).

[I speak to you, New York

. . . .

from any corner of Harlem, / the proud humanity that waits and sings / sheltered in its blues of sarcastic sadness.]

Work Song

Another mode of singing that reappears in two new poems of the later edition of *Tambores en la noche* is the work song tradition of Africa. Although less prominent than in the earlier composition "Barrio abajo," the custom of uniting song with work achieves in the poems "Palenque" [Maroon Village] and "Alto Congo" [Upper Congo] a more original and sophisticated expression. In "Palenque" Artel realizes this originality by using zeugma, a rhetorical device by which he applies to two objects—in this case, corn (*maíz*) and song (*canción*)—a verb (*cultivar*) that usually and semantically governs only one of them. The old patriarch ("aquel abuelo") of the former maroon settlement,

Apoyado en el crepúsculo
contempla a las mujeres
cultivar el maíz y la canción . . .

[Leaning on the twilight of day / contemplates the women / cultivating corn and song . . .]

In "Alto Congo" the poet imagines himself on the central African river in a boat propelled by ten black rowers whose synchronized, harmonious rhythm delivers only one stroke in the water ["un solo golpe en el agua"] (95). As the men row, they also sing—"Los hombres cantan y reman" (96), thus exemplifying and carrying on the work song tradition. Stanza five offers a cumulative summation of the simultaneous actions of the boatmen—shouting, rowing, singing—who work and chant in unison:

Un grito unánime junta
ritmo, golpe, canto y remo.
Uno solo. (96)

[A unanimous shout unites / rhythm, stroke, song and oar. / Just one.]

So strong is the poet's identification with the harmony, rhythm, and strength of the African boatmen that he can easily imagine their country to be his own (i.e., ancestral) homeland and envision himself as one of them:

Esta pudo ser mi patria
y yo uno de estos remeros! (96)

[This could be my land / and I one of these rowers!]

The ease with which Artel is able to place himself in this African setting derives from his personal identification with the river boatmen (*bogas*) of Colombia, whom he esteemed and regarded as his forebears. To reconfirm this association we need only turn to the final metaphorical lines of "La voz de los ancestros":

Oigo galopar los vientos,
temblores de cadena y rebelión,
mientras yo—Jorge Artel—
galeote de un ansia suprema
hundo remos de angustias en la noche. (1940: 17)

189

[I hear the galloping of winds, / tremblings of chain and rebellion, / while I—Jorge Artel— / galley slave of a supreme longing / sink oars of anguish into the night.]

Here the word *galeote,* meaning galley slave, invokes an image of a captive condemned to labor on an oar in a sailing ship, not unlike the drudgery of poling *bongos* and *champanes* that enslaved Africans were forced to perform on the Magdalena and other rivers.[14]

The Drum: Symbol and Substance

As explained in chapter 5, no other aspect of the African heritage dominates the first edition of *Tambores en la noche* as does the drum. This also holds true for the 1955 volume, as evidenced by the overt mention of the instrument, or indirect allusion to it, in twelve of the twenty-one new poems. In fact, several of the poems reiterate the drum motif and the sanctified role of the drummer, thereby reinforcing the poet's self-imposed responsibility as medium between the past and the present, between Africa and America. For example, in "El lenguaje misterioso" [The Mysterious Language], which contains a rare, and yet restrained, instance of onomatopoeia ("—Dum . . . dum . . . dum . . . !"), Artel characterizes the drums as "liturgical" (93). In this way he restores to them the ceremonial significance and hallowed position they enjoyed in traditional African and Afro-American societies (Aretz 199) and symbolically removes them from easy reach of those versifiers who would attempt to exploit them without respecting and appreciating their sanctified role within the religions and cultures of those societies.

For Artel, a poet fiercely proud and keenly aware of his African heritage, the drum is a sacred instrument. Therefore, one must render to it a profound and sincere respect, and not treat it frivolously. Understandably, he who plays the drum has been chosen and trained to perform an important role in the life of the community, not unlike that of an acolyte or a priest. Therefore, in Artel's poetry the drummer takes on, at times, the attributes and powers of a divinity. We need only recall, for example, the poem "La cumbia," wherein the drummers ("tamborileros") are described as "new sleepwalking gods who ring out joy" ["sonámbulos dioses nuevos que repican alegría"] and who "learned to make thunder with their knotted, all powerful hands" ["aprendieron a hacer el trueno con sus manos nudosas, todopoderosas"] (1940: 23–24).

"Al 'drummer' negro de un Jazz-Session" [To the Black Drummer of a Jazz Session], which is based on a performance that Artel witnessed in New York, reinforces the image of the percussion player as divine being. The drummer is surrounded by "sinister archangels" ["arcángeles siniestros"] (109) and his arms, in constant motion, are "two restless wings / sunken in a cosmos of bronzes and cowbells" ["dos alas zozobrantes / hundidas en un cosmos / de bronces y cencerros"]. At the musician's feet,

> Los árboles caen . . .
> con sus cantos y sus nidos,
> levantando un estrépito hasta el cielo. (110)

[The trees fall . . . / with their songs and their nests, / raising an uproar to the sky.]

The drummer's "demonic" movements stir the poet to imagine dynamic, mythic scenes of the African bush that might well inspire and explain the impassioned and frenzied outpouring of so much kinetic energy:

> El jabalí, furioso, te persigue
> y a su paso despiertan elefantes,
> grises hipopótamos,
> hambrientos cocodrilos.
> Cien guerreros jóvenes te buscan
> con sus rostros pintados
> y sus lanzas sedientas.
> Aullan los chacales,
> el rinoceronte ruge.
> Cien guerreros jóvenes te buscan
> y gira entre sus pies,
> sonámbula, la tierra. (110)

[The wild boar, furious, pursues you / and in its passing elephants, / gray hippopotamuses, / hungry crocodiles awake. / A hundred young warriors seek you / with their faces painted / and their spears thirsty. / The jackals howl, / the rhinoceros roars. / A hundred young warriors seek you / and between their feet / the earth, sleepwalking, whirls.]

All of these images, when combined with the first two lines of the last strophe—

> En la emoción yoruba de tus manos
> estalla una tormenta! (111)

[In the Yoruba emotion of your hands / a torment breaks forth!]—

make for a powerful ritualistic evocation of the Yoruba deity (or *orisha*) Shangó, god of thunder and lightning. So potent and moving is the music created by the drummer's hands that a storm of rhythm erupts from within them.

I must point out here that Artel incorporates wild African animals not for an exotic effect, but to create a vivid impression of a mythic and mysterious reality, consistent with his vision of a distant and traditional African homeland (which might also have been influenced by films and readings). Taken together, the presence of vegetable, animal, human, and celestial elements project and enhance the image of power and authority that the drummer-deity exercises on these various worlds and kingdoms and even on the earth itself. In "Al 'drummer' negro de un Jazz Session," as in other poems we have seen, Artel again pays homage to the deeper, spiritual dimension of black creativity, which, paradoxically, has too often been muffled or overshadowed by the excitement and merriment that very creativity (e.g., the drummer, the dancer) produces and inspires. Interestingly, the final lines of the poem—"y la noche ha sentido / el peso de la selva" [and the night has felt / the weight of the jungle]—recall somewhat the last verses of "Dancing": "Un pedazo de selva cayó en el salón!" [A piece of jungle fell into the ballroom!] The jazz drummer's furious, cosmic playing evokes the drumming of ancient African peoples who dwelled in the jungle or bush. The beating of the drums, however, does not exalt the primitive for its own sake, but rather emphasizes the continuity of the dynamic presence and creative heritage of black Africa in yet another geographical and cultural arena of America. Both the sophisticated black percussionist of the jazz session and the empirical drummers of the popular musical groups of Cartagena's barrios offer eloquent testimony to that presence and heritage.

For many traditional African peoples and also for Artel, to play the drum is a privilege and an honor. It is also, however, an art that must be mastered to perfection because the instrument is the sacred vehicle of communication with the ancestors and deities. If the drummer errs, the communication also fails and the musician may suffer the symbolic and fatal penalty described in the poem "Superstición" [Superstition]:

> Le cercenaron las manos
> porque dio una nota falsa.
> Qué ley tan terrible aquella
> del tamborero de Africa! (113)
>
> . . . .
>
> Que van sus manos en pena,

como llamas angustiadas
redoblando los tambores
más allá de las montañas. . . .

Y a todos hieren muy hondo
sutiles garfios de hielo
si rugen las sordas voces
de algún tambor en el viento. . . . (115)

[They cut off his hands / because he made a false note. / What a terrible
law that / of the drummer of Africa! /

. . . .

His suffering hands go, / like anguished flames / rolling the drums way
beyond the mountains . . .

And all are wounded deeply by subtle icy hooks / if the
    muffled voices / of some drum rumble in the wind. . . .]

Insistence on the ritual significance and the symbolic and ancestral value of
the African-descended drum finds especially unique expression in the poem
"Soneto más negro," cited above. The first verse of this beautiful and moving
sonnet demonstrates clearly the poet's ability to see beyond the shallow,
insensitive imitation of the drum beating in much *negrista* verse, and to
form more profound associations. The initial line—

Tambor, lágrima errante, a la deriva! (99)

[Drum, wandering teardrop, adrift!]—

is also a masterful example of verbal synthesis and metaphorical concentration. In just six words the poet has created a bold image evoking the painful
history of African peoples in America—exploited, scorned, oppressed—and
symbolizing the diaspora that left the African bondmen lost and adrift in the
New World, far from the maternal lands and cultures from which they were
so violently uprooted.[15]

Furthermore, by using apostrophe to address the drum directly, Artel
personifies the instrument, thereby endowing it with human qualities, which,
in turn, enhances its significance as a viable symbol of the living spiritual
and cultural presence of Africa in America. At the same time, use of this
rhetorical device also serves to intensify the poet's own reverence for the
sacred instrument:

conjuro voduísta del Caribe,
tu alma torturada y sensitiva
se pierde en el silencio que la inhibe.

Desde el transfondo oceánico, intuitiva,
mi dársena sonora te percibe
y me llega tu luz mucho más viva
y es más negro el soneto que se escribe.

[voodooistic conjuration of the Caribbean, / your tortured and sensitive soul / is lost in the silence that inhibits it.

From the oceanic background, intuitive / my resonant inner harbor perceives you / and your light reaches me much brighter / and the sonnet that is written is blacker.]

Although the music of the drum often has been submerged into silence by the cruel repression of slavery and the slave trade and by the inexorable passage of time, the poet's own intuitive, inner being, made more sensitive by his identity as a coastal native, is able to discern and apprehend the music.

Notwithstanding the difficulty posed by the individual metaphors and images, the significance of the verses is clear and consistent with Artel's earlier representation of the drum as repository of the prolific legacy of Africa in America. It is also consistent with his efforts to transcend the trite, superficial, and noisy creations purported to be black poetry, but that too often merely perpetuated old, harmful stereotypes. Especially noteworthy in this regard is the contrast between the inhibiting silence ("silencio que inhibe") and the resounding inner harbor ("dársena sonora") of the poetic voice. As in "Tambores en la noche," "Ahora hablo de gaitas," and other earlier poems, Artel emphasizes in "Soneto más negro" the individual's internal music or intuitive power, which, penetrating the stifling silence imposed from without, is able to reach and reestablish contact with the lost group heritage or collective unconscious. Thus the poem also reinforces Artel's contention that the black poet who seeks to fulfill the mission of reconnecting the present generations with the past must necessarily be a select spirit.

For Artel the drum is a potent representation and symbol of the beliefs, experiences, and identity of the Afro-American. It also serves, however, as a continuous source of inspiration, allowing the poet to explore in depth the heart and soul of his people. The presence of the drum throughout many of Artel's other new poems (e.g., "Barlovento," "Canción en tiempo de porro," "La ruta dolorosa," "Palabras a la ciudad de Nueva York," "Playa de Varadero") creates a recurrent motif whose silent reverberations suggest a deeply painful longing, a distant remembrance of Africa, which informs and stirs the soul. For that reason the overt sound of the drum continues to be less perceptible in Artel's verse than in much of the *negrista* literature written up to that time. Within Artel's decidedly racial aesthetic, the drum is neither a toy for children nor, as he states in "Negro soy," a "decorative jewel / for tourists" (14). Indeed, for this proud, Afro-Colombian poet, the frequent mention and the all too often capricious, onomatopoeic exploitation of the drum for the purpose of sonorous and rhythmic effects have obfuscated or distorted the cultural significance and function of black poetic expression in Colombia and Spanish America. This distortion, in turn, has truncated the transcendental value of the drum as a "metaphor and symbol standing in both its secular and sacred forms not only for the immediate Black experience . . . , but for history and heritage and the acceptance of one's self in a positive and regenerating relationship to that heritage" (S. A. Williams 140–41).[16]

Fortunately, in Artel's second book the drum remains a constant and fecund "personal symbol," one that, to paraphrase Philip Wheelwright, has continuing vitality and relevance for the poet's imaginative and even actual life (202). Reverently and carefully played, the drum in Artel's poems evokes the anguish and the joy, the power and the beauty, and the dignity and the faith that underlie the history and culture of Afro-America. In so doing, it serves to remind the poet and his audience of the emotional wealth and spiritual strength that is the proud and true heritage of the African experience in the New World.

AFRICAN-AMERICAN EXPERIENCES: SLAVERY AND OPPRESSION

> Strictly speaking, Black slavery cannot yet be considered merely as a part of the Latin American past.
>
> Germán Carrera Damas 23

In the first *Tambores en la noche,* it will be recalled, the drama of slavery is largely hinted at, rather than directly depicted. That is, through the constant allusions to hurt and nostalgia, the reference to captive hands and ancestral screams, and the image of winds throwing themselves into the sea, Artel recreates the emotional turmoil of deracination, exile, and loss that the Africans and their descendants endured as a result of displacement, the Middle Passage, and subsequent enslavement in America. Similarly, as some of Artel's critics pointed out, references to contemporary Afro-American problems are virtually absent from the 1940 book.

Diverging substantially from that approach, the second *Tambores en la noche* abounds in elements that not only reveal a more direct and assertive

confrontation with the slavery experience, but also—and often simultaneously—inveigh against racial prejudice, discrimination, and injustice in the
contemporary world. For example, whereas in "La voz de los ancestros" the
poet identifies himself as a descendant of slaves and imaginatively envisions
the vessels of the port as "the sorrowful ships wherein perhaps came those
who could be our grandparents" (1940: 36), in "La ruta dolorosa" [The
Sorrowful Route] he himself becomes one of the millions of slaves who
endured the transatlantic journey. Addressing the unnamed man of the
Caribbean ("Hombre de los crepúsculos flotantes"), the poetic voice inquires:

> En qué salto de la sangre
> tú y yo nos encontramos
> o en qué canción yoruba nos mecimos
> juntos, como dos hermanos?

> Lo sabrán los mástiles remotos
> de la galera que nos trajo,
> el Congo impenetrable
> donde nuestros abuelos transitaron. (102)

[In what leap of blood / do you and I meet / or in what Yoruba song do
we rock ourselves / together, like two brothers?

The remote masts / of the galley that brought us, / and the impenetrable
Congo / where our forefathers traveled, must know.]

Here mention of the slave ship produces a greater sense of immediacy and
pathos via the personal involvement of the poetic voice.

Other lines from the poem also attest to a more overt and direct confrontation with the legacy of slavery, as the penultimate stanza shows:

> No ves en mis palabras
> el tatuaje del látigo,
> no intuyes las cadenas
> y los tambores lejanos? (103)[17]

[Do you not see in my words / the tatoo of the whip, / do you not intuit
the chains / and the distant drums?]

Of the three objects mentioned above—whip, chains, drums—the first two
pertain directly to involuntary servitude, while the third alludes more to

the disjunction occasioned by the slave trade. "Chains," or more precisely its singular form "chain" ("cadena"), already appears in "La voz de los ancestros": "temblores de cadena y rebelión" (1940: 37). Within that earlier context, the mention of the shackles signals an unmistakable reference to the odious commerce in human beings.

With the poem "El mismo hierro" [The Same Brand], however, Artel gives an ironic and original twist to the chains motif.[18] That which has been historically an instrument of control and restraint and a sign of bondage is transformed into a symbol of common heritage and experience that, transcending time and space, serves to bind peoples of African descent throughout the Americas. "El mismo hierro," one of two poems inspired by the flagrant injustice and indignities endured by black people in the United States, expresses the poet's emotional encounter with the characteristic anguish of the Afro-American soul. The unnatural inequity that Artel witnessed is vividly yet simply stated in the opening stanza:

> Este sol que ahora baña
> los campos de la tierra
> se le niega a otros hombres
> en el hogar de América. (105)

[This sun that now bathes / the fields of the earth / is denied to other men / in the hearth of America.]

Recollections of separate waiting rooms, of the "poison of sadness" debuting in the eyes of the children, and of the taboo of the white woman move the poet to testify:

> He visto perseguirlos como fieras,
> lincharlos,
> sin que importe su afiebrada queja
> ni su muerte en los pantanos. (106)

[I have seen them hunted down like wild animals, / lynched, / with neither their feverish lament / nor their death in the swamps making a difference.]

It is precisely in the anguish and suffering of segregation and degradation, however, that the poet discovers the common, inexorable linkage between himself and the black humanity of North America:

> Este sol que ahora baña
> los campos de la tierra

197

se le niega a otros hombres
en el hogar de América . . .

Y sin embargo,
un hierro idéntico eslabona
aquel dolor de siglos
que asciende a nuestros labios. (106)

[This sun that now bathes / the fields of the earth / is denied to other men / in the hearth of America . . .

And yet, / an identical brand links / that pain of centuries / that ascends to our lips.]

Allusion to the stinging whip, the other slavery-related element mentioned in "La ruta dolorosa," also appears in the 1940 book. There, however, the connections with African bondage are less precise, or more ambiguous. For example, in "Mi canción" we find not "*látigo*" but "*fusta*," which can refer to a long and slender whip used by teamsters to drive their horses on, as well as to a small, lateen-rigged boat with one or two oars:

Una playa foeteada
como espaldas morenas,
por las fustas ardientes,
y un pedazo de mar—hermano mayor
que me enseñó a ser rebelde—,
me dieron la canción. (1940: 227)

[A beach lashed / like brown backs, / by the red hot boats [whips], / and a piece of sea—older brother / who taught me to be a rebel—, / gave me the song.]

Although the two meanings aptly fit the context of the poem, the subordinated simile ("like brown backs") reinforces the superiority of the marine image. Nevertheless, by adeptly exploiting the dual meaning of *fusta* and other words (see the discussion of "*rostro sombrío*" in "Noche del Chocó" above), Artel is able to convey simultaneously to the discerning reader two situations of black coastal life: the everyday reality of the warm fishing coast and the brutal experience of slavery. To the less perceptive reader, however, perhaps accustomed to a more patent, less demanding representation of black experience, Artel's poetics of metaphorical ambiguity has meaning on only the obvious or literal level.[19]

On the other hand, mention of the whip ("*látigo*") in "La ruta dolorosa" and other new compositions is unquestionably and clearly associated with the inhumane treatment—physical and otherwise—inflicted upon African slaves and their descendants. The following lines from "Encuentro" [Encounter], the second poem resulting directly from Artel's observations of degraded black life in the southern United States, also bear this out:

> He aprendido a sentir
> la mirada larga y azul del hombre blanco
> cayendo sobre mi carne
> como un látigo. (118)

> [I have learned to feel / the long blue gaze of the white man / falling upon my flesh / like a whip.]

By inserting in a contemporary context an instrument commonly associated with the historical experience of black subjugation in America, Artel exemplifies the continuous pattern of domination, hatred, and fear that characterized racial relations in mid-twentieth-century United States. This pattern is further substantiated by the poet's ironic likening of the ignominious Jim Crow signs to "lacerating tatoos" ("tatuajes lacerantes"), a process that transfigures a common skin decoration among seafarers into the agonizing mark or wound made by the slave master's whip:[20]

> Ya puedo interpretar la tristeza de túnel
> que envuelve a los que aguardan bajo aquellos letreros,
> como tatuajes lacerantes,
> con los labios plegados
> y en el cerrado puño
> todo el silencio de las horas.

> [Now I can interpret the tunnel sadness / that envelops those who wait beneath those signs, / like lacerating tatoos, / with their lips folded / and in their clenched fist / all the silence of the hours.]

Although they do not sear or scar the flesh, the Jim Crow signs perpetuate the indignity and injustice of the slave past, and, in so doing, tear at the souls of black people.

In light of these observations, both the previously cited verses from "La ruta dolorosa" as well as other lines from the poem acquire even greater significance. Thus when Artel asks

CHAPTER 7

No escuchas cimbreantes sicomoros
creciéndome en la voz;
no miras en mis plantas el cansancio
de infinitas arenas
atándome los pasos?

. . . .

No ves en mis palabras
el tatuaje del látigo,
no intuyes las cadenas
y los tambores lejanos? (102–03)

[Do you not hear the swaying sycamore trees / growing in my voice; / do you not observe on my feet the fatigue / of infinite sands / tying my steps?

Do you not see in my words / the tatoo of the whip, / do you not intuit the chains / and the distant drums?]

he seems to be addressing those critics who, like a modern doubting Thomas, either failed to appreciate the social implications and racial foundations of his poetry or denied his standing as a black poet. In fact, further interrogation of this and other poems reveals a strong intertextuality with Holy Scripture.[21] For example, referring to his poetry ("mis palabras" above) Artel does not use the verb *oír* [hear], but *ver* [see]. While the former is consonant with aural comprehension, as in a recital, the latter pertains to visual apprehension, as in the printed page of a book. Significantly, it is precisely through the sense of sight that the resurrected Christ convinced His incredulous disciples of His presence: "*Behold* my hands and my feet; that it is I myself: handle me, and *see;* for a spirit hath not flesh and bones, *as ye see* me have" (Luke 24: 39; emphasis added).[22]

The title of "La ruta dolorosa" also pertains to New Testament texts and offers yet another example of Artel's art of creative ambiguity. On the one hand, phrases such as "islas de alcohol y tabaco" [islands of alcohol and tobacco], "océanos de plomo / sobre rutas de espanto" [oceans of lead / on routes of terror], and "la galera que nos trajo" [the galley which brought us], confirm a reference to the inhumane and excruciatingly torturous experience of the Middle Passage, by which captured Africans were brought to the New World. Also, the use of the adjective "*dolorosa*" reaffirms Artel's insistence on the ancestral pain originated in the slave trade and seared upon the soul of the African bondmen and their descendants. On the other hand, the title also evokes the Via Dolorosa, or Christ's route to Golgotha, a symbol of sublime suffering but also of the promise of resurrection. In effect, the imagery and vocabulary of "La ruta dolorosa" transmute the enslaved and tormented African into a messianic figure who, upon overcoming the trials and tribulations of bondage and in keeping the faith, leaves to his "followers" an enviable example of sacrifice, struggle, and triumph.[23] In this way too, Artel subverts the European-imposed practice of associating the demonic with the black African (see the discussion of *mandinga* in chapter 2).

The messianic tone of "La ruta dolorosa" becomes more evident in the poem's final verses, which bring to mind Christ's admonition to His disciples to take up the cross and follow Him (Matthew 16: 24):

> Toma tu canción y sígueme
> con su latido entre los labios,
> trasmutada la cruz en el acento
> de un grito liberado.

[Take your song and follow me / with its beat between your lips, / the cross now transformed into the accent / of a liberated shout.]

Here, however, the poet apostolically[24] urges his fellow Atlantic coast dweller ("Hombre del litoral") to pick up his own song (of blackness) and to follow him. By so doing, the descendant or follower of the slave-Christ figure will show his willing acknowledgment and acceptance of the African heritage that infuses the culture and people of the broad Caribbean Basin.

The last two lines quoted—"trasmutada la cruz en el acento / de un grito liberado"—also express a transformation of the Christian cross from a burden to be borne into a bold, unrestrained shout or assertion of freedom, marking the first step toward true and total liberation. Released from the fears and hatreds that repress it, the shout (*grito*) in Artel's new poems occurs primarily as a forceful sign of black struggle and identity, rather than as an expression of *costeñismo* and musical merriment, as is often the case in the earlier poems. Some examples that may be cited are: "gritos de rebelión," from "Encuentro" (117); "el aire fraternal de México / te devolvió tu grito," from "Yanga" (135); and "gritan, claman, lloran, cantan," from "Poema sin odios ni temores" (146). Further corroboration of the black-as-Christ figure is found in the poem "Playa de Varadero" [Varadero Beach], inspired by Artel's visit to Cuba in 1950. In its repudiation of the imposed segregation of the beach—

> de un lado negros
> y de otro lado mestizos,
> flor de albayalde que pone
> polvos de arroz a la raza! (131)[25]—

[on one side blacks / and on the other mestizos, / flower of white lead that puts / rice face powder on the race!]

the poem equates the despised blacks with the crucified Christ, who, as Scripture states, was mocked with the sign "INRI," meaning "*I*esus *N*azarenus, *Rex I*udaeorum" (Jesus of Nazareth, King of the Jews) (John 19: 19). Apostrophizing the divided beach, Artel laments:

> Sí, playa de Varadero,
> tan criolla y tan extraña!
> Cómo podrías oírme
> si mi voz americana,
> desde mi lado de negro
> —que es el lado que en mí canta—
> entre dos mares humanos
> sola en su angustia naufraga,
> mirando atrás a los míos
> bajo el INRI despiadado
> y al frente a quienes esconden,
> con vano empeño de castas,
> el mismo INRI, que llevan
> si no en la piel en el alma! (133–34)[26]

[Yes, Varadero Beach, / so native and so foreign! / How could you hear me / if my American voice, / from my black side / —which is the side that sings in me— / between two human seas / sinks alone in its anguish, / looking back at my people / beneath the merciless INRI / and ahead at those who hide, / with vain caste persistence, / the same INRI, they bear / if not on their skin in their soul!]

Artel's more militant and fearless depiction of the African slave past and of the repressive contemporary conditions of Afro-American peoples also finds expression in the less favorable delineation of white people. If the African slaves and their posterity are identified with the Christ, it is logical that their oppressors—that is, those who have inflicted upon them the horrors and violence of enslavement, segregation, and racial discrimination—are associated with the forces of evil. Thus a line in "La ruta dolorosa" speaks of "the diabolical presence of the white man" (102) in the Africa of the slave trade era. Similarly, Artel, possibly appalled by the wanton murder of young Emmett Till in Mississippi in 1954, points in "El mismo hierro" [The Same Brand] to the mortal danger that merely eyeing a white woman can pose for a black person: "Una mujer blanca / los arrastraría al cadalso / si ellos la miraran" (106) [A white woman would drag them to the scaffold if they were to look at her]. Notwithstanding these unflattering images of whites, Artel reserves his harshest condemnation for those who, out of fear or self-hatred, turn their back on blackness and seek to cover themselves with whiteness, as the verses from "Playa de Varadero" (above) and other poems soon to be discussed show.

New Visions of Traditional and Contemporary Africa

Although Artel's travels during the 1940s and 1950s were limited to countries of the Americas, his poetic vision and inspiration moved beyond the geographical confines of the Western Hemisphere to traditional and contemporary Africa. Indeed, a more tangible and pronounced emphasis on the continent—its peoples, rivers, flora, and fauna—is especially evident in this second edition of *Tambores en la noche*. Whereas in the earlier book, overt, indisputable mention of Africa occurs largely through the adjective "*africana*" (1940: 28, 74) or through metonymical association (e.g., jungle), several elements of the new edition indicate a closer approximation—both geographical and psychological—to the ancestral homeland. Immediately noticeable is the frequent and explicit use of the noun "*Africa*" in several poems:

> Ultimo patriarca de Palenque:
> Bien sabes
> que desde tus fogones crepitantes
> Africa envía sus mensajes! ("Palenque" 84)

[Last patriarch of Palenque: / you know well / that from your crackling fires / Africa sends its messages!]

> Tienen las notas denso sabor a noche,
> a lumbre viva de Africa. ("Barlovento" 82)

[The notes have a dense taste of night, / of intense fire of Africa.]

> Le cercenaron las manos
> porque dio una nota falsa.
> Qué ley tan terrible aquella
> del tamborero de Africa! ("Superstición" 113)

[They cut off his hands / because he made a false note. / What a terrible law that / of the drummer of Africa!]

> ... porque allí puso su risa
> con su angustia y su esperanza
> para que fueran testigos
> de la presencia de Africa. ("Playa de Varadero" 132)

[... because there [blackness] placed its laughter / with its anguish and its hope / so that they would be witnesses / to the presence of Africa.]

> Te habían robado al suelo de tu Africa,
> donde eras también el horizonte, el río y el camino.("Yanga" 135)

[They had stolen you from the soil of your Africa, / where you were also the horizon, the river, and the road.]

Reiteration of the continent's name, it should be noted, is not for sonorous or exotic effect. Rather, it contributes to a cogent evocation of traditional, unspoiled lands and cultures, which for Artel are the primary source of the emotional and spiritual power that motivates Afro-American peoples and their cultural manifestations.

Prominent also in this new focus on the African continent are specific toponyms (e.g., Brazzaville, Guinea, Angola, Mozambique, Algeria), rivers (Congo, Niger, Senegal, Zambesi), and cultural-linguistic entities (Yoruba, Congo, Bantu, *griot*) of Africa, all of which are unique to the 1955 book. There is even mention, as noted above, of indigenous animals, such as the hippopotamus, the crocodile, the jackal, and the rhinoceros. Again, none of these elements, I believe, is intended to create an exotic tone or to heighten acoustical effect, as occurs, for example, in the poems of Palés Matos (e.g., "Danza negra," "Bombo").[27] Rather, as presented in "La ruta dolorosa," "Palenque," "Alto Congo," "Superstición," "Al 'drummer' negro de un jazz-session," and "Poema sin odios ni temores," the geographical and zoological references usually serve to enhance the sense of authentic location and, more importantly, to acknowledge and strengthen the historical, cultural, and emotional links that not only unite the poet with ancestral traditions, but also bind Africans and Afro-Americans.

In two other poems, however—"Argeliana" [*sic*] [Algerian Girl][28] and "Mapa de Africa" [Map of Africa]—, attention to Africa's geography poignantly conveys not only the painful contemporary reality of the continent, suffering under colonialist domination and exploitation, but also Artel's awareness of and solidarity with African peoples' struggles for national sovereignty and independence. "Argeliana" communicates the sadness and loneliness of a young native woman of French-occupied Algeria who anxiously awaits the return of her beloved.

> Niña argeliana que suspiras
> por el amuleto perdido
> a la sombra de los dátiles,
> en un oasis del Sáhara;
> dulce pastora sin caricias
> bajo cuya piel aceitunada
> está esperando la sangre. (97)

[Algerian girl you who sigh / for the lost amulet / in the shade of the date trees, / in an oasis of the Sahara; / sweet shepherdess without caresses / beneath whose olive-colored skin / the blood is waiting.]

Specific topographical, racial, and cultural features (viz., Sahara desert oasis, date trees, olive-colored skin, amulet) help to create a vivid and convincing atmosphere of a North African reality. Against this background implications of foreign oppression and anticolonialist sentiment emerge:

> No importa si los soldados franceses te desean.
> Sólo piensas en el sueño nupcial
> que sugieren los trigales con sus altas espigas,
> en la promesa redonda del naranjo.
>
> Por qué no cambias la amargura
> por alegres collares de músicas,
> y danzas junto a los árboles
> donde un día maduraron las palabras?
>
> Hoy no quieres saber si eres hermosa.

[It doesn't matter if the French soldiers desire you. / You only think about the nuptial sleep / that the wheat fields with their high spikes suggest, / about the round promise of the orange tree.

Why don't you exchange the bitterness / for joyful necklaces of music, / and dance beside the trees / where one day the words grew ripe?

Today you do not wish to know if you are beautiful.]

Implicit in the young woman's refusal to trade her grief for jingling frills and to conceal or ignore her pain by engaging in entertaining dance is a deep sense of commitment and loyalty, not merely to her beloved but also to her people and herself. Her suffering cannot be assuaged with baubles and distractions. There can be no genuine joy or merrymaking while the painful injustice of colonialism, which may well have precipitated her lover's absence, continues to exist. Indeed, under such circumstances dancing and merrymaking are no longer authentic manifestations of individual or group sentiment, but become escapist acts of denial or of collaboration with the oppressor.[29]

"Mapa de Africa" confronts the reality of colonialism in a less romantic and more straightforward way. Written just a few years before the colonial Gold Coast achieved its independence in 1957 and reclaimed the name Ghana, the poem is a meditation on the continent's history and colonialized status, as represented by variously assigned colors. Remembering ancient kingdoms and bygone empires of sub-Saharan Africa, Artel asks rhetorically:

Qué fue de Ghana,
Songoi [sic], Hamasá, Fulki y Bambara? (138)

[What became of Ghana, / Songhai, Hamasá, Fulki y Bambara?]

Then contemplating the long Slave Coast, the poet cannot help but wonder if that area might be the lost homeland of his own ancestors:

Costa de los Esclavos
—tal vez mi tierra—
perdida en los submundos hiperbólicos del sueño!

[Slave Coast / —perhaps my land— / lost in the hyperbolic underworlds of dream!]

The configuration of the Atlas Mountains range, linking the colonialized countries of North Africa, creates an ironic image of concatenation

—cadena de montes, cadenas y cadenas!—

[mountain chain, chains and chains!]

which is not lost on the poet's sensibility. Exploiting the suggestion of confinement that the image suggests, he asks:

Por qué no soltar estas montañas [sic]

estas tierras, estas aguas,
estos picos, libres junto al cielo
y, sin embargo, presos, atados por un rótulo
brutal: "colonia"?

Cuándo podrán saltar estos colores,
tirar las letras—sus amarras—
que los clasifican como *posesiones*
y tomar su color, el único,
el verdadero color de Africa?

[Why not release these mountains(,) / these lands, these waters, / these peaks, near the sky free / and, nevertheless, imprisoned, tied by a brutal / label: "colony"?

When will they be able to skip these colors, / cast off these letters—their moorings— / which classify them as *possessions* / and take on their color, the only one, / the true color of Africa?] (Original emphasis)

Discerning the common experience of exploitation and pain shared by both colonialized and enslaved Africans and implicit in the reference to the branding iron, Artel ends the poem by expressing an urgent desire to see Africa free,

sin la marca,
puesta como un hierro candente,
sobre el lomo del mapa. (139)

[without the mark, / placed like a red-hot brand, / on the back of the map.][30]

MESTIZAJE AND BLACKNESS: DISCOURSE OF RECLAMATION AND LIBERATION

In reviving and reliving through his poetry the pain of slavery, and in raising his poetic voice against the evils of racism and colonialism, Artel sought not to create divisions or antagonisms but to forge a new consciousness of the African past and present; to foster acceptance of the spiritual and cultural significance of the African-American experience; and, concomitantly, to promote a stronger, prouder, integrated American identity based on an appreciation of its popular and too often despised roots. The implications of such a consciousness for the individual and collective Latin American psyche (and for the well-being of peoples of all the Americas) were obvious to Artel. Fearing, despising, and shunning the "shameful" past and degraded forebears only connoted a continued weakness of character, a false sense of security rooted in enslavement to whiteness and European ancestry, and an inability to actualize one's own potential and forge one's own destiny. On the other hand, confronting, comprehending, and embracing the black presence would contribute to a new sense of wholeness, self-confidence, and empowerment conducive to realizing substantive change and true liberation.

As I have shown elsewhere in this book, this vision of American culture and identity, which I choose to call a discourse of reclamation, reconciliation, and liberation, is inherent in much of Artel's poetry. No one poem, however, articulates Artel's racial poetics and his cultural-spiritualist approach to black literary expression as eloquently and forcefully as "Poema sin odios ni temores" [Poem without Hatreds or Fears]. The final piece of the 1955 edition of *Tambores en la noche,* "Poema sin odios ni temores" signifies the culmination of the poet's journeys, discoveries, and encounters—both real and imaginary—within the Afro-American world. It recapitulates the principal concerns and motifs that distinguish and inform his poetry: the affirmation of black identity and the reality of *mestizaje;* revaluation of the African heritage and remembrance and reverence of the ancestors; rejection of the ersatz, false "black" poetry and restoration of the sacred and ethnic value of the drum; emphasis on the redemptive pain of exile and slavery; and insistence upon universal brotherhood and the oneness of the human family. Composed in customary free verse, yet lucid and vigorously poetic language, "Poema sin odios ni temores" pays homage to the unique, prolific, and enriching presence of Africa in the Americas and reminds African-ancestored peoples (and others) of their invaluable contribution to the moral and spiritual development of the New World. In view of its significance, "Poema sin odios ni temores" is deserving of close examination.

The first stanza of the poem is an apostrophe to the departed Afro-Argentines, made all the more poignant and earnest by the references to specific aspects of black life and culture in the River Plate region, such as the *candombe* dance and the historically black areas of Buenos Aires:

Negro de los candombes argentinos,
bantú, cuya sombra colonial se esparce
quién sabe en cuáles socavones del recuerdo.
—Qué se hicieron los *barrios del tambor*?— (141)

[Black man of the Argentine candombes, / Bantu, whose colonial shadow disperses / in who knows what caverns of memory. / —What became of the *the drum quarters*?—][31]

Although most of the African element in the land of the tango is barely a memory, and its remnants often lie hidden, the poet discerns its voice alive in music (e.g., the tango) widely assumed to be of European origin.

> Aunque muchos te ignoren
> yo sé que vives, y despierto
> cantas aún las tonadas nativas,
> ocultas en los ritmos disfrazados de blanco. (142)[32]

[Though many may not know you / I know that you live, and awake / you sing still the native airs, / hidden in the rhythms disguised in white.]

The suggestion that the rhythms are merely disguised as white recalls Artel's early poem "Careta trágica," with its insinuation that the true identity is concealed behind the mask. Indeed, *mestizaje* and white appropriation have often masked the true origins of dances, music, language, and other cultural manifestations of African derivation, giving the impression that they are creations of people of European descent.[33]

In the second strophe Artel pays tribute to the indelible imprint of Africa upon the land and people of Brazil. Just as the anguish and hope of black laughter bear witness to the African presence in Cuba's "Varadero Beach" (132), the joys and sorrows of Afro-Brazilians—that is, the infectious merriment, profound pain, and mysterious magic implicit in their musical and religious expressions—have also made their nation strong and whole.

> Negro del Brasil,
> heredero de antiquísimas culturas,
> arquitecto de músicas,
> en el sortilegio de las macumbas
> surge la patria integral,
> robustecida por tus alegrías y tus lágrimas. (142)

[Black man of Brazil, / inheritor of most ancient cultures, / architect of music, / in the magic of the macumbas, / your country arises whole, / strengthened by your joys and your tears.]

Furthermore, by assuring these descendants of Africa that they are the legatees of venerable cultures, the poet also debunks the disparaging and false epithet of barbarism so often attached to Africa, and encourages the people to take pride in their heritage.

Turning his attention to black peoples of the Antilles, Panama, Colombia, Mexico, and, more generally, of all the southern coasts, the poet enjoins them—regardless of their mixed-race lineage—to rediscover and reclaim (together with him) their black heritage, and to apprehend and keep faith with the emotional consciousness that is their birthright:

> Negro de las Antillas,
> de Panamá, de Colombia, de México,
> de todos los surlitorales,
> —donde quiera que estés,
> no importa que seas nieto de chibchas,
> españoles, caribes o tarascos—
> si algunos se convierten en los tránsfugas,
> si algunos se evaden de su humano destino,
> nosotros tenemos que encontrarnos,
> intuir, en la vibración de nuestro pecho,
> la única emoción ancha y profunda,
> definitiva y eterna:
> somos una conciencia de América. (142)

[Black man of the Antilles, / of Panama, of Colombia, of Mexico, / of all the southern shores, / —wherever you may be, / whether you are the grandchild of Chibchas, / Spaniards, Caribs or Tarascans—/ if some become the turncoats, / if some flee from their human destiny, / we have to find ourselves, / to intuit, in the vibration of our breast, / the only wide and deep, definitive and eternal emotion: / we are a conscience of America.]

Artel emphasizes not merely the importance, but also the necessity, of African-descended peoples remembering, espousing, and learning to identify with the disdained, forgotten ancestries, since they alone, as history shows, are in a position to do so.

> Porque sólo nuestra sangre es leal
> a su memoria. Ni se falsifica ni se arredra
> ante quienes nos denigran
> o, simplemente, nos niegan. (142–43)

[Because only our blood is loyal / to its memory. It neither falsifies itself nor draws back / before those who denigrate us / or, simply, deny us.]

Foreshadowing Manuel Zapata Olivella's prize-winning novel *Changó, el gran putas* (1983), "Poema sin odios ni temores" strongly suggests here that what African-descended people carry in their blood (or soul)—that is, the active, emboldening spirit of the deceased ancestors—prevails and emerges true, even when others forget or betray the past.

Speaking, as Colombians would say, "sin pelos en la lengua" (i.e., without biting his tongue), Artel denounces the onerous and bitter shame internalized by so many descendants of enslaved Africans and degraded Amerindians:

> Esos que no se saben indios,
>
> o que no desean saberse indios.
>
> Esos que no se saben negros,
>
> o que no desean saberse negros.
>
> Los que viven traicionando su mestizo,
>
> al mulato que llevan—negreros de sí mismos—
>
> proscrito en las entrañas,
>
> envilecido por dentro. (143)

[Those who do not know themselves as Indian, / or who do not want to know it. / Those who do not know themselves as black, / or who do not want to know it. / Those who live betraying their mestizo, / the mulatto whom they—slave traders of themselves— / carry condemned in their marrow, / debased on the inside.]

This fervid condemnation of the opprobrious entombment of blackness reiterates and expands upon Artel's earlier rebuke of "those who hide, / with vain persistence of castes, / the same INRI, which they carry / in their soul if not on their skin!" ("Playa de Varadero" 134).

To facilitate the necessary process of mental and psychological decolonization, those alientated from themselves and their ancestry need only to observe and become aware of their own history and their own surroundings. The fortress walls of Cartagena and of other cities bear lasting witness to the laborious, fecund presence of Africa:

> Muros impertérritos nos han traducido a piedra,
>
> como un eterno testimonio;
>
> su victoriosa voz prolonga,
>
> bajo la acústica de los siglos,
>
> nuestra feraz presencia. (143)

[Dauntless walls have translated us to stone, / like an eternal testimony; /

their victorious voice prolongs, / beneath the acoustics of the centuries, / our fertile presence.]

Sweeping away the dust of history and forgetfulness and unmasking the whitening myth of *mestizaje,* Artel the teacher-poet reminds us that the massive wall defenses of so many colonial ports (e.g., Colombia's Cartagena, Puerto Rico's San Juan, Cuba's Havana) were constructed by the labor of enslaved Africans. Still standing erect, the imposing stone walls personify, "like an eternal testimony," the forced labor and fruitful presence of African peoples in America.

Echoing verses from "Negro soy," Artel reaffirms here, too, his self-imposed role as poet-griot, proudly declaring:

> A través de nosotros
> hablan innumerables pueblos,
> islas y continentes,
> puertos iluminados de pájaros
> y canciones extrañas,
> cuyos soles
> mordieron para siempre
> el alma de los conquistadores
> cuando un mundo amanecía en Guanahaní. (143)

[Through us / speak innumerable peoples, / islands and continents, / ports illuminated with birds / and strange songs, / whose suns / pierced forever / the conquistadors' soul / when a world was dawning in Guanahaní.]

Consistently using the first person plural (*nosotros*), Artel melds his voice with that of his audience, thereby also maintaining a sense of community, continuity, and identification with the autochthonous American cultures. For just as Artel regards descendants of African slaves as an integral part of America, so too does he, a black man, speak as a poet of America, as one who understands that the Europeans themselves were influenced and transformed by the reality they sought to conquer.

Fully aware of the continued debasement and distortion of African ancestry perpetrated by those benighted countrymen for whom Europe alone offers an honorable background, the poet-teacher rewrites history to reveal truths generally unknown, forgotten, or ignored. Exploding the myth of racial purity and the fallacy of European superiority, which have long alienated the people from their culture, from themselves, and from each other, Artel urges:

Y, oígase bien,
quiero decirlo recio y alto.
Quiero que esta verdad traspase el monte,
la cumbre, el mar, el llano:
no hay tal abuelo ario!
El pariente español que otros exaltan
—conquistador, encomendero,
inquisidor, pirata, clérigo—
nos trajo con la cruz y el hierro,
también, sangre de Africa.

Era en realidad un mestizo,
como todos los hombres y las razas! (144)

[And, listen carefully, / I want to say it loud and strong. / I want this truth to cross the woodland, / the mountain, the sea, the plain: / there is no such Aryan ancestor! / The Spanish kinsman whom others exalt / — conquistador, encomendero, / inquisitor, pirate, cleric— / [who] brought us with the cross and the chain, / [is] also Africa's blood.

In reality, he was a mestizo, / like all men and races!]

(The mention of the cross and the chain is clearly a reference to the forced imposition of Christianity and slavery, both of which suppressed the Africans and inextricably bound them to the culture and economy of the New World. More common, perhaps, are the metaphors of cross and sword, which usually refer to the physical and cultural destruction of indigenous peoples in America.)

As for those who persist in claiming noble lineage based on parchment instead of character and who take refuge "tras los follajes del árbol genealógico" [behind the foliage of the genealogical tree], Artel admonishes them to

mirarse al rostro
—los cabellos, la nariz, los labios—
o mirar aún mucho más lejos:
hacia sus palmares interiores,
donde una estampa nocturna,
irónica, vigila
desde el subfondo de las brumas . . . (144–45)

[look at their faces / —their hair, nose, lips— / or look much further still: / toward their interior palm groves, / where a nocturnal stamp, / ironically watches / from the bottom of the mists . . .]

I must point out here an exceptionally fine example of Artel's artistic ingenuity and insistence on reclaiming the African heritage. Through a kind of parody that does not so much mock as it rectifies and reverses, Artel insinuates an antithesis or contrast between the studied pretentiousness of Eurocentrism and the natural simplicity of an integrated (Afro-)American identity. While the former is embodied in the artificial and lifeless "genealogical tree" ["árbol genealógico"], emblematic of elitist European ancestry and devotion and of a nobility conferred from without, the latter is represented by the "real," life-giving palm trees ["palmares interiores"], symbolic of an authentic African and tropical presence that dwells deep within the collective psyche of America.

Ever mindful of the ancestral pain of separation and irrecoverable loss that is the source of his poetic inspiration, Artel reaffirms his chosen role as a bridge between the remote African past and the living descendants of those who were forcibly removed from their homelands:

Nuestra voz está unida, por su esencia,

a la voz del pasado,

trasunto de ecos

donde sonoros abismos

pusieron su profundidad, y el tiempo

sus distancias. (145)

[Our voice is united, through its essence, / to the voice of the past, / a reflection of echoes / where resonant abysses / placed their depth, and time / its distances.]

For this reason, Artel rejects the burlesque, ludicrously provocative caricatures of black people and their culture that much of *negrista* verse created or perpetuated:

No lleva nuestro verso cascabeles de "clown",

ni—acróbata turístico—

plasma piruetas en el circo

para solaz de los blancos.

[Our verse does not bear jingling clown bells, / nor—[like a] touristy acrobat— / does it perform pirouettes in the circus / for the solace of whites.]

The lines just cited should not be taken as a denial or rejection of humor in Artel's poetics nor in his conception of black poetry. As he explained in "Importancia del folklore," the essay written for the *La Prensa* newspaper in New York:

> En cuanto al acento humorístico que invariablemente se le pretende imprimir, él es saludable cuando se emplea para resaltar la ingenuidad espiritual de los personajes, su bondad, su fe sencilla, sus emociones rudimentarias, y su sentido festivo de la vida, con el cual el negro del cautiverio y sus descendientes suelen sublimar su dolor. (12)

> [Regarding the humoristic accent that invariably one tries to impress upon the poetry, it is healthy when it is used to project the spiritual ingenuity of the characters, their goodness, their simple faith, their rudimentary emotions, and their festive sense of life, with which the blacks in captivity and their descendants are accustomed to sublimate their pain.][34]

Rather, Artel opposed the exaggerated effects of authors—and, no doubt, of professional declaimers he had seen and heard—that reduced the black poetic persona to comic entertainment. "The only drama in all this," he wrote in his essay, "is that when we laugh in front of the reciter-interpreter [of such poems] we are laughing at something which, to the chagrin of many, the majority of us carry in our blood" (12).

Although Guillén's verses did not fall into that reductive mode, in Artel's eyes the Cuban's representation of the African ancestors left much to be desired, as lines from the penultimate stanza of "Poema sin odios ni temores" reveal. Apparently deriding Guillén's treatment of the forebears in "El abuelo" [The Grandfather] and "Balada de los dos abuelos" [Ballad of the Two Grandfathers], Artel contrasts without malice or envy his own poetry, remarking that:

> En su pequeño mar
> no huyen los abuelos fugándose en la sombra,
> cobardes, omnubilados [*sic*]
> por un sol imaginario.

> [In their small sea / the grandfathers do not flee escaping into the shadow, / cowards, dazzled / by an imaginary sun.][35]

When we consider the reverence in which Artel holds the sacrifice and suffering of the African ancestors and the importance he attaches to their living spiritual legacy, it is no wonder that he rejects their "fleeting" image in Guillén's works. For the Colombian poet the ancestors are not dead or

215

vanished; rather, as African religions teach, they continue to accompany and speak through the living.

> Ellos están presentes,
> se empinan para vernos,
> gritan, claman, lloran, cantan,
> quemándose en su luz
> igual que en una llama! (145–46)

[They are present, / they stand on edge to see us, / they shout, clamor, weep, sing, / burning in their light / just as in a flame!]

Of the lines just cited the third is an obvious and intentional appropriation or parody of one of the final verses of Guillén's "Balada de los dos abuelos," which reads: "gritan, sueñan, lloran, cantan" (*Summa poética* 92). However, to add his own touch of originality and to eliminate any suggestion of unconscious activity, Artel replaces *sueñan* with *claman,* vigorously reinforcing the meaning of the first verb (*gritan*), variations of which, as we have seen, appear frequently throughout Artel's work.

Finally, in a tone befitting a crusade, Artel addresses all African-Americans who have kept the faith, suggesting once more the messianic import of his poetic mission and reassuring his brethren of the transcendental meaning of their presence in the New World:

> Negros de nuestro mundo,
> los que no enajenaron la consigna,
> ni han trastrocado la bandera,
> este es el evangelio:
> somos—sin odios ni temores—
> una conciencia en América! (146)

[Blacks of our world, / those who did not discard the order, / nor have abandoned the flag, / this is the gospel: / we are—without hatreds or fears— / a conscience in America!]

In fine, "Poema sin odios ni temores" is a firm reminder to Americans of African descent that they are the heirs of rich and venerable cultures, of a remarkable history of struggle and sacrifice, and of an unrivaled legacy of creative achievement, made all the more notable because of the unique and adverse circumstances under which it emerged and developed. At the same time, the poem is a challenge to African-Americans to be both mindful and respectful of that very heritage inasmuch as it has sustained them throughout centuries of oppression, exploitation, and degradation. Moreover, because the courage, resilience, perseverance, and creativity ingrained in that history and legacy have strengthened and enriched the many lands to which captive Africans were transported as slave labor, the descendants of Africans are entitled to full recognition as legitimate citizens not only of their respective countries but of the Americas as a whole. For that reason Artel insists upon a black literary expression that goes beyond the facile, sonorous verse of humorous stereotype and entertaining spectacle and renders something of the depth and intrinsic value of the African-American experience.

Finally, the poem is also a call to acknowledge the inescapable reality of biological and cultural blending to which African peoples have contributed in no small measure, without that implying, however, a desire for "ethnic bleaching." Indeed, it is clear that Artel rejects the widespread assumptions of racial purists and supremacists who have promoted *mestizaje* as a means of "improving the [black] race," while at the same time condemning it as a setback in genetic advancement or an obstacle to the social and political development of Latin America.

As the title and last two verses indicate, Artel asserts his claims without hatreds or fears, without animosity or apprehension. Simultaneously, he teaches through this poem that others need not be afraid or ashamed of calling themselves—or of being called—*negro* or *indio;* that there is no reason to hate oneself or others because of skin color, hair texture, or facial features; and that there is no just cause or need to disdain one's ancestral origins or shun one's cultural heritage. Rather, African-Americans must lay claim to their whole racial selves and all their ethnic roots, for in doing so they will maintain their dignity and achieve true liberation. Artel's *Tambores en la noche* thus confirms the creative possibilities inherent in the unique group experience and the liberating potential of an authentic black art.

CONCLUSION

If there is no struggle, there is no progress.
Frederick Douglass

In the previous pages of this book I have examined the two editions of Jorge Artel's *Tambores en la noche* against the backdrop of, first, a few early, uncollected poems; second, his literary career; and third, several salient factors that help to explain the low profile given to writers of African descent in Colombia and the relative absence therein of a tradition of self-assertive black writing. The discussion of fundamental historical and contemporary Colombian realities (chapter 1) and the comparison of slavery, race relations, and literature in Cuba and Colombia (chapter 2) have shown that in the South American nation a number of variables effectively retarded among the nation's sizeable black population a steady outpouring of written texts in which an unequivocal discourse of racial consciousness, ethnic pride, and group solidarity could be easily discerned. These variables include geographical diversity, inveterate regionalism, the nature of African slavery, the lack of a demographic critical mass, intense racial mixing and the subsequent creation of a multiethnic society, the absence of overt discrimination and violent racial hostilities, the lack of educational opportunities and of access to cultural institutions and experiences dominated by the privileged classes, a genteel and elitist tradition of literary production, and the chronic ills of the publishing industry.

The extensive—but by no means exhaustive—biographical sketch of Artel (chapter 3) has provided helpful details and valuable insights about his background and experiences, literary pursuits, major publications, and sociocultural thought, which in turn have illuminated his writing. The consideration of a few of Artel's initial compositions (chapter 4) has permitted a penetrating appreciation of the poet's artistic affinities and generational roots, which effectively link him to Spanish-American post-Modernism, the European avant-garde, and writers of the African diaspora. The close study of the poems of the 1940 edition of *Tambores en la noche* (chapter 5) has affirmed the author's intent and ability to explore the psychic depths of blackness within his corner of America and thus transcend the often superficial treatment of black music, dance, and religion and the common stereotypical representations of black peoples by the practitioners of poetic *negrismo*.

The ensuing examination of critical responses to Artel's poetry (chapter 6) has demonstrated, however, that too many critics and commentators either failed to distinguish the significance of the racial nuances and ethnic implications of Artel's aesthetics or, imposing their narrow "theoretical assumptions, critical perspectives, and value judgments" (Ashcroft, Griffiths, and Tiffin 18) on black-inspired writing in general, devalued Artel's poems and relegated the experiences privileged therein to the margins of artistic worth and significance. Contrary to the fears and misapprehensions of critics and contemporaries, however, Artel's attention to the African heritage is not an instigation to racial hatred, ethnic exclusion, or feelings of superiority, but rather an attempt to promote a salutary self-regard and an all-inclusive sense of community and well-being. To paraphrase the authors of *The Empire Writes Back*, although Artel's poetry, on the surface, deals with racial, historical, and cultural differences that seem to divide, at bottom it contains the seeds of a common past and shared destiny, which, upon germinating and growing in the reader's mind, begin to break down the apparently insurmountable barriers to a community's knowledge, actualization, and liberation of self (Ashcroft, Griffiths, and Tiffin 35).

The reading of the second, revised edition of *Tambores en la noche* (chapter 7) has evinced Artel's appropriaton of an earnest, more assertive poetic voice and his adoption of a less equivocal racial posture. In this work he not only provides moving testimony of the material condition and spiritual richness of Afro-American peoples, but also subtly confronts and challenges the failure of critics, like Guillén, to understand his message and artistry. Although Artel, unlike the Cuban, did not challenge directly the social and economic inequities resulting from the legacy of slavery, racial prejudice and discrimination, and class exploitation, he lay bare the spiritual void and perennial paradox of a nation whose citizens lived relatively free from political oppression and racial persecution but were heavily burdened by shame and fear of the "colored" roots of their reputedly proud mestizo identity. Artel's poetry, therefore, exposed the hypocrisy and irony of Spanish America's disdain for African and Amerindian heritage and the all too common flight from blackness.

For reasons mentioned previously, the poems of the second edition apparently had little direct impact on black writing in Colombia at the time of their publication. Resonant with experiences that affected Artel personally, the book remains, nevertheless, an eloquent example of the continuing struggle of Afro-Colombian writers to inscribe blackness into the literary and cultural consciousness of their nation and, by so doing, to abrogate the silence of ignorance, hatred, fear, and neglect, that would deny and render invisible the all-important African presence in Colombia. Viewed from this vantage, *Tambores en la noche* (1955) represents a major step forward in the development of a more vocal and comprehensive Afro-Colombian discourse.

Although other Afro-Colombian poets wrote verses and published books during the decades of the 1930s, 1940s, and 1950s, none revealed like Artel an unequivocal and proud identification with the African ancestors, nor conveyed as profound, unwavering, and dignified a concern for the historical experience and cultural creations of the nation's black populations. Through his poems and prose writings on race and ethnicity and other intellectual and cultural endeavors, Artel stimulated a greater appreciation for the legacy of Africa and a deeper awareness and acceptance of the *costeño* as an integral and important element of Colombia's peoples, literature, and culture.

As a result, it can be said that Artel came to occupy a position within Afro-Colombia not unlike that of the griot in traditional African societies. Cognizant of the problematics of black identity and black writing in his homeland, Artel took on the task of creating a poetics of memory and reconnection that was true to Colombian reality but that also sought to change it. His efforts to make the inhabitants and traditions of the Atlantic coast better known to fellow Colombians, to advance their role in creating a multiracial democracy in Colombia, and to promote a multicultural consciousness signified a serious and unique challenge to the centrist orientation of the dominant national groups. Similarly, Artel's insistence upon embracing and reconstructing the despised African and indigenous heritages constituted an act of subversion in the face of the Eurocentrism and insidious racism that permeated Colombian (and, by extension, Latin American) society and culture.

Artel's contributions to black literary expression in Colombia do not end there, however. His determination to promote the values and traditions of the coastal regions, to reevaluate the African presence and heritage in America, and to enhance and edify the discourse of Afro-Spanish-American poetry have also influenced, to a greater or lesser degree, the cultural and intellectual development of younger Colombian writers. Undoubtedly, the one whose writings most manifest a clear consonance and solidarity with those of Artel is Manuel Zapata Olivella, many of whose novels and essays reveal an indisputable intertexuality with ideas, perspectives, and phrases found in the poet's own work. Prominent in Zapata Olivella's prose are the same preoccupations that characterize Artel's labors: elevating and promoting *costeño* folklore, reestablishing African nexus, and bringing about an integration of the coastal, the African, and the indigenous with the nation's other regions and peoples to ensure an authentic and whole national identity (see Prescott, "Sin odios ni temores" 301–03).

In sum, through *Tambores en la noche* and other writings on black literature, music, and art, Jorge Artel has given his countrymen an important and lasting legacy. That legacy consists in having awakened the consciousness of his fellow *costeños* and other compatriots to the geographical, cultural, and spiritual value of the nation's marginalized communities; in having undertaken an almost single-handed struggle to exorcize the stigma of slavery and the shame associated with African heritage and black identity; and in having created an original and sincere Afro-Colombian poetics that (cor)responded to the national reality, but that also defied racial and cultural presumptions. In this way, Artel not only promoted a more propitious climate for black artistic creativity and serious and disciplined research on the African presence in Colombia, but also helped to pave the way for the emergence of later authors.

All of these accomplishments would seem to suffice to include Artel and his work in the canon of Colombian and Spanish- American literature. It is important to understand, however, that a canon "is not simply a body of texts *per se,* but rather a set of reading practices (the enactment of innumerable individual and community assumptions, for example, about genre, about literature, and even about writing)"; and that "[t]hese reading practices, in their turn, are resident in institutional structures, such as education curricula and publishing networks" (Ashcroft, Griffiths, and Tiffin 189). Viewed in this light, the struggle of black literary expression to reach a mature stage of development and to win due acceptance and recognition—not merely in order to survive but to thrive—seems destined to continue for years to come. Notwithstanding the continuing literary output of older, established authors and the emergence of a number of promising younger poets and writers (see Prescott, "Perfil histórico del autor afro-colombiano" 118–21, and "Negras, morenas, zambas y mulatas" 191–92), their publications still receive little or no critical attention, are not included in canon-forming anthologies and collections, and generally do not reach the hands of a wide reading public. Moreover, it seems safe to say that as long as black and other disadvantaged peoples of color in Colombia lack the power to effect fundamental change in their lives; as long as they possess little control over the means of literary production and communication, are excluded from school and university textbooks, or are limited to certain narrow roles and stereotypical representations reminiscent of a shameful past of enforced servitude and subordination; and as long as Eurocentric cultural values prevail and whiteness remains the privileged and authorized condition of humanity, the formation and acceptance of a viable literary tradition that foregrounds and validates black experiences, perspectives, and identities—without hatreds or fears—will continue to be a struggle. If that struggle, however, also continues to produce more poets and writers who match or, better yet, surpass the quality, sensibility, and courageous commitment of Jorge Artel's artistry, Afro-Colombian literature may yet flourish, find its voice(s), and fulfill its creative and liberating potential.

APPENDIX A:
Poems of *Tambores en la noche,* 1940 and 1955

TAMBORES EN LA NOCHE 1940

"Tambores en la noche"
"La cumbia"
"Negro soy"
"La voz de los ancestros"
"Danza, mulata!"
"Barrio abajo"
"Bullerengue"
"La canción"
"Ahora hablo de gaitas"
"Mr. Davi"
"Velorio del boga adolescente"
"Dancing"
"Sensualidad negra"
"El líder negro"
"Romance mulato"

Otros Poemas

"Versos para zarpar un día
"Sobordo emocional"
"Canción de los matices íntimos"
"Meridiano de Bogotá"

"Poema incoherente con fondos de
    distancia"
"Añoranza de la tierra nativa"
"Canción para ser cantada desde un
    mástil"
"Canción en el extremo de un retorno"
"Canción para un ayer definitivo"
"Silencio"
"Breve canción para Zoila"
"Cartagena 3 a.m."
"Canción en el aire y sobre el mar"
"Poema para ser trazado al carbón"
"Los turistas"
"Juan el holandés"
"Rincón de Mar"
"El minuto en que vuelven"
"Muelles de medianoche"
"Puerto"
"Ese muchacho"
"Sabiática"
"Hélices"
"Navy Bar"
"Playa"

"Poema del corazón capitán"
"Balneario"
"Extramuros"
"Mi canción"
"Canto nuevo para loar a Barranquilla"
"La canción imposible"

TAMBORES EN LA NOCHE 1955

"Negro soy"
"La voz de los ancestros"
"Danza, mulata!"
"La cumbia"
"Tambores en la noche"
"Velorio del boga adolescente"
"Ahora hablo de gaitas"
"Barrio abajo"
"Mr. Davi"
"Sensualidad negra"
"Bullerengue"
"El líder negro"
"Dancing"
"Romance mulato"
"Puerto"
"Canción en el extremo de un retorno"
"El minuto en que vuelven"

"Extramuros"
"La canción"
"Ese muchacho negro"
"Cartagena 3 a.m."
"Mi canción"
"Noche del Chocó"
"Barlovento"
"Palenque"
"Isla de Barú"
"Canción en tiempo de porro"
"Los Chimichimitos"
"El lenguaje misterioso"
"Alto Congo"
"Argeliana"
"Soneto más negro"
"La ruta dolorosa"
"El mismo hierro"
"Harlem"
"Al 'drummer' negro de un Jazz-Session"
"Superstición"
"Encuentro"
"Palabras a la ciudad de Nueva York"
"Playa de Varadero"
"Yanga"
"Mapa de Africa"
"Poema sin odios ni temores"

APPENDIX B:
Latin American Newspapers and Periodicals Consulted

Colombian sources are arranged alphabetically by location. An abbreviation of place is indicated to facilitate identification in the bibliography of sources bearing the same title.

COLOMBIAN SOURCES

Barranquilla [Barr]

Civilización
Diario del Caribe
Divulgaciones Etnológicas
Dominical
El Heraldo
La Nación
La Prensa

Bogotá [Bog]

Boletín Cultural y Bibliográfico
Crítica
Cromos
La Crónica Literaria (supplement of El País)
Diario de Cundinamarca
El Espectador
Espiral
El Estudiante
Jornada
Letras Nacionales
El Liberal

Mito
Mundo al Día
El Nuevo Tiempo
El Pasatiempo
Papel Periódico Ilustrado
La Patria
Presencia Negra
La Razón
La República
Revista Colombiana de Antropología
Revista Colombiana de Folclor
Revista de las Indias
Revista Javeriana
Revista Mefisto de la Literatura Latinoamericana
Sábado
El Siglo
Sucesos
El Tiempo
Universidad Nacional
Vida
Vínculo Shell

Bucaramanga

Diario de Occidente

Cali

Diario del Pacífico
Páginas de Cultura
El Relator

Cartagena [Car]

Boletín Liberals
Cartagena de Indias
Costa; La Revista del Litoral Atlántico
Diario de la Costa
El Fígaro
El Mercurio
Muros
La Patria
El Universal
Voces de América

Lorica

Rojas Garrido

Manizales [Man]

La Patria

Medellín

El Colombiano
El Diario
Universidad de Antioquia
Universitas Humanística

Pasto

Anales de la universidad de Nariño

Popayán

Revista de la Universidad del Cauca

Quibdó

Occidente

Tunja

Repertorio Boyacense

OTHER COUNTRIES

Brazil

Toda a América

Costa Rica

Diario de Costa Rica
Repertorio Americano

Cuba

Alerta
Bohemia
Diario de Cuba
Diario de la Marina
Orientación Social
Revista Cubana
Revista Cubana Contemporánea

Ecuador

El Universo

El Salvador

La Prensa Gráfica

Mexico

El Día
Estado de Guanajuato
Fraternidad
Provincia
Revista de México
Vida Universitaria

Panama [Pan]

Calle 6
Crítica
El Día
La Hora
Lotería
Mundo Gráfico
La Nación
El País
El Panamá-América

Puerto Rico

Alma Latina
El Mundo
Revista/Review Interamericana

Dominican Republic [DR]

El Caribe
La Nación

Venezuela [Ven]

Panorama
El Nacional
El Universal
Viernes

United States

Américas
Diario Las Américas
La Prensa [NY]

NOTES

INTRODUCTION

1. Kutzinski has also stated the same in her recent book, *Sugar's Secrets.* For an earlier discussion of the Afro-Cuban or Afro-Antillean hegemony within Spanish-American *negrista* poetry, see Prescott, *Candelario Obeso* 33–48.

2. For a brief comparative treatment of Artel and Guillén, see Prescott, "Jorge Artel frente a Nicolás Guillén."

3. The closest approximation of a lengthy critical study on Artel is the unpublished thesis by Betsabé E. Henríquez Del R.

4. In a future study I hope to examine in greater detail the work of specific Afro-Colombian authors who can only receive passing attention in these pages.

CHAPTER 1

1. Carlos Calderón Mosquera has claimed that "El testamento del negro," a famous stanza long considered anonymous, was actually composed in the nineteenth century by Antonio Kalonge, a freedman of the Chocó ("Facetas" 54). For the text of the poem see Sanz y Díaz 331.

2. For information concerning commerce and the slave trade through Cartagena, see Palacios Preciado, *La trata de negros por Cartagena;* and Juan and Ulloa 41.

3. See also Mina 45–49.

4. Regional pride seems to have especially encouraged the *paisas,* as Antioqueños are called, to defend and extol their countrymen and women who have brought prominence and positive attention to the *patria chica,* or regional homeland. This is evident, for example, in the commitment of Antioquian intellectuals such as Antonio

José Restrepo, Juan de Dios Uribe, A. Escobar Uribe, and Benigno Gutiérrez, to keeping alive and publicizing the memory of friends, political comrades, and regional compatriots.

5. As the following discussions of *mestizaje* and slavery will show, regional location and occupation also influenced the way African slaves and their descendants lived, the treatment they received, and the nature and extent of their interaction with other groups. Group interaction, in turn, affected the degree to which Africans and their descendants mixed with other groups, maintained or developed a relatively separate existence and distinct ethnic traits, or were assimilated into the cultural mainstream and thus better prepared to participate in the literate culture. Group interaction also would be instrumental in shaping racial self-perception and black identity in different regions.

6. Influenced no doubt by geographical determinism, Colombian intellectual José María Samper declared that within this geo-racial division lay the key to understanding "very important social phenomena and almost all the revolutions which have shaken and are shaking the republics of that origin" (*Ensayo* 71). See also Smith 63.

7. Several writers have paid homage to this notion: S. Pérez 73; Vergara y Vergara 295; M. Samper 34–35; Camacho Roldán 1: 114; Triana 48; Foción Soto, *Memorias . . . de la dictadura de Rafael Núñez, 1884–1885* (1913), cited in Tirado Mejía, *Aspectos sociales de las guerras civiles* 314; and Bowman 306. The Colombian llanos also were considered by some as suitable only for blacks or others acclimated to the tropics (Rausch 65).

8. Writing more than sixty years apart, Atlantic coast authors Candelario Obeso (*Lectura para ti*), and Manuel Zapata Olivella ("Genio y figura") also offer eloquent testimony of regional distinctions and Andean highlanders' reactions to the coastal presence.

9. Tirado Mejía illustrates the manner in which political conflicts took on regional characteristics with racial overtones: "To fight on strange soil could imply that regional sentiment might take precedence over that of party and that native inhabitants might unite against invader. . . . Beginning with the entry of Caucano divisions into Antioquia during the war of 1860, the partisan struggle became racial with regional manifestations. Mosquera entered with the Caucano soldiery composed in large part of Negroes and they, like any other troops in the same circumstances behaved like an invading army. From that point on considerations of the 'whites of Antioquia' against the 'blacks of the Cauca' outweighed other reasons of a doctrinal nature" (*Aspectos sociales* 46).

10. Antonio José ("El Negro") Cano (1874–1942) and Francisco Botero (?–1938), African-descended authors of Antioquia and Caldas, respectively, reflect a profound identification with region rather than race. While expressions of sentimental ties to the local homeland inform many of their poems, overt racial feeling or identity is virtually nonexistent. Even Cano's eulogistic sonnet to the Afro-Colombian statesman Luis A. Robles, a native of the Atlantic coast who served as the lone Liberal Party congressional representative from Antioquia, offers no indication of racial identity or comradeship (see Cano 64). Indeed, one would have to be familiar with Robles in order to know that the poem's subject is a black man.

11. Black enlistment seems to have been obtained via coercion, appeals to patriotism, promises of economic improvement, and other enticements (see Tirado Mejía, *Aspectos sociales* 45).

12. According to Mina, slave labor continued to be the principal source of the opulence and culture of privileged classes in the Cauca Valley even after independence (41).

13. See also Velásquez, *El Chocó en la independencia* 29.

14. Pereira corroborates the high degree of racial conflict (159).

15. The freedmen's distrust of whites and their desire to escape white control and exploitation may also explain any failure to organize and present frequent petitions as a group within a system that generally favored whites. Nonparticipation in the system, encouraged or exacerbated by the freedmen's lack of authority, of arms, and of education and training, could well be interpreted as an expression of group pride and resistance.

16. Although the Atlantic region also yielded gold, its richest deposits do not compare with those of western Colombia. What is more, the deposits seem to have been limited to the Sierra Nevada area, virtually the only mountainous section of the Atlantic littoral (see Juan and Ulloa 26; Gilij 352). Escalante provides documentary descriptions of mines on the Atlantic coast (*El negro en Colombia* 123–24).

17. See, for example, Juan and Ulloa 43; and Colmenares, *Historia* 103, who gives an example of an escaped artisan slave in Medellín who obtained his freedom by self-purchase.

18. Such opportunities, of course, were not restricted to the Atlantic coast, as Colmenares shows (see note 17 above).

19. Devis Echandía supports the contention that privileged persons of African descent tended to forget about the black masses (167).

20. Even attempts to maintain separate military units based on racial or caste grouping gave way in the face of miscegenation. As Kuethe states, "So blurred were racial distinctions in New Granada that in some instances the military leadership itself differed concerning the proper classification of companies" (*Military Reform and Society* 31). For a useful discussion of racial classifications in Spanish America, see Diggs.

21. In addition, *negro* and *negra*—especially in their diminutive forms *negrito* and *negrita*—have also been used as terms of endearment, even for persons who are not phenotypically black. For example, José María Obando, a Creole military leader and one-time president of Colombia, frequently addressed his wife in letters as "Mi negra" while also referring to himself as "Tu chino" (Rodríguez Plata 312–14, 369, 494–96). This custom astonished North American traveler Isaac F. Holton, who interpreted the epistolary salutation "Mi querida negra" literally as "My dear negress" [*sic*] (481). Also worth noting is the observation by philologist Rufino J. Cuervo that "words that indicate *a defect* [my emphasis] are in an affectionate tone expressions of endearment: *mi negra, mi chato, mi china* are flattery for one who hears them, although they contain nothing of the sort" (661). Note, too, that the nineteenth-century radical writer and journalist Juan de Dios Uribe Restrepo was popularly known as "El Indio," although presumably he was not of discernibly indigenous blood (see Escobar Uribe).

22. Taking note of this situation, Zelinsky states: "The record has at all times been obscured by the fact of racial mobility—'passing'—and the practice of claiming membership in the social-racial stratum just above one's own. The very definition of the Negro is an apparently insuperable problem. Which among the various genotypes obtained by miscegenation shall we classify as Negro?" (173). It should also be remembered that racial terminology and identity varied from place to place (cf. Solaún and Kronus 43n35).

23. Cf. Juan and Ulloa: "there are other Whites, in mean circumstances, who owe either their origin to Indian families, or at least to an intermarriage with them, so that there is some mixture in their blood; but when this is not discoverable by their colour, the conceit of being Whites alleviates the pressure of every other calamity" (27).

24. See also J. M. Samper, *Ensayo* 259–60. In 1953 a letter to the editor of a newspaper proudly noted as an example of Colombia's racial democracy a previously published photograph that pictured the daughter of the president of the Republic dancing with a black man ("Ultimo Grado de Democracia"). Belief in *mestizaje*'s power to override racial prejudice is not limited, of course, to Colombia, but is popular throughout much of Latin America. See, for example, Steiner 65.

25. According to Valenilla Lanz, Manuel Murillo Toro, twice president of Colombia (1864–66, 1872–74), is credited with the phrase "todos somos café con leche," which he applied to Colombians (262).

26. A case in point is the nineteenth-century poet and writer Candelario Obeso, who is discussed in the following chapter. Also revealing is the reaction in 1973–74 of some nonblack Colombians in Bogotá upon learning that this researcher was investigating their country's writers of African descent. Much to my dismay, they quickly declared that racial discrimination did not exist there and implied that I was creating racial problems. It did not take me long to realize the wisdom and value of resorting at times to euphemism. Reaction to the topic "coastal writers of Colombia" was more favorable, even though few noncoastal persons seemed to be familiar with any writer of that region other than Gabriel García Márquez.

27. In June of 1943 black and mulatto university students from the coastal and Cauca regions organized in Bogotá the first (and only) "Day of the Negro," an exhuberant expression of black pride, solidarity, and faith in democracy. Inspired in part by racial disturbances in Detroit, Michigan, the event consisted of a march along a main street of downtown Bogotá, the broadcast of recorded musical selections by Afro-North American artists Marian Anderson and Paul Robeson, and readings of poems written by Afro-Colombian poets Obeso and Artel. The participants also issued a manifesto, which, apparently, did not receive much publicity. For a participant's account of this event and detailed information on media reactions and the manifesto, see Karabalí, "Estudios"; and Prescott, "Natanael Díaz," respectively. For a more recent reaction of the press to expressions of black ethnicity, see "Sin discriminaciones."

28. According to Londoño, "In [blacks and Indians] there is a powerful aspiration to the white race; therefore mixture reaches astounding proportions, and when it has not come from lustfulness, it has come from desperation, from an eagerness to rise, from a desire for lightening. Whiteness brings with it great advantages, among them

the increase in social or professional respect, a matter of definite importance" (141). See also Solaún and Kronus 124.

29. According to Lalinde Botero, "In greater Antioquia our ancestors acquired the ugly custom of applying the modifier 'Negro' to every person who was on the lower rungs of the social scale" (66). For epithets of laziness see Pereira 87; Brisson 106; Eder 165, 197, 205.

30. Representation of the black as devil and of the devil as black is fairly common in Spanish-American culture and literature as demonstrated by Sola 57–66, and Carvalho-Neto 83–89. Strangely, in Colombia even the popular sobriquet for a person with Down's syndrome is "cari-negro" [black face] (see Pardo Umaña 5).

31. That is not to say, however, that all Afro-Colombians have necessarily rejected black identity. Rather, many have refused to embrace and identify with the distorted, unflattering, reenslaving representations of themselves that the dominant literature and media have created and disseminated. Given that these representations are often taken as authentic aspects of blackness, it is understandable that many Afro-Colombians would reject that vision imposed by the Other. As W. E. B. DuBois suggested in 1920, "It is not that we are ashamed of our color and blood. We are instinctively and almost unconsciously ashamed of the caricatures done of our darker shades. Black *is* caricature in our half conscious thought and we shun in print and paint that which we love in life" (Tuttle 53).

32. For example, according to Porto de Portillo, *Plazas y Calles de Cartagena,* in late nineteenth-century Cartagena the meeting places of the black organizations known as *cabildos* were ordered closed by the governor (qtd. in Escalante, "Notas" 224–25). For other documentation of official efforts to suppress black cultural expression, see Escobar Escobar; and Tejado Fernández, chaps. 4 and 5.

33. Much has been written about this maroon community. Especially useful are Escalante, "Notas"; Zapata Olivella, "Los negros palenqueros"; and Friedemann and Patiño Roselli.

CHAPTER 2

1. According to Knight, a settler society was one where people went to "make a fortune, produce a family, and spend their lives" (*African Dimension* 45).

2. Cuba's 1846 census reported 565,000 whites, 220,000 free Negroes and mulattoes, and 660,000 slaves in the total population (Blutstein et al. 32).

3. For a listing of Manzano's published writings see Trelles 33; and Jackson, *Afro-Spanish American Author* 88–89.

4. Manzano's singular work records his life as a slave and his efforts to learn how to write and compose poetry. Del Monte was so impressed with Manzano that he had him recite poems before his Havana *tertulia* and later took up a collection to purchase his freedom. Del Monte's interest in Manzano, however, was not as noble as it may sound. As a nationalist, he wanted to rid Cuba of Spanish dominance; but as a member of the white planter class, he wanted to maintain control over Afro-Cubans. (See Knight, "Slavery" 214–15.)

5. A century before Manzano, a woman poet of color ("poetisa parda") named

Juana Pastor is said to have written several compositions, of which only one or two, regrettably, have survived (Trelles 33; Fernández de Castro 23).

6. In the January 1883 number of the *Revista de Cuba,* a reviewer disputed the identification of Plácido as a *"negro,"* insisting that he was really a mulatto ("Miscelánea - Plácido" 96).

7. Cf. Strauss: "Persecution . . . gives rise to a peculiar technique of writing, and therewith to a peculiar type of literature, in which the truth about all crucial things is presented exclusively between the lines. That literature is addressed, not to all readers, but to trustworthy and intelligent readers only" (25).

8. Insurrections and uprisings involving free Negroids often had as a goal "the destruction of white rule" (Rout 295).

9. According to Ramiro Guerra, "The black population was united, at heart, by a solidarity of race and collective vindications, in the face of the white man's stocks, shackles and whip, and his laws and customs, which subjected the free black to a social, juridical and economic position of inferiority and to constant vexation" (*Manual de Historia de Cuba* [La Habana, 1971] 237; qtd. in Castellanos and Castellanos 212).

10. As early as 1842, Afro-Cubans, among them Antonio Medina y Céspedes, founded the newspaper *El Faro* in Havana. Fourteen years later (1856) *El Rocío,* "the first literary review edited by individuals of the colored race," also appeared there (Deschamps Chapeaux 50; 101–03). According to Knight, slaves in Cuba "managed to salvage some of the religious and cultural values and practices of their native Africa and to form the type of society that gave meaning to their lives" ("Slavery" 218). Their various organizations and religious cults afforded interaction with free Negroids, promoted community stability, and even facilitated mobility toward freedom.

11. According to Henríquez Ureña, these biographical essays or sketches began appearing in the periodical *La Revolución* of New York in 1868. Ten years later Calcagno published them in the *Revista de Cuba* and also in book form under the title *Poetas de color . . . (Plácido, Manzano, Rodríguez, Echemendía, Silveira, Medina)* (*Panorama histórico* 2:190). The Medina of the title seems to be the same Antonio Medina y Céspedes mentioned in note 10 above (Henríquez Ureña, *Panorama histórico* 2:116).

12. A fourth edition of Calcagno's work, consisting of 110 pages, was published in Havana in 1887.

13. Murray also points out that the bill to end the trade was promulgated as a royal decree in September of 1866 and was proclaimed in Cuba in September of the following year. For the likelihood of continued importations, see Scott 39–40.

14. According to Knight, Afro-Cubans, slave or free, were not heavily involved in the revolutionary forces of the Ten Years War (*Slave Society* 167–68).

15. It should be noted also, however, that a black presence is prominent in Cuba's earliest literary work, *El espejo de paciencia* (1608), by Silvestre de Balboa. For a discussion of this narrative poem, see Olivera 25–33. Costumbrista writers such as Francisco Baralt, author of the 1846 sketch "Escenas campestres. Baile de los negros," also took a literary interest in the cultural expression of Afro-Cubans (see Bueno 151–60).

16. Del Monte's *Romances cubanos* (1829–33) included several verses evoking the

cruelty and injustice of slavery; these verses, however, were suppressed by the censors (Henríquez Ureña, *Panorama histórico* 1:194; Schulman 33), as were "El negro alzado" (1835) and other poems by Milanés. Sanz's poem "Ante la tumba de un negro esclavo," composed in 1865, appeared in *El Porvenir* of Cartagena, 16 March 1879, and in *El Pasatiempo* of Bogotá the following month, more than twenty-five years after slavery had been abolished in Colombia. For this and other poems by Sanz, see his *Poesías*. For information about the prose fiction of the other authors mentioned, see Rivas; and L. Williams.

17. This is not to imply, however, that opposition to ending slavery in Colombia was small or weak. Indeed, proslavery forces mounted much resistance to the prospect of losing their labor force and their fortunes, and attempted to undermine or otherwise evade the process of gradual manumission. Recalcitrant opposition to emancipation of the slaves became a crucial factor leading to the civil war of 1851 (Tirado Mejía, "El estado y la política" 368; Taussig, *Devil and Commodity Fetichism* 48; Castellanos, *La abolición de la esclavitud* 103–04).

18. Sharp states that in 1782 the ratio of blacks to whites in the Chocó was about thirty to one ("Manumission" 110n56). According to Jaramillo Uribe, the slave and free black populations of Cartagena in the second half of the eighteenth century exceeded that of all the other sectors, while slaves in the city of Cali came to outnumber whites (*Ensayos* 12–13).

19. Shortly after abolition, the young writer and future president Santiago Pérez (1830–1900) traveled throughout the Pacific region of Colombia as a member of the Comisión Corográfico, taking account of the populations and conditions there. Both Pérez (43–44, 82, 85) and Holton (469–70) confirm the lack of schools and other hardships that precluded educational advancement for Afro-Colombians in those regions.

20. For a discussion of the two novels, see Curcio Altamar 65–68; and R. Williams 25, 93–100. Notwithstanding Nieto's primary position in Colombian literary history, critics of the Colombian novel have largely ignored his work, as Williams points out.

21. See also Cabrera Ortega. Describing the young *costeño* as "a husky boy, with light sallow (or dark tawny) skin, greenish light-blue eyes, straight and full nose, thin lips, arched eyebrows and black, medium curly hair," Fals Borda concludes that Nieto was "a person of mixed-blood or of the tri-ethnic 'cosmic' race, composed of variable mixtures of white, Indian and black, that has come to characterize Colombian coastal people" (31A).

22. This is supported by Fals Borda 41A, 150A. It is also worthwhile to recall here the observations on identity among persons of mixed-race parentage made by Juan and Ulloa, the royal visitors to eighteenth-century Cartagena (see above, chap. 1:29).

23. For information on Nieto's conflicts and comments on his character, see Cordovez Moure, *Reminiscencias* 207, 251, 1011. Significantly, Nieto was one of the members of the Colombian Congress of 1851 who introduced the bill that became the law abolishing slavery in Colombia (see Hernández de Alba 73; Fals Borda 2:105A, 107A–08A; and Castellanos, *La abolición de la esclavitud* 101–2).

24. More accessible but less reliable than the 1877 edition is that of 1950 prepared by the Colombian government on the occasion of the centennial of the poet's birth

and which also includes other works by Obeso. For a comprehensive bibliography of his writings, see Prescott, *Candelario Obeso* 207–09.

25. For the original Spanish, see Prescott, "Negro nací" 14n33.

26. This work is also reproduced in Obeso, *Cantos populares* (1950) 51–52.

27. Zubiría states that Obeso died of *negredumbre,* i.e., gloom of being black or a heavy sorrow of blackness. For an evaluation of some of these comments, see Prescott, "*Negro nací*" 4, 8–9.

28. For twentieth-century affirmations and denials, see Correa R. 66; Arango Bueno 159; "Sin discriminaciones"; "¿Cuál discriminación?"; and Velasco Ibarra 40–51.

29. Rpt. in *Cantos populares* 1950:30. Rout points out that in March of 1837 a royal decree was issued which prohibited Negroids from landing in Cuba. Black and mulatto sailors from other countries who disembarked were imprisoned until their ships were ready to depart (299–300).

30. According to John Stewart, two uprisings in 1836 by the black population of Mompós were quickly put down by the authorities (50). It is worthwhile, too, to remember that during the independence struggle, José Prudencio Padilla, Leonardo Infante, and Manuel Piar, all high-ranking military men of African origin who enjoyed much popularity and influence among the colored masses of New Granada, were executed by the patriot authorities on charges of conspiracy, insubordination, or other crimes. Still, as Park notes, Creole leaders expressed privately no little anxiety about the possibility of black unrest in such areas as the Cauca Valley and the Patía Valley (176).

31. On these points, see Samper, *Ensayo* 259, and Cordovez Moure, *Reminiscencias* 480. The North American traveler Holton reports meeting a Negro judge in the Cauca Valley (447–49). These realities, however, did not prevent members of the privileged classes from exercising a subtle form of discrimination against Afro-Colombians. Tirado Mejía has noted that when authors of contemporary writings on the civil wars of Colombia mentioned an officer or soldier of African descent, they did not merely give his rank but also identified him as "black," "mulatto," or "colored" (*Aspectos sociales* 47).

32. A rare, first-person expression of group discontent and resistance by ex-bondsmen appeared shortly after the final and total decree of slave emancipation in Colombia. The author(s) of an 1852 editorial in *El Picol,* a short-lived newspaper of Barranquilla, demanded that the children of ex-slaves, in accordance with the legislation, be allowed to return to their families (Gómez Olaciregui 25–26).

33. The emphasis on individual or family advancement had historical precedence, having received encouragement during the latter years of the colonial period in the form of the aforementioned certificate of whiteness. This document, it will be recalled, was occasionally granted or sold by the Spanish Crown to select individuals of color who, usually possessing fair skin, wealth, and other evidence of worth, sought to gain for themselves or their male progeny access to educational institutions and the priesthood. According to Rout, the intention of the Crown seems to have been, in part, "To reward successful Negroids and thereby prevent their possible subversion" and "To remove from the ranks of the blacks, mulattoes, and *zambos* potential revolutionary leaders." As Rout also observes, however, "the *gracias al sacar* writ

may be characterized not as a pass to the reserved seats, but a ticket into the bleachers from where the black or mulatto bearer could sneer disdainfully at other Negroids unable to enter the stadium" (159).

34. Cf. Zapata Olivella, ¡Levántate, mulato!, cited above in chap. 1:32. Although after abolition one rarely finds mention of any public expression of black group discontent and resistance on a racial basis (see note 32), it would be incorrect to say that Afro-Colombians totally lacked racial consciousness or that they did not make racial or ethnic distinctions. Indeed, as both the actions of blacks in the Cauca and remarks by Obeso and other intellectuals reveal, Afro-Colombians were well aware of the subtle forms of ostracism and discrimination that impeded their social, economic, and political progress. Often, however, the inveterate regionalism, the political turmoil, and the class distinctions inherent in the society served to disguise, counteract, or dilute racial tensions, inasmuch as the elites marginalized, divided, and generally took advantage of the common people and otherwise exercised power in ways that benefited themselves (see Tirado Mejía, Aspectos sociales 39, 40, 42–43).

35. For a brief summary of the conflicting opinions on Obeso's death, see Prescott, "Negro nací" 3–4.

36. Nevertheless, while Afro-Colombian writers of the late nineteenth century did not emulate Obeso's work, a few, such as the popular Panamanian-born poet Federico Escobar (1861–1912) and the obscure Cenón Fabio Villegas, of the Cauca, ostensibly paid him homage. Escobar placed as an epigraph to his own poetic avowal of blackness, a racially assertive stanza that he attributed to his fellow costeño (see Prescott, "Negro nací"); and Villegas's moving though less defiant paean to "El Vate Negro" [The Black Bard], published in his literary journal El Lirio (1898–99?), suggests striking parallels with aspects of Obeso's life.

37. Colombian poems related to slavery include "A un esclavo" (1850) by Rafael Pombo; "El esclavo Pedro" (1865) by Jorge Isaacs; and "La esclava" (1890) by Venancio Ortiz. As noted above, Cuban antislavery poems, such as Gerónimo Sanz's "Ante la tumba de un negro esclavo," also appeared in the Colombian press. It is noteworthy, too, that Isaacs's novel María (1867), which depicts black enslavement prominently, is another postabolition work. This delayed response might suggest either a certain nostalgia for the halcyon days of the plantation or a sense that the institution could only be poeticized once it had ceased to exist; or it could be a subtle indictment of the prolongation of patterns of the past.

38. According to Blutstein et al., "Leadership in Cuban political life and government was the special province of a relatively small group of men who had achieved prominence in the war of independence; their chief political interest was in gaining and keeping control of the spoils of office. . . . Cuban politics was almost divorced from the main social and economic developments of the country" (39).

39. Rout is rather blunt regarding racial problems in postwar Cuba: "[I]ndependence meant the continuation of the old patterns of racial discrimination and the introduction of the Yankee variety as well" (302). For an example of the latter, see Fernández Robaina 41–42.

40. For a detailed summary of the efforts and tragic end of this group, see Fernández Robaina 46–103; Helg 142–226.

41. *West Indies Ltd.* (1934) and *Cantos para soldados y sones para turistas* (1937) contain some of Guillén's best known compositions in this vein.

42. For other evidence of black adherence to the Liberal cause, see Taussig, *Devil and Commodity Fetishism* 52, 67–68.

43. Admittedly, my research (e.g., Prescott, "From Coast to *Costa*") has dealt primarily with literary publications. Thus my conclusions can only be tentative until more definitive evidence is presented. Taussig's investigations suggest that occasional and ephemeral periodicals may have existed among Afro-Colombians of the Cauca. Certainly, as already noted above, there is also a rich oral tradition, which has served the people well.

44. In the eyes of many Colombians—both black and white—Robles was not only a powerful voice for the minority Liberal Party but also a dignified man of high character and accomplishment. Even though, from all indications, he was not a "race man," or Afro-Colombian spokesperson, Robles did not hesitate to counter those who attempted to degrade his color or his ancestry (see Porto del Portillo, "Efemérides colombianas.") Upon and long after Robles' death, several poets wrote verses in his memory and honor.

45. Perhaps the best-known and possibly highest-ranking black combatant was Gen. Ramón Marín of the Liberal faction, who achieved considerable fame as an astute guerrilla fighter and intelligent tactician. An illiterate man of humble origins who had been a miner before the war, Marín seems to have been all but forgotten by his countrymen after 1902, dying penniless in 1923. For more information about Marín, see Osorio Lizarazo. Taussig mentions other black guerrilla leaders of that conflict (*Devil and Commodity Fetishism* 65, 75–77).

46. For additional views, see Sánchez Santamaría; López de Mesa, "Introducción"; and Gómez.

47. For more discussion of this series of lectures, see Wade, *Blackness and Race Mixture* 15–16. This racist approach to improving the nation's cultural, social, and economic base was common throughout Latin America (see Conniff and Davis 270).

48. Concerning comparison with the United States on racial matters, see Randall 257.

49. In his biography of Padilla, Carlos Delgado Nieto offers as an example of the subtlety of Colombia's racial discrimination the bust of the mulatto naval hero found on the Bogotá street that bears his name. The straight hair, Delgado Nieto notes, is barely wavy, reflecting the general insistence that such heroes be white (108). Cf. Artel: "Nations, like people, have their defects. One of the defects of the Colombian nation is its eagerness to discriminate. And to Colombians—as to people in general—we must admit it, if, that is, we are willing to admit it" ("El Canciller Colombiano").

50. Cf. R. C. Jones: "In those countries where Negroes are treated almost as equals by other groups, such an enumeration [of their number and status] tends to lose its importance and may, in fact, promote the continuation of distinctions rather than be an aid in promoting plans to equalize opportunities" (46). Writing in the late 1940s, Zelinsky asserted: "The most appalling shortcomings in our knowledge of the Latin American Negro occur in Colombia where the Negro and mulatto population is quite large but where no census has ever listed population by race" (189). His statement

lends support to Londoño, who declares that nothing regarding blacks and Indians is presented in Colombian history (143).

51. Giraldo Jaramillo's pique at a traveler's description of Colombia as a black country—based largely on a visit to Cartagena (131)—seems to be indicative of such concerns.

52. Years after Caldas's remarks, these and other conditions described in the following pages remained virtually unchanged (see J. I. Arango F. 37–38).

53. As a student Obeso lacked the means to buy his books and to maintain himself (Añez 18; Caraballo 15, 16–17). When Zapata Olivella disclosed his ambitions to pursue medical studies in Bogotá, his father, who had studied the first two years of law at the University of Cartagena, informed the future novelist that he would have to finance his own education. He did so in part by managing a billiards parlor owned by an uncle (¡Levántate, mulato! 176–77).

54. I have seen, for example, only two extant copies of the first edition of Obeso's Cantos populares de mi tierra—one in Colombia and the other in the United States. Zapata Olivella's second book, Pasión vagabunda, consisted of only five hundred copies (Prescott, "Perfil histórico del autor afro-colombiano" 115).

55. Only three institutions in the United States list this first edition of Artel's book among their holdings: Columbia University, Princeton University, and the University of Texas.

56. This is not an unusual occurrence. Between lending, losing, and giving away books, several writers I know, eager to have their work circulated and read, have found themselves without a single copy of a particular publication.

57. See, for example, José Francisco González's review of Tierra mojada, Zapata Olivella's first novel. For a lucid commentary on the centrist bias in Colombian literary criticism, see Zárate Moreno.

58. Prior to Truque's observations, writers Arnoldo Palacios and Evaristo Calonje Puche had noted that a small coterie, or "literary clan," impeded the emergence of new and unknown authors—especially those from the provinces—into the literary establishment (Zapata Olivella, "Problemas del libro" 9, 49).

59. Twelve years before Nieto's query, Guillermo Abadía had opined that the book was a luxury item in Colombia (Zapata Olivella, "Problemas del libro" 9). See also Guerra 408, who concurs.

60. For an example of the disastrous fires that have menaced the Pacific coast, see Arenas. It is important to note that the Pacific coast is an area rich in Afro-Colombian oral traditions, of both anonymous and identifiable authorship. Of the unlettered or self-taught poets, one of the better known was the late Pastor Castillo, much of whose work remains uncollected and unpublished. For information on this extraordinarily gifted empirical poet, see Marulanda. I am indebted to Ms. Maria Nelly Bazán G. for making available to me published poems by Castillo.

61. In its edition of June 24, 1946, the newspaper El Siglo informed its readers that the Caucano poet Natanael Díaz had come to the capital to publish a book of poems that he had just finished. Some eight years later, on October 19, 1954, La República, also of Bogotá, noted that Díaz had announced the publication of two volumes of poetry and a novel at the end of that year. The same edition also mentioned that

Argentina's Editorial Losada would publish Carlos Arturo Truque's short stories and that Truque had already begun negotiations with the publishing house. Regrettably, Díaz never published a book and Truque's new volume did not materialize. Truque's widow, Nelly Vélez de Truque, however, has persisted in keeping his work in print.

62. Deceased in 1975, Airó was a true promoter of Colombian literature and culture through his publishing house, his literary magazine *Espiral,* and the literary contests he sponsored. Awarded in several genres, the Espiral prizes included a handsome edition of the winning work and undoubtedly gained the authors much public attention. Truque's *Granizada y otros cuentos* and Zapata Olivella's *Hotel de vagabundos* received the 1953 prize for short story and the 1954 prize for theater, respectively. Although Natanael Díaz never published a book, some of his early writings appeared in *Espiral.* In recent years a new generation of poets, novelists, essayists, and short story writers of the Chocó have had their works printed by Editorial Lealón of Medellín. Although this press apparently does not handle promotion and distribution, several talented and promising authors have found in Editorial Lealón a ready and viable means of getting their works into print.

63. For information on Botero's hardships, see Prescott, "Perfil histórico del autor afro-colombiano" 117.

CHAPTER 3

1. Most of the published criticism on Artel appeared more than fifty years ago, mainly in newspapers and literary magazines, many of which have long ceased publication and are difficult to consult. Consequently, these sources are virtually unavailable both to the general public and to the researcher. The lack or inaccessibility of indexes for most Colombian newspapers and journals of the period 1925–45 also makes it difficult to know or to ascertain the whereabouts of useful biographical and critical material on Artel published in his native land.

2. See, for example, Armando Romero, *Las palabras están en situación,* which, despite the chronological limitations of its subtitle, includes an overview of Colombian poetry from the beginnings of the twentieth century up to the 1960s. Nevertheless, Romero makes no mention whatsoever of Artel and his work. Neither does Fernando Charry Lara, who emphasizes that his book, *Poesía y poetas colombianos,* seeks to enhance interest in *some* twentieth-century Colombian poets and does not pretend to be a history of the poetry that might encompass *all* those poets whom others may consider worthy of inclusion. This explanation notwithstanding, the editor does not mention Artel among those excluded from the anthology and who continue to be outstanding figures of Colombian poetry (11). Similarly, Camacho Guizado, in his "Itinerario de las letras colombianas," also overlooks him; and Alstrum et al., in their *Historia de la poesía colombiana,* limit mention of Artel to his inclusion in poetry anthologies.

3. In conversations during the summer of 1981 Artel informed me that early poems of his appeared in the journal *Plus Ultra,* which I have been unable to examine.

4. The Colombian Communist Party came into existence in 1930. For a detailed account of economic, political, and social happenings of the early twentieth century, see Bushnell 161–80, and Uribe Celis.

5. According to the author of a study of communism in Latin America, Artel, representing the Asociación de Intelectuales Revolucionarios, became a member in 1935 of the Comité Central del Frente Popular Colombiano, composed of liberal and Communist elements (Silva 312). An earlier source states that Artel was secretary general of the Frente Popular Nacional ("El poeta Jorge Artel huésped de nuestro país").

6. It is interesting to note that the poem appears on the same page as excerpts taken from Lorca's book. Artel's poem was reproduced a few months later in *La Patria*. Although he did not include "Gitana" in any of his published books, Artel did incorporate it (under the title "Gitana en puerto") into his unedited collection *Un marinero canta en proa*.

7. For a more detailed discussion of Artel's relationship with the literary avant-garde in Colombia, see chapter 4.

8. The Colombian press also carried many articles and poems on Josephine Baker. See, for example, Ruiz Herazo, "Josefina Backer" [*sic*]; and Labarca.

9. For the promotional announcement that includes the citation, see *La Nación* [Barranquilla] 29 Dec. 1929: 7. An advertisement for Whiteman's film "El rey del Jazz" [The King of Jazz] appears in *Mundo al Día* 31 Jan. 1931: 62; and another for Whiteman and his band is found in *El Espectador* 20 Jan. 1932: 9. Petit de Murat offers further substantiation of Whiteman's fame and standing.

10. Two poems by Artel—"Siglo XV" and "Canción pierrotesca en gris y blanco mayor," written in 1928 and 1930, respectively—accompanied the article.

11. For further corroboration, see Cuervo's comments in *Apuntaciones críticas*, cited in chapter 1, note 21, of this volume.

12. For example, the second number (1931) of *mañana*—a short-lived review of the "literary extreme left" published in Bogotá under the editorship of Juan Roca Lemus, Salvador Mesa Nicholls, and Angel de Dolarea—included a little-known poem by Artel titled "silencio," illustrated with a sketch by Gonzalo Gutiérrez. (From a scrapbook in the possession of Zoila Esquivia Vásquez de Artel.) For information on *mañana*, see "Cosas del Día," *El Tiempo* 19 Sept. 1931: 5.

13. For reports of Singermann's Colombian visits and her impact, see *Mundo al Día* 27 Aug. 1932: 32; Díaz, "Berta Singermann y la poesía negra"; and *El Tiempo* 11 June 1949: 11.

14. Examples of poems dedicated to Cosme may be found in Morales.

15. One of Artel's students in this course seems to have been Manuel Zapata Olivella, later to become an outstanding novelist and writer in his own right. See Zapata Olivella, "Jorge Artel."

16. Less than a year later *Repertorio Americano* published four poems submitted by Artel ("4 [i.e., Cuatro] poemas de Jorge Artel").

17. For mention of Artel in the Caracas group's journal, see *Viernes* Año I, no. 7 (February 1940): 35.

18. For example, "Poema del corazón capitán" and "Canción para ser cantada desde un mastil," as the note accompanying their publication states, were written in Bogotá in 1935. It is likely that the poems of the first section of the book were composed during the years indicated.

19. Esquivia Vásquez, "Artel, poeta porteño," indicates that the book originally was to be titled "La voz de los abuelos." The phrase "tamboriles en la noche" also appears in Uruguayan poet Ildefonso Pereda Valdés' "El candombe," which is included in his *Raza negra* 15, and also in Sanz y Díaz 359.

20. Recalling the years of his youth in Bogotá, Artel remarked in 1944: "Around that time I carried a great number of dreams, many illusions, a lot of desire for life; all of that had turned for me into a pleasant and flippant conception of existence. Naturally, I fit right into the youthful bohemia of the time and my friends were those who, like myself, dreamed of little and had made life a gay sport, living in a purely aesthetic way" (Moreno Blanco).

A few years earlier Gregorio Espinosa had pointed out that "The recollection of those somewhat distant days tends not to be to Artel's liking, for he has determined to erect upon the corpse of bohemia a professional renown. Its evocation, however, is indispensable to an explanation of the poet." Espinosa's comments, written under his pseudonym "PALMERIN," sometime in 1940, are taken from an imperfect copy in a scrapbook belonging to Jorge Artel.

21. Decades later Artel himself confessed: "I have never been fond of publishing a lot of books and it seems to me that one should be more an author of verses than of books" ("Habla Jorge Artel"). In that respect Artel's attitude certainly seems to coincide with Eduardo Galeano's criticism that in Latin America making literature is confused with writing books (264–65).

22. I do not recall having seen any advertisements promoting the sale of the book.

23. In both major and minor international anthologies of *poesía negra* published prior to 1950—namely, those of Pereda Valdés, Sanz y Díaz, Ballagas, *Antología de la poesía negra*, Pérez Echavarría, and Devieri—, Artel's poetry is noticeably absent. Occasionally Colombia is represented by Candelario Obeso.

24. The dates of the three critical commentaries in the book led one Panamanian reviewer (Ruiz Vernacci) to infer that it was not the first edition.

25. Palés Matos's *Tuntún de pasa y grifería* came out in 1937, a few years after Guillén's *Motivos de son* (1930), *Sóngoro cosongo* (1931), and *West Indies, Ltd.* (1934). Ballagas's *Cuadernos de poesía negra* appeared in 1934; Del Cabral's *12 poemas negros* in 1935; and Rodríguez Cárdenas's *Tambor* in 1938. Pereda Valdés had published his small volume *La guitarra de los negros* in 1926.

26. It is also worthwhile mentioning that Alejo Carpentier had published his Afro-Cuban novel *Ecué-Yamba-O* in 1933.

27. For similar reasons, perhaps, the publication of Ecuadorian writer Adalberto Ortiz's *Tierra, sol y tambor: cantares negros y mulatos* (1945) also seems to have had less impact than books published in the 1930s. It is likely too, however, that Ortiz's critically acclaimed novel, *Juyungo* (1943), overshadowed his subsequently published poetry.

28. It is general knowledge that Unamuno, in response to a poem sent him by Nicolás Guillén, wrote to the young Cuban poet in 1932 an enthusiastic letter with an original *negrista* poem, which later appeared as a prologue to *Sóngoro cosongo y otros poemas* (1942), Guillén's sixth book of poetry. Undoubtedly, the plaudits of the respected Spanish poet, novelist, and essayist, as well as reviews of Guillén's work in

Spanish journals (e.g. , Altolaguirre), helped to enhance the Cuban poet's name and circulate it far and wide. Guillén's travels to Spain and France in the late 1930s in support of the Spanish Republican cause and to attend international congresses were also instrumental in furthering his reputation and broadening his poetic horizons. In Europe he met and established close relationships with such major figures as Pablo Neruda, César Vallejo, Langston Hughes, Ernest Hemingway, and Jacques Roumain.

29. In an article on *Tambores en la noche,* written shortly before his untimely death, essayist and critic José Camacho Carreño (1903–40) took issue with the opinion of Lozano y Lozano, whom he perceived to be "the most fanatic of traditionalists" ("Blanco y negro").

30. Addressing Artel in April of 1940, *cronista* Jacinto Fernández wrote: "You know that in this city . . . a futurist-oriented youth is being initiated in the fronds of literature, and you know so precisely because you are the central figure of the movement. Without your inspiration and without your savory conversational dialogues, that nucleus would not be bending today like thirsty grape clusters towards the river branch of prose" ("Una carta para Jorge Artel").

31. Information about Artel's 1941 trip is based in part on an August 1941 article, "Jorge Artel en Colón," shown me by a friend of the poet, and on Henríquez Del R. 30. *Calle 6,* a Saturday weekly founded in 1941 by Panamanian writer and journalist Gil Blas Tejeira, reproduced Artel's poem "Velorio del boga adolescente" in its January 3, 1942, issue, with the following introductory note: "Jorge Artel, Colombian and, more than Colombian, *costeño,* is the most colorful poet of the new Spanish American lyric. Proud of his African ancestry, he sings it without complexes. He is the Negro with the black soul, not, however, in the derogatory sense, but rather in the highest sense which a racial consciousness gives" (4).

32. An article titled "Jorge Artel hizo examen de la poesía colombiana" appeared in the February 19, 1944, issue (Año IV, no. 115: 1, 4) of *Calle 6,* and Esquivia Vásquez reports that no. 140 (1944) of this publication carried a commentary by Artel on Cartagena's artistic and literary ambience (Menelik, "Hilazas"). Regrettably, the numbers of *Calle 6* corresponding to December 17, 1942, through December 2, 1944, are unavailable, having been removed from the collection of the founder whose widow kindly permitted me to examine the extant volumes during my visit to Panama in 1982. The serial does not appear to be available in any public institution.

33. Artel's introduction was published later in *Voces de América.* No bio-bibliography of the Cuban poet, however, records it.

34. For Artel's preliminary remarks, see "Hay que fijar las pertenencias europeas en la cultura criolla." Artel may well have envisioned the staging of the racial poems in *Tambores en la noche* as one means of fomenting a nativist culture. An article on that prospect written by Artel's friend, journalist and writer José Morillo, appeared in October 1947 under the title "El teatro negro en Colombia."

35. This poem and two others were published together under the title "La poesía de Jorge Artel."

36. For critical commentary on the novel, see Lewis, "The Poet as Novelist" 63–72.

37. Chaired by Manuel Zapata Olivella, the session included a reading of several

of Artel's poems by his elder son, Jorge Nazim, and a paper presented by this writer (Prescott, "La presencia y la herencia").

38. Misinformation about Artel continued after his death. The notice in *El País* erroneously included Artel's novel, *No es la muerte, es el morir,* among his collections of verse.

CHAPTER 4

1. Lewis offers a notable exception to this one-dimensional tendency ("In Search of Blackness" 132–57).

2. Significantly, in 1936 critic and anthologist Achury Valenzuela deplored the low profile of contemporary Colombian poets within the Hispanic world and urged his fellow Colombians "to abandon this attitude of ours, insular and disconnected from the spiritual life of America" ("Aleluya de poetas nuevos" 9).

3. For examples of the "state of society" approach to the study of Artel's poetry, see Jackson, "Afro-Colombian Literature of Commitment" 116–19; and Lewis, "In Search of Blackness" 132–57.

4. Pierrot and Columbine are stock characters from the Italian commedia dell'arte, developed between the sixteenth and eighteenth centuries. The former acted the part of a dreamer with a sad, whitened face. Columbine was the sweetheart of Harlequin, a buffoonlike, masked character who wore multicolored, diamond-patterned tights and carried a wooden sword. According to Jean Franco, Pierrot and Columbine are symbols taken from Parnassianism (125), a French literary movement that influenced Spanish-American Modernists. Darío alludes to Pierrot and Columbine in his poem "Canción de Carnaval," which forms part of his *Prosas profanas* (1896). The Greek goddess Pallas Athena is the theme of Darío's poem "Palas Athenea," from the year 1915. For these compositions, see Darío, *Poesías completas* 628–30 and 1262–67, respectively. Poet and short story writer Edgar Allan Poe (1809–49) figures among the writers treated by Darío in his book *Los raros* (1896). See also Henríquez Ureña, *Breve historia* 30.

5. Quotations are taken from *The Dehumanization of Art and Other Writings on Art and Culture,* translated by Willard R. Trask. In one or two cases I have modified the citations to maintain clarity.

6. In his discussion of the mask, J. E. Cirlot explains:

All transformations are invested with something at once of profound mystery and of the shameful, since anything that is so modified as to become "something else" while still remaining the thing that it was, must inevitably be productive of ambiguity and equivocation. Therefore, metamorphoses must be hidden from view—and hence the need for the mask. Secrecy tends toward transfiguration: it helps what-one-is to become what-one-would-like-to-be; and this is what constitutes its magic character, present in both the Greek theatrical mask and in the religious masks of Africa or Oceania. The mask is equivalent to the chrysalis." (195–96)

Elsewhere, speaking of the chrysalis, Cirlot adds: "The ritual mask, as well as the theatre-mask, is probably closely connected with the idea of the chrysalis and metamorphosis. For, behind this mask, the transformation of an individual's personality is hidden from view" (44).

7. In "Saludo a Cartagena," a poetic prose text, Artel presents a more elaborate, objective, and even ironic description of the carnivalesque atmosphere that accompanies the local celebration of the holiday commemorating Cartagena's declaration of independence (November 11). Despite his occasionally incisive tone, there is little doubt that the poet delights in the revelry and even identifies with the peculiarly coastal manner of celebrating the occasion.

8. In this respect, as we will soon see, Artel's poetry shares in the antipopular attitude of the polemical avant-garde literature and art described by Ortega y Gasset.

9. Dunbar's poem may be found in Brown, Davis, and Lee 310. Although it may be risky, or even groundless, to read any racial insinuation into "Careta trágica," it is not far-fetched to discern in the poem a veiled allusion to a common and deceptive Colombian stereotype mentioned previously: that of the naturally cheerful, and invariably loud and festive *costeño*. This interpretation is borne out by statements Artel made years after the appearance of the cited poems. Thinking, perhaps, about his own experiences, Artel criticized the tendency of highland Colombians to misinterpret and generalize about the *costeño* on the basis of outer appearances, reminiscent of Carnivalesque behavior. He admonished them to understand the true, inner nature of their coastal countryman, whom he described as "a man gentle on the inside, with a limpid concept of life, which is to say respectable," and therefore "the least false in the world" (Moreno Blanco). Reinterpreting the élan vital of the coastal inhabitant, Artel declared that *costeños,* because of their pelagic sense of life, squandered everything: health, energy, joy, money—but that what they most squandered were dreams.

10. In this regard León de Greiff (1895–1976) and Luis Vidales (1900–90) are exceptional. Still, Corvalán holds that "Los Nuevos" represented a timid rebellion against the Modernist masters (*Modernismo y Vanguardia* 92). For firsthand information about the aims of this group, see Zalamea.

11. At least two early commentators on Artel's poetry linked the poet with the movement. Valerio Grato noted that "At times he enjoys spending his leisure moments in the house of the labyrinth, cultivating *the Futurists' art;* it is a whim like that of putting on one's coat backward in a carnival spree" (emphasis added). José Morillo remarked that "other [verses of Artel's] are like greguerías of dreams gone by, wandering poems which the gray life of the outlying wards twisted *into Futurist rhythm* on warm nights" ("Tamboriles en la noche"; emphasis added).

12. Cf. Achury Valenzuela: "Artel has saved himself from the poetic influence of the European schools. Artel is an avant-gardist without the need to be enrolled in the "isms" nor in some night course of literary psychoanalysis. He has imposed on his poetry a rhythm, a rhyme, a prosody and a meter that are unmistakable" (*12 poetas* 96).

13. Neither does the poet's early adoption of the pseudonym that became his legal name seem to have been a capricious act. Attending only to the second element ("Artel"), we descry through normal reading the word *arte* (art); reading in reverse brings out the word *letra* (letter). And it is the art of the letter (i.e., literature) to which Artel devoted his life. It is also worth noting that the word *artel* denotes a Russian

trade union, which may be a subtle indication of the poet's political orientation and social commitment to humanity as a whole.

14. Cf. Ortega y Gasset: "The modern inspiration . . . is invariably waggish. The waggery may be more or less refined, it may run the whole gamut from open clownery to a slight ironical twinkle, but it is always there . . . the art itself is jesting. . . . Serious people of less progressive taste . . . will not be convinced that to be a farce may be precisely the [radical] mission and virtue of art" (*Dehumanization of Art* 43–44; the word "radical" appears in the original Spanish).

15. In a similar vein López Estrada has stated, "The new poetry is a work that is found in the learned direction of literature; its condition is fundamentally minority even when the poet proposes to write a work of social intent, and even though its content may include the strongest opposition to the culture of the period" (111).

16. Moreover, what López Estrada, referring to Spain, says about the centuries-old infiltration of the popular element into the learned poetic forms and its leaning toward freedom in both metrical composition and content (105), is probably also true of Spanish America.

17. Although a number of women writers were active in Colombia during this period, there is no mention of their involvement or participation in the male-dominated groups.

18. For Arciniegas's description of his own poetry, see Ortega Torres 254.

19. Cf. Juan Orrego Salas: "The war had developed the taste for rapid action, for the almost instinctive expression of the most contradictory sentiments, for the violent changes that affect both the rhythm of social life and that of music. 'Jazz'—with its pronounced dynamic restiveness, with its characterisitc harmonious audacities, with that constant ridicule of any symmetric organization of rhythm—was called, among others, to be one of the inspiring elements of the new music of those days."

20. For example, according to Francisco Grandmontagne, the first International Congress of Dancers, held in Paris (circa 1924), "condemned the ultramodern dances, especially the jazz-band and the shimmy" (423).

21. Also illustrative of the anti-jazz-band reaction is a cartoon published in a Bogotá newspaper that depicts an exasperated Beethoven standing before a group of gaily performing black jazz musicians. The translation of the caption, which expresses the German composer's ironic lament, reads: "They could not have chosen after one hundred years a better way to celebrate my centennial! . . ."

22. Similar images may be found in other contemporary poems by Artel included in *Tambores en la noche* (1940), e.g., "En las calles vacías / —crucificadas de misterios" [On the empty streets / —crucified with mysteries] ("Silencio" 147); "Mástiles sin banderas, / —enarbolados de silencio" [Masts without flags, / —hoisted with silence ("Muelles de media noche" 185); and "el negro silencio del puerto" [the black silence of the port ("Puerto" 189).

23. For an assessment of García Rovira's remarks, see Mendoza Pantoja, "Un caso de daltonismo literario."

24. Versions of the poems examined by García Rovira differ somewhat from those that appear in *Tambores en la noche*. It is also evident, however, that Artel revised several previously published poems before collecting them into his book.

CHAPTER 5

1. The dedication of Dominican poet Colón Echavarria's *Tambor de negros* ("A Nicolás Guillén, Emilio Ballagas y Luis Palés Matos, Maestros del verso negro" [7]), would appear to support this opinion.

2. It should be remembered that following the Cuban-Spanish-American War, the United States not only imposed the right of intervention in Cuba via the Platt Amendment, but also annexed Puerto Rico. During the early decades of the twentieth century, the United States also had marines stationed in the Dominican Republic and in Nicaragua.

3. A typical example from Colombia is "Bamba," by Arturo Camacho Ramírez (in Achury Valenzuela, *El libro de los poetas* 121–22), a contemporary of Jorge Artel and a member of the later *Piedra y Cielo* group. Camacho Rodríguez's poem is the sole Colombian representative of black-inspired verse cited in R. Valdés-Cruz's *La poesía negroide en América* (1970).

4. A certain arrogance of Cuban precedence in Afro-Hispanic poetry is also evident here in Ballagas's appropriation of Candelario Obeso as one of several "precursors of Afro-Cuban poetry" ("La poesía afro-cubana" 82).

5. All translations are mine, unless otherwise noted. A revised or condensed version of the essay appears in Moreno Fraginals (ed.), *Africa in Latin America* 251–72.

6. Citations are taken from Moreno Fraginals 103–44.

7. According to Perdomo Escobar, *bomba* is a large, two-headed drum (317). Citing an article from 1895 on the bambuco dance, H. C. Davidson mentions without elaboration that a "*bomba*" formed part of the orchestra's instruments (1: 198). It is noteworthy that Palés Matos lists *bomba* as a Negro dance of Puerto Rico (*Tuntún de pasa y grifería* 127). Moliner offers a variety of meanings for "bomba," including "globo; pompa o burbuja," and "versos que se improvisan en las fiestas populares" (1: 396).

8. Significantly, José Camón Aznar regards the Spanish avant-garde writer's own literary work to be "one whole *shout of freedom,* of experiences, of border situations, of decomposition, of rupture of classical lines, of a releasing of all caged doves" (410; emphasis added).

9. There is evidence that "Poema para ser trazado al carbón" [Poem to be Drawn in Charcoal] (163–65) and "Navy bar" [Navy Bar] (205–06), two of Artel's poems that allude to a jazz hangout frequented by sailors, had a basis in fact. Farson mentions a "Navy Bar at Cartagena," which is described as an "enterprising jazz roadhouse" whose owner was a Jamaican Negro (65, 66–67).

10. The *grito* is not limited to the above-mentioned contexts. It also appears in reference to the sea: "esta angustia en mis ojos, / tendidos como flechas / sobre el grito del mar" ("Poema del corazón capitán" 214); and to the blaring horn of a departing ship: "De cuál dolor humano será el grito mecánico / que ahora se alarga sobre el lomo / movedizo del mar?" ("Sobordo emocional" 103). Likewise, Artel also uses the word *algarabía* in nonhuman contexts: "la terca algarabía del férreo cabrestante" ("Sobordo emocional" 104); "despertó la mañana, / colmando el fragrante paréntesis de playa / con su muda algarabía de colores" ("Playa" 209).

11. See, for example, the entry for *¡juepa!* in Günther Haensch and Reinhold Werner 229.

12. For a discussion of Obeso's poem, see Prescott, *Candelario Obeso* 92–96.

13. It is worthwhile to note Hughes's awareness and sanction of the shout, especially as present in certain Afro-American religions. Of "the low-down folks, the so-called common element," Hughes says: "Their joy runs bang! into ecstasy. Their religion soars to a shout. . . . These common people are not afraid of spirituals . . . , and jazz is their child. . . . They still hold their own individuality in the face of American standardizations" ("The Negro Artist" 168).

14. Two films which depicted such scenes are "Trader Horn" and Paul F. Hoefler's "Africa Speaks," both of 1931 (see *Diario de Costa Rica* 5 Jun. 1931: 8; and "Cosas del Día," *El Tiempo* 3 July 1931: 5).

15. According to Fraser, one of "two widespread misconceptions about drums and drumming in Africa . . . is the popular belief that drums are to be found among all African peoples . . ." (6). Kwabena Nketia corroborates Fraser: "In spite of the importance attached to drums, some societies either do not possess drums or do not emphasize them nearly as much in their music as one would expect" (157).

16. According to Kwabena Nketia, "Instrumental sounds may be used as speech surrogates, that is to say they may be organized in such a way as to reflect the intonation and rhythms of specific texts. . . . Any instrument that can reproduce . . . [the tones of words, phrases, and sentences] and the rhythm of speech texts, therefore, can be used as a speech surrogate. Wooden slit drums, drums with parchment heads, double bells, flutes and trumpets are the most widely known. . . . [Drums with parchment heads] are made in all sorts of shapes and sizes and used for conveying signals and imitating speech as well as for playing music" (152, 155; cf. Harrison 51).

17. Concerning the original title, see Morillo's unsigned article, " 'Tamboriles en la noche.' " According to Moliner, the *tamboril* is a small drum that is carried hanging from one arm and played with a single stick (2: 1258). It is considered to be of Spanish origin whereas the larger *tambor*, especially the *tambor macho* of the Atlantic Coast, is of African derivation. For more on the distinction between *tambor* and *tamboril,* see H. C. Davidson 3: 113–17 and 125–26. Coincidentally, the phrase "tamboriles en la noche" is found in the opening stanza of Ildefonso Pereda Valdés's poem, "El candombe," which reads: "Gritos salvajes cortan el aire; / suenan tamboriles en la noche, / que los negros ponen más negra, / con tristeza africana trasplantada a la América" (*Raza negra* 15).

18. For a full discussion of these African concepts of time, see Mbiti 19–36.

19. Although the poem appeared twice in 1933 under the title "La luz de los ancestros," Artel assured me in 1975 that the title that appears in *Tambores en la noche* is the original and correct one. He recited "La voz de los ancestros" on January 9, 1934, during the testimonial to "Miss Simpatía" of Barranquilla, which took place in the city's Rialto Theater.

20. Artel's apprehension of the wind as poetic element is especially felicitous. As a symbol, Cirlot explains, the wind "is air in its active and violent aspects, and is held to be the primary element by virtue of its connexion with the creative breath or exhalation. Jung recalls that in Arabic (and paralleled by the Hebrew) the word

ruh signifies both 'breath' and 'spirit' . . ." (353). We also note the interrelationship of wind (as breath) and life in Scriptures: "And the Lord God . . . breathed into his nostrils the breath of life" (Gen. 2:7).

21. According to French linguist and ethnologist Maurice Delafosse (1870–1926), whom Artel cites in his 1940 address, the griot refers to members of the castes or corporations of intellectual workers who are the repositories of the "unwritten learned [or 'professional'] literature. . . . There are all categories of griots: some are musicians, singers, poets, story-tellers, mimes, dancers, mountebanks; others have the task of learning by memory the genealogies of noble families, the important facts relating to great personages, the annals of States or of tribes, political, juridical or social customs, religious beliefs, and their transmission to the next generation. . . . Each one of these men is a veritable living dictionary whom the prince, the magistrate, or the priest consults when he is embarrassed on a point of history, of law or of liturgy. It is their knowledge that contributes to the summary education of youth during its initiation into adult life" (*The Negroes of Africa* 268–69. Artel may have consulted the Spanish translation of the original French work: *Los negros*).

22. The *cumbia* is said to be an amalgam of African, Native American and European sources. For information about the African roots and indigenous origins of the dance, see M. Zapata Olivella, "Del folklore musical," "La música colombiana," and "La cumbia, baile del litoral Atlántico"; and Delia Zapata Olivella, "La cumbia, síntesis musical de la nación colombiana." Another recent source (orig. published in 1986) is Correa Díaz Granados.

23. Cf. RoseGreen-Williams. I am not unmindful that a reading of Artel's poem that focuses on gender representation would analyze closely the representations of female gender. My emphasis here, however, is on Artel's attempt to establish a reconnection between Afro-Colombia and the ancestral homeland. This perspective should not let us forget, however, that African cultures, as Alice Walker reveals in *Possessing the Secret of Joy,* are not free of patriarchal structures.

24. Also, as African scholar T. Adeoye Lambo observes, dance provides a healthy psychological outlet: "The rhythm, vigorous movements, their coordination and syn-chronization, tend to induce some degree of catharsis. . . . The essential psychological function of the dance, in fact, is the prevention of depression and accumulation of other psychic stresses" ("The Place of the Arts in the Emotional Life of the Africa [*sic*]," *AMSAC Newsletter* 7.4 (1965):41 [*sic*]; qtd. in Hanna, *To Dance is Human* 68. Although the citation indicates the page noted, the bibliography lists the total pagination as 1–6.) At a lecture I gave on Artel's poetry in 1993, a graduate student from Sierra Leone volunteered that common everyday events such as the arrival and departure of friends and relatives, were an occasion for dance, and that one particular purpose for dancing was to rid people of too much sadness or too much joy.

25. Undeniably, as we have indicated, Artel's poems and verses dealing with women were not entirely immune to Spanish-American *negrismo* or Latin American machismo. The ones that operate under those influences often appear to be less original and more ambivalent in their representations.

26. The symbolic significance accorded the drum, or tom-tom, in Hughes's early writing is worth noting. In 1926 he wrote: "Jazz to me is one of the inherent expressions

of Negro life in America: the eternal tom-tom beating in the Negro soul—the tom-tom of revolt against weariness in a white world . . . the tom-tom of joy and laughter, and pain swallowed in a smile" ("The Negro Artist" 171).

27. One cannot help but note, too, similarities of expression between a few of Artel's poems (e.g., "Sensualidad negra" and "Danza, mulata!") and certain compositions by Francophone African poets, such as David Diop's "A une danseuse noire" [To a Black Dancer] and "Rama Kam (Song for a Black woman)," and Léopold S. Senghor's "Black Woman."

28. Gómez de la Serna ascribed African origins to jazz-band music (181–183). Not everyone, however, shared this opinion. Notably, Delafosse, whom Artel had read, adamantly disagreed: "In France when we speak of Negro music we immediately evoke the diabolical harmonies and cacophony of a jazz-band. Now nothing less resembles the music of the Negroes, at least the Negro music of Africa, than the music of the jazz-band. I do not know from what source the latter is derived, but it is certainly not from Africa" (*The Negroes of Africa* 262). Artel's "Dancing" suggests, however, that the Colombian was not swayed by the learned Frenchman's thinking.

29. The use of the word jungle (*selva*) in Artel's poem also seems to coincide with dance scholar Pearl Primus's opinion that "it suggests the music of the interior—whether that music be of voices, birds, instruments, rivers or silence" (174). One might think that Duke Ellington and his Jungle Band (1926) would have been more illustrative of this trend and a natural choice for inclusion in Artel's poem. His name and music, however, do not seem to have penetrated Colombia as Whiteman and his band did in the late 1920s and early 1930s. Moreover, and somewhat paradoxically, Whiteman's group was regarded as the consummate "black" jazz band, serving as a paragon to all the rest, and he was credited with making the music contagious ("Jazz"; Sexton; see also Petit de Murat).

30. Artel's poem is reminiscent of a scene depicting collective female work and song, narrated in René Maran's prize-winning novel, *Batouala:* "The women, as soon as they arrived, set right to work with their *koufrou* to pound the maize and millet and manioc into meal, and while pestles banged in wooden mortars they sang the song of the *kouloungoulou*" (67–68). Maran, it will be remembered, is one of the black authors whom Artel cites in "La literatura negra en la Costa." A Spanish translation of his novel appeared in 1922.

31. Erroneously equating the Colombian *gaita* with the Spanish bagpipe of the same name, some critics have produced translations of Artel's poetry that contravene the racial and cultural connotations discussed below (e.g., "Dance, Mulatto" in Young, *The Image of Black Women* 99). For more information on the instrument, see H. C. Davidson 2:225–27; Abadía Morales 244.

32. Although other instruments, such as the accordion, maracas, bells, marimba, and trombone, appear in *Tambores en la noche*, their mention does not match that of the drum and the *gaita* in frequency or importance.

33. Statements by Artel in the 1940s tend to reinforce the poet's subtle criticism of his fellow countrymen's disdain for *lo colombiano*. In a 1943 interview Artel recognized the intellectual distinction and position of poet and critic Jorge Zalamea, but he also considered him "a dogmatic Eurocentric mentor, who refuses to believe in the future

of a South American culture, often scorning the elements of our geography and our humanity with which a work oriented toward the unique destiny of America can be constructed" (Nieto, "Los Poetas Colombianos.") Less than a year later another interviewer quoted Artel as saying: "Colombian poetry . . . has evolved slowly, among other reasons because—and this is the main one—it is a copy, a reflection of the great poetic movements of Europe. Symbolists, Parnassians, Modernists, etc. The majority of our poets have ignored the voice of the land, that seeks in them an aroused expression, without finding it" (Moreno Clavijo).

34. Cf. M. Zapata Olivella: "Artel does not believe in race. . . . He carries within himself the resentments of many ancestral influences. We can say that his only gods are the ancestors. . . . He believes in the forefathers that live wide-awake in his blood, that are on the lookout for the seagull's flight, that leap with the notes of a *gaita* . . ." ("Jorge Artel").

35. For Artel's insistence on the union of African and indigenous musical elements, see "Modalidades artísticas," where he refers to "el maridaje en que entraron la gaita y el tambor" (20) [the union into which the gaita and the drum entered].

36. Cf. the following lines from the poem "Añoranza de la tierra nativa" [Longing for the Native Land], where the beach is compared, again in metaphor, to black (female) bodies:

Las playas—negras hembras desnudas,
tendidas al sol—,
impregnadas de yodos balsámicos,
brindan al aire
su risa rosada de caracoles. (122)

[The beaches—nude black females, / laying in the sun—/ saturated with soothing iodines, / offer to the air / their rosy laughter of seashells.]

37. Undoubtedly, as Artel correctly stated, Colombia did not manifest "those crude antagonisms of race" that have been present in the United States, Brazil, and Cuba. It had not experienced any race war like that of 1912 in Cuba, nor did Afro-Colombians suffer the legal injustices and violent acts of degradation—individual and collective— that their (U.S.) Afro-American brothers and sisters were forced to endure. In that respect, as Artel suggests, Afro-Colombians did enjoy equality with other citizens. Although today one might question Artel's assertions in light of recent reflections and research on race in Colombia (e.g., Solaún and Kronus; Mosquera; Friedemann; Mosquera M.; Wade, *Blackness and Race Mixture*), it is important to note that he made them about six months after the first celebration of the controversial "Día del Negro" in Bogotá (June 1943). This black student event, it will be recalled, had provoked much concern, confusion, and criticism in several parts of the country. It is likely, therefore, that the poet was sensitive to the possibility of adverse reactions to any unqualified statements about race.

38. Commenting upon black poetry during the height of the Allied struggle against the Axis forces of fascism and racial supremacy, Artel assured his fellow Colombians

that "this art, of course, is not demanding the disappearance, not by any means, of the art of other races. It merely aspires to locate itself, and it has done so, on an aesthetic plane of aesthetic evolutions" ["este arte, desde luego, no está reclamando la desaparición, ni mucho menos, del arte de otras razas. Apenas aspira a situarse, y se ha situado, en un plano estético de evoluciones estéticas" ("El poeta Artel ofrecerá varios recitales" 2).

CHAPTER 6

1. Humberto Jaramillo Arango, on the other hand, saw Artel's book as one "with a flavor of struggle and with the fire of combat" ("*Tambores*").

2. Commenting upon poems of Artel's unpublished collection, *Un marinero canta en proa,* Luis Palés Matos stated: "In this work, the poet moves from the typically environmental and folkloric and falls fully into the universal and anguished theme of the drama of man, of all men, worn down by love, ignorance and misery" ("Dolor que se cuece"). Cf. Moreno Blanco: "For us, nevertheless, broadening now the concepts in view and leaving for a few minutes the main part of Artel's poetry, there arise in this artist of the verse other lyrical shades far removed from the black and marine elements, poems of a refined nostalgia, transparent in their intonation, where man is bound to the purest love, to life and to dream."

3. In yet another example of this dualist or Manichean ordering, the anonymous author of the article "Candelario Obeso" also suggested that Obeso's "black poetry" is exclusivist while "white poetry" is universal (61–62).

4. Haitian critic René Piquion refers to Langston Hughes as "the racist and lyric poet" (77). J. H. Ferguson found that Latin American blacks deprecated the "self-consciously Negro literature," and recalled having overheard "a coloured Jamaican lady . . . telling one such racist poet in her own country: 'I could write the kind of stuff you do' " (79–80).

5. I am referring here to the definition of *racism* presented by James M. Jones: "Racism results from the transformation of race prejudice and/or ethnocentrism through the exercise of power against a racial group defined as inferior, by individuals and institutions with the intentional or unintentional support of the entire culture" (117).

6. Cf. the following newspaper headline: "El pleito de las credenciales. La Lucha de los Negros Puros contra los Mestizos y Blancos Es la Causa. Dijo Arriaga Andrade en su segunda intervención. En el Chocó no hay problema racial. El problema es del 'racismo.' " [The Dispute over Credentials. Blacks against Mixed-Race Persons and Whites Is the Cause. Arriaga Andrade Said in His Second Statement. In the Chocó There Is No Racial Problem. The Problem Is of "Racism."]

7. Vicente Caraballo's *El negro Obeso* renewed interest in Colombia's first avowedly black poet and led to the collection and republication of several of his works (see *Cantos populares* [1950]). José Morillo's 1949 essay, "Candelario Obeso," sparked a heated polemic on *poesía negra* in the pages of *El Universal,* which eventually involved several leading intellectuals of the city (see H. R. L.; and Vargas Prins 150–69).

8. Mártán Góngora would later publish several volumes of poetry inspired in black

life and culture of his native littoral and other areas. For a listing of his works, see Alfonso Martán Bonilla 9–28.

9. See also "Conversando con Jorge Artel" 7: "Poetry, from the philosophical point, is essential and unique, it has no color. It is neither white, nor blue, nor black. But the critics and even the poets ourselves, we have been bent on giving the name black poetry to an aesthetic function of the spirit because of the color of those who practice it, that function in which are sung the anguish and pains of a long-suffering race, that was humbled in the jungle by the European, brought as a prisoner in chains to the lands of America to be sold in the markets like dogs for hire."

10. The other interviewer was the young poet Marco Fidel Chaves, of Puerto Tejada. The Fernando González mentioned by Artel is the nonconformist and acerbic writer from Antioquia whose works include *Los negroides* (see Ayala Poveda 394–95).

11. Cf. Juan Marinello's remarks in his prologue to Guillén's *Cantos para soldados y sones para turistas* (1937), reprinted as "Hazaña y triunfos americanos de Nicolás Guillén": "For Nicolás Guillén a crucial moment in his life as artist and man has arrived. He possesses the word—colored by the vital movements of Africa and Spain and shaken by old rancors and new hopes—which his land and his time require. The long and hard struggle of his island against the mighty who bleed it as well as the immediate awareness of the cruelest oppressions, impose upon him an energetic and combative stand [and] demand of him a service of liberation via his art" (376). Some of Guillén's own words recall Roca Lemus's earlier criticism of Artel's poetry. Given the political orientation of both critics, the similarity is not surprising.

12. For Guillén's opinion on the indigenous presence in Cuba, see Fuenmayor, "No soy un poeta negro" 69.

13. The author of an unsigned review of Artel's book observed that "Through the verses of Jorge Artel the spirit of a race speaks, with all its nostalgia" (Review, *Revista de las Indias* 310). A statement by Ballagas also seems to support Artel's claim to greater racial spirit: "We Cubans do not have in black poetry 'spirituals' nor melancholy blues. Our black poetry has on many occasions the joy of a land of constant sun; *less profundity but more musical nuances*" ("La poesía afro-cubana" 87; emphasis added).

14. Comments made by Artel in late 1939 precipitated a polemic in Cartagena concerning foreign music on the coast. For some reactions, see M. Zapata Olivella, "La crítica cartagenera"; and Leal Baena, "Negro de sociedad."

15. In a brief note on a recital by Artel in Barquisimeto, Venezuela, Guillermo Morón wrote: "He recalled Nicolás Guillén, the interpreter of Antillean passion with the sorrowful *sones. Artel—he said so expressly—keeps away from the son, from the sound, and with everyday words he pries into the heart of Negro humanity*" (emphasis added).

16. For more on the *declamadores,* see Lebrón Saviñón 147–53.

CHAPTER 7

1. One of these is the unsigned review "Meridiano Cultural. Poemas de Jorge Artel," published in *El Universal* of Caracas. The writer assumed, however, that the book was a reissue of the first edition and failed to acknowledge or mention existence

of any new material. Future references to and citations from the second edition are indicated by page number in the text; references to the 1940 book include the year of publication.

2. Interest in Afro-Spanish-American life and culture, however, did not disappear. This is especially evident in countries such as Colombia, Panama, Ecuador, and Peru, where the black presence in literature was traditionally less prominent than in the Antilles, and where more writers of African descent were beginning to emerge and project the rich, heretofore ignored African heritage of their native lands. Indeed, one may well argue that if the decade of the 1940s marks a turning away from blackness—no longer a novelty—in the literature of mainstream (white) Spanish America, the writings of many Afro-Hispanic authors evince a notable, but not exclusive, pursuit and exploration of the African heritage and black identity. In any case, the publication, between 1940 and 1960, of a number of individual collections and general anthologies of poetry related to the black presence in Spanish America suggest an abiding interest in this lyrical vein. For examples of individual works, see Lewis, *Afro-Hispanic Poetry;* for anthologies, see Sanz y Díaz; Ballagas, *Antología* and *Mapa;* Devieri; Pérez Echavarria; Pereda Valdés, *Antología* (1953); and Toruño, *Poesía negra.*

3. I wish to express again my thanks to poet Meira del Mar [Olga Chams], director of the Biblioteca Departamental del Atlántico, for allowing me to conduct research in the library's periodical collection. This institution deserves support to improve its facilities and to microfilm its unique holdings so that they may be preserved for future generations of students, scholars, and general readers.

4. While it is regrettable that Cartey does not devote more space to Artel's work, even more so are the several errors in page references to Artel's book and an erroneous attribution to Artel of verses that belong to another poet (74). It is also lamentable that a printing error—i.e., a period in lieu of the original question mark—in the lines cited from "La ruta dolorosa" (50) distorts the meaning of the poem and results in a faulty translation.

5. A similar alteration occurred when the poem was published in *Presencia negra,* under the title "Poema sin odios ni rencores" [Poem Without Hatred or Rancours].

6. Errors noted include "suelo" instead of "suele" ("Superstición"); the suppression of the third strophe of "El lenguaje misterioso"; "Tienen la noche" instead of "Tienen las notas" ("Barlovento"); and "el suelo" instead of "al suelo" ("Yanga").

7. He also removed the dedications from the poems "Velorio del boga adolescente" (27), "Ahora hablo de gaitas" (31), and "Extramuros" (67), but retained the one to his aunt, doña Carmen de Arco, in "La voz de los ancestros."

8. Bonivento Fernández offers additional evidence about the racial background of the *bogas* of the Atlantic coast: "The Negro type has practically disappeared in the Department of the Magdalena. Only on the right bank of the Magdalena River does one find the the type of man who most resembles that racial conformation, commonly called 'boga,' who preserves the character and appearance of the Negro, but who under the influence of other races, has been changing. He is distinguished by his strong constitution which allows him to defend himself as well as possible from the inclemency of the climate and the severity of the labor" (31).

9. The suggestion of a religious context or meaning within the fishermen's song brings to mind the *bogas,* or river boatmen, of the Magdalena, who were known to compose songs for ritualistic occasions (see Samper, *Viajes* 13; Prescott, *Candelario Obeso* 134–35). Another possible example of religious insinuation in Artel's earlier poetry is the phrase "agua bautismal" in the poem "Playa" (210). Morillo gives the phrase as "agua lustral" ("Teatro negro"). I have not found, however, any publication of the poem with that variant.

10. It is difficult not to sense in these lines an echo of Langston Hughes's famous poem "I, Too," which Artel had cited in his 1940 address "Modalidades artísticas de la raza negra" (16).

11. For Artel's account of this visit, see "Barro y oro del Chocó."

12. In "Los Chimichimitos" (89–91), a poem inspired by Venezuelan legend, Artel perforates Spanish-American folklore's cultural and racial melding to discover a mythic variation on the theme of African exile and suffering. According to the glossary, the poem's title denotes elves or goblins who carry away unbaptized children, luring them with gifts only to subject them to eternal penance (148). Olivares Figueroa confirms that Chimichimito refers to goblin (252), but also notes that it is a folk dance of indigenous origin with African nuances (ix–x; 131).

13. Paradoxically, while the title of ten poems in the first edition contain words denoting song (i.e., *canción, canto*), only one title among the new poems carries that distinction: "Canción en tiempo de porro."

14. Romoli reports that during the colonial era the Marquesa of Torre Hoyos, "the great lady of Mompós, . . . had a galère rowed by slaves in livery and a coach to go abroad in the narrow limits of town" (228). Artel's poem "La ruta dolorosa" refers to a slave ship in the phrase "la galera que nos trajo" (102).

15. As if emphasizing the sorrowful nature of the African experience in America and affirming the integrity of Artel's poetry, lines from "La ruta dolorosa," the poem immediately following "Soneto más negro," reiterate the teardrop metaphor: "En la reminiscencia de una lágrima / residen nuestros dolores heredados (103)" [In the reminiscence of a tear / our inherited sorrows reside].

16. Williams's statement refers to the activity of music and not to the drum per se. Still—and probably because of that referent—the statement is especially apposite here.

17. Cf. "el tatuaje de un látigo" [the tatoo of a whip] in *Antología poética* (1979) 50. The use of the definite article in the original version ties the whip to the specific experience or scourge of slavery.

18. Literally meaning "iron," the word *hierro* here may denote the iron chains or fetters that bound the ankles and wrists of slaves. At the same time, and in other poems, it refers both to the hot branding iron applied to the skin of the bondmen to mark their condition and to the mark it makes. Used with *eslabonar* (to link), *hierro* conveys both literal and figurative meanings.

19. As I show in the following discussion of "Poema sin odios ni temores," an indirect, "surrealistic" representation of the African experience, based on subconscious recollection, is a recurrent feature of Artel's poetic art and evinces the characteristic suppression and repression of blackness in Colombian history and society. For the

possible Modernist and avant-garde origins of this aspect of Artel's poetics, see chapter 4.

20. Cf. the analogous metaphor "el tatuaje del látigo" in "La ruta dolorosa" (103), cited previously (p. 196). In fact, the tatoo figures in both editions of *Tambores en la noche*, although in different contexts and with different meanings. For example, the poem "Palabras a la ciudad de Nueva York" contains a strikingly realistic allusion to the familiar markings on sailors' arms: "la serpiente con rostro de mujer / o el laurel apuñalado *que decoran / los brazos* de algún marinero sin buque" (120–21; emphasis added) [the serpent with a woman's face / or the dagger-shaped laurel *that decorate / the arms* of some boatless sailor]. The tactile and visual image of the tatoo, however, contrasts with the more abstract usage in the earlier poems "Canción en el extremo de un retorno" and "Cartagena 3 a.m.," respectively: "poner a mis días tatuajes de nostalgia" [to put tatoos of nostalgia on my days] and "Ciudad de los mil colores, / puerto tatuado de sol" [City of a thousand colors, / port tatooed with sun] (1940: 132, 155).

21. The allusion to the sycamore, a relative of the common fig tree, also supports biblical intertextuality. The fig tree, per se, appears frequently in Jesus' parables (cf. Matthew 21:18–22; Luke 13: 6–9; 21: 29–33) to illustrate specific lessons. The sycamore, indigenous to Egypt and the Near East, was used by ancient peoples to make funeral boxes for mummies. The application of the adjective "cimbreantes" (swaying) implies the movement of the wind, which, as explained in chapter 5, bears the voices of ancestral spirits (cf. "las palmeras cimbreantes" ["the swaying palm trees"] in "Mi canción" [1940: 229]). Consequently, the presence of the sycamore tree in the verses cited evokes both the deep African roots and the gospel-like message to Afro-Americans and other peoples that inform Artel's poetry.

22. Regarding the skepticism of the disciple Thomas, see John 20: 24–29. Two lines from "Encuentro" also suggest an image of the wounded Christ: "Yo soy aquel que te busca tras la huella sangrante" ["I am the one who seeks you behind the bleeding track"] and "Reminiscencias / de otros días, gritos de rebelión, / alimentan la llaga que te enseño" ["Reminiscences / of other days, cries of rebellion, / nourish the wound I show you"] (117). It is also interesting to note that Artel uses in "La canción imposible," not reproduced in the 1955 edition, the verb *crucificar* (crucify) and other images of Christ's suffering to convey the agonizing difficulty of expressing the myriad voices and sentiments within him: "La canción imposible / crucifica mis ansias bajo un gotear de hieles" [The impossible song / crucifies my yearnings beneath a dripping of sorrows] (1940: 246).

23. Cf. Harding: "For much of his life [W. E. B.] Du Bois saw the black people of the nation as critical transformers and redeemers of the destiny of the world. . . . We define his deepest hopes and convictions as those of a Black Messianism stretched over the boundaries of humanity. This, in his thought, was the calling of Africa's rejected children" (53). Du Bois "had grasped an Old Testament understanding of the messianic people and nation. That is, those who have a sense of common encounter— experience with the acts of God in their history and who are called by their prophets to a common vocation on behalf of all men" (58).

24. According to Arroyo, Artel described his efforts to win full acceptance for the expression of the genuinely American as an "apostolic mission" (4).

25. Artel's use of the phrase "pone / polvos de arroz a la raza!" not only criticizes the false, cosmetic face that minimizes blackness, but also acknowledges the warning that Arturo Regueros Peralta gave him decades earlier (see chapter 6).

26. As early as 1949, in a discussion of the impact of racial discrimination upon black poetry and music in the United States, Artel described Afro-Americans there as a race "vejada constantemente y tatuada por un "inri" infamante" [constantly vexed and tatooed by a slanderous "Inri"] (Gerbasi). In a more direct manner, other poets and writers, such as Countee Cullen, Virginia Brindis de Salas, Helcías Martán Góngora, and Teresa Martínez de Varela, have also depicted the scorned and sacrificial black man as Christ, or the suffering Christ as black.

27. It is probable, however, that Artel discovered in Palés Matos's use of such elements new possibilities for his own writing. In any case, he admitted to admiring the "liturgical poetry" of his Puerto Rican confrere (see Portela).

28. In the third edition of *Tambores en la noche* the title reads "Argelina," which is the correct feminine adjectival form of *Argel* (i.e., Algiers in Spanish).

29. It hardly seems inconsequential that Artel refers here to music and dance, two activities that exercise important functions within the cultural life of African peoples. Moreover, the rejection of the decorative and sonorous ("alegres collares de músicas") and of rhythmic movement ("danzas") inherently parallels Artel's own repudiation of *negrismo*'s continuing emphasis on the escapist gaiety of black music and dance, and of the failure of its practitioners to appreciate the historical and ethnic significance that those art forms often embody.

30. Unlike its usage in "El mismo hierro" (see note 18), *hierro* here refers to the "red-hot iron" or brand burned onto the slaves' skin. Rodríguez Molas corroborates this barbaric practice (5).

31. The *barrios del tambor* were black quarters or wards located in the center of Buenos Aires. The name derives from the African drums that resounded throughout the area and indicated the places where the *candombe* dances took place (Rossi 79–80; cf. Rout 190). Becco confirms the primacy of the Bantu influence in the River Plate region (13).

32. According to Daniel Granada, with the passing of the Africans and the conservators of their customs, the only part of the *candombe* dances that was not lost was the name (see *Vocabulario Rioplatense Razonado* [1889] 68, cited in Rossi 79).

33. For example, the popularity and cinematic representation of the Charleston, a U.S. African-American creation, often gave the impression that the dance was originated by whites.

34. Compare the title of Langston Hughes's *Laughing to Keep from Crying* (1952) and his poem "Minstrel Man" with the following lines from Artel's "La voz de los ancestros": "—Anclados a su dolor anciano / iban cantando por la herida" [Anchored to their ancient pain / they went singing through the hurt].

35. According to Moliner, the correct spelling of the word should be *obnubilado* (2: 540). Nevertheless, it is unquestionable that Artel is repudiating here what he sees

as the symbolic erasure of the African ancestors in the Cuban's work. Certainly, as Guillén's two poems suggest, the African and the Spaniard unite, giving way to a new entity, the mulatto: "la dulce sombra oscura del abuelo que huye, / el que rizó por siempre tu cabeza amarilla"; "los dos en la noche sueñan, / y andan, andan. / Yo los junto" (*Summa poética* 96; 92) [the sweet dark shadow / of the grandfather that flees, / the one who curled forever your yellow hair; the two in the night dream, / and walk, walk. / I bring them together]. Just as Guillén had understated the racial import of *Tambores en la noche* and suggested that Artel undertake a more socially oriented art, Artel now took his Cuban confrere to task for reinforcing an image of a vanishing black presence, especially in the face of whiteness or for the sake of *mestizaje.*

BIBLIOGRAPHY

This bibliography lists mainly works cited in the text and notes and other works consulted. It is divided into two main sections: Publications by and about Jorge Artel; and General Sources, subdivided into Literature, and History, Society, and Culture. To avoid unnecessary repetition, place of publication for Colombian periodicals is indicated only for titles in common, with priority of omission given to coastal publications. For the sake of clarity, place of publication is specified also for non-Colombian Spanish-language serials whose titles overlap, with priority of omission given to the one most cited. The reader may refer to the appendix for a list of Latin American serials.

PUBLICATIONS BY JORGE ARTEL

Books

Antología poética. Bogotá: Ecoe Ediciones, 1979.
Antología poética. Medellín: Universidad de Antioquia, 1986.
Cantos y poemas. [Bogotá: Presidencia de la República, 1983.]
No es la muerte, es el morir. Bogotá: Ecoe Ediciones, 1979.
Poemas con botas y banderas. Barranquilla: Ediciones Universidad del Atlántico, 1972.
Sinú, riberas de asombro jubiloso. Barranquilla: Ediciones Universidad del Atlántico, 1972.
Tambores en la noche. Cartagena: Editora Bolívar, 1940.

Tambores en la noche. [2nd ed.] Guanajuato: Ediciones de la Universidad de Guanajuato, 1955.

Tambores en la noche. [3rd ed.] [Bogotá]: Plaza y Janés, 1986.

Poems in Periodicals and Anthologies

"Al oído de Reagan." *Revista Mefisto de la Literatura Latinoamericana* 2.4 (Dec.
1986/Jan.–Feb. 1987): 26.

"Ancestro." *Letras Nacionales* 35 (1977): 25–26.

"Añoranza de la tierra nativa." *El Tiempo* 8 Nov. 1931, "Lecturas Dominicales": 2.

"Barrio abajo." *El Tiempo* 4 Dec. 1932, "Lecturas Dominicales": 6.

"Breve Canción para Zolia." *El Mercurio* 10 Jan. 1932: 5.

"Canción de los matices íntimos." *La Crónica Literaria* 2.56 (22 Apr. 1933): 3.

"Canción del hombre sin retorno." *El Tiempo* 12 Dec. 1948, sec. 2: 3.

"Canción para ser cantada desde un mástil." *Civilización* 31 Dec. 1935: n.p.

"Canción pierrotesca en gris y blanco." *Mundo al Día* 28 Feb. 1931: 19.

"Careta trágica." *La Patria* 17 May 1929: 5.

"Carnavales." *La Patria* 5 May 1930: 8.

"Cartagena 3 a.m." *El Tiempo* 4 Dec 1932, "Lecturas Dominicales": 12.

"Cartagena, 3 a.m." *Los poetas (de la naturaleza).* Selección Samper Ortega de Literatura Colombiana. Poesías 84. Bogotá: Editorial Minerva, [1936]. 46.

"4 [i.e., Cuatro] poemas de Jorge Artel." *Repertorio Americano* 24 Feb. 1940: 77. ["La
voz de los ancestros"; "Poema para ser trazado al carbón"; "Bullerengue"; "Muelles
de media noche."]

"La cumbia." Achury Valenzuela, *12 poetas, 24 poemas* 97–99. Rpt. in Achury Valenzuela, *El libro de los poetas* 125–26.

"Dancing." *El Tiempo* 5 June 1932, "Lecturas Dominicales": 5.

"Dansa, Mulata!" *Toda a América* [Rio de Janeiro] Feb.–Apr. 1939: 52.

"Danza, mulata!" *Los poetas del amor y de la mujer.* Selección Samper Ortega de
Literatura Colombiana. Poesías 83. Bogotá: Editorial Minerva, [1936]. 71–72.

"Dos poetas nuevos de Colombia." *Repertorio Americano* 25 Mar. 1939: 190–91.

"Elegía de los veinte años." *La Patria* 26 Apr. 1930: 3.

"Evocación de la tierra nativa." A Zoila de Artel. *Cartagena de Indias* 2nd ser., 18 July
1936: n.p.

"Exodo." *La Patria* 18 Jan. 1930: 3.

"Extramuros." *La Crónica Literaria* 26 Aug. 1933: 3.

"Las gaitas." *El Fígaro* 25 Nov. 1940: 6.

"Gitana." *Civilización* 15 Dec. 1929: n.p. Rpt. in *La Patria* 15 Mar. 1930: 3.

"Good Evening, Colón." *El Tiempo* 26 Sept. 1948, sec. 2: 3.

"La luz de los ancestros" [*sic*]. *La Crónica Literaria* 24 June 1933: 5. Rpt. in *Dominical*
9 July 1933: 3.

"Meridiano de Bogotá." *El Tiempo* 26 Nov. 1933, "Lecturas Dominicales": 7.

"Playa." *El Tiempo* 12 June 1932, "Lecturas Dominicales": 5.

"Poema del corazón capitán." *Civilización* 31 Dec. 1935: n.p.

"Poemas de Jorge Artel." *El Tiempo* 8 Nov. 1931, "Lecturas Dominicales": 2, 12.
Includes: "Añoranza de la tierra nativa" (A Juan Roca Lemus), "Sinfonía de la
hora más gris," "Sabiática" [sic], "La cumbia."

"Poemas de Jorge Artel." *El Tiempo* 24 Apr. 1932, "Lecturas Dominicales": 7. Includes: "Canción en el extremo de un retorno," "Canción" [i.e., "Mi canción"], "Puerto."

"Poemas de Jorge Artel." *El Tiempo* 26 Nov. 1933, "Lecturas Dominicales": 6, 7, 12. Includes: "Meridiano de Bogotá" (A Olaf de Greiff), "El minuto en que vuelven," "Mr. Davi"; "Rincón de mar"; "Juan el holandés."

"Poema sin odios ni rencores." *Presencia Negra* 37 (1983): 8.

"La poesía de Jorge Artel." *Boletín Cultural y Bibliográfico* 9 (1966): 704–08. ["Poema del corazón capitán"; "El itinerario jubiloso"; "La tintorera del mar."]

"Sabática." *Civilización* 15 Apr. 1930: n.p.

"Siglo XV." *Mundo al Día* 28 Feb. 1931: 19.

"Signos." *La Patria* 27 July 1929: 7.

"Soneto del hielo," *El Panamá-América* 12 Sept. 1947, ARTES, LETRAS Y CIENCIAS: 17.

"Tamboriles en la noche." *El Tiempo* 24 July 1932, "Lecturas Dominicales": 12.

[Tres poemas.] *Civilización* 30 Dec. 1933: 70. ["Meridiano de Bogotá"; "Mr. Davi"; "El minuto en que vuelven."]

"Velorio del boga adolescente." Achury Valenzuela, *12 poetas, 24 poemas* 101–02. Rpt. in Achury Valenzuela, *El libro de los poetas* 127–28; *Calle 6* [Colón] 3 Jan. 1942: 4; *Fraternidad* 1 Dec. 1945: 16.

"Versos para zarpar un día." *El Tiempo* 24 July 1932, "Lecturas Dominicales": 7. Rpt. in *Dominical* 31 July 1932: 11.

"La voz de los ancestros." *El Mercurio* 14 Jan. 1934: 5. (See also "La luz de los ancestros.")

Prose Writings in Periodicals

"Artel visto por Artel." *El País* 15 Sept 1959: 5.

"Barro y oro del Chocó." *Américas* 9.4 (1957): 7–10.

"El Canciller Colombiano y el Acercamiento Colombo-Panameño." *Vida Universitaria* 21 Oct. 1959: 5.

"Carboncillo de Luis Palés Matos." *La Prensa Gráfica* 8 Mar. 1959, Revista Dominical: 6.

"Carne de Africa contra los negros." *Costa* 7 (Nov. 1937): n.p.

"Cuestión de Minutos. López, El Bodegón. VII." *El País* 8 Aug. 1960: 4.

"De Cartagena a Bogotá." *Mundo al Día* 11 Aug. 1931: 27.

"Desde el Mirador. Declamador." *Panorama* 8 Oct. 1949: 10.

"Desgobierno en Cartagena." *Jornada* 27 May 1948: 4.

Editorial. *Costa; la Revista del Litoral Atlántico* 1 (May 1937): n.p.

"En Bolívar se presencia un movimiento de renovación." *El Espectador* 4 Apr. 1932: 4.

"Glosario Dominical" [Column]. *Panorama* 1 May 1949: 16; 22 May 1949: 9; 18 Aug. 1949: 10; 6 Sept. 1949: 10; 8 Oct. 1949: 10.

"Hacia una interpretación de Santander." *Muros* 3.14 (Jan. 1942): 36–45, 47–48.

"Importancia del folklore. (Síntesis de una conferencia)." *La Prensa* [NY] 18 May 1952: 10, 12–13.

"Instantáneas antillanas. El 'porro' invade las Antillas." *El Nacional* [Ven] 13 Feb. 1950: 8.

"Leyenda y realidad de la Costa Atlántica." *Cromos* 20 Nov. 1948: 4–5, 37–38.

"La Literatura negra en la Costa. Carta de Jorge Artel a Gregorio Espinosa." *El Tiempo* 15 July 1932: 6.

"Modalidades artísticas de la raza negra." *Muros* 1 (June 1940): 16–20.

"Pasión y Muerte del Cuarto Panameño." *La Hora* 21 Oct. 1963: 8–9.

"Presentación de Nicolás Guillén." *Voces de América* 21 (June 1946): 385–90.

"Saludo a Cartagena." *El Tiempo* 11 Nov. 1931: 5.

"Visiones: Panamá: Recuerdo y Perspectiva." *Lotería* 72 (1961): 45–48.

"Versión directa de la cumbia." *Costa* 3 (July 1937): n.p.

————, et al. "El pleito de las generaciones: un manifiesto de los ultra-jóvenes." *El Tiempo* 14 Oct. 1931: 2.

Interviews

"El Dr. Alfonso López No Volverá al Poder. J. Artel. 'Soy marxista, pero mi marxismo termina en cuanto colinda con mi religión.'" *Mundo Gráfico* 2nd ser., 5 Feb. 1944: 7.

"En mi concepto, la genuina cubanidad está en Oriente." *Diario de Cuba* 23 Jan. 1951: n.p.

"Jorge Artel habla en Bogotá de la situación en Bolívar." *El Universal* 1 May 1948: 1, 7.

"Habla un gran lirida cartagenero: 'Siempre querré ser el poeta negro de Colombia y pasear la voz de mis ancestros,' dice Artel." *El Colombiano* 1 Oct. 1943, "Literario": 5.

Olier M., Edgardo, and Jorge García U. "Artel habla de su sangre en una terraza de Malambo." *El Universal* 18 May 1986, "Dominical": 12.

Ossa, Jesús María, and Farid Numa. "Jorge Artel, un poeta que toma aliento en la savia de su pueblo." *Revista Aleph* 26 (July-Sept. 1978): 22–24, 29–30.

"El poeta colombiano Jorge Artel habla para el *Panamá-América.*" *El Panamá-América* 15 Dec. 1946: 5, 7.

"El poeta colombiano Jorge Artel opina sobre la poesía negroide." *La Nación* [DR] 7 Jan. 1950: 8.

Santos Molano, Enrique. "Habla Jorge Artel. 'Hay Divorcio Notorio entre Artista y Público.'" *El Tiempo* 22 May 1966: 12.

Unpublished Writings

"Defensa Preventiva del Estado, o El Derecho Penal frente a los Problemas de la Cultura Popular en Colombia." Diss. U of Cartagena, 1945.

De Rigurosa Etiqueta. Theater.

Un marinero canta en proa. Poems.

Phonograph Recordings

"Tambores en la noche." Read by Jorge Artel and song versions by Leonor González Mina ("La Negra Grande de Colombia"). Sonolux LP 12–523.

"La Voz de Jorge Artel; antología." Colección Literaria (Emisora H.J.C.K.); vol. 29.

PUBLICATIONS ABOUT JORGE ARTEL

"Actividades del Comité. Artel." *Fraternidad* 1 Nov. 1944: 7.

Angulo Bossa, Jaime. "Tres paréntesis sobre Jorge Artel." *Diario de la Costa* 14 July 1945, Sábado Literario: 4.

Arroyo, Anita. "Notas hispanoamericanas. Mensaje y voz del poeta Jorge Artel: Insistencia en América." *Diario de la Marina* 30 Nov. 1950: 4.

Auqué Lara, Javier. "Artel, el Guillén colombiano." *Cromos* 10 Dec. 1949: 5, 27.

Becerra y Córdoba, Esaú. "La nueva poesía de Jorge Artel." *El Diario* 11 Oct. 1943: 5.

Benítez, José A. Letter. *La Prensa* 4 May 1952: 5.

Berrueto Ramón, Federico. "Jorge Artel, misionero de su raza." *Provincia* [Saltillo, Coah.] 1.12 (1954): 6–7.

Bruges Carmona, Antonio. "Poetas jóvenes de la Costa. Jorge Artel." *Civilización* 30 Dec. 1933: 69.

Burgos Ojeda, Roberto. "Unos minutos con Jorge Artel." *El Heraldo* 14 Jan. 1938: 5.

Camacho Carreño, José. "Blanco y negro. Una interpretación de la poesía nueva a través de la obra de Jorge Artel.—De lo clásico y de lo moderno." *El Tiempo* 4 June 1940: 4. Rpt. in *El Fígaro* 6 June 1940: 3, 6.

Caneva [Palomino], Rafael. "Jorge Artel." *Universidad de Antioquia* 18.69 (1945): 90

Cárdenas, Alfonso. "El poeta de la cumbia y de los puertos. Jorge Artel." *Cromos* 2 Oct. 1948: 6, 36.

Carranza, Eduardo. "La poesía negra de Jorge Artel." *El Tiempo* 28 July 1940, sec. 2: 1, 4.

Castro, Ariel H. " '*Tambores en la noche*' grabados por su autor." *Crítica* [Pan] 3 Mar. 1967: 24.

Comité Mexicano Contra el Racismo. "Actividades del Comité. Artel." *Fraternidad* 1 Nov. 1944: 7.

"Conversando con Jorge Artel." *Diario del Pacífico* 2 Nov. 1943: 1, 7.

"Un cronista cartagenero." *Civilización* 30 Nov. 1929: 34.

Cuchí Coll, Isabel. "Poeta Jorge Artel recuerda Isla en Nueva York." *El Mundo* 6 Dec. 1951: 15.

" 'De Rigurosa Etiqueta' va a escena." *El Día* [Pan] 1 June 1967: 12.

Delgado, Oscar. "Jorge Artel." *El Tiempo* 8 Nov. 1931, "Lecturas Dominicales": 11.

"Día a día. Jorge Artel." *La Prensa* 1 Feb. 1938: 4.

Dr. Argos [Lorenzo Ortega]. "Apuntes literarios. Jorge Artel y su obra." *El Heraldo* 19 Feb. 1938: 11.

"Eminente Conferencista Discriminado." *El Día* [Monclova, Coah.] 21 Feb. 1957: 1, 4.

Esplandián [Gil Blas Tejeira]. "Aquí está Jorge Artel." *La Nación* [Pan] 2 Dec. 1946: 2.

———. "Por aquí anda Jorge Artel." *La Nación* [Pan] 9 Jan. 1948: 2.

Esquivia Vásquez, Aníbal. "Artel, poeta porteño." *El Mercurio* 5 Nov. 1933: 4.

Fernández, Jacinto. "Artel y nosotros." *El Fígaro* 29 Apr. 1940: 6.

———. "Una carta para Jorge Artel." *El Fígaro* 8 Apr. 1940: 6 ("Lunes Literarios").

Franco, José. Letter. *La Prensa* 29 Apr. 1952: 4.

García Márquez, Gabriel. "Un Jorge Artel Continental." *El Universal* 15 Sept. 1948: 4. Rpt. in *Textos costeños*. Comp. Jacques Gilard. Vol. 1. Bogotá: Edit. Oveja Negra, 1983. 94.

García Ochoa, Edgar. "Flash. Murió Artel." *Diario de la Costa* 14 Feb. 1982: 5.

Gerbasi, Vicente. "Creyón de la Semana. Jorge Artel: el porvenir cultural del mundo está en el Africa." *El Nacional* 27 Nov. 1949: 20.

Grato, Valerio [Carlos Arturo Soto]. " 'Jorge Artel,' el poeta negro." *Mundo al Día* 28 Feb. 1931: 19.

"Un grupo de intelectuales y universitarios lanzará candidato a Jorge Artel. Obreros y trabajadores liberales respaldarán con su voto el nombre del escritor." *El Fígaro* 28 Nov. 1938: 2.

Guarín, Martha, and Marta Cantillo. "Adiós al poeta de las negritudes." *El Heraldo* 21 Aug. 1994: 13A.

Guillén, Nicolás. "Nota sobre Jorge Artel." *El Nacional* 7 Jan. 1951: 12.

"Hay que fijar las pertenencias europeas en la cultura criolla." *El Heraldo* 17 Sept. 1947: 3.

Henríquez Del R., Betsabé E. "La poesía negra de Jorge Artel." Trabajo de graduacion para optar al título de Licenciada en Filosofía y Letras, Universidad de Panamá, 1964–65.

Herrera Torres, Juvenal. Prólogo. Artel. *Antología poética* 1979. V–XIV.

Hoepelman, Virgilio. "El recital de Jorge Artel. Su arte y su estilo poético." *La Nación* [RD] 25 Jan. 1950: 5, 11.

Ibarra, Gustavo. "Los temas de dos generaciones." *Muros* 3.15 (Apr. 1942): 13–19.

Jackson, Richard L. "Afro-Colombian Literature of Commitment. Jorge Artel." Jackson, *Black Image* 116–19.

———. "Jorge Artel." Jackson, *Afro-Spanish American Author* 51–52.

Jaramillo Arango, Humberto. "*Tambores en la noche:* libro de poemas de Jorge Artel." *El Fígaro* 2 Sept. 1940: 2.

"Jorge Artel." *Alerta* 16 Nov. 1950: 6.

"Jorge Artel en Puerto Tejada." *Diario del Pacífico* 8 Nov. 1943: 1.

"Jorge Artel hizo examen de la poesía colombiana." *Calle 6* 19 Feb. 1944: 1, 4.

"Jorge Artel, Poeta de América." *La Prensa* [NY] 21 Nov. 1951: 4.

"Jorge Artel renuncia su candidatura para diputado." *Boletín Liberal* 23 Feb. 1939: n.p.

"Jorge Artel y Alfonso Castro están en libertad desde ayer." *El Universal* 25 Apr. 1948: 1, 8.

"*La Hora* se anotó dos . . . Artel triunfa en reportaje y en la Foto M. Fernández." *La Hora* 9 Nov. 1963: 16.

Leal Baena, Tomás. "Negro de sociedad." *Diario de la Costa* 11 Jan 1940: 12.

Lewis, Marvin A. "In Search of Blackness: The Afro-Colombian Poet." *Afro-Hispanic Poetry, 1940–1980.* 132–57.

———. "The Poet as Novelist: Jorge Artel." *Treading the Ebony Path: Ideology and Violence in Contemporary Afro-Colombian Prose Fiction.* Columbia: U of Missouri P, 1987. 63–72.

"Una Librería que se niega a vender la obra *Tambores en la Noche.*" *Estado de Guanajuato* 3 Mar. 1956: 1, 4.

"El libro de Jorge Artel." *El Fígaro* 17 May 1940: 3.

"Lo exótico frente a lo autóctono," *El Universal* 24 Oct. 1948: 4.

López, Galo Alfonso. "Jorge Artel, premio en Antioquia." *El Universal* 11 May 1986: n.p.

Lozano Garcés, Donaldo. "Horizontales. Jorge Artel." *Occidente* 27 June 1948: n.p.

Lozano y Lozano, Juan. "Tambores en la noche." Artel, *Tambores en la noche* (1940) 5–7.

Martá, Adolfo. "Carbón de Jorge Artel." *El Heraldo* 12 Feb. 1938: 15. Rpt. in Artel, *Tambores en la noche* (1940) 13–15.

Mendoza P[antoja], Reginaldo. "Jorge Artel." *La Patria* 21 Aug. 1929: 1.

Menelik [Aníbal Esquivia Vásquez]. "Hilazas." *Diario de la Costa* 30 Aug. 1944: 3.

"Meridiano Cultural. Poemas de Jorge Artel." *El Universal* [Ven] 24 Mar. 1956: 18.

"Meridiano de la Cultura. Ilustre poeta y ensayista Jorge Artel visitó *El Universo.*" *El Universo* [Guayaquil] 3 Sept. 1968, sec. 2: 3.

Morales Benítez, Otto. "La poesía de Jorge Artel." *El Colombiano* 3 Oct. 1943: 5.

Moreno Blanco, Lácides. "Conversando con Jorge Artel: El poeta habla de su generación." *El Siglo* 22 Jan. 1944, Páginas Literarias: 2.

Moreno Clavijo, Jorge. "Quince minutos con Jorge Artel." *El Nuevo Tiempo* 14 Jan. 1944: 2.

Morillo, José. "Artel, el poeta de costa morena." *El Mercurio* 20 Nov. 1931: 4.

[———]. " 'Tamboriles en la noche.' " *El Mercurio* 8 Mar. 1932: 3.

———. "El teatro negro en Colombia." *El Siglo* 25 Oct. 1947, Páginas Literarias: 1, 2.

Morón, Guillermo. "Jorge Artel." *El Nacional* 25 Nov. 1949: 4.

"Murió el poeta Jorge Artel." *El Colombiano* 18 Feb. 1982: 4-A.

"Necrológicas. Jorge Artel." *El País* [Madrid] 29 Aug. 1994, Edición Internacional: 23.

"El negro Artel." Editorial. *La Razón* 26 Feb. 1937: 7.

Negroni, Germán. "El verso negro de Jorge Artel." *Diario Las Américas* 2 June 1956: n.p.

Nieto, José. "Los Poetas Colombianos. Jorge Artel." *El Tiempo* 20 June 1943, sec. 2: 2.

"Notas breves. *Tambores en la noche.*" *Muros* 1.4 (19 July 1939): 12, 31.

"Noticiero Cultural. Homenaje." *El Tiempo* 15 Feb. 1952: 5.

Orellano, José. "Donde vivieron Obregón y Cepeda. Artel evoca sus nostalgias." *El Heraldo* 3 July 1983, "Revista Dominical": 8–9.

Palés Matos, Luis. "Dolor que se cuece: Presencia de Jorge Artel." *Alma Latina* 8 Apr. 1950: 6–7, 50. Rpt. in *El Tiempo* 14 May 1950, Suplemento Literario: 2.

Palmerín [Gregorio Espinosa]. "Actualidades." *El Fígaro* n.d., n.p. [ca. 1940].

"El poeta Jorge Artel ofrecerá varios recitales en la Ciudad." *El Relator* 1 Nov. 1943: 2.

"El poeta Jorge Artel huésped de nuestro país." *El Panamá-América* 4 Dec. 1943: 4.

Portela, Francisco V. " 'Lo afroantillano no ha logrado aún el tono patético de lo negro,' J. Artel. 'El primer gran poeta marino de Colombia' cuenta para los lectores de *La Prensa* sus impresiones." *La Prensa* [NY] 16 Oct. 1951: 4.

Prescott, Laurence E. "Aniversario de un poeta y un libro. Jorge Artel y sus *Tambores en la noche.*" *Diario del Caribe* 5 Oct. 1975, Suplemento: 1, 4–5.

———. "Del postmodernismo al vanguardismo: Una primera etapa en la poesía de Jorge Artel." *De Ficciones y Realidades: Perspectivas sobre literatura e historia colombianas.* Comp. Alvaro Pineda Botero and Raymond L. Williams. Bogotá: Tercer Mundo Editores/Universidad de Cartagena, 1989. 147–60.

————. "Jorge Artel frente a Nicolás Guillén: Dos poetas mulatos ante la poesía negra hispanoamericana." *Ensayos de literatura colombiana.* Comp. Raymond L. Williams. Bogotá: Plaza y Janes, 1985. 129–36.

————. "La presencia y la herencia de Africa en la poesía de Jorge Artel." *Contribución africana a la cultura de las Américas.* Ed. Astrid Ulloa. Bogotá: Instituto Colombiano de Antropología, 1993. 363–74.

————. "Remembering Jorge Artel." *Afro-Hispanic Review* 15.1 (1996): 1–3.

————. "Sin odios ni temores: El legado literario y cultural de Jorge Artel." *Memorias - IX Congreso de la Asociación de Colombianistas.* Ed. Myriam Luque, Montserrat Ordóñez, and Betty Osorio. Santafé de Bogotá: Universidad de los Andes / Pennsylvania State U, 1997. 293–303.

————. "Spirit-Voices: Jorge Artel's Poetic Odyssey of the Afro-American Soul." *Perspectives on Contemporary Literature* 8 (1982): 67–76.

————. "*El tambor:* Symbol and Substance in the Poetry of Jorge Artel." *Afro-Hispanic Review* 3.2 (1984): 11–14.

"Recital poético." *Diario de Occidente* 3 July 1949: 13.

Rev. of *Tambores en la noche. El Liberal* 7 June 1940: 5.

Rev. of *Tambores en la noche. Revista de las Indias* 6 (1940): 309–10.

Rey, Max. "Una Entrevista con Jorge Artel." *El Liberal* 15 Aug. 1948, Nuestro Tiempo: 2.

Roca Lemus, Juan. "Los cantos de Artel, el marinero que nació en un tambor." *El Tiempo* 26 Nov. 1933, "Lecturas Dominicales": 6.

Ruiz Herazo, Arturo. "El hombre que parecía un bull-dog." *Civilización* 15 Apr. 1930: n.p.

R[uiz] V[ernacci], E[nrique]. "Feria de ingenuos. 'Tambores en la noche.'" *El Panamá-América* 31 Aug. 1941: 2.

Santos Molano, Enrique. "Habla Jorge Artel. 'Hay Divorcio Notorio entre Artista y Público.'" *El Tiempo* 22 May 1966: 12.

Sarmiento Colley, Rafael. "Jorge Artel. El repatriado poeta de los negros." *El Tiempo* 1 April 1984, "Lecturas Dominicales": 12–14.

Solano Barrio, Lucía Teresa. "Me cansé de ser extranjero.' Las andanzas del poeta Jorge Artel." *El Colombiano* 10 May 1979, sec. C: 1.

"Tambores en la noche." *El Liberal* 7 June 1940: 5.

Toruño, Juan Felipe. "Artel. ¿Poesía Negra? ¿Negroide?" *Los desterrados.* Vol. 1. San Salvador-El Salvador: Tipografía "La Luz" de *DIARIO LATINO,* [1938]. 21–29.

Tuñón, Federico. "Acerca de la poesía negra." *El Panamá-América* 13 Sept. 1941: 6–7.

"Un Jorge Artel Continental." *El Universal* 28 Aug. 1994, Dominical: 1, 8–11.

Vesga Duarte, Carlos. "El libro de Jorge Artel." Artel, *Tambores en la noche* (1940) 9–11.

Zapata Olivella, Manuel. "Jorge Artel, marinero de un mar mulato." *El Tiempo* 12 June 1949, Suplemento Literario: 4.

GENERAL SOURCES

Literature

Achury Valenzuela, Darío. "Aleluya de poetas nuevos." Achury Valenzuela, *12 poetas, 24 poemas* 5–10. Rpt. in *El libro de los poetas*. Ed. Darío Achury Valenzuela. Bogotá: Tipografía "Colón"-Casa Edit., 1937. 3–7.

———, comp. *12 poetas, 24 poemas*. Bogotá: Edit. Santafé, 1936. 2nd ed. *El libro de los poetas*. Bogotá: Tipografía "Colón" - Casa Edit., 1937.

Alegría, Ciro. Prólogo. *Tierra mojada*. By Manuel Zapata Olivella. Bogotá: Ediciones Espiral, 1947. 9–15.

Alstrum, James, et al. *Historia de la poesía colombiana*. [Bogotá]: Casa de Poesía Silva, 1991.

Altolaguirre, Manuel. "*Sóngoro cosongo*." *Revista de Occidente* 108 (1932): 381–84.

Alvarez D'Orsinville, J. M. *Colombia literaria; entrevistas*. 3 vols. Bogotá: Ministerio de Educación Nacional; División de Extensión Cultural, 1957–1960.

Alvarez Garzón, Juan. "Pórtico" [al libro *Costa azul* de Lino Antonio Sevillano]. *Anales de la Universidad de Nariño* 4.32–33 (1950): 144–50.

Amaya González, Víctor. "La danza ardiente o la cumbiamba." *El Tiempo* 19 Sept. 1931: 2.

Añez, Julio. "Candelario Obeso." *Papel Periódico Ilustrado* 1 Sept. 1884: 18–19. Rpt. in *Cantos populares de mi tierra*. By Candelario Obeso. Biblioteca Popular de Cultura Colombiana, 114. Bogotá: Prensas del Ministerio de Educación Nacional, 1950. 7–10.

Anzola Urdaneta, Gonzalo. "El Poema Vanguardia." *El Mercurio* 24 July 1932: 5.

Arango F., Juan Ignacio. *El libro en Colombia*. Santafé de Bogotá: Centro Regional para el Fomento del Libro en América Latina y el Caribe, 1991.

Arango Ferrer, Javier. *Dos horas de literatura colombiana*. Medellín: Ediciones La Tertulia; Imprenta Departamental de Antioquia, 1963.

———. *La literatura de Colombia*. Buenos Aires: Imp. y Casa Edit. Coni, 1940.

Arciniegas, Ismael Enrique. "Canto a la rima." *El Tiempo* 7 June 1931, "Lecturas Dominicales": 7.

———. "El Negro Infante." *El Tiempo* 31 May 1931, "Lecturas Dominicales": 5.

"Artes y Letras: *Las Estrellas son Negras*." *El Liberal* 26 Apr. 1948: 5.

Ashcroft, Bill, Gareth Griffiths, and Helen Tiffin. *The Empire Writes Back: Theory and Practice in Post-colonial Literatures*. London: Routledge, 1989.

Ayala Poveda, Fernando. *Manual de literatura colombiana*. Bogotá: Educar Editores, 1984.

Baehr, Rudolf. *Manual de versificación española*. Trans. K. Wagner and F. López Estrada. Madrid: Edit. Gredos, 1973.

Baena, Manuel. *Aventuras de un estudiante*. Bogotá: Imp. de San Bernardo, 1914.

———. *Cómo se hace ingeniero un negro en Colombia*. Murcia: Tip. M. Arenas Apóstoles, 1929.

Baldwin, James. *Notes of a Native Son*. 1955. New York: Bantam, 1964.

Ballagas, Emilio, comp. *Antología de la poesía negra hispanoamericana*. Madrid: Aguilar, 1944.

——. "Comparsa habanera." Ballagas, *Antología* 50.

——. *Cuadernos de poesía negra*. La Habana-Santa Clara: [Imp. "La Nueva"], 1934.

——, comp. *Mapa de la poesía negra americana*. Buenos Aires: Edit. Pleamar, 1946.

——. "La poesía afro-cubana." *Revista de la Biblioteca Nacional de Cuba* 2nd ser. 2.4 (1951): 6–18. Rpt. in Fernández de la Vega and Pamies, *Iniciación* 78–87.

——. "Poesía negra liberada." *Revista de México* 4 (July 1937): 5–6. Rpt. in *La Prensa* 4 Apr. 1938: 4.

——. "Situacion de la poesía afro-americana." *Revista Cubana* 21 (1946): 5–60. Rpt. in Fernández de la Vega and Pamies, *Iniciacion* 37–77.

Barrera Parra, Jaime. "Notas del Week-End. Los negros dentro de la civilización actual." *El Tiempo* 20 Oct. 1929, "Lecturas Dominicales": 12.

"Bibliografía." *El Tiempo* 23 Aug. 1931: 5.

Botero, Francisco. *Fruto de lucha*. Bogotá: Edit. Minerva, 1931.

Bousoño, Carlos. *Teoría de la expresión poética*. 4th ed. Madrid: Edit. Gredos, 1966.

Brathwaite, Edward Kamau. "The African Presence in Caribbean Literature." *Daedalus* 103.2 (1974): 73–109. Rpt. in Moreno Fraginals 103–44.

Brown, Jonathan C. "The Genteel Tradition of Nineteenth-Century Colombian Culture." *Americas* 36 (1980): 445–64.

Brown, Sterling A., Arthur P. Davis, and Ulysses Lee, eds. *The Negro Caravan; Writings by American Negroes*. New York: Dryden, 1941; New York: Arno P and the *New York Times*, 1970.

Bruges Carmona, Antonio. "Algo sobre poesía negra." *Costa* 3 (July 1937): n.p.

Bueno, Salvador, ed. *Costumbristas cubanos del siglo XIX*. [Barcelona]: Biblioteca Ayacucho, [1985].

Bustamante, José Ignacio. *Antología poética*. Popayán: n.p., 1951.

Caballero Escovar, Enrique. "Bogotá y las letras colombianas. Por el federalismo literario." *El Tiempo* 30 Aug. 1931, "Lecturas Dominicales":12.

Caicedo M., Miguel A. *La palizada* (novela). Quibdó: Dirección de Educación Pública, 1952. (Impreso en la Edit. Iqueima de Bogotá.)

Calcagno, Francisco. *Poetas de color . . . (Plácido, Manzano, Rodríguez, Echemendía, Silveira, Medina)*. Habana: Imp. militar de la v. de Soler y compañía, 1878.

Camacho Guizado, Eduardo. "Itinerario de las letras colombianas." *Sobre literatura colombiana e hispanoamericana*. Biblioteca Colombiana de cultura. Colección Autores Nacionales 27. Bogotá: Instituto Colombiano de Cultura, 1978. 25–121.

Camacho Ramírez, Arturo. "Bamba." Achury Valenzuela, *El libro de los poetas* 121–22.

Camón Aznar, José. *Ramón Gómez de la Serna en sus obras*. Madrid: Espasa-Calpe, 1972.

"Candelario Obeso." *Revista de las Indias* 39.106 (1948): 59–70.

Caneva [Palomino], Rafael. *1 y 9 poemas*. Ciénaga: Ediciones del "Grupo Magdalena," 1939.

Cano, Antonio José. *Madrigales y otros poemas*. Medellín: [Imprenta del Departamento], 1935.

Caraballo, Vicente. *El negro Obeso (apuntes biográficos) y escritos varios*. Bogotá: Edit. A B C, 1943.

Cardona Jaramillo, Antonio. "Notas de humo. Poeta de color." *El Tiempo* 24 June 1948: 5.

Carpentier, Alejo. *Ecué-Yamba-O.* Madrid: Editora España, 1933.

Cartey, Wilfred. *Black Images.* New York: Teachers College P, 1970.

Castañeda Aragón, Gregorio. "Micro-Poemas." *El Tiempo* 3 Apr. 1938, sec. 2: 2. Rpt. in *La Prensa* 29 Mar. 1954: 8. Copyright *El Heraldo.* Quoted by kind permission of *El Heraldo.*

Charry Lara, Fernando. *Poesía y poetas colombianos.* Bogotá: Procultura, 1985.

Cobo-Borda, Juan Gustavo. *Poesía colombiana, 1880–1980.* Colección Literaria Celeste 5. [Medellín]: Universidad de Antioquia, [1987].

Cordovez Moure, J. M. *Reminiscencias de Santafé y Bogotá.* Ed. Elisa Mújica. Madrid: Aguilar, 1962.

———. *De la vida de antaño.* Biblioteca Aldeana de Colombia 34. [Bogotá]: Edit. Minerva, 1936.

Coronel, Juan. *Un peregrino.* 1894. Cartagena: Editora Bolívar, 1944.

Correa R., Flavio. *Mundo abierto (reseña de un viaje).* Medellín: Tipografía Olimpia, 1950.

Corvalán, Octavio. *Modernismo y Vanguardismo.* New York: Las Américas, 1967.

Coulthard, G. R. *Race and Colour in Caribbean Literature.* London: Oxford UP, 1962.

"Las Críticas de Valencia a la Literatura de Vanguardia. Una polémica literaria ha surgido con tal motivo en la costa atlántica." *El Espectador* 4 Mar. 1932: 6.

Curcio Altamar, Antonio. *Evolución de la novela en Colombia.* Bogotá: Instituto Caro y Cuervo, 1957.

Darío, Eugenio. *Caminante sin sitio.* Bogotá: Edit. "Nuevo Mundo," 1953.

———. "De mi otra agenda. La poesía negra es un mito." *El Liberal* 4 July 1948: 9, 15.

———. *Mi hacha y tu cántaro.* Bogotá: Edit. Iqueima, 1948.

Darío, Rubén. *Poesías completas.* Ed. Alfonso Méndez Plancarte. Madrid: Aguilar, 1961.

Del Cabral, Manuel. *12 poemas negros.* [Santo Domingo: Tip. "Femina," 1935.]

Del Real Torres, Antonio. "La influencia geográfica en los escritores." *Diario de la Costa* 24 Nov. 1940, sec. 2: 7.

———. "El Vanguardismo." *El Mercurio* 7 Jan. 1932: 5.

Depestre, René. *Buenos días y adiós a la negritud.* Cuadernos Casa 29. Havana: Casa de las Américas, 1985. 19–34.

Devieri, Hugo, comp. *Versos de piel morena.* Buenos Aires: Edit. Mayo, [1945].

Díaz, Natanael. "Berta Singermann y la poesía negra." *El Estudiante* 16 July 1941: 2.

Diop, David. "A une danseuse noire / To a Black Dancer." Shelton 78–81.

———. "Rama Kam (Song for a Black woman)." Kennedy 187.

Dr. Argos [Lorenzo Ortega]. "Breve incursión por la lírica de color." *El Heraldo* 3 June 1946: 6.

Drachler, Jacob, ed. *African Heritage: Intimate Views of the Black Africans from Life, Lore, and Literature.* New York: Crowell-Collier, 1964.

Du Bois, W. E. B. *The Souls of Black Folk; Essays and Sketches.* 1903. Greenwich, Conn.: Fawcett, 1961.

Echavarria, Colón. *Tambor de negros.* [Buenos Aires]: Edit. Norte, 1946.

Escobar, Federico. *Hojas secas; versos.* . . . Panamá, 1890.

Esquivia Vásquez, Aníbal. *Lienzos locales.* 4th ed. Cartagena: [Tip. Hernández] 1961.

Fernández de Castro, José Antonio. *Tema negro en las letras cubanas (1608–1935).* La Habana: Ediciones Mirador, [1943].

Fernández de la Vega, Oscar, and Alberto N. Pamies. "Ebano y Canela. Motivo y propósito." Fernández de la Vega and Pamies, *Iniciación* 9–17.

———, eds. *Iniciación a la poesía afro-americana.* Miami: Ediciones Universal, 1973.

Fernández Moreno, César. *Introducción a la poesía.* México: Fondo de Cultura Económica, 1962.

Franco, Jean. *An Introduction to Spanish American Literature.* Cambridge: Cambridge UP, 1969.

Fuenmayor, Alfonso. "No soy un poeta negro, dice Nicolás Guillén. 'La poesía se hará más social.'" *Cromos* 27 Apr. 1946: 28–29, 69–70.

Galeano, Eduardo. *Nosotros decimos no; crónicas (1963/1988).* Madrid: Siglo Veintiuno Editores, 1989.

García Borrero, Joaquín. "Gitana." *El Tiempo* 23 Oct. 1927, "Lecturas Dominicales": 328.

García Lorca, Federico. *Primer romancero gitano (1924–1927).* Madrid: Revista de Occidente, 1928.

García Rovira, Julio. "Arrancando Postillas. -Poetas Nuevos." *El Mercurio* 6 Sept. 1932: 4.

Gómez de la Serna, Ramón. *Ismos.* 1931. Madrid: Ediciones Guadarrama, 1975.

Gómez Kemp, Vicente (Ramiro). *Acento negro; poemas.* La Habana: [Edit. Hermes], 1934.

González, José Francisco. "*Tierra mojada* (glosa)." *Revista Javeriana* 29.142 (1948): 114.

Guillén, Nicolás. "Canción del bongó." Guillén, *Summa poética* 77–78.

———. *Cantos para soldados y sones para turistas.* México: Edit. Masas, 1937.

———. *Motivos de son.* Guillén, *Summa poética* 59–73.

———. "Pequeña oda a Kid Chocolate." *El Tiempo* 26 Jan. 1930, "Lecturas Dominicales": 4.

———. "Recuerdos colombianos." *Bohemia* 26 Sept. 1948: 20–21, 91, 105.

———. "Secuestro de la mujer de Antonio." *El Tiempo* 17 May 1931, "Lecturas Dominicales": 10.

———. *Sóngoro cosongo; poemas mulatos.* La Habana: Ucar, García y Cía., 1931.

———. *Sóngoro cosongo y otros poemas.* La Habana: Imp. La Verónica, 1942.

———. *Summa poética.* Ed. Luis Iñigo Madrigal. 6th ed. Madrid: Ediciones Cátedra, 1986.

———. *West Indies, Ltd.; poemas.* La Habana: Ucar, García y Cía., 1934.

———. "Yambambó (Canto negro)." *El Tiempo* 9 Nov. 1930, "Lecturas Dominicales": 9.

Guirao, Ramón. *Bongó; poemas negros.* [San Cristóbal de la Habana: Talleres de Ucar, García y Cía., 1934].

H. R. L. "La vida literaria en Cartagena." *El Siglo* 25 Sept. 1949: 2.

Henríquez Ureña, Max. *Breve historia del modernismo*. 2nd ed. México: Fondo de Cultura Económica, 1962.

———. *Panorama histórico de la literatura cubana*. 2 vols. La Habana: Edit. Arte y Literatura, 1979.

Hughes, Langston. *I Wonder as I Wander; An Autobiographical Journey*. 1956. New York: Hill and Wang; American Century Series, 1964.

———. "The Negro Artist and the Racial Mountain." *Nation* 23 June 1926: 692–94. Rpt. in *The Black Aesthetic*. Ed. Addison Gayle, Jr. Garden City, N.Y.: Anchor-Doubleday, 1972. 167–72.

———. "Our Land." *The New Negro*. Ed. Alain Locke. 1925. New York: Atheneum, 1968. 144.

———. *Selected Poems*. New York: Vintage-Random, 1974.

Isaacs, Jorge. "El esclavo Pedro." *La Patria* [Bog] 2 (1878): 16.

Jackson, Richard L. *The Afro-Spanish American Author; An Annotated Bibliography of Criticism*. New York: Garland, 1980.

———. *The Black Image in Latin American Literature*. Albuquerque: U of New Mexico P, 1976.

———. *Black Writers in Latin America*. Albuquerque: U of New Mexico P, 1979.

Kennedy, Ellen Conroy, ed. *The Negritude Poets; an Anthology of Translations from the French*. 1975. New York: Thunder's Mouth P, 1989.

Kent, George. *Blackness and the Adventure of Western Culture*. Chicago: Third World P, 1972.

Kutzinski, Vera M. *Sugar's Secrets: Race and the Erotics of Cuban Nationalism*. Charlottesville and London: UP of Virginia, 1993.

Lagos, Ramiro, comp. *Poesía liberada y deliberada de Colombia*. Bogotá: Ediciones Tercer Mundo, 1976.

León, María Teresa. "Romance del enamorado de la gitana." *Diario del Comercio* 30 Nov. 1929: 14

Lewis, Marvin A. *Afro-Hispanic Poetry, 1940–1980: From Slavery to Negritude in South American Verse*. Columbia: U of Missouri P, 1983.

Locke, Alain, ed. *The New Negro*. 1925. New York: Atheneum, 1968.

López, Eduardo. *Cosas viejas (poemas)*. Bogotá: Escuela Tipográfica Salesiana, 1931.

López Estrada, Francisco. *Métrica española del siglo XX*. Madrid: Edit. Gredos, 1969.

McKay, Claude. *Cock-tail negro*. Trans. A. Rodríguez de León and R. R. Fernández-Andés. Madrid: Ediciones Ulises, 1931. Trans. of *Home to Harlem*. 1928.

———. *Selected Poems*. New York: Harcourt Brace & World, 1953.

Mansour, Mónica. *La poesía negrista*. México, D.F.: Ediciones Era, 1973.

Manzano, Juan Francisco. *Autobiografía de un esclavo*. Ed. Ivan A. Schulman. Madrid: Ediciones Guadarrama, 1975.

———. *Obras*. Ed. José Luciano Franco. [La Habana?]: Instituto Cubano del Libro, [1972].

Maran, René. *Batouala*. London: Jonathan Cape, 1922.

———. *Batuala; Verdadera novela de negros*. Trans. José Mas. Madrid: Imp. y Edit. V. H. De Sanz Calleja, 1922.

Marchese, Angelo, and Joaquín Forradellas. *Diccionario de retórica, crítica y terminología literaria.* Barcelona: Edit. Ariel, S.A., 1986.

Marinello, Juan. "Hazaña y triunfos americanos de Nicolás Guillén." *Cantos para soldados y sones para turistas.* By Nicolás Guillén. México: Edit. Masas, 1937. Rpt. in *Cuba: Cultura.* By Juan Marinello. Comp. Ana Suárez Díaz. La Habana: Edit. Letras Cubanas, 1989. 372–80.

Martán Bonilla, Alfonso. "La poesía de Martán Góngora." *Poeta del mar; antología temática.* By Helcías Martán Góngora. Cali: Ediciones Universidad del Valle, 1993. 9–28.

Martán Góngora, Helcías. "Presentación de un Poeta: Hugo Salazar." *El Liberal* 23 May 1948, "Nuestro Tiempo": 2.

Martínez de Varela R., Teresa. *Mi Cristo Negro.* [Bogotá?]: Imprenta Fondo Rotatorio Policía Nacional, [1983].

Marulanda, Octavio. "Pastor Castillo, rimado extraño." *Páginas de Cultura* 9 (1965): 1, 5.

Mateus, Jorge. "Elegía risueña del jazz band." *El Tiempo* 7 Dec. 1930, "Lecturas Dominicales": 2.

Maya López, Rogelio. "Un nuevo poeta y un nuevo libro." *La Patria* [Man] 29 May 1948: 4.

Mendoza P[antoja], Reginaldo. "Un caso de daltonismo literario." *El Mercurio* 10 Sept. 1932: 4.

Micromegas. [José Gerardo Ramírez Serna]. "Poetas negros." *El Relator* 28 Feb. 1946: 4.

Miller, James E., Jr., Robert O'Neal, and Helen M. McDonnell, eds. *Black African Voices.* Glenview, Ill.: Scott, 1970.

Moore, Gerald. "Poetry in the Harlem Renaissance." *The Black American Writer.* Ed. C. W. E. Bigsby. Vol. 2. Baltimore: Penguin Books, 1971. 67–76. 2 vols.

Morales, José Luis, comp. *Poesía afroantillana y negrista (Puerto Rico - República Dominicana - Cuba).* Río Piedras: Edit. Universitaria; U de Puerto Rico, 1976.

Morejón, Nancy, comp. *Recopilación de textos sobre Nicolás Guillén.* [Havana]: Casa de las Américas, 1974.

Morillo, José. "Candelario Obeso." *El Siglo* 16 Jan. 1949, Páginas Literarias: 4.

[———]. "Una evocación de Langston Hughes." *El Mercurio* 29 June 1932: 3, 4.

Mullen, Edward. "The Emergence of Afro-Hispanic Poetry: Some Notes on Canon Formation." *Hispanic Review* 56 (1988): 435–53.

Nieto, José. "Entrevista literaria con el poeta José Nieto." By Antonio del Real Torres. *Diario de la Costa* 27 Jan. 1942: 11.

———. "Problema de la Actualidad Permanente. Por qué no hay escritores en Colombia?" *El Tiempo* 19 Apr. 1959, "Lecturas Dominicales": 2.

Obeso, Candelario. *Cantos populares de mi tierra.* Bogotá: Imprenta de Borda, 1877. Rpt. in *Cantos populares de mi tierra.* 1950. 11–46.

———. *Cantos populares de mi tierra.* Biblioteca Popular de Cultura Colombiana, 114. Bogotá: Prensas del Ministerio de Educación Nacional, 1950.

———. *Las cosas del mundo. La familia Pygmalion.* Bogotá, 1871.

————. *Lectura para ti,* publicación por entregas. Bogotá: Imprenta de Guarín y Compañía, 1878. Rpt. in *Cantos populares de mi tierra.* 1950. 47–89.

————. *Lucha de la vida.* Bogotá: Imprenta de Silvestre y Compañía, 1882.

————. "Palabras al aire." *La Ilustración* 8 Sept. 1874: 276.

Olivera, Otto. *Cuba en su poesía.* Colección Studium 49. Mexico: Ediciones de Andrea, 1965.

Onís, Federico de, ed. *Antología de la poesía española e hispanoamericana (1882–1832).* Madrid, 1934. Rpt. New York: Las Américas, 1961.

Orjuela, Héctor H., comp. *Bibliografía de la poesía colombiana.* Bogotá: Instituto Caro y Cuervo, 1971.

Ortega Torres, José J. *Poesía colombiana; Antología de 490 composiciones de 90 autores.* Bogotá: Edit. de la Litografía Colombia, 1942.

Ortega y Gasset, José. *The Dehumanization of Art and Other Writings on Art and Culture.* Trans. Willard R. Trask. Garden City, N.Y.: Doubleday, n.d.

————. *La deshumanización del arte.* 1925. Madrid: Revista de Occidente en Alianza Edit., 1983.

Ortiz, Adalberto. *Juyungo; Historia de un negro, una isla y otros negros.* Buenos Aires: Américalee, 1943.

————. *Tierra, sol y tambor: Cantares negros y mulatos.* México: Ediciones La Cigarra, 1945.

Ortiz, Fernando. *Hampa afro-cubana. Los negros brujos.* Madrid: Librería de F. Fe, 1906; Madrid: Edit. América, 1917.

————. *Hampa afro-cubana. Los negros esclavos.* La Habana: Revista Bimestre Cubana, 1916.

————. "Más acerca de la poesía mulata. Escorzos para su estudio." *Revista Bimestre Cubana* 37 (1936): 23–39, 218–27, 439–43. Rpt. in Fernández de la Vega and Pamies, *Iniciación* 172–202.

————. "Los últimos versos mulatos." *Revista Bimestre Cubana* 35 (1935): 321–336. Rpt. in Fernández de la Vega and Pamies. 156–71.

Ortiz, Venancio. "La esclava." *El Orden* 14 Feb. 1890: 61–62.

Osorio T., Nelson, ed. *Manifiestos, proclamas y polémicas de la vanguardia literaria hispanoamericana.* Caracas: Biblioteca Ayacucho, [1988].

Palacios, Arnoldo. *Las estrellas son negras.* Bogotá: Edit. Iqueima, 1949.

————. "Sangre Nueva" *El Liberal* 22 Oct. 1946: 11.

Palés Matos, Luis. "Danza negra." *El Tiempo* 6 July 1930, "Lecturas Dominicales": 6.

————. "Tambores." *Tuntún de pasa y grifería* 98–99.

————. *Tuntún de pasa y grifería; poemas afro-antillanos.* Biblioteca de Autores Puertorriqueños. San Juan: Imp. Venezuela, 1937. 3rd. ed. San Juan: Cultural Puertorriqueña, 1988.

Payán Archer, Guillermo. "Breve nota sobre Natanael Díaz." *El Liberal* 18 Aug. 1946, "Suplemento Literario": 8.

Pereda Valdés, Ildefonso, comp. *Antología de la poesía negra americana.* Santiago de Chile: Ediciones Ercilla, 1936.

————, comp. *Antología de la poesía negra americana.* 2nd ed. Montevideo: B. U. D. A., 1953.

———. *La guitarra de los negros*. Montevideo: [La Cruz del Sur], 1926.

———. *Raza negra*. [Montevideo]: Edición del periódico negro *La Vanguardia*, 1929.

Pérez Echavarría, Miguel Román, comp. *La poesía negra en América; Antología*. Buenos Aires: Nocito y Raño, 1946.

Pérez y Soto, Simón. "A las palabras sin rima." *El Tiempo* 28 June 1931, "Lecturas Dominicales": 8.

Piquion, René. *Langston Hughes, un chant nouveau*. Port-au-Prince, Haiti: Imprimierie de l'Etat, [1940].

Pombo, Rafael. "A un esclavo." *Poesía inédita y olvidada*. Ed. Héctor H. Orjuela. Vol. 2. Bogotá: Instituto Caro y Cuervo, 1970. 23–27. 2 vols.

Portuondo, José Antonio. *Bosquejo histórico de las letras cubanas*. La Habana: Ministerio de Relaciones Exteriores, 1960.

Prescott, Laurence E. *Candelario Obeso y la iniciación de la poesía negra en Colombia*. Bogotá: Instituto Caro y Cuervo, 1985.

———. "A Conversation with Nicolás Guillén." *Callaloo* 10 (1987): 352–54.

———. "From Coast to *Costa:* Race Consciousness and Afro-Colombian Periodicals." Unpublished paper, Sixth Annual Conference of the Association of North American Colombianists, Lawrence, Kansas, 9–11 Nov. 1989.

———. "Natanael Díaz y la lucha por la identidad del negro en Colombia: un capítulo desconocido de la historia afroamericana." Unpublished paper, Eleventh International Congress of the Latin American Studies Association, Mexico City, 29 Sept.–1 Oct. 1983.

———. "Negras, morenas, zambas y mulatas: Presencia de la mujer afro-americana en la poesía colombiana." *Colombia: Literatura y Cultura del siglo XX*. Ed. Isabel Rodríguez Vergara. [Washington, D.C.]: OEA/OAS, c1995. 179–95.

———. "*Negro nací:* Authorship and Voice in Verses Attributed to Candelario Obeso." *Afro-Hispanic Review* 12.1 (1993): 3–15.

———. "Perfil histórico del autor afro-colombiano: Problemas y perspectivas." *América Negra* 12 (Dec. 1996): 107–28.

Rampersad, Arnold. *The Life of Langston Hughes*. Vol. 2. New York: Oxford UP, 1988. 2 vols.

Realpe Borja, Marco. *Un canto civil a Whitman y otros poemas*. Grupo Funcionalista. Bogotá: [Edit. S-I-P-A], 1959.

Redmond, Eugene B. *Drumvoices: The Mission of Afro-American Poetry. A Critical History*. Garden City, N.Y.: Anchor- Doubleday, 1976.

Restrepo Maya, Bernardo. "Poetas del Litoral Atlántico." *Sábado* 22 July 1944: 16.

Rivas, Mercedes. *Literatura y esclavitud en la novela cubana del siglo XIX*. Sevilla: Escuela de Estudios Hispano-Americanos de Sevilla, 1990.

Rodríguez Cárdenas, Manuel. *Tambor (poemas para negros y mulatos)*. Caracas: Edit. "Elite," 1938.

Romero, Armando. *Las palabras están en situación; un estudio de la poesía colombiana de 1940 a 1960*. Bogotá: Procultura, 1985.

RoseGreen-Williams, Claudette. "The Myth of Black Female Sexuality in Spanish

Caribbean Poetry: A Deconstructive Critical View." *Afro-Hispanic Review* 12.1 (1993): 16–23.

Ruiz Herazo, Arturo. "Josefina Backer [sic]." *Mundo al Día* 28 Mar. 1931: 20.

Said, Edward W. *The World, the Text, and the Critic.* Cambridge: Harvard UP, 1983.

Salazar, Adolfo. "Claudio MacKay y el sionismo de color." *El Tiempo* 25 Oct. 1931, "Lecturas Dominicales": 11.

Salazar Valdés, Hugo. *Carbones en el alba; poemas.* Bogotá: Edit. Iqueima, 1951.

———. *Sal y lluvia.* Cali: Tip. Lutamon, 1948.

Salgar Pérez, Alicia. "Gitanerías." *El Tiempo* 24 Jan. 1932, "Lecturas Dominicales": n.p.

Samper, Darío. "Nacionalismo y cultura." *El Tiempo* 18 May 1930, "Lecturas dominicales": 5.

Sánchez, Luis Alberto. *Historia de la literatura americana (desde los orígenes hasta 1936).* Santiago de Chile: Ediciones Ercilla, 1937.

Sánchez López, Luis María. *Diccionario de escritores colombianos.* 3rd ed. [Bogotá]: Plaza y Janés, Editores Colombia Ltda., 1985.

Sanz, Gerónimo. "Ante la tumba de un negro esclavo." *El Pasatiempo* 12 Apr. 1879: 583.

———. *Poesías de Gerónimo Sanz.* Habana, 1881.

Sanz y Díaz, José, ed. and comp. *Lira negra (selecciones españolas y afroamericanas).* Colección Crisol 21. Madrid: M. Aguilar, 1945.

Schulman, Ivan A. Introducción. *Autobiografía de un esclavo.* By Juan Francisco Manzano. Madrid: Ediciones Guadarrama, 1975. 11–54.

Senghor, Léopold Sédar. "Black Woman." Drachler 129–30.

Sevillano Quiñones, Lino Antonio. *Costa azul.* Pasto: Edit. "Cultura," 1949.

Shelton, Austin J., ed. *The African Assertion; A Critical Anthology of African Literature.* New York: Odyssey P, 1968.

Sola, Sabino. *El diablo y lo diabólico en las letras americanas (1550–1750).* Publs. de la Universidad de Deusto, 3. Bilbao: Universidad de Deusto, 1973.

Strauss, Leo. *Persecution and the Art of Writing.* Glencoe, Ill.: Free, c1952.

Torre, Rogelio de la. *La obra poética de Emilio Ballagas.* Miami: Ediciones Universal, 1977.

Torres Caicedo, J. M., ed. *Ensayos biográficos y de crítica literaria.* Vol. 2. París, 1868. 3 vols. 1863–1868.

Torres León, Fernán. "La poesía a través de 4 poetas jóvenes." *El Tiempo* 19 Apr. 1959, "Lecturas Dominicales": 3.

Toruño, Juan Felipe, ed. *Poesía negra; Ensayo y antología.* México, D.F.: Colección Obsidiana, 1953.

———. *Poesía y poetas de América; Trayecto en ámbitos, fisonomías y posiciones.* [San Salvador, El Salvador: Imprenta Funes, 1944.]

Trelles, Carlos M. "Bibliografía de autores de la raza de color de Cuba." *Revista cubana contemporánea* 43 (1927): 30–78.

Truque, Carlos Arturo. *El día que terminó el verano y otros cuentos.* Bogotá: Instituto Colombiano de Cultura, 1973.

———. *Granizada y otros cuentos.* Bogotá: Ediciones Espiral Colombia, 1953.

———. *¡Vivan los compañeros!* Bogotá: Colcultura, 1993.

———. "La vocación y el medio: historia de un escritor." *Mito* 6 (1956): 480–86. Rpt. in *El Colombiano* 22 Apr. 1956, "Literario": 2.

Valdés-Cruz, Rosa E. *La poesía negroide en América.* New York: Las Américas, 1970.

Valencia, Gerardo. "La negra de los sahumerios." *El Tiempo* 7 Dec. 1930, "Lecturas Dominicales": 12.

Vanín Romero, Alfredo. *Alegando que vivo; poemas.* [Popayán: Edit. López Ltda.], n.d. [1976?].

Vargas Prins, P[edro] P[ablo]. *Crítica y prosas (Filosofía, literatura e ideas).* Cartagena: n.p., 1949.

Velásquez [Murillo], Rogelio. *Las memorias del odio.* Bogotá: Ediciones de la Alianza de Escritores Colombianos; Edit. Iqueima, 1953.

Vélez, Victoriano. *De mis breñas; cuentos y cantos.* Bogotá: Ediciones Colombia, 1926.

Vergara y Vergara, José María. "La Semana Santa en Popayán." 1866. *Museo de cuadros de costumbres.* Vol. 1. Biblioteca de "El Mosaico." Bogotá: Banco Popular, 1973. 4 vols. 293–307.

Villegas, Cenón Fabio. "El Vate Negro." *El Lirio* 11 (1899): 83–84.

Walker, Alice. *Living by the Word. Selected Writings 1973–1987.* New York: Harcourt, 1988.

———. *Possessing the Secret of Joy.* New York: Harcourt, 1992.

Wheelwright, Philip. *Metaphor and Reality.* Bloomington: Indiana UP, 1962.

Williams, Eric. "Four Poets of the Greater Antilles." *Caribbean Quarterly* 2.4 (1952): 8–15.

Williams, Lorna V. *The Representation of Slavery in Cuban Fiction.* Columbia: U of Missouri P, 1994.

Williams, Raymond L. *The Colombian Novel, 1844–1987.* Austin: U of Texas P, 1991.

Williams, Sherley Anne. *Give Birth to Brightness; A Thematic Study in Neo-Black Literature.* New York: Dial, 1972.

Wilson, Leslie N. *La poesía afro-antillana.* Miami, Fla.: Ediciones Universal, 1979.

Young, Ann Venture. "The Black Woman in Afro-Caribbean Poetry." *Blacks in Hispanic Literature: Critical Essays.* Ed. Miriam DeCosta. Port Washington, N.Y.: Kennikat P, 1977. 137–42.

———, ed. and tr. *The Image of Black Women in Twentieth-Century South American Poetry; A Bilingual Anthology.* Washington, D.C.: Three Continents, 1987.

Zalamea, Jorge. "El 'programa' de 'Los Nuevos,'" "Editorial de *Los Nuevos.*" *Crítica* 1 Sept. 1950. Rpt. in *Literatura, política y arte.* Ed. J. G. Cobo Borda. Bogotá: Instituto Colombiano de Cultura, 1978. 594–97.

Zapata [Vásquez], Antonio María. "Nuestros ideales." Editorial. *Rojas Garrido* 10 June 1917: 1–2.

Zapata Olivella, Manuel. *He visto la noche; relatos.* Bogotá: Edit. "Los Andes," 1953.

———. *Hotel de vagabundos; Teatro.* Bogotá: Ediciones Espiral Colombia, 1955.

———. *¡Levántate, mulato!* Bogotá: Rei Andes Ltda., 1990.

———. *Pasión vagabunda (relatos).* Bogotá: Edit. Santafé, 1949.

———. *Tierra mojada; novela.* Bogotá: Edit. Iqueima, 1947.

Zárate Moreno, Jesús. "La actualidad literaria en Colombia. La crítica contra la crítica." *El Espectador* 22 Jan. 1950, "Dominical": 6.

Zubiría, Tito de. "Poetas de América. Paul Laurence Dunbar." *El Fígaro* 9 Dec. 1940: 6.

History, Society, and Culture

Abadía Morales, Guillermo. *Compendio general de folklore colombiano.* 3rd ed. Biblioteca Básica Colombiana 24. Bogotá: Instituto Colombiano de Cultura, 1977.

Acosta Hoyos, Luis Eduardo. *Bibliografía anotada del Departamento de Nariño.* Pasto: Imprenta del Departamento, 1966.

"Actualidades." *El Mercurio* 29 Apr. 1932: 3.

Alakija, Oluwole Ayodele. "Is the African Musical?" *Negro: An Anthology.* Comp. and ed. Nancy Cunard. Ed. and abridged by Hugh Ford. 1934. New York: Frederick Ungar, 1970. 249–51.

Alba, Victor. *The Latin Americans.* New York: Praeger, 1969.

Ames, David W. "Contexts of Dance in Zazzau and the Impact of Islamic Reform." *African Religious Groups and Beliefs. Papers in Honor of William R. Bascom.* Ed. Simon Ottenberg. Meerut, India: Folklore Institute, 1982. 110–47.

Arango Bueno, Teresa. *Precolombia.* 3rd ed. Bogotá: Edit. Minerva, 1963.

Arango F., Juan Ignacio. *El libro en Colombia.* Santafé de Bogotá: Centro Regional para el Fomento del Libro en América Latina y el Caribe, 1991.

Arboleda, Gustavo. "Apuntes sobre la imprenta y el periodismo en Popayán." *Revista de la Universidad del Cauca* 15–17 (1952?): 219–[420?].

Arenas, Ismael Enrique. "Tumaco Arrasado por las Llamas." *El Tiempo* 13 Oct. 1947: 1, 2.

Aretz, Isabel. "Music and Dance in Continental Latin America, with the Exception of Brazil." Moreno Fraginals 189–226.

Arocha Rodríguez, Jaime. "Afro-Colombia Denied." *Report on the Americas* 25.4 (1992): 28–31.

Baquero, Gastón. "Panorama." *Diario de la Marina* 21 Apr. 1949: 4.

Barrett, Leonard. "African Religion in the Americas: The Islands in Between." *African Religions: A Symposium.* Ed. Newell S. Booth, Jr. New York: NOK Publishers Ltd., 1977. 183–215.

Becco, Horacio Jorge. "Vicente Rossi y su obra rioplatense." *Cosas de negros.* By Vicente Rossi. 7–28.

Blutstein, Howard I., et al. *Area Handbook for Cuba.* Washington, D.C.:U.S. Government Printing Office, 1971.

Bohannan, Paul. *Africa and Africans.* American Museum Science Books. Garden City, N.Y.: Natural History, 1964.

Bonivento Fernández, José Alejandro. *Aspectos socio-geo-económicos del Departamento del Magdalena.* [Bogotá]: Gráficas del F. R. Judicial Penitenciaría Central "La Picota", [1963].

Bossa Herazo, Donaldo. "En un gran duelo. Carmen de Arco de la Torre," *El Universal* 9 May 1948: 4.

Bowman, Isaiah. *South America; A Geography Reader.* Chicago: Rand, McNally & Co., 1915.

Bowser, Frederick P. "Colonial Spanish America." *Neither Slave nor Free: the Freedmen of African Descent in the Slave Societies of the New World*. Ed. David W. Cohen and Jack P. Greene. Baltimore: Johns Hopkins UP, 1972. 19–58.

Brisson, Jorge. *Viajes por Colombia en los años de 1891 a 1897*. Bogotá: Imprenta Nacional, 1899.

Bushnell, David. *The Making of Modern Colombia: A Nation in Spite of Itself*. Berkeley and Los Angeles: U of California P, 1993.

Cabrera Ortega, M. Aurelio. "Breve historia del general Juan José Nieto." *El Heraldo* 11 Oct. 1947: 8.

Caldas, Tito Livio. *Industria editorial, cultura y desarrollo en Colombia*. Bogotá: Edit. Minerva, 1970.

Calderón Mosquera, Carlos. "Facetas del Departamento del Chocó." *Vínculo Shell* 17.127 (1965): 54–56.

Camacho Roldán, José María. *Notas de viaje (Colombia y Estados Unidos de América)*. Vol. 1. 1890. Bogotá: Banco de la República, 1973. 2 vols.

Carlson, Fred A. *A Geography of Latin America*. New York: Prentice-Hall, 1937.

Carrera Damas, Germán. "Flight and Confrontation." Moreno Fraginals 23–37.

Carvalho-Neto, Paulo de. *El folklore de las luchas sociales: un ensayo de folklore y marxismo*. Colección Mínima 64. México: Siglo Veintiuno, 1973.

Castellanos, Jorge. *La abolición de la esclavitud en Popayán, 1832–1852*. Cali: Departamento de Publicaciones, Universidad del Valle, 1980.

Castellanos, Jorge, and Isabel Castellanos. *Cultura afrocubana*. Vol. 1. *El negro en Cuba, 1492–1844*. Miami: Ediciones Universal, 1988. 4 vols. 1988–1994.

Ceyte, J. I. "Ayer y Hoy. A la juventud liberal." *Rojas Garrido* 5 Aug. 1917: 2–3.

Cirlot, J. E. *A Dictionary of Symbols*. Trans. Jack Sage. New York: Philosophical Library, 1962.

Colmenares, Germán. "La economía y la sociedad coloniales, 1550–1800." *Manual de historia de Colombia*. 1:223–300.

———. *Historia económica y social de Colombia*. Vol. 2. *Popayán: una sociedad esclavista, 1680–1800*. Bogotá: La Carreta Inéditos Ltda. [Edit. Lealón, Medellín], 1979. 2 vols. 1978–1979.

Conniff, Michael L., and Thomas J. Davis. *Africans in the Americas: A History of the Black Diaspora*. New York: St. Martin's, 1994.

Correa Díaz Granados, Ismael. "La cumbia cienaguera." *La cultura popular en el Caribe*. Comp. Javier Moscarella. Bogotá: Organización de Estados Iberoamericanos O.E.I., n.d. 29–34.

Corwin, Arthur F. *Spain and the Abolition of Slavery in Cuba, 1817–1886*. Austin: U of Texas P, 1967.

"Cosas del Día," *El Tiempo* 3 July 1931: 5.

Crist, Raymond E. "La personalidad de Popayán." *Revista de la Universidad del Cauca* 14 (1950): 5–16.

"¿Cuál discriminación?" Editorial. *El Tiempo* 2 Sept. 1977: 4.

Cuervo, Rufino José. *Apuntaciones críticas sobre el lenguaje bogotano con frecuente referencia al de los países de Hispanoamérica. . . .* 9th ed. corrected. 1872. Bogotá: Instituto Caro y Cuervo, 1955.

Davidson, Basil. *Black Mother: The Years of the African Slave Trade.* Boston: Little, Brown, 1961.

Davidson, Harry C. *Diccionario Folklórico de Colombia: música, instrumentos y danzas.* 3 vols. Bogotá: Publicación del Banco de la República, 1970.

Delafosse, Maurice. *The Negroes of Africa; History and culture.* Trans. F. Fligelman. 1931. Port Washington, N.Y.: Kennikat P, 1968.

———. *Los negros.* Trans. Joaquín Gallardo. [Barcelona: Edit. Labor, 1931].

Delgado Nieto, Carlos. *José Padilla; estampa de un almirante.* Bogotá: Instituto Colombiano de Cultura, 1973.

Deschamps Chapeaux, Pedro. *El negro en el periodismo cubano en el siglo XIX; Ensayo bibliográfico.* La Habana: Ediciones Revolución, 1963.

Devis Echandía, *La ciudad vencida: La Cartagena de ayer, la Cartagena de hoy.* Bucaramanga: Edit. Gómez y Páez, 1937.

Diallo, Yaya, and Mitchell Hall. *The Healing Drum: African Wisdom Teachings.* Rochester, Vt.: Destiny Books, 1989.

Diario de Costa Rica 5 Jun. 1931: 8.

Diggs, Irene. "Color in Colonial Spanish America." *Journal of Negro History* 38 (1953): 403–27.

Dolinger, Jane. "Colombia's Happy and Free Negroes." *Sepia* Apr. 1960: 55–58.

Eder, Phanor James. *Colombia.* London: T. Fisher Unwin, 1913.

Empson, Charles. *Narratives of South America; illustrating manner, customs, and scenery: containing also numerous facts in Natural History, collected during a four years' residence in tropical regions.* London, 1836.

Escalante, Aquiles. *El negro en Colombia.* Bogotá: Universidad Nacional, 1964.

———. "Notas sobre el Palenque de San Basilio, una comunidad negra en Colombia." *Divulgaciones Etnológicas* 3 (1954): 207–358.

Escobar Escobar, Hernán, ed. *Algo de lo nuestro.* [Medellín: Edit Bedout, 1960].

Escobar Uribe, Arturo. *El Indio Uribe (o la lucha por la libertad en el siglo XIX.* Bogotá: Edit. y Tip. Hispana, [1964].

Essien-Udom, E. E. *Black Nationalism: A Search for an Identity in America.* New York: Dell, 1965.

Fals Borda, Orlando. *El Presidente Nieto.* Bogotá: Carlos Valencia Editores, 1981. Vol. 2 of *Historia doble de la costa.* 4 vols. 1979–86.

Farson, J. S. Negley. *Transgressor in the Tropics.* 2nd ed. New York: Harcourt, 1938.

Ferguson, J. Halcro. *Latin America: The Balance of Race Addressed.* London: Oxford UP, 1961.

Fernández Robaina, Tomás. *El negro en Cuba, 1902–1958: Apuntes para la historia de la lucha contra la discriminación racial.* La Habana: Edit. de Ciencias Sociales, 1990.

Fisher, John R., Allan J. Kuethe, and Anthony McFarlane, eds. *Reform and Insurrection in Bourbon New Granada and Peru.* Baton Rouge: Louisiana State UP, 1990.

Forrest, A. S. *A Tour through South America.* London: Stanley Paul, 1913.

Francés, José. "El despertar de la noche humana. 'El Hermano Negro' y 'El Cocktail Negro' [sic]." *El Tiempo* 7 Feb. 1932, "Lecturas Dominicales": 11.

Franklin, John Hope, and Alfred A. Moss, Jr. *From Slavery to Freedom: A History of Black Americans.* 6th ed. New York: McGraw-Hill, 1988.

Fraser, Elizabeth. "African Drums and Drumming." *African World* [London] Nov. 1966: 6–7.

Friedemann, Nina de. "Estudios de negros en la antropología colombiana: presencia e invisibilidad." *Un siglo de investigación social; antropología en Colombia.* Ed. Jaime Arocha Rodríguez and Nina de Friedemann. Bogotá: Etno, 1984. 507–72.

Friedemann, Nina de, and Carlos Patiño Roselli. *Lengua y sociedad en el Palenque de San Basilio.* Bogotá: Instituto Caro y Cuervo, 1983.

Galvis Noyes, Antonio José. "La esclavitud en Colombia durante el período republicano (1825–1851)." *Universitas Humanística* 5–6 (1973): 227–37.

Geografía económica de Colombia. Tomo V. *Bolívar.* Bogotá: Edit. El Gráfico, 1942.

Gilij, Felipe Salvador. *Ensayo de historia americana, o sea Historia natural, civil y sacra de los reinos, y de las provincias de Tierra Firme en la América meridional.* Trans. Mario Germán Romero and Carlo Bruscantini. Bogotá: Edit. Sucre, 1955.

Giraldo Jaramillo, Gabriel. *Bibliografía colombiana de viajes.* Biblioteca de bibliografía colombiana 2. Bogotá: Edit. A B C, 1957.

Góez, Ramón Carlos. *Geografía de Colombia.* Colección Tierra Firme 26. México: Fondo de Cultura Económica, 1947.

Gómez, Eugenio J. *Problemas colombianos; La unidad política.* Bogotá: Talleres Gráficos *Mundo al Día,* 1941.

Gómez Olaciregui, Aureliano. *Prensa y periodismo en Barranquilla; siglo XIX.* [Barranquilla: Imp. Departamental], 1967.

Grahn, Lance R. "Cartagena and its Hinterland in the Eighteenth Century." Knight and Liss 168–95.

———. "An Irresistible Dilemma: Smuggling in New Granada, 1713–1763." Fisher, Kuethe, and McFarlane 123–46.

Granada, Daniel. *Vocabulario Rioplatense Razonado.* Montevideo, 1889. Cited in Rossi 79.

Grandmontagne, Francisco. *Páginas escogidas (1920–1935).* Madrid: Aguilar, 1966.

Guerra, José. "El problema editorial. Vicisitudes del libro colombiano." *Universidad de Antioquia* 25 (Jan.–Feb. 1950): 401–9.

Guglielmini, Homero H. "Negros y Blancos en los Estados Unidos." *El Tiempo* 2 Apr. 1933, "Lecturas Dominicales": 7.

Guillenar, Pedro. "El Paraíso de los Negros es París. Allí tienen los mismos derechos que los Blancos." *Mundo al Día* 28 Nov. 1931: 24, 26.

Guzmán Izquierdo, Manuel. "Raza negra." *Repertorio Boyacense* 163–64 (1952): 2524–26.

Haensch, Günther, and Reinhold Werner, eds. *Nuevo Diccionario de Colombianismos.* Vol. 1 of *Nuevo Diccionario de Americanismos.* Santafé de Bogotá: Instituto Caro y Cuervo, 1993.

Hamnett, Brian R. "Popular Insurrection and Royalist Reaction: Colombian Regions, 1810–1823." Fisher, Kuethe, and McFarlane 292–326.

Hanna, Judith Lynn. *To Dance is Human; A Theory of Non-Verbal Communication.* Austin: U of Texas P, 1980.

———. "What is African Dance?" *New African Literature and the Arts.* Ed. Joseph Okpaku. Vol. 1. New York: Apollo-Thomas Y. Crowell, 1970. 312–17. 2 vols.

Harding, Vincent. "W. E. B. Du Bois and the Black Messianic Vision." *Black Titan: W. E. B. Du Bois; An Anthology.* By the editors of *Freedomways.* Boston: Beacon P, 1970. 52–68.

Harris, Rex. *Jazz.* 3rd ed. Harmondsworth, Middlesex: Penguin Books, 1954.

Harrison, Daphne D. "Aesthetic and Social Aspects of Music in African Ritual Settings." *More than Drumming: Essays on African and Afro-Latin American Music and Musicians.* Ed. Irene V. Jackson. Westport, Conn.: Greenwood P, 1985. 49–65.

Helg, Aline. *Our Rightful Share: The Afro-Cuban Struggle for Equality, 1886–1912.* Chapel Hill: U of North Carolina P, 1995.

Hernández de Alba, Gregorio. *Libertad de los esclavos en Colombia.* Publicaciones de la Sociedad Colombiana de Etnología 4. Bogotá: Edit. A B C, 1956.

Holton, Isaac F. *New Granada: Twenty Months in the Andes.* New York: Harper and Brothers, 1857.

hooks, bell. *Black Looks; Race and Representation.* Boston: South End P, 1992.

———. *Yearning: Race, Gender, and Cultural Politics.* Boston: South End P, 1990.

Illidge, José. "To Benigno A. Gutiérrez." 19 June 1955. Letter in *El cancionero de Antioquia.* Comp. Antonio José Restrepo. 1928. Ed. Benigno A. Gutiérrez. Medellín: Edit. Bedout, 1955. 149–59.

Jahn, Janheinz. *Muntu: An Outline of the New African Culture.* Trans. Marjorie Grene. New York: Grove P, 1961.

James, Preston. *Latin America.* 1942. 3rd ed. New York: Odyssey P, 1959.

Jaramillo Uribe, Jaime. *Ensayos sobre historia social colombiana.* Bogotá: Universidad Nacional de Colombia, 1968.

Jaramillo [Uribe], Jaime, et al. "Regiones y nación en el siglo XIX." *Aspectos polémicos de la historia colombiana del siglo XIX; memoria de un seminario.* Bogotá: Fondo Cultural Cafetero, 1983. 185–229.

"Jazz. Negros norteamericanos (Música de los)." *Enciclopedia universal ilustrada europeo-americana.* Vol. 7. (Apéndice.) Bilbao: Espasa-Calpe, 1932. 989–90. 10 vols.

Jiménez López, Miguel, et al. *Los problemas de la raza en Colombia.* [Bogotá: "El Espectador," 1920.]

Jones, James M. *Prejudice and Racism.* Reading, Mass.: Addison- Wesley, 1972.

Jones, Robert C. "Negroes in Latin America." *Sociology and Social Research* 30.1 (1945): 45–51.

Juan, Jorge, and Antonio de Ulloa. *A Voyage to South America.* The John Adams Translation [abridged]. 1806. New York: Knopf, 1964.

Karabalí, Manuel [Manuel Zapata Olivella]. "Estudios del negro en Colombia." *Cromos* 13 Sept. 1947: 8–9, 44–46.

King, James Ferguson. "Negro Slavery in New Granada." *Greater America: Essays in Honor of Herbert Eugene Bolton.* Berkeley and Los Angeles: U of California P, 1945. 295–318.

King, Martin Luther, Jr. *Strength to Love.* New York: Harper & Row, 1963.

Kinney, Esi Sylvia. "Africanisms in Music and Dance of the Americas." *Black Life and Culture in the United States.* Ed. Rhoda L. Goldstein. New York: Apollo-Thomas Y. Crowell, 1971. 49–63.

Knight, Franklin W. *The African Dimension in Latin American Societies.* New York: Macmillan, 1974.

——. "Slavery, Race, and Social Structure in Cuba during the Nineteenth Century." Toplin 204–27.

——. *Slave Society in Cuba during the Nineteenth Century.* Madison: U of Wisconsin P, 1970.

Knight, Franklin W., and Peggy K. Liss, eds. *Atlantic Port Cities: Economy, Culture, and Society in the Atlantic World, 1650–1850.* Knoxville: U of Tennessee P, 1991.

Kuethe, Allan J. *Cuba, 1753–1815: Crown, Military and Society.* Knoxville: U Tenn P, 1986.

——. "Havana in the Eighteenth Century." Knight and Liss 13–39.

——. *Military Reform and Society in New Granada, 1773–1808.* Gainesville: UP of Florida, 1978.

Kwabena Nketia, J. H. "The Musical Heritage of Africa." *Daedalus* 103.2 (1974): 151–61.

Labarca, Eugenio. "El jazz de Josefina Baker." *El Tiempo* 4 June 1933, "Lecturas Dominicales": 2.

"La Gran Compañía de Artistas Negros ('The Black Stars Dancing')." *La Patria* 5 Apr. 1930: 12.

Lalinde Botero, Luis. *Diccionario "jilosófico" del paisa.* [1st ed.] Medellín: Edit. Bedout, [1966].

Lebrón Saviñón, Carlos. *Este negro nuestro que debemos querer: Un estudio etnológico acerca del negro en América.* Santo Domingo: Editora Cultural Dominicana, 1978.

Levine, Lawrence W. *Black Culture and Black Consciousness: Afro- American Folk Thought from Slavery to Freedom.* New York: Oxford UP, 1977.

Linares, Antonio G. de. "Charleston - City." *El Tiempo* 23 Oct. 1927, "Lecturas Dominicales": 332–33.

——. "Josefina Baker, o la Reina negra de Europa." *El Espectador* 13 Oct. 1927, Suplemento Literario Ilustrado: 7.

Londoño, Julio. *Nación en crisis.* Bogotá: [Edit. Santafé], 1955.

López de Mesa, Luis. "Introducción a la historia de la cultura en Colombia." *El Tiempo* 25 Jan. 1930: 3.

"Lo que suena." *Diario de Cundinamarca* 29 Aug. 1874: 980.

Lugo, Jesús M. "Rojas Garrido." *Rojas Garrido* 10 June 1917: 1–2.

Manual de historia de Colombia. 3rd. ed. 3 vols. Bogotá: Procultura, 1984.

Martín, Juan Luis. "El oído musical del negro de Cuba. Apuntes sobre la música afrocriolla." *El Tiempo* 9 Nov. 1930, "Lecturas Dominicales": 9.

Masferrer, Marianne, and Carmelo Mesa-Lago. "The Gradual Integration of the Black in Cuba: Under the Colony, the Republic, the Revolution." Toplin 348–84.

Mbiti, John S. *African Religions and Philosophy.* New York: Anchor-Doubleday, 1970.

Melo, Jorge Orlando. "La evolución económica de Colombia, 1830–1900." *Manual de historia de Colombia.* Vol. 2. 133–207.

Mina, Mateo. *Esclavitud y libertad en el Valle del Río Cauca.* Bogotá: Fundación Rosca de Investigación y Acción Social, 1975.

"Miscelánea - Plácido." *Revista de Cuba* 13 (January 1883): 96.

Moliner, María. *Diccionario del uso español.* 2 vols. Madrid: Edit. Gredos, 1983.

Moreno Fraginals, Manuel, ed. *Africa in Latin America: Essays on History, Culture, and Socialization.* Trans. Leonor Blum. New York: Holmes & Meier; Paris: UNESCO, 1984.

Mörner, Magnus. *Race Mixture in the History of Latin America.* Boston: Little, Brown, 1967.

Mosquera, Jesús Lácides. *El poder de la definición del negro.* Ibagué: Universidad del Tolima, 1975.

Mosquera M., Juan de Dios. *Las comunidades negras de Colombia; Pasado, presente y futuro.* 1985. Medellín: Edit. Lealón, 1986.

"El mundo está dominado por Africa. El último baile de los salones cosmopolitas." *Mundo al Día* 25 Apr. 1931: 51–52.

Murray, David R. *Odious Commerce: Britain, Spain and the Abolition of the Cuban Slave Trade.* Cambridge: Cambridge UP, 1980.

Naranjo M., Enrique. "Prejuicios raciales. El criollismo." *La Nación* [Barr] 10 Jan. 1929: 7.

"Un negro linchado y después quemado vivo." *Mundo al Día* 14 Feb. 1931: 1.

"Noticiero Cultural. Recital." *El Tiempo* 12 Nov. 1943: 5.

Ocampo, Victoria. "En Harlem, el barrio negro de Nueva York." *El Tiempo* 12 Oct. 1930, "Lecturas Dominicales": 4–5.

Olivares Figueroa, R. *Folklore Venezolano.* Vol. 1. *Versos.* Caracas: Ediciones del Ministerio de Educación Nacional, 1948. 2 vols. 1948–54.

Orrego Salas, Juan. "Música de Medio Siglo." *El Liberal* 12 Mar. 1950: 2.

Osorio Lizarazo, José A. "El Negro Marín." *Sábado* 2 June 1945: 3.

Osorio T., Nelson, comp. *Manifiestos, proclamas y polémicas de la vanguardia literaria hispanoamericana.* Caracas: Biblioteca Ayacucho, [1988].

Ospina, Joaquín, ed. *Diccionario biográfico y bibliográfico de Colombia.* 3 vols. Bogotá: Edit. Aguila, 1927–39.

Palacios Preciado, Jorge. "La esclavitud y la sociedad esclavista." *Manual de historia de Colombia* 1:303–46.

———. *La trata de negros por Cartagena de Indias (1650–1750).* Tunja: Universidad Pedagógica y Tecnológica de Colombia, 1973.

Pardo Umaña, Emilia. "El Cordero 'cari-negro.'" *El Tiempo* 30 Sept. 1951: 5.

Park, James William. *Rafael Núñez and the Politics of Colombian Regionalism, 1863–1886.* Baton Rouge: Louisiana State UP, [c1985].

Perdomo Escobar, José Ignacio. *Historia de la música en Colombia.* 3rd ed. Biblioteca de Historia Nacional 103. Bogotá: Edit. A B C, 1963.

Pereira, Ricardo S. *Les Etats-Unis de Colombie. Précis d'histoire et de géographie, physique, politique et commerciale . . .* Paris, 1883.

Pérez, Santiago. "Apuntes de viaje." *Selección de escritos y discursos de Santiago Pérez.* Ed. Eduardo Rodríguez Piñeres. Biblioteca de Historia Nacional 81. Bogotá: La Librería Voluntad, 1950. 29–86. (Rpt. of *Apuntamientos de viaje por Antioquia y las Provincias del Sur.* Bogotá, 1853).

Petit de Murat, Ulises. "Jazz. Las canciones del norte." *El Tiempo* 11 Jan. 1931, "Lecturas Dominicales": 2.

"El pleito de las credenciales." *La Razón* 10 Feb. 1938: 1.

Porto del Portillo, Raúl. "Efemérides colombianas." *Diario de la Costa* 22 Sept. 1944: 4.

―――. *Plazas y Calles de Cartagena.* [Cartagena]: Dirección de Educación Pública de Bolívar, Extensión Cultural, 1945.

"El primer intérprete de la poesía negra en Medellín." *El Colombiano* 17 Mar. 1944: 4.

Primus, Pearl. "African Dance." Drachler 172–180.

"Problema Racial." [Editorial]. *El Heraldo* 21 June 1943: 3.

"Problema Racial en la Univ. de Tunja. (Un problema de regiones)." *Sucesos* 21 Oct. 1960: 14.

Quijano Mantilla, Joaquín. "Berlín visto por un hombre mudo. Así Conoció Joaquín Quijano Mantilla a Josefina Baker." *El Tiempo* 4 Aug. 1929, "Lecturas Dominicales": 4.

Randall, Stephen J. *Colombia and the United States; Hegemony and Independence.* Athens: U of Georgia P, 1992.

Rausch, Jane M. *A Tropical Plains Frontier: The Llanos of Colombia, 1531–1831.* Albuquerque: U of New Mexico P, 1984.

Restrepo, Antonio José. *Sombras chinescas (tragicomedia de la regeneración). Núñez.* Cali: Edit. Progreso, 1947.

―――, comp. *El cancionero de Antioquia.* 1928. Ed. Benigno A. Gutiérrez. Medellín: Edit. Bedout, 1955.

Restrepo, Huberto, S.S. *La religión de la antigua Antioquia (estudio teológico-pastoral sobre Tomás Carrasquilla).* Medellín: Edit. Bedout, 1972.

"Revista de Libros." *Viernes* 7 (Feb. 1940): 33–37; 8 (Mar. 1940): 30–35.

Rivera y Garrido, Luciano. *Memorias de un colegial.* Bogotá: Edit. Minerva, 1936.

Rocca, Marie L. "The Negro in Colombia: An Historical Geography." *Columbia Essays in International Affairs* 7. The Dean's Papers, 1971. Ed. Andrew W. Cordier. New York and London: Columbia UP, 1972. 36–68.

Rodríguez Molas, Ricardo. *La música y la danza de los negros en el Buenos Aires de los siglos VVIII y XIX.* Buenos Aires: Ediciones Clio, 1957.

Rodríguez Plata, Horacio. *José María Obando, íntimo (archivo- epistolario-comentarios).* Vol. 1. Academia Colombiana de Historia. Biblioteca Eduardo Santos, 12. Bogotá: Edit. Sucre Ltda., 1958.

Romero, Emilio. *Geografía del Pacífico sudamericano.* Colección Tierra Firme 32. México: Fondo de Cultura Económica, 1947.

Romoli, Kathleen. *Colombia, Gateway to South America.* Garden City, N.Y.: Doubleday, Doran & Co., 1944.

Rossi, Vicente. *Cosas de negros.* [2nd ed.]. Estudio preliminar y notas de Horacio Jorge Becco. Colección "El pasado argentino." 1926. Buenos Aires: Librería Hachette, [1958].

Rout, Leslie B., Jr. *The African Experience in Spanish America, 1509 to the Present Day.* Cambridge: Cambridge UP, 1976.

Samper, José María. *Ensayo sobre las revoluciones políticas y la condición social de las repúblicas colombianas (hispano-americanas),* con un apéndice sobre la orografía y la población de la Confederación Granadina. 1861. Biblioteca Popular de Cultura Colombiana 52. Ensayos 5. Bogotá: Edit. Centro - Instituto Gráfico Ltda., n.d. [1944?].

———. *Viajes de un colombiano en Europa*. Paris, 1862.

Samper, Miguel. *La miseria en Bogotá*. Bogotá, 1867. Rpt. in *Selección de escritos*. Comp. Hector Charry Samper and Santiago Samper Trainer. Bogotá: Instituto Colombiano de Cultura, 1977. 27–98.

Sánchez Santamaría, I. M. *Vicios de la raza*. Bucaramanga: Tip. Mercantil, 1919.

Scott, Rebecca J. *Slave Emancipation in Cuba: The Transition to Free Labor, 1860–1899*. Princeton, N.J.: Princeton UP, 1985.

Sexton, Susie. "Paul Whiteman Made Jazz Contagious." *American Magazine* June 1924: 74–75.

Sharp, William F. "Una imagen del negro." *Universidad Nacional* 2 (1969): 171–85.

———. "Manumission, *Libres*, and Black Resistance: The Colombian Chocó, 1680–1810." Toplin 89–111.

———. *Slavery on the Spanish Frontier (1680–1810)*. Norman: U of Oklahoma P, 1976.

Silva, Lautaro. *Latinoamérica al rojo vivo*. Madrid: Aguilar, 1962.

"Sin discriminaciones." Editorial. *El Tiempo* 3 Nov. 1975: 4A.

Smith, T. Lynn. *Studies of Latin American Societies*. Garden City, N.Y.: Anchor Books-Doubleday, 1970.

Solaún, Mauricio, and Sidney Kronus. *Discrimination without Violence*. New York: Wiley, 1973.

Steiner, Stan. *The Islands: The Worlds of the Puerto Ricans*. New York: Harper & Row, 1974.

Stevenson, William Bennet. *A historical and descriptive narrative of twenty years' residence in South America. . . .* Vol. 2. London: Hurst, Robinson, and Co., 1825. 3 vols.

Stewart, John. *Bogotá in 1836–37, being a Narrative of a Expedition to the Capital of New Grenada, and a Residence there of eleven months*. New York: Harper & Brothers, 1838.

Taussig, Michael. *The Devil and Commodity Fetishism in South America*. Chapel Hill: U of North Carolina P, 1980.

———. "The Evolution of Rural Wage Labour in the Cauca Valley of Colombia, 1700–1970." *Land and Labour in Latin America; Essays in the Development of Agrarian Capitalism in the 19th and 20th Centuries*. Ed. Kenneth Duncan, Ian Rutledge, and Colin Hardings. Cambridge: Cambridge UP, 1977. 397–434.

Tejado Fernández, Manuel. *Aspectos sociales de Cartagena de Indias en el siglo XVII*. Sevilla: Escuela de Estudios Hispanoamericanos, 1954.

Tirado Mejía, Alvaro. *Aspectos sociales de las guerras civiles en Colombia*. Bogotá: Edit. Andes, 1976.

———. "El estado y la política en el siglo XIX." *Manual de historia de Colombia* 2:325–84.

Toplin, Robert Brent, ed. *Slavery and Race Relations in Latin America*. Westport, Conn.: Greenwood P, 1974.

Torre, Guillermo de. *Minorías y masas en la cultura y el arte contemporáneos.* Colección El Puente. Barcelona: E.D.H.A.S.A., 1963.

Triana, Miguel. *Por el sur de Colombia; Excursión pintoresca y científica al Putumayo.* 1908. Biblioteca Popular de Cultura Colombiana 122. [Bogotá]: Ministerio de Educación Nacional, 1950.

Tuttle, William M., Jr., ed. *W. E. B. DuBois.* Englewood Cliffs, N.J.: Prentice-Hall, 1973.

"Ultimo Grado de Democracia." *El Espectador* 13 Dec. 1953, "Dominical": 4.

Uribe, Juan de Dios. *Sobre el yunque; obras completas.* Ed. Antonio José Restrepo. Vol. 2. Bogotá: Imprenta de "La Tribuna editorial, 1913. 2 vols.

Uribe Celis, Carlos. *Los años veinte en Colombia: Ideología y cultura.* [Bogotá]: Ediciones Aurora, 1985.

Valenilla Lanz, Laureano. *Críticas de sinceridad y exactitud.* Caracas: [Imp. Bolívar] 1921.

Vega, Fernando de la. *Cartagena, la de los claros varones.* Cartagena: Empresa Edit. "El Mercurio," 1929.

Velasco Ibarra, J. M. *Servidumbre y liberación.* Buenos Aires: Américalee, 1965.

Velásquez [Murillo], Rogelio. "Apuntes socio-económicos del Atrato Medio." *Revista Colombiana de Antropología* 10 (1961): 157–225.

———. *El Chocó en la independencia de Colombia.* Colección Síntesis 11. Bogotá: Edit. Hispana, 1965.

"La 'Venus Negra' en Buenos Aires." *La Patria* 6 Aug. 1929: 2.

Villaselva, Hector de. "El Divino Arte en Peligro. La música de negros ejecutada por 'Jazz-Band', cava la sepultura." *El Mercurio* 4 Jan. 1931: 4.

Wade, Peter. *Blackness and Race Mixture: The Dynamics of Racial Identity in Colombia.* Baltimore: Johns Hopkins UP, 1993.

———. "Patterns of Race in Colombia." *Bulletin of Latin American Research* 5.2 (1986): 1–19.

———. "Race and Class: The Case of South American Blacks." *Ethnic and Racial Studies* 8 (1985): 233–49.

Whitten, Norman E., Jr. *Black Frontiersmen; A South American Case.* New York: Wiley; Schenkman, 1974.

Wilson, Olly. "The Association of Movement and Music as a Manifestation of a Black Conceptual Approach to Music-Making." *More than Dancing: Essays on Afro-American Music and Musicians.* Ed. Irene V. Jackson. Westport, Conn.: Greenwood P, 1985. 9–23.

Wolf, Donna M. "The Cuban People of Color and the Independence Movement: 1879–1895." *Revista/Review Interamericana* 5 (1975): 403–21.

Wright, Winthrop R. *Café con leche: Race, Class, and National Image in Venezuela.* Austin: U of Texas P, 1990.

Zapata Olivella, Delia. "La cumbia, síntesis musical de la nación colombiana. Reseña histórica y coreográfica." *Revista Colombiana de Folclor* 3.7 (1962): 187–204.

Zapata Olivella, Manuel. "La crítica cartagenera." *Diario de la Costa* 4 Jan. 1940: 9.

———. "La cumbia, baile del litoral Atlántico." *Cromos* 26 Apr. 1954: 12–13, 58.

————. "Del folklore musical. Origen africano de la cumbia." *Vida,* 2nd ser., 22 (1948): 53–55, 64.

————. "Genio y figura." *Diario de la Costa* 1 Mar. 1942, sec. 2: 12.

————. *El hombre colombiano.* Bogotá: Canal Ramírez-Antares, 1974.

————. "La música colombiana. Origen americano de la cumbia." *El Liberal* 16 Jan. 1949, "Nuestro Tiempo": 1.

————. "Los negros palenqueros." *Cromos* 13 Mar. 1948: 28–29, 45–46.

————. "El porro conquista a Bogotá." *Cromos* 31 May 1947: 8–9, 53, 56.

————. "Problemas del libro en Colombia. Los inéditos." *Cromos* 16 Aug. 1947: 8–9, 49, 53.

Zárate, Manuel F., with the collaboration of Dora P. de Zárate. *Tambor y socavón.* [Panama, R. P.]: Imprenta Nacional, 1962.

Zelinsky, Wilbur. "The Historical Geography of the Negro Population of Latin America." *Journal of Negro History* 34 (1949): 153–221.

INDEX

This index lists names and subjects. Full name is given for persons cited by same in the text; surname and initial(s) are given for others. Page numbers in italics refer to illustrations.

Books in the African American Life Series

Coleman Young and Detroit Politics: From Social Activist to Power Broker, by Wilbur Rich, 1988

Great Black Russian: A Novel on the Life and Times of Alexander Pushkin, by John Oliver Killens, 1989

Indignant Heart: A Black Worker's Journal, by Charles Denby, 1989 (reprint)

The Spook Who Sat by the Door, by Sam Greenlee, 1989 (reprint)

Roots of African American Drama: An Anthology of Early Plays, 1858–1938, edited by Leo Hamalian and James V. Hatch, 1990

Walls: Essays, 1985–1990, by Kenneth McClane, 1991

Voices of the Self: A Study of Language Competence, by Keith Gilyard, 1991

Say Amen, Brother! Old-Time Negro Preaching: A Study in American Frustration, by William H. Pipes, 1991 (reprint)

The Politics of Black Empowerment: The Transformation of Black Activism in Urban America, by James Jennings, 1992

Pan Africanism in the African Diaspora: An Analysis of Modern Afrocentric Political Movements, by Ronald Walters, 1993

Three Plays: The Broken Calabash, Parables for a Season, and The Reign of Wazobia, by Tess Akaeke Onwueme, 1993

Untold Tales, Unsung Heroes: An Oral History of Detroit's African American Community, 1918–1967, by Elaine Latzman Moon, Detroit Urban League, Inc., 1994

Discarded Legacy: Politics and Poetics in the Life of Frances E.W. Harper, 1825–1911, by Melba Joyce Boyd, 1994

African American Women Speak Out on Anita Hill–Clarence Thomas, edited by Geneva Smitherman, 1995

Lost Plays of the Harlem Renaissance, 1920–1940, edited by James V. Hatch and Leo Hamalian, 1996

Let's Flip the Script: An African American Discourse on Language, Literature, and Learning, by Keith Gilyard, 1996

A History of the African American People: The History, Traditions, and Culture of African Americans, edited by James Oliver Horton and Lois E. Horton, 1997 (reprint)

Tell It to Women: An Epic Drama for Women, by Osonye Tess Onwueme, 1997

Ed Bullins: A Literary Biography, by Samuel Hay, 1997

Walkin' over Medicine, by Loudelle F. Snow, 1998 (reprint)

Negroes with Guns, by Robert F. Williams, 1998 (reprint)

A Study of Walter Rodney's Intellectual and Political Thought, by Rupert Lewis, 1998

Ideology and Change: The Transformation of the Caribbean Left, by Perry Mars, 1998